How to Do *Everything* with Your

iMac

Third Edition

How to Do *Everything* with Your iMac

Third Edition

Todd Stauffer

Osborne/**McGraw-Hill**

New York   Chicago   San Francisco   Lisbon
London   Madrid   Mexico City   Milan   New Delhi
San Juan   Seoul   Singapore   Sydney   Toronto

Osborne/**McGraw-Hill**
2600 Tenth Street
Berkeley, California 94710
U.S.A.

To arrange bulk purchase discounts for sales promotions, premiums, or fund-raisers, please contact Osborne/**McGraw-Hill** at the above address. For information on translations or book distributors outside the U.S.A., please see the International Contact Information page immediately following the index of this book.

How to Do Everything with Your iMac, Third Edition

567890 CUS CUS 0198765432

ISBN 0-07-213172-1

Publisher:	Brandon A. Nordin
Vice President &	
Associate Publisher:	Scott Rogers
Acquisitions Editor:	Jane K. Brownlow
Project Editor:	LeeAnn Pickrell
Acquisitions Coordinator:	Emma Acker
Technical Editors:	John Rizzo, Greg Titus
Copy Editor:	Claire Splan
Proofreaders:	Stefany Otis, Susie Elkind
Indexer:	Karin Arrigoni
Computer Designers:	Lauren McCarthy, Lucie Ericksen, Tabitha M. Cagan
Illustrators:	Lyssa Wald, Michael Mueller
Series Design:	Michelle Galicia
Cover Design:	Dodie Shoemaker

iMac™ is a trademark of Apple Computer, Inc., registered in the U.S. and other countries. iMac photo courtesy of Apple Computer, Inc.

This book was composed with Corel VENTURA™ Publisher.

About the Author...

Todd Stauffer is the author or co-author of over two dozen books on computing, including the previous editions of *How to Do Everything with Your iMac* and *How to Do Everything with Your iBook*. He's written for a number of publications, including *Silicon Alley Report*, *MacAddict*, *Publish,* and MacCentral.com. He's the publisher of Mac-Upgrade.com as well as a humor columnist and travel writer.

About the Reviewers...

John Rizzo is the author of several books about Macs, a computer magazine columnist, a consultant, and the founder of the MacWindows.com Web site. He was an editor at *MacUser* magazine and a columnist for *MacWeek* magazine.

Greg Titus is a Senior Software Engineer and Manager with The Omni Group where he works as both a Cocoa/WebObjects consultant and as a developer of shrink-wrap software for Mac OS X. Acting as a project manager and networking/database specialist, his consulting clients have ranged from Fortune 500 companies in the areas of finance and telecommunications, to major search engine providers, to dot-coms. You can reach Greg at greg@omnigroup.com.

Contents at a Glance

Contents

Acknowledgments

The original *How to Do Everything with Your iMac* was the result of a fairly unique idea: a big book about a little computer. With the help and support of some great people, I took a stab at putting together a book that I hoped would help many readers get the most—for business, pleasure, or education—out of their iMac.

But the iMac product line is changing swiftly; new Mac OS versions are coming out, and even more exciting capabilities are being built into and bundled with the iMac. Those changes, coupled with the success of the first and second editions, have us at it again to bring you this third edition covering all the latest applications and capabilities of the iMac.

My thanks go first to Heidi Poulin, project editor on the first edition, who helped shape the original content and much of the structure that continues into this edition. Likewise, thanks to Bob LeVitus for his technical review and preface for the original edition.

Jane Brownlow, acquisitions editor for all three editions, was largely responsible for the success of the first edition and made it possible for me to write the second and third. My thanks to her for flexible deadlines as we tried to get this book done in a way that could touch on nearly every aspect of computing with your iMac.

For the third edition, I thank Emma Acker for managing the schedule and LeeAnn Pickrell for overseeing the editing and production. Claire Splan was our invaluable copy editor, once again cleaning up tenses, conjugations, and all those grammatical elements with which I have only a passing relationship.

Very heartfelt thanks go to John Rizzo and Greg Titus for their technical edits. Splicing both Mac OS X and Mac OS 9 into this book was an interesting undertaking. With John and Greg watching my back, I feel confident that you're getting great, accurate information in this book.

Finally, my thanks to Donna, who put up with "book mode"—and, more to the point, me—while I completed this revision.

Introduction

The original idea of *How to Do Everything with Your iMac* was a simple one. The iMac is a complete computer with a wonderful bundle of applications that enable you to do just about anything you need a computer to do. So, I wanted my book on the iMac to be as comprehensive as possible, teaching the reader how to be productive while enjoying this exciting little tool.

It was a risk, though, because the prevailing winds suggested that iMac owners might want thin books with only the basics to get up and running with their easy-to-use iMac. A 600-page book on the iMac? To some, it didn't make sense. Would readers buy this book?

The results speak for themselves, with the first two editions of the book selling tens of thousands of copies in each edition—a bestseller in the computer-book business. The folks at Osborne/McGraw-Hill were tickled enough to create an entire series of *How to Do Everything* books.

Now, we've put together this third edition, largely to tackle all of the new software and capabilities that Apple continues to pile onto the iMac. Not the least of these is Mac OS X— arguably the first all-new Mac OS since the advent of the Macintosh. While Mac OS X is still a work in progress, many iMac users will no doubt be exploring Mac OS X, if not using it on a regular basis.

But the newness of Mac OS X necessitates covering both Mac OS 9 and Mac OS X in this book. That way, you're sure to get a sense of what both operating systems are capable of, as well as how they differ. As we go forward with Mac OS X, there will still be a lot of Mac OS 9 to contend with, in the form of the Classic environment and older applications. I hope you'll enjoy the hybrid approach, which I feel will truly tell you "everything" you need to know about the modern iMac's operating systems.

In *How to Do Everything with Your iMac, Third Edition,* we've extended the book's focus to include coverage of Mac OS X, including some of the applications that come bundled with Mac OS X, such as the Apple Mail application. Likewise, it's been updated to discuss new iMac capabilities, such as burning CD-RW media, and to cover the latest iMac models, including the flat-panel iMac G4, and the latest application versions.

Coverage of the Internet is rearranged to get you up and running more quickly, starting with Chapter 6's quick guide to the Internet. That's in addition to Chapters 18–23, where you'll find extensive coverage of e-mail (both Outlook Express and Mail), the World Wide Web and Apple's iTools applications, which make it easy to transfer files online, create Web pages, and display images and movies on the Web. There you'll also find coverage of America Online and some advice and instruction for using your iMac with a high-speed Internet connection.

In this book, you'll learn, in detail, how to accomplish important computing tasks with your iMac, from the first time you press the Power button. Because the iMac comes bundled with AppleWorks 6, I show you how to create documents, reports, memos, newsletters, spreadsheets, databases, and charts. And I mean how to *use* them in real-world situations to oversee projects, turn in to teachers, present to your clients, or manage your hobbies.

You'll see how to create slide-show presentations. How to create a mail-merge form letter. How to use templates and assistants for all sorts of things. How to manage your calendar, task list, and contacts with aplomb. How to create databases to track just about anything—sports teams, weddings, recipes, projects, or classroom assignments.

The iMac is about creativity and fun, too. You can draw, paint, and even create a newsletter or high-end report. You'll learn about QuickTime, digital audio, digital video, and even a little about creating your own movies and burning your own audio CDs. Plus, there's an entire chapter on games and multimedia: how to play the iMac's games and how to get the best gaming experience.

Beyond that, you'll learn about printing documents, adding fonts, scanning photos, backing up data, adding a removable drive, synchronizing with your Palm handheld and customizing your settings. You can even work with Microsoft Windows applications and network your iMac to a group of other Macs. Plus, you'll read about AirPort technology, which allows you to create a connection between your iMac and other Macs or the Internet without any cables at all.

The book communicates all this information very simply. It has four major parts: "Get Started," "Get Things Done," "Get Online," and "Customize Your iMac." The book is both a reference and a tutorial. It's arranged so you can move quickly to an interesting topic you look up in the index, or you can just read straight through to get a complete understanding of a given topic. Plus, special elements help you along the way, including notes, tips, shortcuts, and cautions. And every chapter includes special "How To…" and "Did You Know…" sidebars that explore one special feature to show you how to make the most of your iMac.

An important note: Throughout the book I'll refer to "Mac OS 9" and "Mac OS X" generically—in most cases, when I say that, I'm discussing a feature or issue that has been present in those operating systems since they were introduced. But don't let that generic approach confuse you—it's always a good idea to have the latest version of Mac OS 9 (at the time of writing, Mac OS 9.2) and Mac OS X (version 10.1, currently). See Chapter 29 for details on updating your Mac OS versions. You should also look into Apple's Mac OS X Up-To-Date program (**http://www.apple.com/macosx/uptodate/**) to determine whether you're eligible for free or inexpensive upgrades to the Mac OS.

Want to reach me? You can, through my Web site for this book. It's **http://www.mac-upgrade .com/imac_book/** on the Web. Or send e-mail directly to **questions@mac-upgrade.com**. You'll also find a bonus chapter (once it's completed) on the Web site for this book. The bonus chapter covers Quicken software for Mac OS X, which wasn't available at the time of writing. Other corrections, explanations, discussion, and frequently asked questions will also be posted on that site, so please visit regularly or whenever you have a question.

Part I

Get Started

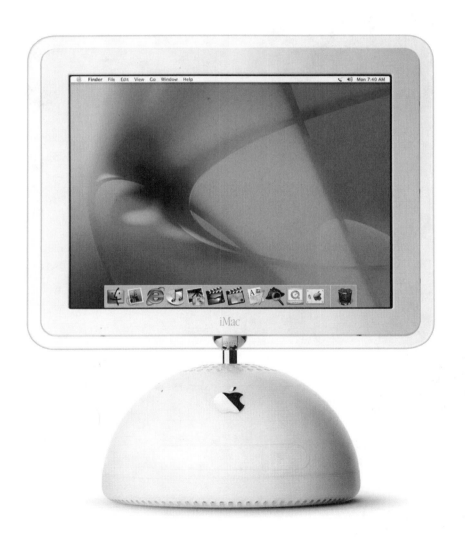

Chapter 1

Welcome to iMac

How to...

- ■ Prepare yourself for using your iMac
- ■ Figure out all the parts of the iMac
- ■ Set up and move your iMac
- ■ Start, restart, and put iMac to sleep

In 1998, Apple Computer set out to create a different sort of computer from those that had been seen in the past—one designed specifically for consumer users who wanted to get on the Internet. They called it the iMac, to suggest that it was the first "Internet" Macintosh marketed. It used a lot of the parts and software that a regular Power Macintosh computer uses, but it offered enough differences to make it a whole new idea. And it's a very exciting idea—a friendly, easy-to-use computer that can still do just about anything at all.

In the fall of 1999, Apple refreshed the iMac line with a new iMac called the iMac DV. The major difference, aside from speed and memory, was the inclusion of DVD drives (for watching DVD movies) and FireWire, a special port that enables high-speed connections for digital camcorders and peripherals.

By the spring of 2001, Apple added another interesting twist—Mac OS X, the company's new, high-end operating system. iMacs introduced in early 2001 can also sport CD-RW drives in place of DVD drives, which enable the iMac to "burn" audio and data CDs. (All iMacs introduced in the summer of 2001 have CD-RW drives.)

In 2002, Apple released the first all-new iMac since the original. The flat-panel iMac features a PowerPC G4 processor, a SuperDrive for creating DVD media (in some models), powerful audio speakers, and an innovative tilt-and-swivel LCD display, which offers more on-screen space while taking up less room on your desk. And the latest iMacs feature even more software—AppleWorks, iTunes, iMovie—to make you productive.

As if this weren't enough, it turns out that the iMac is great looking. The appearance of the iMac is meant to please you even when the iMac isn't on. But don't let the fashionable looks fool you. The iMac is a full computer, based on the Macintosh operating system (called *Mac OS*). Your iMac can run just about any Macintosh program, read and edit just about any computer document, and it can certainly take full advantage of the Internet. In fact, it's designed to be just as functional in a school or small business as it is at home.

As the title of this book suggests, if you have an iMac, you can do just about anything you can do with any other sort of computer. You're ready to go.

What Makes iMac Different and Cool

iMac offers a number of distinguishing features beyond looks. The iMac is a powerful computer, based on Apple's PowerPC G3 processors. Ease of use was important when Apple created iMac. The iMac is designed to help you get on the Internet, connect peripherals, and even attach to a network easily. It has all the important stuff built in—a modem, Ethernet port, graphics—plus two easy, modern ways to add extras: Universal Serial Bus and FireWire ports. Moreover, it comes with applications already installed that you can use for a variety of home or home-office tasks.

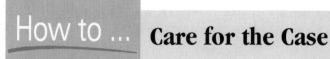

How to ... **Care for the Case**

Wondering how to clean your iMac's case? The plastics are durable, but they can still be scratched by abrasives or hard-edged objects. The iMac's case just won't look the same with scratches.

To clean the case, Apple recommends you shut down the iMac, pull its plug (from the wall socket or surge protector), and wipe the case with a dry, lint-free cloth. Avoid using water or liquid cleaners, since the iMac's case has seams where liquid could conceivably penetrate the case and damage the electronics.

On the flat-panel model, you can wipe the display with the included lint-free cloth. To clean the screen on any iMac, use a slightly damp, clean, lint-free cloth or a cloth designed specifically to clean computer monitors (you can get them at computer and office-supply stores). Don't spray liquids directly on the iMac (spray water lightly on the cloth itself) and don't use any harsh cleaners.

The iMac is also designed to work collaboratively with other computers over the Internet or a local area network of Macs or PCs. It offers some special ways to transmit, share, and translate files that other computers use so you can edit and share them with others.

What Is the Internet?

It's obvious just from the "i" in iMac's name that the Internet will be a huge focus of this book and your experience with the computer, so you'll need to know what it is. The Internet is the name given to a global system for connecting computers to one another using various sorts of cable, wire, and even wireless technologies. Once connected, these computers can share documents and transfer files between one another. The result is electronic mail, message areas, and the World Wide Web.

The Internet began as a government project to move data over long distances, with redundanies to survive some sort of wartime or natural disaster. Eventually, it became an imporant way to connect university computing centers and, later on, individuals. In the early 1990s the corporate world caught on and electronic mail and messaging became two of the most popular ways to use a personal computer.

So what makes it the Internet? Any computer using a particular language called the Transmission Control Protocol/Internet Protocol (TCP/IP) can connect to the Internet. All you need is a modem or a network connection and an Internet connection through an Internet service provider (ISP). The ISP gives you an address on the Internet, called an IP address, which gives your iMac a unique identity on this global network. Once you have an address, you're ready to send and receive Internet documents.

 *To learn more about using the iMac with the Internet, see "Get Online with the Assistants," later in this chapter, Chapter 6 and Chapters 18 through 23, where I discuss the Internet in detail.*

iMac Is Still a Mac

The iMac, ultimately, is a Macintosh computer. It's been simplified, designed in very clever ways, and made to work well on the Internet. At the heart of the iMac, though, is a standard PowerPC G3 processor and the Mac OS.

Any of those Macintosh programs (designed for your iMac's version of the Mac OS) available in the store or through mail order will work with your iMac. Even new versions of the Mac OS available from stores support the iMac automatically—you don't have to buy special software that's only for iMac. There are really only four things you need to look for when shopping for software:

■ *Does it install or run from CD-ROM?* Remember, the iMac doesn't have a floppy drive. Many slot-loading iMac models can also support software that runs on a DVD-ROM.

■ *Is it designed for PowerPC?* Some older Macintosh programs aren't specifically designed for PowerPC processors like the powerful processor in an iMac. Those old programs should still run if you're using Mac OS 9.1, but they might slow down the system. (And they may not work at all in Mac OS X.)

■ *Is it designed for your iMac's version of the Mac OS?* Make sure the program is designed to be compatible with the version of the Mac OS that your iMac is running. That means, specifically, that it is compatible with Mac OS 8.1-9.1 (or higher), depending on the version you have.

■ *Does it run in Mac OS X?* If you use Mac OS X as your primary operating system, you'll want to use "native" applications whenever possible. Any iMac running Mac OS X is still capable of running older Mac applications—in fact, you can boot into Mac OS 9.1 (or later) if you need to work in the "Classic" environment. It's more efficient and effective, however, to use applications designed specifically for Mac OS X, which offer more features and better performance from within Mac OS X.

The iMac does not run software specifically written for DOS, Windows, Windows 95/98, or Windows NT/2000, although many programs are written in both PC and Macintosh versions. Sometimes you'll even find both versions on the same CD-ROM.

And that's not to say the iMac can't run PC software at all—it just can't run PC software right out of the box. Special software programs, such as Connectix Virtual PC and FWB Software's RealPC, allow you to run those programs on your iMac (see Chapter 26). That software, called *emulation* software, can trick Windows programs into believing that they're being run on a Windows-based machine, even as they're being run on your iMac. It's a neat tool and it can be done pretty inexpensively.

Computers that use Intel-compatible processors and DOS, Windows, or Windows NT are often called "PCs" for the sake of convenience and to differentiate them from Macs and iMacs. I'll follow that convention despite the fact that your iMac is a "personal computer."

iMac Uses the Latest Hardware

Get your iMac home and there's a decent chance that you'll soon want external peripherals for it—you may want a printer, a document scanner, and a digital camera, or you may want to connect your iMac to other computers and copy files between them. Part of the excitement of the iMac stems from its Universal Serial Bus (USB) and, on recent models, FireWire ports that can be used to connect high-speed peripherals.

USB is incredibly easy to use—you pretty much just plug things in and they work. Plus, it's a standard that the latest Mac and PC computers can both use. That means many USB devices are compatible with iMacs right out of the box. That said, some USB devices require special *driver software,* so read the box carefully, ask a salesperson, or just focus on USB devices that show up in the Mac section of the store. If it has a Mac or iMac logo on the box, then it likely includes the software drivers you need.

In some cases, you'll need a Mac OS X-specific driver if you wish to work with the device in Mac OS X. See Chapter 26 (or Chapter 25, if the device is a printer) for details.

If you have an iMac DV model or any iMac made in the summer of 2000 or later, your iMac includes additional ports, called FireWire ports. These high-speed ports are included for copying data between your iMac and a digital camcorder so you can edit video. But that's not all FireWire is good for. It is also popular for connecting other devices, including high-speed external hard disks and removable disks. You'll find that many external devices are available with FireWire connections. (FireWire ports are based on something called the IEEE-1394 standard, so you'll sometimes see devices that say they use the "1394 port.") As an added bonus, FireWire is easy to set up, with the same "hot-pluggability" that USB offers.

You need to watch out for peripherals made for older Mac computers. These days, all of Apple's new products use USB ports, but older Mac printers and scanners may use either *serial* ports or *SCSI* ports for their connections. That's not the end of the world—actually, many of those other peripherals made for older Macintosh computers can still be used, but you'll need an adapter and some know-how. We'll discuss various peripherals in Chapter 26.

iMac: A Quick Tour

Before you get into the heart of setting up your iMac, let's take a quick look at it to get an idea what everything is and how things connect. You'll find that the iMac has some interesting and surprising nooks and crannies.

Different iMac Models

Throughout the book I'll refer to the different iMac models for two important reasons. First, some iMac models offer particular software bundles that other iMacs don't. If I discuss a program that you don't have, you'll want to be sure that it's because you have a different iMac model, not because you've lost the CD. Second, the iMac models differ significantly in how you work with them, such as different ways to plug in devices and insert CD-ROMs.

Original iMacs

There are four distinct versions of the original iMac series. Each of these iMac versions had a tray-loading CD-ROM drive, and differed primarily in the colors offered, and performance specifications. These iMacs generally shipped with Mac OS 8.6 through Mac OS 9, although they do support Mac OS X, as long as you've upgraded the RAM—128MB or more is recommended.

NOTE   *Although the original iMacs are still covered in this book, this edition focuses on issues involving later versions of most of the software, including the Mac OS, than the versions that shipped with the original iMacs. If you haven't updated your iMac with the latest versions of the Mac OS and the various applications, see Chapter 26 and Appendix A for details.*

Slot-Loading iMacs

All slot-loading iMacs feature improved sound thanks to better speakers. Some, originally called the iMac DV, have DVD drives and FireWire ports. These iMacs have also been designed to avoid using an internal fan, so they run quieter than most other computers.

In early 2001, Apple changed things around, offering slot-loading iMacs that could feature a CD-ROM, DVD-ROM, or a CD-RW (rewriteable) drive. In the summer of 2001, all iMacs began shipping with CD-RW drives as the standard. In May of 2001, Apple began shipping iMacs that include both Mac OS X and Mac OS 9.1 (or 9.2, in some cases) on the hard disk.

Flat Panel iMacs

In early 2002, Apple introduced the flat-panel iMac, complete with a PowerPC G4 processor and a radical new 15" flat-panel display on a swiveling neck. Its design marks the return of the tray-loading CD/DVD drive, albeit more automatic. The iMac G4 ships with both Mac OS 9 and Mac OS X; unlike all previous iMacs, it defaults into Mac OS X.

From the Front

Here you can get acquainted quickly with all the different ways you'll interact with your iMac on a daily basis. Figure 1-1 shows a slot-loading iMac from the front.

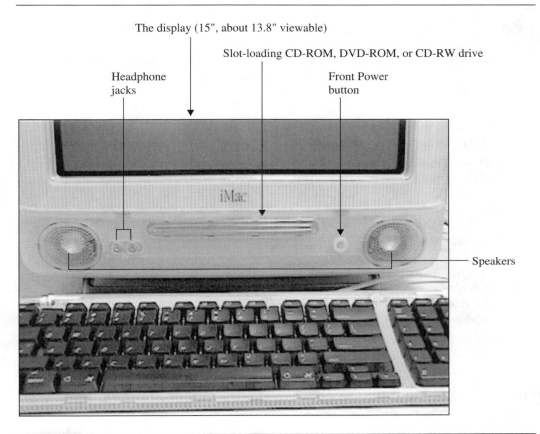

The display (15", about 13.8" viewable)

Slot-loading CD-ROM, DVD-ROM, or CD-RW drive

Headphone
jacks

Front Power
button

Speakers

FIGURE 1-1   The slot-loading iMac from the front

Here are some basic notes about the front of your iMac:

■ Place your mouse close to the keyboard and on a mousepad, which is recommended
for smooth movement and to help keep the inside of the mouse clean. (The Pro Mouse,
shipped with slot-loading iMacs and the iMac G4, doesn't require a mousepad due to
its optical design.)

■ The Power button on the original iMac's keyboard can be used to turn off the iMac or to
display a window with various power-off options. On slot-loading and iMac G4 models,
you can use the Power button on the front or side of the iMac for an emergency restart of
the iMac (when it crashes or freezes) by holding down the button for six or more seconds.
You can also press the button on those models quickly to put the iMac to sleep.

NOTE   *On the slot-loading iMac, the Power button on the front of the iMac pulses while the iMac is in sleep mode.*

■ The iMac has shipped with two different keyboards—the space-saving original Apple USB Keyboard and the newer Pro Keyboard design. The Pro Keyboard offers two sets of modifier keys (⌘, OPTION, and SHIFT) as well as special keys for changing sound volume and for ejecting CD media.

■ Feel free to switch the mouse from one side to the other. USB devices can be unplugged and plugged back in even while the iMac is turned on and active.

■ On the original iMac, the CD-ROM drive needs to be worked with carefully. If you don't have a CD in the drive already, you can open it by pressing the colored button on the front. The drive pops open. (If you do have a CD in the drive, drag the CD icon on the iMac's desktop to the Trash icon. This is explained more in Chapter 2.) You'll need to pull the CD-ROM drive tray out with a finger. Then, place CDs as you would in any CD player and lightly push the tray back until it clicks shut.

■ On the slot-loading iMac, CDs and DVDs are a little easier to deal with. Just slide the disc lightly into the drive until the drive catches and pulls it in the rest of the way. (If you don't feel the drive catch, don't force it—make sure you don't already have a disc in the drive first.) When a CD is ejected, be careful not to grab it too quickly; make sure it's completely ejected by the iMac first, then grab it.

■ With the iMac G4, you'll open and eject CDs by pressing the EJECT key on the keyboard; it's in the upper-right corner, just to the right of the MUTE key.

From the Side or Back

The ports for your iMac's peripherals and Internet or network connections are on the side or back of the iMac. On the original iMac, you open the port door by putting your finger in the hole and lightly pulling down and away to expose the ports for connecting your iMac to devices.

The slot-loading iMacs and iMac G4 models don't have a port door. Figure 1-2 shows the ports for an iMac G4. Earlier tray-loading iMacs have the same ports with the exception of FireWire; on all three models the ports are arranged somewhat differently, but labeled the same. Note that the iMac G4 has three USB ports; others have only two.

Here are some things to keep in mind about the ports on your iMac:

■ The modem and Ethernet ports look similar, but they accept different types of cable. The modem port accepts a typical RJ-11 "modular" telephone cable connector. The Ethernet port accepts an RJ-45 10BaseT cable (also called "twisted-pair") connector. If your connector isn't fitting properly, examine the cable and the ports carefully.

■ On the original iMac, the Reset and Programmer's buttons are best selected with a straightened paperclip. On the slot-loading iMac, the Reset button is an actual button.

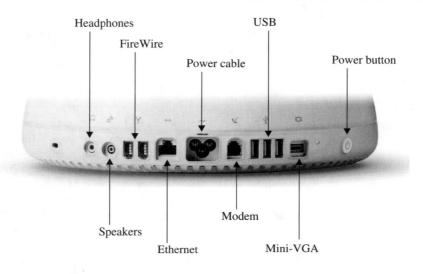

Headphones

FireWire

Power cable

USB

Power button

Modem

Speakers

Ethernet

Mini-VGA

FIGURE 1-2   The ports on the iMac G4

Be careful though—pressing either while your iMac is running will immediately restart the iMac and cause you to lose data! (The iMac G4 has no special reset buttons.)

■ USB ports accept USB cables in one direction only, so if the USB connector doesn't fit easily, turn it over. FireWire ports are the same way.

■ The ports for the external speaker and microphone are stereo miniplug ports. (The latest iMac models don't have a microphone port.) The microphone port will accept a PlainTalk microphone (from Apple), a miniplug-compatible microphone, or a line-in connection from an audio source, like a stereo receiver. The speaker port is a line-out source; it isn't amplified, so it will only work with powered speakers or a stereo receiver, not with headphones or inexpensive, nonpowered PC speakers. The iMac G4 has a special port for its external speakers.

■ Most slot-loading iMac models include a video-out port, which you can use for video mirroring. It's found hidden behind a removable plastic grille on the back of the iMac. This port enables you to connect an external monitor (or a VGA-based overhead projector) that can display the same image as the iMac's screen at the exact same time. The iMac G4's mini-VIA port requires a special adapter that must be bought separately, adapting it for a regular VGA connection.

Before You Set Up iMac

If you've just gotten your iMac and you're waiting for me to tell you how to get started, this is your section. I'll also talk about some relevant issues for users who have their iMac running—stuff not necessarily covered by the iMac manual from Apple. Let's take a quick look.

Get a Surge Protector

Not enough people get surge protectors for their computers, and I suggest you run out and buy one right now (or at least later today) if you plan to start or continue using your iMac. The surge protector is designed to let you plug in a number of peripherals while stopping power surges from reaching your valuable equipment. It keeps your iMac from getting fried, basically, when a power surge occurs thanks to a lightning strike, power outage, or problem with your (or your power company's) wiring.

You need to get the kind of surge protector that includes protection for the phone line, too. In my experience, extreme surges occur more frequently over phone lines than over power lines. Since your phone line will probably almost always be plugged into your iMac's modem port, it's possible for such a surge to go straight into the modem, causing it to cease functioning. In fact, this could affect your entire iMac.

A good surge protector costs at least $25, probably more depending on the features. Don't get an $8 protector and think you're done—often, those are just power strips (giving you more plug receptacles), not protectors. Check the box to see if the manufacturer offers a guarantee or equipment replacement insurance. If so, there's a decent chance the protector actually works well.

Keep Glare to a Minimum

Another important consideration before you set up your iMac is where the windows are. I mean actual windows—those things in the wall that let sunlight in.

In general, avoid having a window directly in front of the iMac (that is, when you sit at the iMac, the window is at your back) or directly behind the iMac (when you look at the iMac's screen, you can see the window behind it). The reason for this is simple—glare and eyestrain. If the window is directly behind you, then sunlight will glare off the screen and make it harder to see text and images on your iMac. If the window is directly behind the iMac, your eyes will have trouble adjusting to the varying levels of light, causing strain and fatigue.

Along those same lines, it's always a good idea to look away from your monitor for a minute or more every 15 minutes. That means looking out the window (which should be directly to your right or left if possible), reading a bit, or just letting yourself relax and perform eye exercises, raise a dumbbell, get up for some water, or do whatever you do to relax.

Don't Forget the Ergonomics

It's also important to consider the ergonomic implications of your setup. While I'm not a doctor or chiropractor, I can pass on some general advice. You might want to consult an expert regarding your setup, especially if you're experiencing any pain or strain.

First of all, your hands and legs should generally approach the table and chair that support your iMac at a 90-degree angle. That means elbows at 90 degrees and knees at 90 degrees with your feet flat on the floor, if possible. Adjust your table and/or chair if neither of these angles is correct.

Next, you shouldn't look far down or far up at your monitor—don't crane your neck, in other words. If you have an iMac G4, position and tilt the display so that the top of the screen is level with your eyes when you're looking straight ahead. With other models, if you're looking down at your monitor, you should consider purchasing a special stand to raise the iMac. (You can also lower your adjustable chair, if you have one, as long as that doesn't adversely affect your sitting and typing position.)

In fact, looking straight ahead is exactly what you want to do. Do you have a desk that positions the monitor off to the side at an angle? They should be illegal. You should look *directly* at a monitor that is in front of you, not to one side. Otherwise, you'll have your neck and/or back cocked sideways for minutes or hours at a time—not a good thing. It's like driving cross-country while looking out the driver-side window. That would start to hurt after a while, wouldn't it?

Do you have padded mouse and wrist accessories? Don't let them allow you to get lazy. The ideal wrist position is actually over the keys slightly, not resting on the wrist pad—at least, according to most things I've heard and read. If you took piano class as a kid, then you know how you're supposed to hold your hands. Keep them aloft for a while. When you're tired, don't rest your wrists on little gel things—quit typing.

Finally, the second you start to feel pain or strain, contact your doctor. (Repetitive strain injuries are serious and often covered by health insurance policies.) You may be able to get add-on keyboards, mice, or some other solution for working with your iMac. Or your doctor may prescribe a vacation to the Bahamas for two weeks. Especially if you slip her five bucks or so.

Set Up iMac

Now for the moment of truth. When you've accounted for surges, glare, and ergonomics, the setup instructions that come with your iMac are perfectly acceptable.

1. Pull the iMac out of the box, place it on the table, and use the little bar to tilt it up slightly, if desired.

NOTE   *Technically the iMac is portable, but it's still heavy at 25-40 pounds, depending on the model. On earlier models, grasp both the handle and the area right under the CD/DVD drive, to lift and carry the iMac in two hands. With the iMac G4, you can lift it using only the metal neck, according to Apple.*

2. Plug the power cord into the power socket on the back of the iMac, then plug it into your surge protector.

3. Using the phone wire that came with the surge protector, connect the phone wire from your wall socket to the Phone In socket on your surge protector. Use the phone cord that came with your iMac to stretch from the Phone Out on the surge protector to the modem socket on the iMac. (Note: You can use a small phone splitter from Radio Shack or a similar store if you want to place a telephone next to your iMac.)

4. Plug the iMac's keyboard cord into one of the USB ports on the iMac's side or back.

5. Plug your iMac's mouse into one of the USB ports on the keyboard (according to your preference).

6. Press the Power button on the front or side of the iMac. The little light on the Power button built into the iMac (or the light on the flat-panel display) will glow.

7. That's it. If all goes well, your iMac should fire up and be ready to go. You'll see the famous Happy Mac, followed by either the "Welcome to Macintosh" or the Mac OS X startup screen. Soon, if this is the first time you've turned on your iMac, the Setup Assistant will greet you.

NOTE *If you don't see anything on the screen, if you see something blinking, or if it's been, say, 20 minutes and nothing is happening and the power light is amber, pulsating, or off, turn to Chapter 29 to troubleshoot your iMac.*

Get Online with the Assistants

Once the iMac has started up, you'll be greeted by the Setup Assistant. The Mac OS's Assistants are designed to walk you through some of the basic settings that your iMac needs to operate without making you dig too deep into all the configuration controls. The Assistant, instead, asks you plain questions and helps you enter the answers.

Both Mac OS X and Mac OS 9 have Setup Assistants, and they're a little different. Which you see first depends on which OS is selected as your primary operating system. But, you will need to set up each operating system the first time you launch it, so you'll likely encounter both Assistants at some point.

NOTE *If the Assistants described in this section don't sound familiar, you may be dealing with an older iMac and/or Mac OS version. (You'll also sometimes see these assistants when you re-install Mac OS 9.1 or higher.) In that case, you'll encounter separate Setup and Internet Assistants, which should be fairly self-explanatory. Simply make choices in the Assistant windows and click the right-facing arrow to move on.*

The iMac Setup Assistant

The first Assistant you'll encounter (if your iMac defaults to Mac OS 9.1 or later) is the iMac Setup Assistant. The point of this series of screens is to retrieve registration information, get you connected to the Internet, and set up other items. After seeing the "Welcome" screen (in many different languages) click the mouse button to run through the Setup Assistant and answer the questions. When you've answered a question, click the Continue button to move to the next screen. If you need to go back to a previous question, click the Go Back button.

You should note that the main purpose of this assistant is to register your computer and send that registration over the Internet. If you prefer not to set up your iMac for Internet access at this point, you can choose the No, Not Right Now option when asked if you'd like to set up Internet access. You can later use the Internet Setup Assistant (in Mac OS 9.1 or later) to create an Internet account.

If you do opt to set up an Internet account, you can use the assistant to set up a special trial account with Earthlink, or you can set up your iMac with an existing account. If you choose an existing account, you'll want to have all information from your ISP handy—with help from the assistant, you'll enter everything by hand. When you're done establishing an Internet account or otherwise working online, you'll be connected to the Internet automatically by the assistant.

> NOTE   *Mac OS 9 has other assistants that, oddly enough, don't seem to launch any more on new iMac models. (They used to with earlier models.) If you open the Applications (Mac OS 9) folder, then the Utilities folder, you'll find an Assistants folder. Double-click the Mac OS Setup Assistant to perform some basic setup tasks, including setting an owner's name and, if desired, a printer. (These are topics that are also covered later in the book, if you'd like to worry about them then.) Double-click the Internet Setup Assistant if you'd like to get some help establishing an Internet connection.*

The Mac OS X Setup Assistant

The Mac OS X Setup Assistant begins in a way similar to the iMac Setup Assistant—after the musical "Welcome" screen, you begin by choosing your country and clicking the Continue button. You continue to answer questions in the Assistant and click the Continue button to move to the next question; click the Go Back button to return to a previous screen. After the initial screens, you'll be asked to enter registration information and some demographic questions—don't forget to check No next to the I Would Like… options if you don't want to be contacted by Apple or third parties.

The next screens are more interesting. On the Create Your Account screen, enter your full name in the Name entry box, followed by an eight-character (or less) user name in the Short Name box. This will be your name on the Mac OS X system, and it will be the name of your personal *home* folder, where your documents and preferences will be stored. Next, enter an eight-character (or less) password in the Password and Verify boxes (since you can't see what you type, you'll enter it twice). Remember that passwords are case-sensitive, so if you use any capital letters, you'll always have to type those letters as capitals. In the Password Hint entry box, enter a hint that doesn't give away your password, but that you can use to help remember it, if desired.

> NOTE   *The password and user name are necessary if you decide to enable Multiple Users, discussed in Chapter 27, or to access your iMac from another computer on a network as discussed in Chapter 28. (You'll also sometimes use the password and user name when installing new software.) Also, the password can be any length, but the first eight characters are the only ones that are looked at by Mac OS X. Remember to keep your password from being easily guessed by combining numbers and letters, preferably using nonsensical words.*

Once you've created a user account, you'll set up your Internet account. If you have your own existing account, select that option and click Continue. You'll then need to select the type of account and enter information provided by your ISP. If you don't yet want Internet access, you can select I'm Not Ready to Connect to the Internet and skip a few steps.

Software Update

If you configured an Internet account using the Mac OS X Assistant, Software Update may automatically launch and check special Apple computers via the Internet for updates to your Mac OS X software. If Software Update finds new versions of your software, the Software Update icon flashes in the Dock at the bottom of the screen; click it and a listing will appear in the Software Update window. Place check marks next to the items you want to install, then click Install. A window will appear asking for your password; enter it in the Password box and click OK. Now, the updates will be downloaded and installed automatically. Note that these updates can take a long time if you have a modem connection, so if you'd like to ignore Software Update for now, click Cancel in the Software Update window and it will disappear. (See Chapter 29 for more on Software Update.)

Next up, you'll choose your local time zone on the Select Time Zone screen, followed by the Set Your Date and Time screen (use the arrows next to the "digital" date and time entries to change them to the current date and time). Click Continue and you'll be reminded to register if you haven't already. Then, the Mac OS X desktop will appear and you're ready to compute.

iMac: On, Off, Sleep, Info

Once you get past the Assistants, you're greeted with the desktop—the space that shows your hard drive icon, a few words across the top of the screen, and even a little Trash can. I'll discuss this area in more depth in Chapters 2 through 5. For now, we need to talk about a few important commands.

Which Mac OS Do You Have?

The first one is the About This Computer command. Throughout this book, I'll be referring to different versions of the Mac OS. In order to know if a particular feature is available to you, you'll need to know if you have Mac OS 9.1, Mac OS X, or a later or earlier version of the Mac OS. To find out, move your mouse pointer to the top of the screen and point it at the little Apple picture. Click the mouse button once. A menu appears.

Now, move the mouse down the menu until it points at About This Computer (in Mac OS 9) or About This Mac (in Mac OS X). Click the mouse button again. The About This Mac window appears (see Figure 1-3).

FIGURE 1-3   On the left, the About this Computer box in Mac OS 9; on the right, About This Mac in Mac OS X

This window tells you some other things about your iMac, including how much system RAM (random access memory) it has and, in Mac OS X, the type of processor your iMac has installed.

Turn Off iMac

You've already turned on your iMac successfully using the Power button on the front or side of the iMac. But what about turning off the iMac? There are a couple of different ways, and it's important to turn it off correctly.

Let's start with the one way *not* to turn off your iMac. Don't just cut power to the machine. That means don't just pull the cord out of the wall or surge protector, and it means don't just throw the power switch on the surge protector. If your iMac ever crashes you may have to resort to this sort of thing, but not yet.

Instead, shut down your iMac gracefully by choosing the aptly named Shut Down command. In Mac OS 9, move the mouse up to the Special menu. (If you don't see the Special menu, click once anywhere on the desktop background.) Click once on the Special menu item and the full menu appears. Now point to the Shut Down command and click the mouse again. Your iMac shuts down.

In Mac OS X, you choose the Shut Down command from the Apple menu (the one that looks like an Apple logo).

 *Another way to Shut Down is to tap the POWER key on your iMac's keyboard, if it has a POWER key. A dialog box appears, allowing you to do a number of power-related things. To shut down, just click the Shut Down button with your mouse.*

You may notice that, after choosing Shut Down, your iMac goes through a few hoops. It will ask all open application programs if they need to save anything, then it tells them to quit. During that process, the application may ask *you* if you want to save something. Once all that business has been taken care of, the iMac quits all those programs, writes some last-minute things to the hard disk, and shuts itself down. To start up again, tap the Power button.

Restart iMac

Sometimes you don't really want iMac to shut all the way down. Instead, you want it to simply restart—maybe you've just installed a new program or you're experiencing odd behavior because of an errant program or similar issue. In that case, you'll click Restart from the Special menu (in Mac OS 9) or from the Apple menu (in Mac OS X). You can also tap the POWER key on your keyboard, if you have such a key, and choose Restart. Your iMac goes through the same procedure as when you issue the Shut Down command, except that the power is never turned off to the iMac, and the Mac OS starts right back up again after the contents of system memory are cleared.

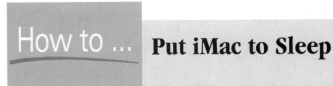

How to ... Put iMac to Sleep

Here's the cool option. Instead of shutting down your iMac, you can choose to put the iMac to sleep instead, so that it wakes up more quickly and is ready to work after only a few seconds. The best part is that the iMac is still using very little power, even though it's technically turned on and working. (In some cases, it can even wake up to accept an incoming fax!)

If your iMac is a slot-loading or flat-panel model, you can put it to sleep by simply pressing the Power button on the front or side of the iMac. Your iMac should immediately power down, plus, the Power button will strobe (on the flat-panel models), almost as if the iMac were snoring.

You can also put any iMac to sleep by choosing Sleep from the Special menu in Mac OS 9, or by choosing Sleep from the Apple menu in Mac OS X. If your iMac has a POWER key on its keyboard, you can press that key, then click the Sleep command that appears in the dialog box onscreen.

To wake up your iMac, just tap any key on the keyboard. The screen will light back up (it may also shimmer), and iMac may beep to acknowledge your command. You're ready to compute.

Chapter 2

Get Acquainted with iMac

How to...

- Figure out what the desktop is for
- Learn how to use the mouse
- Click and drag on the screen
- Get to know icons and windows
- Get some Help
- Boot between versions of the Mac OS

If you've worked your way through Chapter 1, then, hopefully, you've gotten past the Setup Assistant, you have an Internet account, and all your settings are in order. Now let's take a look at what you see once you've powered up your iMac. Your iMac is a combination of hardware—things on the outside that you touch and push like the CD-ROM or DVD-ROM drive, the mouse, and the keyboard—and software—pictures and words on the screen like icons, menu items, and windows.

In this chapter you'll see how those things come together. You'll learn how to move around on the screen, work with the mouse and keyboard, even how to insert CD-ROMs and DVD-ROMs and work with the internal hard disk.

NOTE   *As mentioned in Chapter 1, recent iMac models have shipped with different Mac OS versions, either Mac OS X or Mac OS 9, while many have shipped with both. While the operating systems have some fundamental differences, they're similar enough that this chapter and Chapter 3 can cover both conceptually. Then you can move on to Chapter 4 to study Mac OS X in depth or Chapter 5 to work with Mac OS 9.*

What Is the Desktop?

Let's begin at the beginning. After you've pressed the POWER key on your keyboard or the front of the iMac and your iMac has started up, you'll see one of two things: the login screen or the desktop. If you see a login screen, you'll need to enter your user name and password, as detailed in Chapter 27.

In most cases, you'll see the desktop. The *desktop,* for all practical purposes, is the background pattern or color you see on the main screen of your iMac when it first starts up. Think of it in terms of 3-D: There's the little hard disk picture(s), the menu bar, and the Trash picture. All these items can be thought of as sitting *on top of* the desktop, as shown in Figure 2-1. And if you don't see a desktop like Figure 2-1, which shows Mac OS X version 10.0.4, then your iMac has started up in Mac OS 9, as shown in Figure 2-2.

If it's called the desktop, then clearly this is supposed to have some relationship to a typical desk, right? Sort of. The desktop represents the top of a desk, but there's stuff on it that you wouldn't normally put on the top of your desk, like a trash can and a hard disk. But, for the most part, the metaphor holds up.

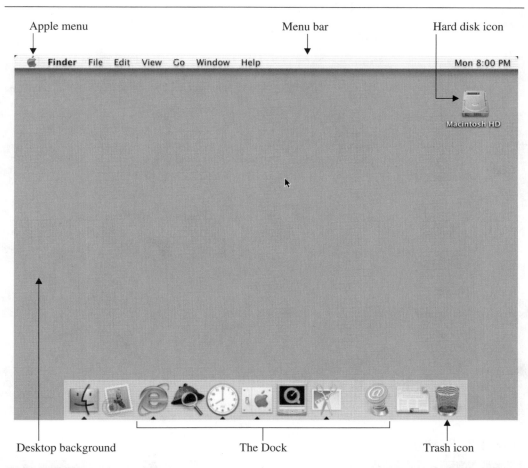

FIGURE 2-1   The Mac OS X desktop is the pattern or color behind other interface elements that comprise your virtual "workspace."

So what are you looking at? The desktop metaphor is made possible by three major elements: icons, menus, and windows. Each represents a real-world idea you'd find near, or on, a desk.

What's an Icon?

Icons are the small pictures that represent parts of your iMac or files on your computer. The Macintosh HD icon, for instance, represents the hard disk that's inside your iMac's case. A hard disk is used for storage—it's sort of a virtual filing cabinet. The icon, then, allows you to open that filing cabinet and root around in the file folders.

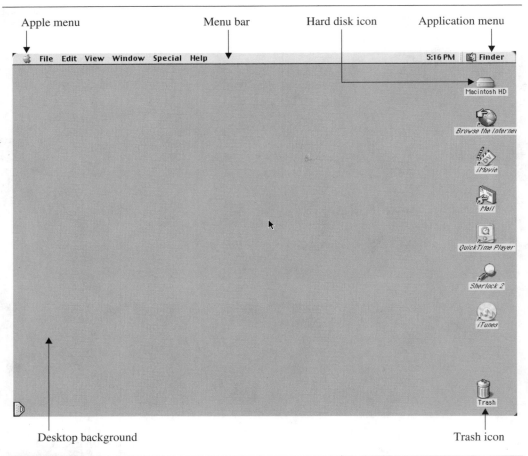

Apple menu   Menu bar   Hard disk icon   Application menu

Desktop background   Trash icon

FIGURE 2-2   Here is the Mac OS 9 desktop, which is similar, but offers some visual differences.

What's a Menu?

The little words at the top of the iMac screen are called *menus*—they're situated in the long, white (or gray) menu bar. Each of these menus holds related commands that allow you to accomplish things on your iMac, almost as if they were the drawers full of pencils, staplers, and scissors you'd find in a real desk.

In Mac OS X, the menu bar offers two distinct menus, shown in the following illustration. Both of these menus will appear no matter what application you're using on your iMac. One is the Apple menu; the other is the "application" menu, which is named for the application that's currently active. Point at the application menu (the menu marked Explorer in the illustration) and click the mouse button and you'll see commands that enable you to hide the current application, show all applications, and, in most cases, quit that application. Point and click on the Apple menu and you can access a number of quick preferences and shortcuts to help make your computing tasks simpler.

In Mac OS 9, the menu bar offers the same two menus, the Apple menu and Application menu, but they're in different places and they do slightly different things. While the Apple menu is still a repository for common commands, it is a bit more full-featured, as discussed in Chapter 5. Likewise, the Application menu is different—it's used to switch between different open applications as well as to show and hide them. (More on that in Chapter 5 as well.)

TIP *If you're familiar with Microsoft Windows, you'll notice that Mac menus work slightly differently. In Windows, each individual window has its own menu bar within that window. On the iMac, the menu bar is always at the top of the screen, and although it may seem like the iMac menu bar is always the same, it actually changes every time you load or switch to a different application.*

What's a Window?

Our final element, the window, is sort of like a piece of paper you might find on your real-world desktop. It's in windows that you'll type things, read things, draw things, and so on. In fact, on the iMac, just about anything you do will take place in a window. If you'd like to see a window, point your mouse at the Macintosh HD icon and click the mouse button twice quickly. (That's called a "double-click" and it almost always *opens* the item you double-clicked.) We'll talk about windows in greater depth later in this chapter.

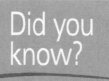

The Dock

Before we move on to the basics of the mouse and keyboard, there's probably one other question you may be asking if you're using Mac OS X—what's the Dock? That area down at the bottom of the screen is a new feature in Mac OS X, and it has some interesting capabilities. As you'll see later in this chapter, the Dock is where you'll always find the Trash can in Mac OS X; in Chapter 4, you'll see that the Dock is one way to switch between applications. In fact, the Dock is many things—you can start applications from it, launch applications using it, and even place your own items on the Dock. For now, just remember that it's there and it's an important part of the Mac experience; in Chapter 4, you'll see how to use and customize the Dock to its fullest.

Using the Mouse and Keyboard

The most basic skill requirement for using a modern computer is the ability to use a mouse and keyboard. The mouse, perhaps, is primary on the Macintosh, since Macs were designed from the outset to use the little guy.

Depending on the age of your iMac, you have one of two mouse designs. The earlier iMac mouse was a round disk with one large button, called the Apple USB Mouse (you can see the name on the underside of the mouse). This mouse is interesting to users because it can be a little tough to orient—"up" is where the mouse cable connects to the mouse, and you need to orient "up" so that it's pointed in the general direction of your iMac. (Not pointed *toward* the iMac, but oriented in that direction, perpendicular to your keyboard.)

The oval mouse (called the Pro Mouse) is interesting in two respects. First, it's an *optical* mouse, meaning it doesn't have a rolling ball that registers movement. This results in good tracking on a normal tabletop, even without a mouse pad. Second, the mouse doesn't appear to have a button—that's because the whole top of the mouse acts as the button. When resting your hand naturally on the mouse, pressing down with your fingers will cause it to "click."

NOTE   *For the sake of convenience I'll refer throughout this chapter, and elsewhere in the book, to "pressing the mouse button." In the case of the Pro Mouse, this simply means the top portion of the mouse under your fingers. You'll hopefully get used to this movement fairly quickly.*

Click with the Mouse

The mouse is used to point at, grab, carry, and activate items on the desktop. It'd be more convenient if you could just reach into your iMac screen to grab things, but that gets expensive really fast since you'd have to buy all those new iMacs. Instead, you use the mouse to point and grab for you.

When you move the mouse, a little arrow on the screen moves around with you to indicate where the mouse is currently pointing. That arrow is called the "mouse pointer," and it's something you'll get to know very well. No matter what you want to do with your iMac, you'll likely do it by rolling the mouse pointer over to an icon (or menu item or window) on your screen and clicking the mouse button.

NOTE   *Mouse movements are relative, not absolute. That means if you pick up the mouse and put it down in a different place, the location of the mouse pointer on the screen won't change. Only rolling (or sliding) the mouse in a particular direction will move the mouse in that direction.*

There are three basic actions that the mouse allows you to perform: select, open, and drag-and-drop. Each of these is a combination of pointing the mouse and clicking the mouse button:

■ **Select**   To select an item, move the mouse pointer until it's touching that item, then press and release the mouse button once. A selected icon becomes highlighted, a selected window comes to the *foreground* (it appears "on top" of other windows), and a selected menu drops down to show you its contents. In the case of a menu, you move your mouse down to the menu item and click again to select that menu item. You'll also find buttons and menus within applications that need to be selected.

■ **Open**   Icons like the Macintosh HD are opened (to reveal their contents) by pointing the mouse at the item and double-clicking the mouse button. Other icons can be opened, too, like document, folder, and application icons.

NOTE   *You can also open icons and folders in the Finder by selecting them (pointing at the icon and clicking once), pointing at the File menu and clicking once, then pointing at the Open command and clicking once.*

■ **Drag-and-Drop**   On the desktop and in the Finder, you can drag icons around to move them from one place to another. Place the mouse pointer on an item, click and hold down the mouse button, and move the mouse. Now you're dragging. To drop the icon in its new location, let go of the mouse button.

You'll also find that the mouse pointer changes sometimes to reflect different things that are happening. It'll turn into a little rotating beach ball, for instance, when the iMac is busy doing something that can't be interrupted in the current application. It'll turn into an *insertion point* (a capital "I"—also called an I-beam) when the mouse is hovering over a window (or sometimes a portion of a window, such as a part of an electronic form) where you can type. Click the mouse once in that window and the *insertion point* is placed in the document. Type with the keyboard and your words appear.

> Directions to Mike's: Take the 6
> train to 14th Street. then switch to
> the L and|

Special Keyboard Keys

Most of the time, you'll find that typing on the iMac keyboard is like typing on any computer terminal, typewriter, or word processor. But there are special keys on the iMac's keyboard and special key combinations you'll use for various things.

The special keys are the CONTROL (Control), OPTION (Option), and ⌘ (Command) keys. These keys, along with the more familiar SHIFT key, can be used in various combinations to perform special commands in your application or in the Finder.

You'll see these special keyboard commands throughout this book. In order to use them, you'll need to hold down all of the keys at once, then release them all together. For instance, ⌘-S can be used to save a document in most applications; press ⌘ first and then the S key, release them together, and the command will execute.

NOTE   *Some of the most common keyboard commands are discussed in Chapters 3 and 7; others are discussed throughout the book.*

This brings up a fourth instance where you can use the mouse to perform some interesting tasks. Hold down the CONTROL key, click the mouse, and then release them both. Do this in the right place (usually when pointing at an object in the Finder or in an application) and you'll get a *contextual menu*—a special "pop-up" menu of options regarding that object, as shown in the accompanying illustration. In essence, iMac is offering a special set of menu commands that are relevant to the object you've chosen.

> NOTE *If you're used to Microsoft Windows, you'll notice that the iMac mouse only has one button. This CONTROL-click scheme is sort of like "right-clicking" in Windows.*

If you have an iMac made in the spring of 2001 or later, you'll also notice some other keys on your extended keyboard. On the far right, above the number pad, are three audio keys (VOLUME DOWN, VOLUME UP, and MUTE) along with an EJECT key. The EJECT key is used to eject media in the CD or DVD drive, and it works whether you're viewing the Finder or not. The volume keys also work whether or not you're in the Finder, with some exceptions. (For instance, the keys will occasionally not be recognized when you're playing a full-screen game.)

> NOTE *These keys didn't work in early versions of Mac OS X, but they're now fully functional in Mac OS X version 10.1 and higher.*

The Mouse and Keyboard Connectors

Your mouse and keyboard both connect to the iMac using one of the two USB (Universal Serial Bus) ports on the side of the iMac. The keyboard is plugged into the iMac, then the mouse is plugged into one side or the other of the keyboard. (You can also plug your mouse into the USB port on the iMac's side, but the keyboard is a better choice.)

If one or both of these plugs works loose, don't worry about it too much. USB is called a *hot-pluggable* technology, which basically means that it's OK to connect and disconnect devices while your iMac is running. Bottom line: If one of the devices comes unplugged, plug it back in. It should work right away.

> NOTE *You'll see more about this in Chapter 26, but your iMac's keyboard actually contains a USB hub. That means its second USB port can be used for connecting another USB device, such as a joystick, trackball, or even an image scanner or printer.*

Work with Icons and Windows

I mentioned that icons are the small pictures on your iMac screen that represent parts of your iMac's internal filing system. And while icons represent different parts, windows are the way you view those parts—when you open a file folder or a document, you'll view its contents using a window. Let's look at icons and windows each in turn.

In Depth with Icons

You can often tell right away what a given item is based on the way its icon looks. There are about five different types of icons you'll encounter on your iMac, and each gives you an idea of what it does based on its general appearance.

■ **Hardware Icons** These icons appear on the desktop to help you interact with some of the hardware in or attached to your iMac. Whenever you start up your iMac, for instance, the internal hard disk is recognized and the Macintosh HD icon is placed on the desktop. Similarly, if you pop a CD-ROM into your iMac's CD-ROM or DVD-ROM drive, that CD's icon appears on the desktop. *Hardware icons generally look like the devices they're representing—the disk icons look like little disks.*

Audio CD

Macintosh HD

■ **Folders** Open your Macintosh HD and a window appears that shows you more icons— most of them will be folders. Folder icons are used by the Finder to help you manage your documents and applications. You can create a storage system by creating new folders that organize your documents and applications. *Folder icons look like file folders.*

Memos

Spreadsheets

■ **Programs** Application programs like AppleWorks or Internet Explorer have their own icons, too. When you "open" an application (by pointing to its icon and double-clicking the mouse) you start up that application, loading all of its menu commands and, probably, a document window. You can then start creating. *Program icons are often the most creative—they tend to be unique icons designed by the application programmers.*

Preview

SimpleText

■ **Documents** Document icons are created whenever you save a document in an application. If you create a report in AppleWorks, for instance, a new document is created when you invoke the Save command, and a new icon appears in the Finder. Just as with a document in a physical filing system, you can move that document icon to a folder where you want it stored. *Documents often, although not always, look like pieces of paper or some variation on that theme—a piece of paper with a special logo, for instance.*

RAM article

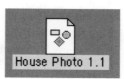

House Photo 1.1

■ **System Icons** This is a catch-all category that we won't discuss too much right now. The Mac OS features many special little icons that perform certain tasks behind the scenes on your iMac. For instance, there are system icons that represent the fonts you use in your documents and the special files used to manage color settings on your iMac. You'll read more about system icons in Part IV of this book.

Arial Narrow

iMac.icc

- **Aliases**   An alias is a special "empty" icon that doesn't really represent a file or a device—instead, it *points* to that file. For instance, an alias allows you to have a pointer to a document or application on your desktop while the actual document or application is stored deep in your hard disk's file folders. Instead of being an entire *copy* of a file, an alias is simply an icon that represents the file. *An alias looks like the document or application it points to, but it has a special, curved arrow as part of the icon.*

Mail

Icons will respond to the mouse commands described early in this chapter. They can be selected, opened, and moved around the screen using drag-and-drop. In fact, you'll find that there's often reason to drag an icon over another icon and drop the first icon on the second icon. For instance, you can drop a document icon on top of a folder icon to store that document in that folder. Similarly, you can drop a document icon onto an application icon to start that application and view the document.

Open Up Windows

So what do you do with these icons? In most cases, you open them. When you open a folder or document icon by double-clicking it, a window appears. Double-click the Macintosh HD icon, for instance, and a window appears that reveals that disk's folders and other icons, as shown in Figure 2-3.

Any window has standard parts that make it easy to deal with. All of these parts allow you to move things around, resize them, stack windows—do different things while you're working with the windows. Here's what the different parts do:

- **Close Button**   Click this to close the window. Note that you're dealing with an application's window, so closing the window doesn't necessarily quit the application. You'll often have a different command to Quit (usually in the File menu).

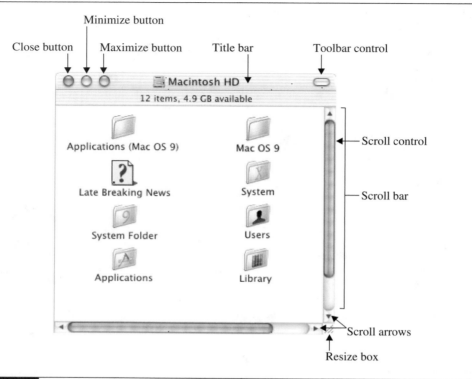

FIGURE 2-3 The parts of a window in Mac OS X

- **Minimize Button**   Click this button to minimize the window to the Dock. This is one way to decrease window clutter—the minimized window will appear as a *tile* on the right side of the Dock, where you can click it to work with it again.

- **Maximize Button**   Click this button to resize the window to optimum size (in many cases). Click it again to revert to the original size.

- **Title Bar**   This part of the window tells you what the window represents. It's also used to drag the window around the screen: Click and drag on the title bar, then release the mouse button to drop the window.

- **Toolbar Control**   In some windows, you can click this control to hide and show the toolbar. For instance, in Mac OS X, the Finder toolbar can be hidden and shown in this way. (More on this in Chapter 4.)

- **Scroll Bar**   This bar shows you that the window can be scrolled. If more information is in the window than can be shown at once, a scroll control will appear, which you can drag to see the rest of the window's contents.

- ■ **Scroll Control**   Click and drag the scroll control to scroll the window's contents up and down (or side to side, if you use the bottom scroll bar).
- ■ **Scroll Arrows**   Click the arrows to scroll up and down or side to side within the window.
- ■ **Resize Box**   Click and drag the resize box to make the window larger or smaller.

If you're working in Mac OS 9, you'll notice that the windows are similar, but not exactly the same. In particular, the top toolbar is different, with the close, minimize, and maximize controls in different places (they're also called "boxes" instead of "buttons" in Mac OS 9).

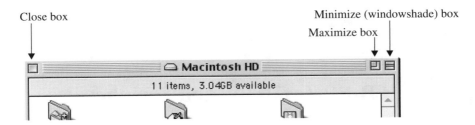

Close box

Minimize (windowshade) box

Maximize box

You'll also encounter some different sorts of windows, called *dialog boxes*. These windows are designed so that the Mac OS can ask you questions or get you to provide information. Usually, dialog boxes require you to click Cancel or OK after you've finished entering information (these tend to look like alerts, pictured next). They don't always, though.

As shown in this illustration, some dialog boxes have to be dealt with in order to move on from the document in question. In Mac OS X (Mac OS 9 doesn't have these special boxes), these are called dialog *sheets,* because they pop out from under the title bar of the document window in question, making it clear which window the dialog sheet's options will affect:

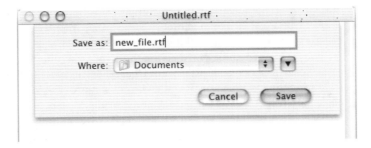

Another type of dialog box is called an *alert*. These messages appear when the Mac OS or an application needs to get your attention because something immediate is happening. This can range from something wrong with a printer or peripheral to a problem with a crashed or misbehaving application. Alerts are like regular dialog boxes, except they don't often give you many options or settings—you simply respond to the question. You can usually dismiss an alert by clicking the Cancel or OK button. (Shown is a Mac OS 9 alert.)

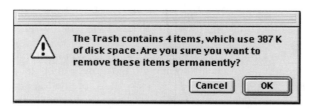

In Mac OS 9 you'll come across another type of alert, called a floating alert. These appear as small yellow strips and are designed to appear but remain unobtrusive, so that you can continue working. Click the alert's Close box to dismiss it.

Hard Disks, CD-ROMs, DVDs, and Peripherals

Your hard disk is where you'll store most of your documents and any new applications that you install on your iMac. The hard disk is a small box inside your iMac that uses magnetic technology to write down the ones and zeros that make up "digital data." Visually, this digital data is

Storage vs. Memory

Storage disks are different from main memory in any computer. Main memory is called *Random Access Memory (RAM)* and is actually comprised of little computer chips—usually arranged on a special plug-in module—that hold digital information. RAM is sort of the short-term memory of your iMac. Anything currently on the screen, anything being printed, and some behind-the-scenes work goes on in RAM. (In Chapter 1 you saw how to get the About This Computer information, which tells you the current status of RAM in Mac OS 9.)

But your iMac can easily forget what's in RAM, since RAM is wiped clean whenever you power down your iMac. In fact, if a power surge, a kicked power cord, or some other uncontrollable circumstance cut power to your iMac, you'd also lose whatever was in RAM at that time. RAM needs power in order to remember things.

That's why you have storage disks. Hard disks and removable disks (like Iomega's Zip disks) are used for writing things down and saving them long term. Whenever you create a document using your iMac, you'll want to save it to a disk—that lets you keep the document over the long term. The same goes for applications. If you bought and wanted to use Microsoft Office, you'd need to "install" the application by copying it to your hard disk. That way it's easily accessible to your iMac—your iMac will remember, long term, how to run Microsoft Office.

represented by folder, application, document, and system icons that are displayed when you double-click the disk icon in the Finder.

CD-ROM and DVD-ROM discs are slightly different. CD-ROM and DVD-ROM are *read-only* technologies because you can't actually save any files to the discs, delete files stored on the discs, or move things to different folders on the discs. Instead, you can only copy from the CD-ROM or DVD-ROM to another disk, start up an application, or open a document directly from the CD-ROM or DVD-ROM. (CD-ROM stands for Compact Disc–Read-Only Memory; DVD-ROM stands for Digital Versatile Disc–Read-Only Memory.)

Of course, not every disc you deal with is a data disc. You can also listen to music stored on audio CDs on your iMac, and you can watch DVD movies on iMacs equipped with DVD players.

The Hard Disk Icon

The hard disk icon is always there on the desktop by default (you can change this in Mac OS X, as detailed in Chapter 4). As the iMac starts up, it looks for the hard disk and other storage disks that are attached to the machine. Any disks found are "mounted" on the desktop. That is, the icon is made to appear on the desktop, available for you to use. If you insert a disk (like a CD) after startup, the Mac OS places the CD's icon as close to the top-right corner as it can get without covering up another icon.

To peer into the hard disk's contents, you can point the mouse at the icon and double-click. This opens the main-level window that shows all of the folders used to store things on your iMac. The hard disk icon can be renamed—you can even change the look of the icon—but you can't throw the icon away or store it inside a folder or on another storage device.

The Trash

Basically, the Trash is the one way you delete things from your hard disks, removable disks, or desktop. You simply drag-and-drop icons onto the Trash. When you've dropped something on the Trash icon, that icon changes to reflect the fact that the Trash has items in it. That doesn't mean that items have been deleted yet, though. More on that in Chapter 3.

The Trash icon is also used for something else—ejecting CDs and other removable disks. It takes some getting used to, but after you've dragged a CD or removable disk icon to the Trash, it will pop out of its drive (or the CD-ROM drive will open up). In Mac OS X, you'll even notice that when you do drag items to the Trash to be ejected, its icon changes to reflect that, as shown.

Disks are not deleted or erased when dragged to the Trash. There's a special command that erases entire disks when it's necessary to do so—in Mac OS 9, it's Special | Erase. In Mac OS X, you use the Disk Utility application, as discussed in Chapter 29.

If you've used Microsoft Windows 95/98/ME, you'll find that the Trash is very similar to the Recycle Bin in Windows. The major difference is that entire folders are stored, intact, in the iMac's Trash, while the Windows Recycle Bin will usually do away with folders.

CDs and DVDs

CD and DVD icons appear when you insert a CD or DVD into the CD or DVD drive of your iMac. How you insert the disc depends on what type of iMac you have. Newer iMac models offer a "slot-loading" CD, DVD, or, on models made in early 2001 and later, CD-RW (Compact Disc-Rewriteable) drive.

 Not all iMacs can play back DVD movies. From late 1999 to early 2001, most iMacs had a DVD-capable drive. These days, Apple offers some models that only support CD or CD-RW, while others can support both CD-RW, DVD and, in some cases, DVD-R (DVD-Recordable).

In this case, you insert discs the same way you slide them into the slot on a car-stereo CD player. If there's no disc currently in the iMac, just slide your disc into the open slot. After you've placed it part of the way in, it will be pulled the rest of the way in by its mechanism.

When iMac has recognized the disc, it puts a new icon on the desktop to represent that disc. If the disc is a data disc designed to store data files that your iMac can access in the form of icons, then you can double-click the icon to open a Finder window and view the files. Data discs include CD-ROM discs as well as CD-R (CD-Recordable) and CD-RW discs that have been created by other users.

 If you insert a blank CD-R or CD-RW disc into a newer iMac that has a CD-RW drive, you'll activate the Disc Burner software, which enables you to copy data to that disc. See Chapter 3 for details.

If the disc is an audio CD, you'll see a generic audio CD icon, probably named "Audio CD." In that case, double-clicking the CD icon will open up a window that shows you the different music tracks on the CD. Double-clicking one of the music tracks will open the Apple CD Player, QuickTime Player, or iTunes and play that track.

If the disc is a DVD video and you have an iMac that supports DVDs, then opening it reveals its contents—movie data—in a window. Double-clicking certain items may launch the Apple DVD Player, or you can launch the Apple DVD Player yourself (it's in the Apple menu in Mac OS 9, or in the Applications folder on your hard disk in Mac OS X) and it will automatically detect the presence of a DVD in the drive.

Since a CD-ROM or DVD-ROM is *read-only,* you can't drag an icon from the desktop or a Finder window to the disc icon or window. You can drag icons the other way, though, causing the items on the disc to be copied to a Finder window or the desktop.

 As mentioned, iMac models with a CD-RW do enable you to copy items to the disc. If you insert a CD-R or CD-RW disc in such an iMac, you'll be asked to prepare the disc—then, you can drag items to it and, eventually, "burn" those files to the disc. More on that in Chapter 3.

To eject the disc, you can do one of two things. You can select the disc icon with your mouse, then choose File | Eject or Special | Eject or press ⌘-E. That ejects the disc. Or, as mentioned before, you can drag the disc icon to the Trash. That ejects the disc; it doesn't erase it.

Removable Disks

If you have an Iomega Zip drive, a SuperDrive, or some other sort of external storage drive, those disks will appear on your desktop as well. Usually, you just pop the disk into the drive and, after a short delay, its icon appears on the desktop. It'll work just like a CD, with the exception that you'll be able to save files to removable storage disks.

You eject removable disks the same way you eject a CD: Select the disk and choose Special | Eject or File | Eject, or drag the disk's icon to the Trash.

Get Help from the Mac OS

The Help Viewer system, found in both Mac OS 9 and Mac OS X, is based on the Web technology using *hyperlinks,* which allow you to move from topic to topic in the Help Viewer system by clicking the blue, underlined text. This makes it easy to learn about a topic, then click to see a related topic.

In order to see help, open the Help menu and choose the *Application Name* Help command. This works both in the Finder (Help | Mac Help) and in other applications, such as iMovie (Help | iMovie Help). While some other applications will use their own help systems, the Help Viewer, shown in Figure 2-4, is the standard set by Apple.

FIGURE 2-4   The Help Viewer is the main online Help system for your iMac (Mac OS X version is shown).

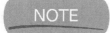 *For other applications, you may see other types of help. In Mac OS 9 or "Classic" applications, you may see the Apple Guide system, for instance, or in Internet Explorer you'll see Microsoft's own help system. See Chapter 5 for Classic help systems.*

You can also often get to the Help Viewer by holding down the CONTROL key and clicking anywhere in a window (for an application) or on the desktop area (for the main Mac Help topics). In the contextual menu that appears, choose the Help entry.

Browse for Help

With the Help Viewer open, you have a couple of choices. You can either browse for help or search for it. To browse, begin by clicking on the hyperlinks—the blue, underlined words—on the page. Clicking a hyperlink causes the Help Viewer to show you that topic. This method is a little like using the Table of Contents in a book. Click the topic that seems most appropriate. When the document for that topic appears in the Help Viewer, you can click the subtopic that seems most appropriate for your situation.

The browsing screen shows you topics that seem to be related to the original topic that you clicked. After you've clicked the subtopic, you'll most likely see an instructional document that walks you through that topic. While you're reading the instructions you'll see different types of hyperlinks:

- If you see a link that says "Tell Me More," then the Help Viewer will return you to a browsing screen filled with similar topics.

- If the link says "Open...for me," then the link is designed to automatically open the item or command that is being discussed in that help document. For instance, "Open System Preferences for me," when clicked, would open the System Preferences application.

- The third type of link points to a Web site on the Internet. These links often begin with "Go..." If your Internet connection is running, you can click one of these links to load your Web browser and view the help that's online. (If you have a modem-based connection, you may need to initiate that connection in the Internet Connect application before you can view help that's Web-based.)

To leave a particular page, you can either click the Back button in the Help Viewer (which returns you to the list of topics) or you can click a link that takes you to another, related topic. Or, click the Help Viewer's Close box to close help and return to your application.

Search for Help

If the Table of Contents approach doesn't work for you, you can search directly for a topic using keywords. In the Search entry box at the top of the screen, enter a few words that suggest the issue you want to learn about. You don't need to enter complete sentences—something like "application menu" or "mail merge" should be good enough. (You *can* enter a full question, though, which may help your search succeed.)

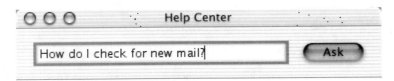

Then click Ask. After your iMac thinks things over, the Help Viewer will display the search results page. You'll notice that the search results include little dots in a second column. These dots represent the *relevance* of the subtopics—five dots means that the subtopic is very relevant to the type of information you're trying to get; fewer dots mean the subtopic is likely less relevant.

When you see a topic that looks good, click its hyperlink to see the associated help document. If you don't see the topic you want, you can click the Next link at the bottom of the page if the Help Viewer has identified other relevant topics. If you don't see the results you're looking for, you can try different keywords or a different search question—just type it in the Ask entry box, then click Ask.

TIP

If you started out in an application-specific help system, such as iMovie's Help, you may see a Search All Help link at the bottom of the results page. This enables you to conduct the same search using all of the Help Viewer help systems—Mac Help, iTunes Help, AppleScript Help, and so forth.

The Help Center

At the bottom of most Help Viewer screens you'll see a small question mark (?) icon. Click this icon and you're taken to the Help Center, which lets you browse or search all application help systems that are compatible with the Help Viewer. The more Help Viewer-compatible applications you have installed, the more options you'll see in the Help Center.

Boot Between OS Versions

As you'll see in upcoming chapters, today's iMac includes both Mac OS X and Mac OS 9 on the same disk. Which you use on a daily basis is largely up to you—I'll cover both in this book, and most of the iMac's bundled applications work in both environments. You should know right up front, though, that if you have Mac OS X and Mac OS 9 installed on your iMac, you have the option of booting into either of them.

Switching between the two is easy—it simply depends on where you start:

■ **If You're in Mac OS X** Launch the System Preferences application and select the Startup Disk icon. If you aren't signed into an Admin account, you'll need to click the locked padlock icon and enter the user name and password of an Admin account. Then, select the Mac OS 9 System folder icon that appears in the Startup Disk pane. Once it's selected, you can restart by clicking the Restart button (in version 10.1) or via Apple menu | Restart. The iMac will shut down, restart, and then Mac OS 9 should boot.

■ **If You're in Mac OS 9** Open the Apple menu and select Control Panels | Startup Disk. In the Startup Disk control panel, click the disclosure triangle next to the hard disk where Mac OS X is installed. Then, select the Mac OS X System folder (you'll see Mac OS X in the Version column). With the correct folder selected, click the Restart button.

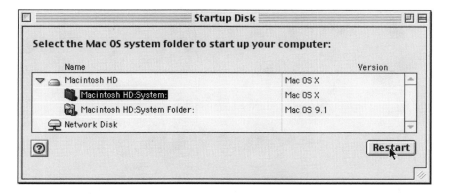

Note that you can use the Startup Disk pane or control panel to select a CD for startup, if desired. You can also select a CD for startup immediately after you've restarted your iMac and heard the startup tone. Simply hold down the C key to start up from a CD. And, if you ever get stuck starting up or restarting up from a CD, you can get out of it by holding down the OPTION key after hearing the startup tone. On the screen that appears, select your main hard disk's icon, then click the right arrow to start up from that disk.

Chapter 3

Manage Your Files

How to...

- ■ Dig into your Mac's folders
- ■ Create folders, duplicate files, and deal with aliases
- ■ Burn data CDs
- ■ Delete files and toss out the Trash
- ■ Get information on your disks, folders, and files
- ■ Change the way you view your folders
- ■ Search for files with Sherlock

When you first start up your iMac, in addition to seeing the desktop, you're also seeing the application that creates the desktop—the Finder. The Finder is a special application that's always active and can't easily be "quit." It's the Mac OS's built-in application for dealing with the files on your hard drive, CD/DVD drive, and removable media. Whether you're using Mac OS 9 or Mac OS X, you'll use the Finder to manage your applications, documents, and other files. In this chapter, I'll discuss some of the Finder behaviors that are common in both versions of the Mac OS—then, in Chapters 4 and 5, you'll see some of the differences. Plus, you'll meet Sherlock in this chapter—the Mac OS's built-in tool for searching for files on your iMac.

Files 101: Open Up Folders

The Finder offers you the tools for a basic filing system on your iMac. It allows you to create and name folders, move documents around, store application programs where you want them, and delete icons of all sorts when necessary. In a way, it's convenient to think of the Finder as an icon management utility.

In fact, your hard disk, accessed via the Finder, works a little like a filing cabinet. Open the cabinet (that is, open a disk), root through folders, and create new ones when you need to file away documents for a new project. The only difference is that you have to do all this on your computer screen. (Oh, and you never have to run out for any of those smelly markers from the office supply store.)

Dig Deep into Finder Windows

The Finder doesn't really help you *search* for things in an automated way—that's for Sherlock to do, as discussed later in this chapter. Instead, the Finder helps you organize and look for things manually. In a way, it's like comparing a library card catalog system to a computerized library search system. With the Finder, you'll be opening a lot of drawers and flipping through a lot of cards.

The most basic way to find something in the Finder is to dig for it. To do that, start out at the desktop and double-click the icon for your hard disk, CD-ROM, or a removable disk. This opens the window for that device so you can see its folders. Then, find the folder you want to look in next and double-click it. In Mac OS 9, a new window for that folder will open. Keep double-clicking folders until you find the item you're looking for, as shown in Figure 3-1.

SHORTCUT   *In Mac OS 9, there's a special trick to getting through many windows while keeping Finder clutter to a minimum: Hold down the OPTION key as you open new windows. Every time you open a new window, the previous one will close behind you if you're holding down OPTION as you double-click.*

3

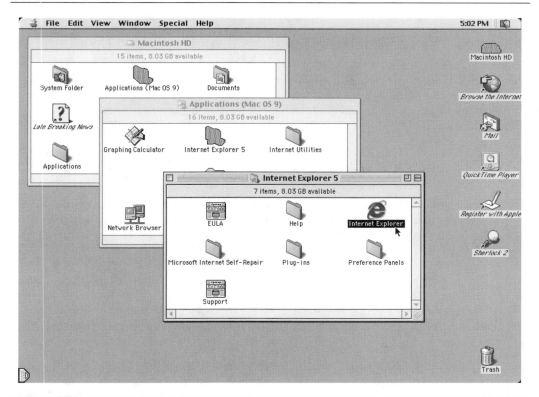

FIGURE 3-1   In Mac OS 9, you dig into your iMac's folders using the Finder.

As you can see, this method of digging can get a little tedious, and it opens up windows all over the screen. That's one reason that Mac OS X has abandoned this approach—when you double-click a folder in Mac OS X, its contents appear in that same window.

At least, that's the default behavior. If you'd prefer to dig through folder windows in Mac OS X, you can do it—simply select View | Hide Toolbar and you'll see the Finder window's toolbar disappear. (You can also click the small toolbar control box on the far right side of the Finder window's title bar.) Now, when you double-click a folder, a new Finder window will appear. To change back, select View | Show Toolbar.

> TIP
>
> *The OPTION key can also be used in Mac OS X; with the toolbar showing, clicking a folder while holding down OPTION will open that folder in a new Finder window. If the toolbar isn't showing, holding down OPTION will open that folder in the same Finder window.*

Understand Your iMac's Folders

So, when you first open up your hard disk (usually called "Macintosh HD") by double-clicking it on the desktop, what are you seeing? If you're working in Mac OS 9.1 or higher (whether or not you have Mac OS X installed on your iMac), you'll see three important folders that appear when you open up your hard disk: Applications (Mac OS 9), Documents, and System Folder. Here's a quick look at each:

- The *Applications (Mac OS 9)* folder is where you'll find all of the applications installed by the Mac OS 9 installer, including utilities, Internet applications, and Apple-provided applications such as iMovie and iTunes.

- The *Documents* folder is where, by default, you can store your personal documents. It's convenient to place your documents here because the Mac OS will often default to showing this folder when you first attempt to open or save documents.

> TIP
>
> *If you have more than one user and you're using Mac OS 9 as your primary operating system, you might want to set up personal home folders, as discussed in Chapter 27.*

- The *System Folder* is where the Mac OS's main files, along with important system files such as fonts and preferences files, are stored. You'll spend some time in this folder, but generally only for installations and troubleshooting, as discussed in Chapters 25, 26, and 29.

Nearly every installation of Mac OS X also includes these folders, since nearly every installation of Mac OS X includes Mac OS 9.1 or higher. (Mac OS X doesn't strictly require Mac OS 9.1 or higher, but having both OS versions is standard on current iMacs, as it enables Mac OS X to run "Classic" applications. See Chapter 5.) In addition to those folders, you'll see a few others that are noteworthy, including the Library folder, the Applications folder, the System folder, and the Users folder. As a rule, the folders in Mac OS X need to be more rigidly adhered to—they shouldn't be moved (and generally can't be) and they're designed for specific functions:

- The *Applications* folder is where the Mac OS X installer places Mac OS X native applications, including utilities and Internet applications. As discussed in Chapter 26, you'll typically install your own applications in this folder.

- The *Library* folder is where important system-level files—preferences, fonts, and other important items—are stored. If you're installing such items, you'll generally put them inside a subfolder of the Library folder.

- The *System* folder is really designed to be off-limits to regular users. This is where Apple's Installer application places important files that keep the Mac OS running.

- The *Users* folder is where each user's home folder is stored. Even if you're the only user of your iMac, you'll still find a subfolder within the Users folder with your name on it, which is your *home* folder. When you're working in Mac OS X, your home folder is the primary place for you to store personal documents and files.

NOTE   *The Users folder also has a special subfolder called Shared, which you can use to place files that you'd like other users of the Mac to be able to access (assuming there are other users).*

As you're working in Mac OS X, you'll find that you often can't drag-and-drop icons to every folder on this disk—this is different from Mac OS 9, where a regular user can alter almost any file or folder on the hard disk. For now, though, realize that you'll want to open the Applications folder to access most of the Mac OS X applications installed on your iMac, and the Users folder is where you'll find your personal home folder for storing files.

TIP   *Here's a neat trick in both Mac OS 9 and Mac OS X. Say you have a window open but you want to view the window of the folder or drive that contains the folder you're looking at. (In computing parlance, we'd call that the "parent folder.") Hold down the ⌘ key and click the name of the folder in the title bar. A little menu appears allowing you to open parent folders to view their contents.*

Select Items in the Finder

Selecting icons, double-clicking icons, and dragging-and-dropping icons are covered in Chapter 2. But what if you want to gather more than one icon at a time? There are two ways to do it. First, you can select more than one icon at a time by dragging a box around the items. Here's how:

1. Place the mouse pointer just above and to the left of the first icon you want to select.

2. Hold down the mouse button and drag the mouse pointer toward the icon you want to select.

3. Once the first icon is highlighted, keep dragging diagonally to expand the box you're creating. As you expand the box, every item inside the box becomes highlighted.

4. When you've highlighted everything you wanted to highlight, release the mouse button.

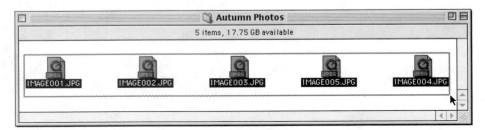

Now you have multiple items highlighted. Click and drag one of the items and they all come along—you can treat them all as if they were a single icon, moving them *en masse* to a different folder, to the printer icon, to the Trash, opening them all using the File | Open command, and so on. To deselect them, just click anything else on the screen (such as part of the desktop or a different icon).

If you want to add icons that aren't grouped together on the screen, you can add them individually by holding down the SHIFT key as you select each icon. Now, each time you click another icon with the SHIFT key held down, it gets added to all the other highlighted items, as shown here:

Remember that these selections don't just work in Icon view windows—you can drag a rectangle around List view windows as well and in Mac OS 9 you can select additional items in List view using the SHIFT key. In Mac OS X, you can use the SHIFT key in List view and Columns view to select a range of items, or use the ⌘ key to add individual items to your selection. (List view is discussed in the section "Change How Folders Are Displayed in the Finder" and Columns view is discussed in Chapter 4.)

Get Information from Finder Windows

If you're using your iMac for video, audio, photos, and all this other creative stuff that your iMac encourages you to do, there's a chance you'll eventually fill up your hard disk—even today's larger disks. But how can you tell if your drive is getting full?

Look at a Finder window. If you open the Macintosh HD's window (or any folder window) and take a look at the top of it, you'll see some information about the Macintosh HD. Specifically, you'll see how many items are in that folder and how much storage space is left on that particular disk. This works just as well with a CD-ROM or removable disk, too. Here's how it looks in Mac OS 9 and higher:

In Mac OS X, you can see the same information, but it's hidden by default. First, select View | Show Status Bar. Now you'll see the status bar in your open Finder window:

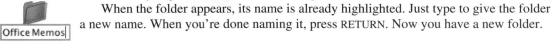

Files 201: Create Folders, Copy Files, Rename Icons, and Create Aliases

Before you get too busy moving things around, you'll need to create some folders you can move things into. You'll also find that it's often important to duplicate items or create aliases to those items. The Finder is designed to help you do just that.

Create a New Folder

You'll probably learn pretty quickly that it's a good idea to create folders of your own and store them on your hard drive or within other folders. For instance, you may wish to create subfolders within the main Documents folder (in Mac OS 9) or within your home folder in Mac OS X. That way, you can begin to organize your documents for easy retrieval. Doing this also makes it easier to copy your important files to a removable drive for safekeeping.

To create a new folder, open and select the window where you'd like the folder to appear. (If you want it to appear on the desktop, you don't need to select a window.) Then, choose File | New Folder. You can also just press ⌘-N in Mac OS 9, or press ⌘-SHIFT-N in Mac OS X.

When the folder appears, its name is already highlighted. Just type to give the folder a new name. When you're done naming it, press RETURN. Now you have a new folder.

Rename Icons

You can rename a folder or any other sort of icon by clicking once on its name (not its icon) and waiting a second or so. Then, the name becomes highlighted, ready for editing. (In Mac OS X, the preferred way to do this is to click once on an icon to select it, then press RETURN to begin editing the name.) With the name highlighted, you can press DELETE to clear the current name and begin typing a new one. When you're done editing the name, press RETURN again to make the name change final.

Move Icons

A big part of using the Finder is mastering drag-and-drop. You'll move files and folders around a lot in the Finder—from one folder to another, for instance. You do that by dragging the icon in question from one part of the Finder and dropping it on another part. For instance, you can drag an icon from one Finder window to another, or from a Finder window to the desktop or vice versa. You can also drag-and-drop icons onto folder icons—even if the icon and folder are in the same Finder window—to move the item to the target folder (see Figure 3-2).

In most cases, dragging an icon to another location *moves* that icon to the new location—it will no longer be in the folder where it started. If you drag an icon to another *disk* however, whether that disk is a remote disk (via a network) or a removable disk, such as a Zip or CD-RW, then you actually create a duplicate of the file, which is placed in the target folder. So, you'll now have two copies—the original and a duplicate.

Create a Duplicate

You can create duplicates on the same disk, if desired. All you have to do is select the item and choose File | Duplicate. You could also select the item and press ⌘-D.

Duplicating creates an exact copy of the file, except that no two items can have the same name and be stored in the same folder, so the duplicate gets the appendage "copy" added to its name. Now, if you like, you can move that duplicate to another folder and rename it.

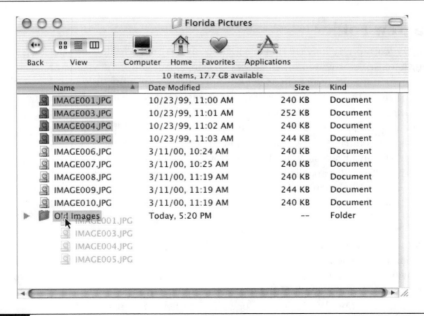

FIGURE 3-2   Dragging icons to a folder in the same Finder window moves those items to that folder.

Remember this is a duplicate of the original and it no longer has a relationship to the original file. For instance, if you had a memo document called *Memo to Bob* and you created a duplicate, you'd now have two memos. If you subsequently opened the duplicate memo in AppleWorks and edited it to say "Dear Sue," the original *Memo to Bob* would not be altered. Only the copy is affected.

Another note about duplicating—it takes up space. Every file you create takes up space on the hard disk in your iMac. If you create many duplicates, then you'll be filling up your hard disk. Instead, you might want to consider creating aliases.

There's a quicker way to duplicate a file. Pick up the original icon you want to duplicate and drag it to the location where you want the duplicate to appear. Now, when you're in the final spot for the duplicate, hold down the OPTION key. Did you see the pointer turn into a plus sign? That means when you let go of the mouse button, a duplicate will be created. While still holding down the OPTION key, release the mouse button. Your duplicate is made.

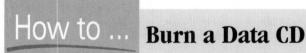

How to ... **Burn a Data CD**

iMac models that include an internal CD-RW drive and Mac OS 9.1 or higher (if you're running Mac OS X, you'll need version 10.1 or higher) can be used to create data CDs directly from the desktop. This is a fairly new feature in the Mac OS—up until now, creating data CDs has required additional software and jumping through some hoops. Now it's much easier.

You begin by inserting a blank CD-R or CD-RW disc in your iMac's CD slot. When the disc is recognized by the Mac, you'll see a dialog box asking if you'd like to prepare the disc for burning. Click Prepare and, after a moment, an icon for the disc will appear on the desktop.

Now, you can name the icon as you would any sort of folder or disk, then you can drag items to the CD icon to add them to the disc. Once you've dragged all the items to the disc that you plan to add, you're ready to burn the CD. In Mac OS 9.1 (or higher) choose Special | Burn CD-RW. (You'll also get the option to burn the CD if you drag it to the Trash icon.) In Mac OS X, choose Finder | Burn CD-RW.

In the dialog box that appears, click Burn if you'd like to continue the process. Now, just sit back and wait while the data is burned to the CD-R or CD-RW disc. When you're done, the disc will eject and you're ready to label it, share it with a friend, or store it away as a backup.

If the disc is a CD-RW (rewriteable), remember that it can be erased and used again, if desired. (You can't add individual files to it; you've got to delete the entire disc and start again. For more flexibility in creating CDs, you'll need a third-party application such as Roxio Toast, described in Chapter 26.) To erase a CD-RW disc, insert it in your iMac's CD slot. When it appears on the desktop, select it and choose Special | Erase Disc in Mac OS 9. (In Mac OS X, you'll need to use the Disk Utility application, described in Chapter 29, to erase a CD-RW.) Click Erase in the dialog box that appears and the disc will be erased and made ready to use again.

Create an Alias

In Mac parlance, an *alias* is simply an icon that represents another file. For instance, when the Mac OS 9 desktop first appears on a brand new iMac, some aliases to iMovie and iTunes appear on the desktop, although the actual program icons are buried in the Applications (Mac OS 9) folder.

There are a couple advantages to creating aliases for your important files:

- **Convenience** Say you have the real AppleWorks icon buried three folders deep on your hard disk. If you like, you can create an alias icon for AppleWorks right on your desktop.

- **Size** Aliases are very small files—unlike a duplicate, an alias isn't a complete copy of the file. It's basically just an icon. So you can have many aliases in different folders on your iMac and still not be taking up too much storage space.

- **Safety** Why is it safer to create aliases? Because if you (or a co-worker, partner, or kid) throw away an alias, the original item doesn't get destroyed. If I take that AppleWorks alias I created and trash it, for instance, then AppleWorks itself is unharmed back in the Applications folder. However, if I had dragged the actual program out to the desktop and trashed it, I'd be in trouble. The actual program would have been deleted.

Convinced? If so, get started creating aliases. In the Finder, select the file for which you'd like an alias. Then, choose File | Make Alias or press ⌘-M in Mac OS 9 or ⌘-L in Mac OS X.

An alias appears, complete with italicized text and the word "alias" appended to the name. Now you can move the alias anywhere you want to and rename it, if desired.

SHORTCUT *Want to create an alias that immediately appears in its final resting place? Here's how: Drag the original icon to the place where you want the alias to appear or just drag it to the desktop. Now, instead of letting go, hold down the OPTION and ⌘ keys. See the pointer turn into a little curved arrow? That means when you drop the icon, it'll create an alias instead of moving the original. Keep holding down OPTION and ⌘, then let go of the mouse button. Voilá! Your alias is ready.*

Find the Alias' Original

Sometimes an alias just isn't good enough—you need to deal with the real file. If that's the case, you can select the alias's icon and choose File | Show Original (or press ⌘-R).

This will cause the folder containing the alias' original file to appear in the Finder.

Fix an Alias

Aliases can break sometimes—suddenly, the alias will no longer point to its original file. This happens for a variety of reasons, but mostly it happens because you move, delete, or otherwise mangle the original file. Perhaps you have an alias to Internet Explorer on your desktop, then you install a new version of Internet Explorer. The alias on your desktop points to the older version (which you've since deleted, let's say) and not the new one.

If an alias can't find its original, a dialog box appears (shown is the Mac OS 9 version):

If you don't need the alias anymore, you can click Delete Alias and the alias will trouble you no longer. (Actually, it's simply been moved to the Trash, not permanently deleted.) If you want to continue to use the alias, click Fix Alias and the Fix Alias dialog box appears. Now, find the file you want the alias to point to, select it in the dialog box, and click Choose. Now the alias is pointing to the chosen file. (The Fix Alias dialog box works just like the Open dialog box, which is discussed in Chapter 7.)

Files 301: Delete Icons

The Mac OS really only offers one way to delete Finder icons—by moving them to the Trash. Actually, this is a good thing, because it makes you think carefully about what you're doing before you make a mistake and accidentally delete something. Plus, the Trash offers a way to recover files before they're permanently deleted, even if they've already been thrown away.

Toss Icons

If you're pretty sure you don't need a particular item anymore, you can drag it straight from its current location in the Finder to the Trash. Just drag the icon over the Trash until the Trash icon (or, in Mac OS X, the Trash *tile* in the Dock) becomes highlighted, then release the mouse button. The item is dropped and the Trash becomes "full." You can throw out multiple files just as easily—select them all by dragging a box around them or holding down the SHIFT key, then drag the group to the Trash.

If this is all too much mousing for you, there are three other ways to move files to the Trash:

- With the file(s) selected in the Finder, choose ⌘-DELETE to move items to the Trash.
- Select the file(s) in the Finder and choose File | Move to Trash from the menu.
- CONTROL-click on a file, then choose Move to Trash from the contextual menu.

In Mac OS X, you may encounter a warning that tells you that you don't have sufficient privileges to move an item to the Trash. This happens because Mac OS X keeps careful track of which users are owners of certain folders or files, and which of those items can't be altered or deleted by other users. If you encounter such a file and you feel you need to be able to delete or change it, see Chapter 29 for a discussion of privileges.

Retrieve Items from the Trash

Just because an item has been thrown in the Trash doesn't mean it's been deleted. If you have something in the Trash that you need to get back, just double-click the Trash icon (in Mac OS 9) or single-click the Trash tile (in Mac OS X). This opens the Trash window, allowing you to see everything that's been thrown away. When you find what you need, you can drag it back out of the Trash onto the desktop or into another Finder window.

Documents and applications can't be launched from the Trash—they must be dragged out to a Finder window or the desktop before they can be used.

Empty the Trash

The step that really gets rid of the items in the Trash is the process of emptying the Trash. Once it's been emptied, you can't get those items back. (Unfortunately, there's no "iMac Dumpster" to go rooting through.)

Think carefully before emptying the Trash. If you delete something accidentally, you'll probably have to buy a special utility program, like Norton Utilities, to get the item back.

If you're sure you want to get rid of the items in the Trash can and reclaim the storage space that they're taking up, then choose Special | Empty Trash (in Mac OS 9) or Finder | Empty Trash (in Mac OS X). You'll see an alert box that tells you the Trash is about to be emptied. If that's what you really want to do, click OK. Once you click OK, the files are gone forever (at least, without a special recovery utility program). Say "Bye, bye!"

Want to skip the alert box that tells you how much stuff will be thrown away? Hold down the OPTION key as you choose Special | Empty Trash. The Trash is emptied immediately.

What do you do if you didn't want to delete a file and you've emptied the Trash? Well, it may require a special purchase. There's a chance it can be recovered, especially if you stop using the iMac immediately, and run out to get a copy of Norton Utilities. (See Chapter 29 for more on disk-fixing utilities.)

Get Info on Files

Another unique Finder responsibility is the Info window, which allows you to learn more about files in the Finder. The Info window can be used to tell you how much storage space an item takes up, who created the item, and any comments that have been stored about that item. You can also view the Info window on disks and folders to learn more about them.

To get info, select the item in the Finder and choose File | Get Info (in Mac OS 9) or File | Show Info (in Mac OS X). The Info window appears, offering you information about the selected file. (Note that the Info window's title bar name changes for the individual item you're getting info on.)

In the Info window you'll see information based on the type of file selected—that is, an alias offers different information from a folder, which is different from an application. You may also see a special pull-down menu, which you can use to switch between General Information about the file and other options, including Sharing (in Mac OS 9), Privileges (in Mac OS X), and others. The Info window is discussed in other chapters, including Chapters 28 and 29.

To close the Info window, click its Close button.

Files 401: Change How Folders Are Displayed in the Finder

Managing the way your Finder windows appear can go a long way toward helping you find files. To change the way you view a Finder window, open that window and select it in the Finder, then choose the appropriate view from the View menu. Between Mac OS 9 and Mac OS X, there are four different ways that folders can be viewed:

- **As Icons** In this view, the window is filled with icons that can be arranged any way you like. This is the default view in most cases.

- **As Buttons** Available only in Mac OS 9, buttons are like icons except they only require a single click to activate them. (To select, rename, and drag-and-drop a button, select its name instead of its icon, since a single click activates them.) Buttons are an odd way to arrange most windows, although not a bad idea for a quick pop-up window at the bottom of the Finder screen that could be filled with application aliases. That makes a quick mini-launcher that can be very convenient. (You can create a pop-up window in Mac OS 9 by dragging a typical Finder window to the bottom of the screen. See Chapter 5 for more on pop-up windows.)

- ■ **As List** If you have a lot of items in a particular folder window, this is the way to go. Viewing as a list allows you to do two things. First, you get a whole lot of files on the screen at once in a very orderly manner. Second, you can use the little triangles to look inside subfolders without doing a lot of double-clicking.

- ■ **As Columns** Unique to Mac OS X, the Columns view enables you to see the contents of a folder and its subfolders in separate columns within a single Finder window. Columns view is discussed in more detail in Chapter 4.

How to ... **Drop Files in List View**

One peril of using the List view (and this occasionally happens in some other views as well) is that it can be tough to drop items in the open folder window, especially if you have a lot of subfolders in that window (or if you're trying to drag something *from* a subfolder in that same window). Here's the trick—if you want to drop something in the current folder, drag it to the little information bar at the top of the window, just below the title bar. Release the mouse button to drop the item. This drops it in the main folder instead of in one of the subfolders.

Customize List View

Once you have a folder in List view, you can do some other things to make that folder work better for you. At the top of the window, you'll find column listings for the different information that's offered about each file. Place the mouse pointer between two columns and it'll change to a little cursor with an arrow coming out of each side. That's your cue that you can drag the column divider to change the width of the column.

Want to change the order of List view columns? Go up to the column head name and click and hold the mouse button. Now drag the mouse pointer to the left or right—the pointer changes to a hand and you're able to move the column to wherever you'd like it in the window. Let go of the mouse button to drop the column in place.

To order the window according to a particular column, just click that column's heading name. To view your files organized by file size, for instance, just click the Size column head. You can also change the order of that listing by clicking the direction control in Mac OS 9.

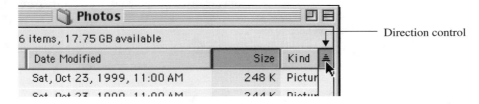

Direction control

In Mac OS X, click the column head itself to change the sort direction, which is indicated by the small triangle.

Don't like what you've done? In Mac OS 9 you can choose View | Reset Column Positions to put the columns back the way you found them. In Mac OS X, you'll just have to undo the changes manually!

Arrange Other Views

If you're not in List view, there's still some arranging you can do. In Icon and Button views, you can select the Finder window, then choose View | Arrange in Mac OS 9. That brings up a menu that lets you choose how you'd like your icons arranged. In Mac OS X, there's only one option—View | Arrange by Name.

If you want your Icon views to appear a bit more uniform, you can select the window in the Finder, then choose View | Clean Up, whether you're working in Mac OS 9 or Mac OS X. This will move the icons or buttons around so that they're equally spaced and as many as possible fit in the open window.

With any Finder window you can click the resize box (the Maximize button in Mac OS X) to automatically reshape the window to display all or as many files as possible. In Mac OS 9, hold down the OPTION key and click the resize box to maximize the window onscreen.

Auto-Arrange the View

Choosing View | Arrange by Name re-arranges your Finder windows just that one time. Would you like it to be arranged all the time? That's easy enough. Select the window in the Finder, then choose View | View Options (View | Show View Options in Mac OS X). In the View Options dialog box, you can choose to have the window automatically arrange icons. The choices are:

- **None**   The icons will not be auto-arranged.
- **Snap to Grid**   The icons won't be put in any particular order, but they will always appear in uniform rows and columns, no matter where you drag-and-drop them within the window.
- **Keep Arranged**   This option allows you to force the window to automatically keep icons in order at all times, even when new icons are dropped into the folder. Choose the radio button next to this option to activate it, then choose *how* to arrange the icons from the pull-down menu.

Files Grad School: Search for Files

Although the iMac's basic interface—all those icons and windows—is called the Finder, it's really not that good at automatically seeking out files and folders on your iMac. That sort of task is left to a program called Sherlock 2 (in Mac OS 9) or just plain Sherlock (in Mac OS X).

The easiest way to launch Sherlock is from the Finder itself—click once on the desktop to make sure you've switched to the Finder. Now, choose File | Find or press ⌘-F on your keyboard. In Mac OS 9, you can also launch Sherlock from the Apple menu; in Mac OS X, you can single-click the Sherlock Holmes-style hat icon in the Dock to launch Sherlock.

When Sherlock launches, its window appears, as shown in Figure 3-3. Notice that the Sherlock interface includes Channels at the top of the window that allow you to switch between the different types of searches. The first channel (represented by the hard disk icon) is where you'll search your local disks (and network disks, in some cases) for files. You can also use this channel to search within documents for particular words or phrases. We'll cover the other channels—for Internet searching—in Chapter 6.

3

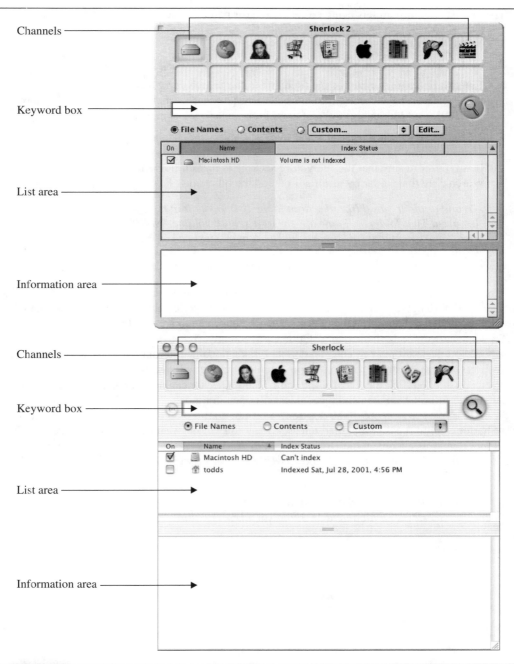

Channels

Keyword box

List area

Information area

Channels

Keyword box

List area

Information area

FIGURE 3-3   On the top, Sherlock 2 in Mac OS 9; on the bottom, Sherlock in Mac OS X

The easiest way to search is using a file's name (or part of a file's name):

1. Select the Files channel at the top of the Sherlock window.

2. Make sure the File Names button is selected.

3. Enter the filename or part of the filename in the Search entry box. Examples might be "letter" if you're searching for business correspondence, "memo" or "invoice," or may be "2001" or "March" if you tend to include dates in the names of your files.

4. In the list area, you'll see disks and folders. Place a check mark next to each disk or folder that you'd like to search. In Mac OS X, you'll also see your home folder listed here; if you're sure that the file you're seeking is in your home folder, you can opt to search only that folder by turning it on and the others off.

TIP *To add a folder you'd like to search to the list, locate it in the Finder and drag it to the list area. That folder will now appear as a search volume—you can click to place a check mark next to it (or remove the check mark) just as you can with other disks.*

5. Click the Find icon—it looks like a large magnifying glass.

That's it. After a few seconds, you'll see the found files in the list area (see Figure 3-4). You can then scroll through the list and click once on each result to see exactly where the file is located. The path to the file will appear in the bottom pane (the information area) of the Sherlock window.

So what can you do in the list area? Quite a lot, actually. You can single-click an item to see its path in the information area. You can double-click a document to open it in its associated application (or, if the result is an application, double-clicking will launch it). In the information area, you can double-click the icon for the same result. Or, you can double-click any folder that appears in the information area and that folder will open in Finder.

Want to move the icon out to the desktop? You can do that, too. Just click and drag the icon from Sherlock out to the desktop, then release the mouse button. You can also drag these icons to open Finder windows, icons in the Dock, or even to the Trash, if you like. Likewise, you can drag items from a Sherlock window to a removable disk or network drive and the items will be copied to that disk.

CAUTION *Be aware that you could accidentally delete important files by moving them to the Trash using Sherlock. Don't delete anything you aren't familiar with.*

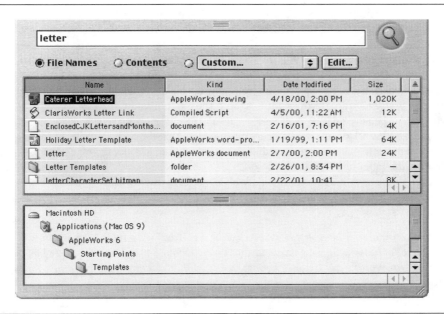

FIGURE 3-4   In Sherlock you'll see results listed in the list area.

Custom Searches

Sherlock allows you to customize file searches beyond simply typing the filename (or part of it) and clicking the magnifying glass. You can actually build sophisticated searches with a ton of search criteria at your disposal. But, first, let's start with something a little easier.

Apple has saved some custom searches that you can experiment with. Select the Custom pop-up menu in Sherlock and you'll see some interesting entries. You can select from: Applications, Larger Than 1MB, Modified Today, and Modified Yesterday. If you select one of those, you can click the magnifying glass and any file that meets the chosen criterion will appear in the list menu.

Of course, it's probably not too often that you'll want to simply know every file on your hard disk that is larger than 1MB. More often, you want to know about files *with certain filenames* that meet other criteria as well. So, you can select a custom search criterion, then enter a filename (or partial filename) in the keyword box. Now your results will include files that meet both criteria—for instance, files with "letter" in their name that are over 1MB in size.

Neat-o, eh? You can do still more. Select Edit from the Custom menu and you can create your own custom searches, complete with tons of different criteria. After you've selected Edit, you'll see the More Search Options window, shown in Figure 3-5 (shown is Mac OS 9's version).

Working with the More Search Options window is a little like playing that old car-trip game called "Mad Libs." It is in the More Search Options dialog box where you build each criterion for your custom search by choosing options from pop-up menus, entry boxes, and so on.

It's actually pretty simple. If you want to search files that are new since 3/30/2001, click the check box next to "date created" and choose "is after" from its pop-up menu. Now, in the date entry box, enter **3/30/2001** or use the little arrows to select that date. Other criterion work similarly; you can create custom searches that check the date modified, the size of the file, the kind of file it is, the label on the file, and so on.

If you'll only be using this search once, click OK in the More Search Options window, then return to the Sherlock window, enter a filename if you want, and click the magnifying glass. Your search is conducted.

If you've created a Search you really like in the More Search Options window, click the Save As button. Enter a name in the Save Custom Settings button and click Save again. Now you've got a new custom search on that custom menu back in Sherlock's main window.

More Search Options

Find items whose:

- ☐ **file name** | contains ⇕ | [   ]
- ☐ **content includes** | [   ]
- ☑ **date created** | is ⇕ | 3/30/2001
- ☐ **date modified** | is ⇕ | 7/28/2001
- ☐ **comments** | contain ⇕ | [   ]
- ☑ **size** | is greater than ⇕ | 500 | K

Advanced Options

- ☐ **kind** | is ⇕ | alias ⇕   ☐ **is** | invisible ⇕
- ☐ **label** | is ⇕ | None ⇕   ☐ **has** | a custom icon ⇕
- ☐ **version** | is ⇕ | [   ] ☐ **name/icon** | is locked ⇕
- ☐ **file/folder** | is locked ⇕   ☐ **file type** | is ⇕ | [   ]
- ☐ **folder** | is ⇕ | empty ⇕   ☐ **creator** | is ⇕ | [   ]

[?]   [Save...]   [Cancel] [OK]

FIGURE 3-5   The More Search Options window is the world's most intimidating Mad Libs game.

How to ...   **Search Inside Files**

What if you could just search the insides of files to find what you're looking for? The Content search option in Sherlock helps you with just that, although content searches are only useful for searching document files—files created in applications like AppleWorks, PageMill, Microsoft Word, Adobe Acrobat, or SimpleText—since those are the files that contain text. If you're searching for images, applications, utilities, or other files, you need to use Find File.

Once you have the indexes created for your hard disks and other disk volumes, searching by content is really very easy. All you need to do is:

1. Make sure the Files channel is active—click the disk icon at the top of the Sherlock window.

2. Click the Contents button to search by contents.

3. Now, put a check mark next to the volumes or folders you want Sherlock to include in its search.

4. Click the Search button and you're off to the races.

When Sherlock is done, you'll see the found documents in the list area. You can work with those files just as you would work with found documents after a regular file search.

As mentioned, in order for Content searches to work properly, your target volume or folder needs to be indexed. The process of indexing simply means that Sherlock pages through a folder or disk and puts together a smaller database of keywords—that's what actually gets searched during a content search. In order to stay current, the index must be updated fairly frequently.

In Mac OS X, Sherlock automatically indexes folders in the list area. Mac OS X disks can't be indexed; but if you happen to have an external disk or a network disk, you may be able to index it. If there's a disk or folder that you'd like to index, select it in the list area, then choose Find | Index Now. To set preferences for future indexing, select Sherlock | Preferences.

In Mac OS 9, you can set up indexing for your disks and folders by selecting Find | Index. In the Index dialog box, select the volumes you'd like to index immediately and click Create Index or Update Index. If you want to schedule future updates, click the Schedule button.

Chapter 4

Go Deep with Mac OS X

How to...

- Dig into and customize the Finder window
- Use the Apple menu
- Use and alter the Dock
- Launch and manage applications from the Dock

Chapter 2 showed you some of the basic concepts involved with either Mac OS 9 or Mac OS X, while Chapter 3 focused on the Finder concepts that are common to both operating systems. In this chapter, I'd like to focus on the interface elements that make Mac OS X different from Mac OS 9—particularly the Finder window, Apple menu, and Dock. So, if you're not using Mac OS X at all, you get a free pass to Chapter 5!

Dig Into the Finder Window

One of the most unique aspects of Mac OS X is its new Finder window, which is something of a departure from earlier Mac OS versions. In some ways, the Finder window is similar to a Web browser window—at least insofar as it now has a button bar with common commands and frequently accessed folders. As you'll see, it's a powerful way to browse through your iMac's files.

NOTE *Mac OS X has special Finder preference settings that you can access at Finder | Preferences. Once there, you can decide whether or not hard disks, removable media, and network disks will appear on the desktop. In Mac OS X version 10.1, you'll see other options, such as what a new Finder window will show by default and whether or not you want to see filename extensions.*

Explore Columns View

As mentioned in Chapter 3, the traditional way to maneuver through an iMac's folders is to double-click the hard disk icon, which opens a window that shows subfolders, which you double-click...and so on. That particular behavior is supported in both Mac OS 9 and Mac OS X. But in Mac OS X, the traditional way isn't always the best. Instead, you can opt to use the Finder window and its special columns view for quickly locating and working with files. To get into columns view, select View | Columns from the Finder menu, or click the Columns button in the View portion of the Finder window toolbar.

In Columns view, you can quickly move throughout the entire hierarchy of your hard disk— simply click a disk or item to start with, then single-click folders to display them in the next column. When you finally reach a document, or application, single-clicking it will bring up information about that item in the rightmost column, as shown in Figure 4-1.

You can drag-and-drop an item from one column to another, if that happens to help you. (For instance, in Figure 4-1, you could drag an item from the Wedding Photos folder that's displayed in the second column back to the Vacation Photos folder icon in the first column.) If you need to

Back button   Change to Columns view   Hide Toolbar button

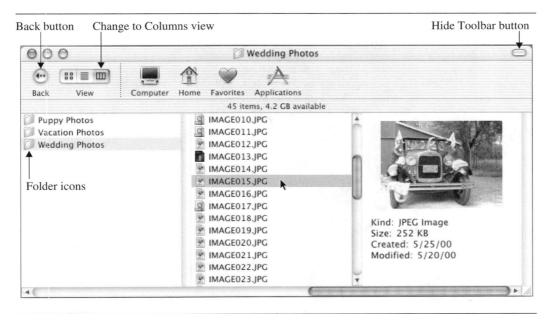

Folder icons

FIGURE 4-1   The Mac OS X Finder window, showing the Columns view

drag an item to another folder, however, you'll find that a second Finder window, also in Columns view, might be the easiest way to accomplish that. To open a new Finder window, press ⌘-N or select File | New Finder Window.

The wider you drag out the Finder window, the more columns you can display. Also, if you view your iMac at 1024 × 768 resolution, you'll see more columns than at 800 × 600. See Chapter 24 for details on screen resolution.

Also, in Mac OS X 10.1, you can drag individual columns to change their width; simply click and hold the mouse button at the bottom of the dividing line between any two columns, then drag the mouse to change the size of those columns. Release the mouse button and the new column widths are set.

Customize the Finder Window Toolbar

The Finder window's toolbar is not only handy for quickly accessing folders and common commands, but you can customize it to do your bidding, if desired. The first way to customize it is to simply drag folders or items from the Finder window to the toolbar. When you drop a folder, document, or application icon on that toolbar, it stays.

Now, it's an easy target for quickly accessing a favorite folder or even for dragging-and-dropping items. To remove it, simply drag it off the toolbar—when you release the button, the icon disappears. The original isn't affected.

The other way to customize the Finder window is to select View | Customize Toolbar from the Finder menu. When you do, a large dialog sheet pops out from the frontmost Finder window. Now you'll see a number of different tools and items that you simply drag up to the toolbar, including commands such as Eject (for removable media and CDs) and Path, which you can use to see a pop-up menu of enclosing folders.

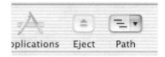

You can drag items around all you like on the toolbar, and you can use the Show menu at the bottom of the dialog sheet to select whether you'd like to see icons, text, or both in the toolbar. To remove an item from the toolbar, simply drag it off and release the mouse button. To return to the default set, drag the entire default set box from the bottom of the dialog sheet up to the toolbar. When you're done making changes, click Done.

Understand the OS X Apple Menu

I'm not one to dwell on the past (if only that were true) but I should point out that the Apple menu in Mac OS X is also a different beast from the Apple menu in previous Mac OS versions. In fact, Apple engineers originally didn't even have an Apple menu in pre-release versions of Mac OS X, but user requests lead them to add it back in. It's a shell of what it once was, but it's a pretty useful shell.

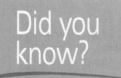

The Go Menu

Mac OS X offers another difference from earlier Mac OS versions in the form of the Go menu, which appears in the middle of the Finder's menu bar. The Go menu is mostly redundant—it allows you to quickly visit some of the same folders that you can click to using the Finder window's toolbar. You can also use the Go | iDisk command to quickly access your iDisk, if it has been configured (see Chapter 20). You'll also find a convenient Recent Folders menu, which you can use to visit folders you've been to recently in the Finder. And, you'll find the Connect To Server command in the Go menu, which enables you to access remote server volumes, as discussed in Chapter 28.

NOTE   *If you're familiar with Mac OS 9, you'll be interested to know that the Mac OS X Apple menu can't be customized—only the Recent Items menu changes, while the rest of the menu is fixed commands.*

Get Information and Set Preferences

But let's begin by taking a look at the Apple menu. Click the Apple icon in the top-left corner of your screen and the Apple menu appears, as shown in Figure 4-2.

At the top of the menu, you'll find the About This Mac command, which you can choose if you'd like to see the exact version of Mac OS X that you're running, the amount of memory you have installed, and the type of processor your Mac has. To close the About This Mac window, click its Close button.

The next command you'll see is the Get Mac OS X Software command, which is something of a marketing ploy. It launches, in your Web browser, Apple's Mac OS X Downloads page, where you'll find updates to Apple's software, additional drivers, and shareware and freeware programs from third parties. If your Internet connection isn't designed to connect automatically, you'll need to connect before issuing this command.

The System Preferences command can be used to quickly launch the System Preferences application, where you can choose settings and preferences for the Mac OS X environment. System Preferences is discussed in detail in Chapter 24 and many others later in this book. Likewise, the Dock menu commands are discussed in the section "Set Dock Preferences," later in this chapter.

The Location menu is used to change the preset location for your network settings—see Chapter 23 for details.

Launch Recently Used Items

The Recent Items menu tracks the most recent five documents that you've worked with and the five applications that you've most recently launched. By selecting this menu and then selecting

FIGURE 4-2   The Apple menu in Mac OS X

one of the documents or applications, you can quickly re-launch that item. If you tend to work with the same small set of applications or documents, you'll find that the Recent Items menu is a handy way to launch them without forcing you to open the Applications folder.

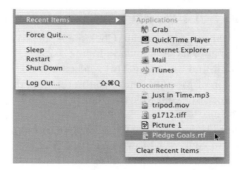

The Recent Items menu has another command, Clear Recent Items (or Clear Menu in Mac OS X 10.1), which you can select to clear the Recent Items menu of its remembered applications and documents.

Force Applications to Quit

The Force Quit command is used as a troubleshooting tool—if you encounter an application that is no longer responding to input, and you've waited more than a few minutes to see if it has an internal problem it's recovering from, then you can force that application to quit. This causes the application to quit without saving any changed data—the Mac OS is *killing* the application's processes, forcing it to go away without giving the application any opportunity to respond. That means it's a last resort, but one that you'll occasionally need to implement. If you want to force an application to quit, select the Force Quit command. The Force Quit Applications window will appear.

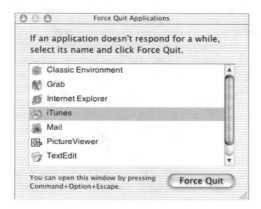

Select the application that you'd like to force quit, then click the Force Quit button. That application should quit—it will disappear from the Dock and the Force Quit Applications window. Click the Force Quit Applications window's Close button to close the window. In most cases, you can now continue to work—with Mac OS X, there is generally no need to restart your Mac after an application has frozen or crashed, unless you notice other odd or problematic behavior with your applications. If you do, that may mean you need to do some troubleshooting—see Chapter 29 for more on dealing with problem applications and trouble with the Mac OS.

Issue System Commands

The final four commands in the Apple menu are the system-level commands that directly affect the Mac OS and the iMac. The first three—Sleep, Restart, and Shutdown—are discussed in Chapter 1.

Select the Log Out command to quit all active applications, close your user account, and display the Login window so that another user can access his or her unique user account. If you've set up multiple users (see Chapter 27), then you'll definitely get used to using the Log Out command. But even if you're the only user of your iMac, logging out is one way to secure your files and applications from interference from others.

Master the Dock

The Dock is all-new in Mac OS X—unlike the Apple menu, it isn't really an update of any particular tool in older versions of the Mac OS. Instead, it sort of combines the capabilities of Mac OS 9's Launcher, Application menu, and even the older Apple menu into a single interface element that is otherwise completely unique.

The Dock is used primarily to launch applications and, once they're launched and running, to switch between multiple applications. But it's also handy for a few other tasks, including quick access to settings via Dock Extras and quickly digging through folders thanks to the folder pop-up feature. We'll look at all those in this section.

Launch and Switch Between Applications

You'll notice immediately that the Dock has some default icons on it—nearly all iMac users will see the same icons, with an exception or two. (In particular, if you have an AirPort card installed in your iMac when you first configure Mac OS X, you'll see a special Signal Strength Dock Extra on your Dock.) Most of the other icons (called *tiles* when they're on the Dock) are standards, though, including the Finder, Mail, Internet Explorer, System Preferences, and others. You'll notice also that the Dock is divided into two different sections by a dividing line. On the left are application tiles and on the right are document tiles.

To launch an item on the Dock, click its tile once. If that item is an application, you'll see the tile's icon "bounce" up and down to indicate that the application is being launched. You'll also see a small triangle appear beneath that application's icon—the triangle is the *running indicator,* which tells you that the application is currently launched and running. Here you'll notice that the Finder and Internet Explorer both have running indicators.

The Dock is the heart of Mac OS X's ability to *multitask,* or run more than one application simultaneously. Using the running indicators, you can see immediately which applications have been launched and are running. You can then click any of those applications in the Dock to switch quickly to it. You can also cycle quickly through your running applications by pressing ⌘-TAB to move forward and ⌘-SHIFT-TAB to move backward along the Dock.

But what about applications that aren't on the Dock? When you launch an application from the Applications folder or elsewhere, that item will add a tile to the Dock while that application is active. When you quit the application, its tile will disappear.

Documents that appear on the right side of the Dock work the same way—click them once and they'll be launched in their associated application. (If that application isn't already on the Dock, a tile and running indicator will appear for that application.) The only difference is that the document doesn't bounce and a running indicator doesn't appear beneath it—running indicators are reserved for applications.

Minimize Windows to the Dock

Although you can drag often-used documents to the Dock, if you like, the right side of the Dock is used more often for minimized windows. When you click the Minimize button in a Finder window or in an application's document window, that window is minimized to the Dock, where it will appear on the document side of the dividing line. That's a convenient way to get open windows off the screen, while one click of the window's tile in the Dock will return it to full-screen. Plus, the windows, when minimized, are actually miniature versions of themselves, making them (hopefully) easy to identify and return to.

If you're not sure what a particular window represents, simply point to it with the mouse (but don't click the mouse button). The *mouseover name* (also shown) will appear just above the Dock to show you what the window's title is. In fact, this works for any type of tile in the Dock, including applications, documents, and even Dock Extras.

Add Items to the Dock

Of course, you can add tiles to the Dock yourself to make it quite a bit more useful as a launcher. You'll probably find that you have applications and documents to which you'd like quick access. That's easy enough to accomplish. All you have to do is drag any application or document from

4

the desktop or a Finder window down to the Dock. If you drag it to the correct side (applications to the left, documents and folders to the right), then a space will open up on the Dock where you can drop that item.

When you drag an item to the Dock, nothing happens to the original application or document—it stays right where it is. Instead, a special alias is created in order to make the new Dock tile possible. That also means that removing items from the Dock has no effect on the original item—if you remove a Dock tile, the original application or document is still safely saved on your hard disk.

So how do you remove a Dock tile? Simply drag the tile from the Dock to the desktop area, somewhere above the Dock. When you release the mouse button, the Dock tile will disappear in an animated poof of smoke. Remember—only the Dock tile has been deleted. The original item is fine.

You can also move items around on the Dock in the same way—simply drag-and-drop the tile from one location to a new location. As you move the tile around on the Dock, space will open up between two other tiles, as long as you don't cross the dividing line.

TIP *Want to resize the Dock? You can do it as easily as you move items around on it. Point the mouse at the dividing line in the Dock and you'll see the mouse pointer change into a two-sided arrow. Now, hold down the mouse button and drag the mouse up the screen to make the Dock (and each tile on it) bigger or drag it down the screen to make the entire Dock smaller.*

Use Pop-up Menus and Docklings

The Dock has another feature we haven't looked at until now. Click and hold the mouse button on a Dock tile and you'll see a small pop-up menu appear.

Each pop-up menu will vary in what it enables you to do. A running application's menu will show you a list of its open windows and a Quit command, while an inactive Dock tile's menu will generally give you the option Show in Finder, which you can select to reveal that tile's original item in a Finder window.

Docklings (also called *Dock Extras*) are special Dock tiles that are specifically designed to take advantage of pop-up menu technology. Instead of launching applications or documents, a Dockling is simply there to give you a convenient pop-up menu—to change settings for your display or AirPort connection, for example. To use a Dockling, just click and hold the mouse button on its tile. A pop-up menu with different options will appear—point to the option that suits you and release the mouse button.

Some Apple-provided Docklings can be found in the Dock Extras folder inside your Applications folder. You can then drag them to the Dock for quick access. Because Docklings are neither applications nor documents, they can be placed on either side of the Dock's dividing line.

*See **http://www.apple.com/macosx/downloads/** on the Web for more Docklings. In Mac OS X 10.1, some Docklings are replaced by menu bar items discussed in Chapter 24.*

Quickly Dig with Folder Tiles

The pop-up menu technology makes another special case possible—pop-up folder navigation. If you drag a folder icon from a Finder window to the Dock, a new folder tile is added. (It might be your Documents folder, for instance, or any personal folder that you like to be able to access frequently.) Click and hold the mouse button on that folder icon and a pop-up menu appears—with the contents of that folder! If there's a subfolder inside that folder, the subfolder appears as a hierarchical menu—select it and that subfolder's contents appear. You can dig down five folders deep to quickly find the document, application, or folder you want to open and use.

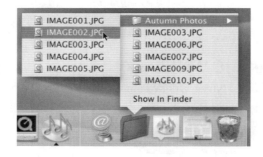

And don't forget that you can define the term "folder" pretty loosely. You can drag your home folder to the Dock, for instance, to quickly gain access to its enclosed items and subfolders. And you can even drag a disk icon—your hard disk or an attached USB or FireWire disk, for instance—to create a tile for it as well.

Change Folder Icons

One problem comes up when you add a few folder tiles to your Dock—they all look kind of the same, making it difficult to tell which is which. The solution to that is to alter the folder's icon before you drag it to the Dock to create a tile. Once the folder is customized, the Dock tile will be as well.

You'll need to begin by actually creating the custom icon. You can do this in a painting program (such as AppleWork's Paint module or Macromedia Freehand) or a third-party application specifically designed to create icons. (Icons are 128 pixels by 128 pixels in Mac OS X.) Then, to change a folder's icon, select the drawn icon in your editing application and choose Edit | Copy. Now, locate the folder in a Finder window, select it, and choose File | Show Info. In the Info window, highlight the folder's icon and choose Edit | Paste in the Finder. If you have the correct file permissions to alter that folder, you should see the new folder icon appear in place of the original.

To return to a standard folder icon, select the icon again in the Info window and select Edit | Cut to remove the new icon.

4

Set Dock Preferences

I mentioned earlier that you can quickly change some Dock options using the Dock menu in the Apple menu. You can also fine-tune those options in the Dock pane of the System Preferences application. To launch the Dock Preferences, choose Dock | Dock Preferences from the Apple menu.

NOTE   *In Mac OS X version 10.1, this menu has additional options, including the ability to change the position of the Dock from the bottom of the screen to the left or right sides.*

In the Apple menu, you can choose Dock | Turn Hiding On to activate hiding; in Dock Preferences, turn on the Automatically Hide and Show the Dock option. When Hiding is turned on, the Dock disappears below the bottom of your screen and only reappears when you point your mouse at the bottom few pixels of the screen to reveal it. This is done to give your applications a little more "screen real estate" so that your application's windows can be maximized without portions of them hiding behind the Dock.

With Magnification turned on (either by selecting Dock | Turn Magnification On in the Apple menu or by turning on the Magnification option in the Dock Preferences pane) individual tiles on the Dock will become larger as you pass the mouse pointer over them. The Dock Preferences slider can be used to choose exactly how large magnified items will become. Magnification is particularly useful when the Dock has many different items on it and the individual tiles are becoming difficult to see.

In the Dock Preferences pane, you have other options, including a slider that changes the size of the Dock and a check box that lets you turn on or off the Animate Opening Applications option to determine whether or not an application icon will bounce in the Dock as its application is loading.

NOTE   *Mac OS X version 10.1 adds one additional option to the Dock Preferences pane, the Minimize Using menu. The Scale Effect is quicker than the Genie Effect.*

When you're done in the Dock Preferences pane, choose System Preferences | Quit to leave the System Preferences application.

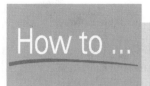

How to...Work with Menu Bar Items

In Mac OS X and higher, Apple has introduced a new, neat little feature—the *menu bar item*. These are small menus that let you quickly access settings for your iMac and, sometimes, for your applications. In fact, if you guessed that they were a replacement for the less-than-popular Dock Extras, you might be right.

To use a menu bar item, simply open it like any other menu—point at it and click the mouse. Then, you'll either see menu options or other controls that enable you to choose a setting—for instance, you might be able to change your iMac's volume or its screen resolution.

You'll generally add menu bar items by turning them on in various places—in the System Preferences application (see Chapter 24), in applications such as Internet Connect (Chapters 6 and 23), and elsewhere. Just look for options that say something like "Show displays in menu bar" or "Show modem status in menu bar." Turn on one of those options and you're turning on a menu bar item.

Chapter 5

Dig into Mac OS 9 and Classic

How To...

- Understand Classic vs. Mac OS 9 vs. Mac OS X
- Identify Classic applications
- Start and manage Classic
- Use the Classic Apple and Application menus
- Perform Mac OS 9 Finder tricks
- Get help in Classic and Mac OS 9

As you've seen by now, the new world of Mac OS X has brought something along for the ride—Mac OS 9. Whether you're using Mac OS 9 as your day-to-day operating system, or you're trying to use Mac OS 9 applications from within Mac OS X, you're probably going to find yourself at least a little familiar with this "classic" OS.

Mac OS 9 and Mac OS X are radically different underneath, but they share many things in common—particularly Finder commands, as discussed in Chapter 3. In this chapter, I'd like to discuss some of the differences when you're working in Mac OS 9, as well as some of the issues you'll encounter when you're running an application with the Classic environment in Mac OS X.

Understand Classic, Mac OS 9, and Mac OS X

Mac OS X, Apple's latest operating system, is more than just an upgrade to Mac OS 9 and earlier versions. It's actually a completely different operating system, with underlying components that are very different from those that make up Mac OS 9. They're so much different that applications need to be rewritten before they can run successfully in both operating systems.

Mac OS X is more powerful, less likely to crash and better designed for efficient networking and Internet tasks than Mac OS 9. Those advantages made the upgrade to Mac OS X an exciting move for Apple. But at the same time, Apple needed a solution that enables older Mac applications, which users have invested in heavily, to run in Mac OS X. In fact, Apple's engineers came up with two.

The first is something called a *Carbon* application, which is designed to run in both Mac OS 9 and Mac OS X. This is accomplished by re-writing an application so that it only uses a subset of programming commands, called the Carbon APIs (Application Programming Interfaces) that both Mac OS 9 and Mac OS X support. While this results in an application that doesn't have every Mac OS X advantage of a fully native application (called a *Cocoa* application), it does allow the application to run in both operating systems while still taking advantage of advanced features in Mac OS X. For instance, AppleWorks 6.2 is a Carbon application, and it's certainly a very useful application, as you'll see in Chapters 8–13.

The other solution to the OS conundrum is called the *Classic environment*, which is simply a way in which Mac OS 9.1 or higher is run as an application within Mac OS X. Once launched, the Classic environment can run Mac OS 9.1-compatible applications that haven't been altered to run in Mac OS X.

You'll find Mac folks tossing around the term "Classic" a lot these days. It can mean a few different things. A Classic application *is one that is designed for Mac OS 9; the* Classic environment *is Mac OS 9 running from within Mac OS X; and the* Classic Mac OS *(or components of it, like the Classic Apple menu, Classic Finder, and so on) refers to pre-Mac OS X versions of the Mac OS, including Mac OS 9 and later.*

Identify Classic Applications

So how can you tell which application is a native Mac OS X application and which is a Classic application? Classic applications will give you two telltale signs. First, they look like older Macintosh applications, if you've seen them (see Figure 5-1). They have a different menu bar and slightly less colorful windows and controls. Second, when you start up a Classic application from within Mac OS X, you'll usually need to launch the Classic environment—which means a delay of a minute or more before the application pops on the screen.

5

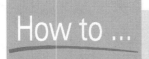 **Decide Which OS to Use**

In previous chapters you've been introduced to both Mac OS X and Mac OS 9, partly because iMacs shipping at the time of writing include both operating systems. (In fact, Chapter 2 shows you how to switch between the two operating systems, if you have them both installed.) Likewise, the fact that Mac OS X relies on Mac OS 9 to create the Classic environment means that Mac OS 9s look and feel as well as some of its commands will be around for a while. But this brings up an interesting question. Since both OSes exist on your iMac, which should you use?

Which you use depends, ultimately, on which applications you need to run on a regular basis. If you'll only be using the applications discussed in this book—those that ship with your iMac— then you should be fine using Mac OS X, as most of the applications I discuss in this book have (or will soon have) Mac OS X versions. For occasionally running Classic applications, you can use the Classic environment. (Note that it's recommended that you have more than 128MB of RAM installed in your iMac if you're going to run Classic applications within Mac OS X. At least double that amount—256MB or more—would be ideal.)

If you plan to run Classic applications most or all of the time—if you have copies of WordPerfect for Mac or Adobe Photoshop or other specialized and important applications that don't have native Mac OS X versions—then you'll likely want to stick with Mac OS 9. In fact, many iMac and other Mac users will likely stick with Mac OS 9 for quite a while, perhaps beyond 2002, as applications are slowly updated. If you're comfortable with it, feel free.

Of course, if you're working directly in Mac OS 9, you can't launch native Mac OS X applications—only Carbon or standard Mac OS 9-compatible applications will launch. In that case, you'll always see an application window that looks something like the right side of Figure 5-1. (Other differences in Classic applications are discussed in Chapter 7.)

Work with the Classic Environment

Whenever you launch a Classic application from within Mac OS X, the Classic environment will first be launched, if necessary. What is the Classic environment? It's really just an *instance* of Mac OS 9 being loaded from the hard disk and placed into memory, just as if the iMac were starting up from a power-off state. The major difference is that this version of Mac OS 9 loads as a *process* within Mac OS X, thus enabling Classic applications to run side by side with native applications.

Once the Classic environment is launched, it can handle one or more Classic applications—you can continue to launch Classic applications until system memory isn't able to accommodate more. (Although, by then, you'll likely see a severe slow-down in application response.)

TIP *If you work with the Classic environment a good deal, you can also set it to automatically load when Mac OS X starts up on your iMac. In Mac OS X, select System Preferences from the Apple menu, then click the Classic icon. In the Classic pane, turn on the Start Up Classic on Login to This Computer option. (See Chapter 24 for more on system preferences.)*

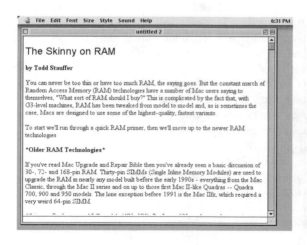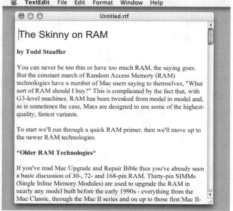

FIGURE 5-1 A Classic application (on the left) has older-style menu bars and window treatments than does the native Mac OS X application (on the right).

One of the caveats of the Classic environment is that trouble in one Classic application can cause trouble for all Classic applications, because they don't have the *protected memory* and other features of both Carbon and Cocoa Mac OS X applications. If you encounter trouble, you should save data in all your other Classic applications, if you can, then see Chapter 29 for troubleshooting help.

Use the Classic Apple and Application menus

When you're working in Mac OS 9—or whenever you switch to a Classic application in Mac OS X—you'll see a slightly different menu bar from the standard one in Mac OS X. In Classic, the menu bar has two familiar menus—the Apple menu and the Application menu— but they're arranged a bit differently, and they have different purposes and tasks, as well.

Explore the Classic Apple Menu

Overall, the Apple menu works like any other menu—you move the mouse pointer up to the Apple icon, click the mouse button, and the menu appears (see Figure 5-2). Then, move the mouse pointer down the menu until you're pointing at the item you want to select. If it's a submenu, it'll have a little arrowhead pointing to the right—another menu will appear directly to the right once the mouse reaches the arrowhead. You can then move to the right and choose something from the new menu.

FIGURE 5-2   The Classic Apple menu is sort of a junk drawer for your iMac.

If there's anything that's remarkably different about the Classic Apple menu, it's the simple fact that you're usually launching something—a desk accessory, a control panel, an alias—instead of choosing a command. Most commands in the Finder and in other applications are for performing a task; the Apple menu, on the other hand, is pretty much a quick-launcher.

So what's on this menu? Lots of things, in four basic categories, including Desk Accessories, Control Panels, Aliases, and Menus.

Desk Accessories

Originally, desk accessories were the only types of program that could multitask on the Macintosh. Very early Macs could only run one application—like a word processor—at a time. So, Apple had to create desk accessories to help out with important tasks that you need to perform while still using the application. That's why they're small, single-function programs like the Calculator or the Note Pad. Here are some of the desk accessories you'll find on the Apple menu in Mac OS 9:

- **Chooser**   The Chooser is a special desk accessory that helps you select printers and connect to networked computers. You can read more about the Chooser in Chapter 25.

- **Key Caps**   This little program helps you figure out what key combinations you need to press in order to type certain characters. Launch it, then choose the font you want to use from the Font menu. Now, try different modifier keys—⌘, OPTION, CONTROL, SHIFT—in various configurations. The letter keys will change to show you the character that will appear when you press that same combination of modifier keys and that letter key.

- **Network Browser**   If your iMac is attached to a network, especially a large one, the Network Browser makes it easy to see all the different machines and hard drives to which you have access. This accessory is discussed in detail in Chapter 28.

- **Scrapbook**   The Scrapbook is designed for cutting and pasting multimedia elements that you'd like to save for the future—stuff like pictures, drawings, audio clips, even QuickTime videos. All you have to do is highlight the desired item in an application, then choose Edit | Copy or Edit | Cut. Switch to the Scrapbook and choose Edit | Paste and your clipping is added at the end of the Scrapbook's pages. Now, when necessary, you can copy the multimedia clipping out of the Scrapbook and into some other applications. (Note: The Scrapbook is fully drag-and-drop aware, so you can drag-and-drop from applications to the Scrapbook, and vice versa, if you prefer.) To close the Scrapbook, click its Close box. Anything you've pasted into the Scrapbook will be there the next time you launch it—it's saved automatically. To remove something from the Scrapbook, view it, then choose Edit | Clear from the menu.

- **Sherlock 2**   Sherlock 2 is Mac OS 9's search utility, discussed in Chapters 3 and 6.

■ **Stickies**   These ought to look familiar. Launch Stickies from the Apple menu and you've got little sticky notes you can add to your screen, sort of. Just type your message on a note, then position it on the screen; you can choose File | New Note if you need more little colorful opportunities to express yourself. (Choose the colors by selecting a note and then choosing the color from the Color menu.) Stickies don't need to be saved unless you want the note to no longer appear on the screen. In that case, click the note's Close box and you'll be asked if you want to save the note as a text file. You can quit Stickies by choosing File | Quit in the Stickies menu.

Control Panels

Control panels are used to customize and make choices about your iMac. They can range from the droll, like setting the clock or deciding what sort of text the OS should use, to the fun, like the Appearance Manager, which allows you to change the colors and appearance of your iMac's interface.

Throughout this book I'll touch on many of these control panels; a lot of the appearance and customization panels are covered in Chapter 24. All you need to know now is that they're there on the Apple menu, they'll pop right open when you select them in the Control Panels menu, and you can close them all by clicking their respective Close boxes.

You might also be interested to know that control panels are stored in the System Folder on your iMac's hard drive in the folder called Control Panels. Any control panels in that folder will appear in the Control Panels menu on the Apple menu.

Aliases

In the Apple menu, you'll also find aliases to applications or utilities that are actually stored elsewhere on the hard drive. Most of these are added by non-Apple installation programs, but you can add items to the Apple menu yourself, including aliases to files or even folders (which appear as submenus). Simply drag them to the Apple Menu Items folder inside the System Folder. You'll see the items the next time you access the Apple menu.

Other aliases are added by Apple or by third-party installers—America Online and FaxSTF, for instance, both add aliases to the Apple menu to make it easier for you to start up an application conveniently or look into things like the status of your fax receiving. Likewise, Apple adds an alias to the Apple System Profiler, a useful utility for seeing the devices installed and recognized by your iMac.

Recent Menus

The Recent menus enable you to quickly re-launch or re-access an item you've been working with recently. To use the Recent menus, just click the Apple menu, then point the mouse at Recent Applications, Recent Documents, or Recent Servers (see Figure 5-3). Then, select the item you'd

5

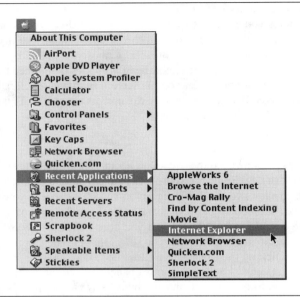

FIGURE 5-3   The Recent menus let you pick documents, applications, or servers that you've worked with recently.

like to re-launch. Your iMac will switch back to the Finder (if necessary) and launch the application and/or open the document you've chosen.

If you choose a server (actually, a server's disk), you may need to log back into the server to access it. If you're not familiar with the process, consult Chapter 28.

NOTE *A server, in this context, is a computer that your iMac is connected to by networking cables or by wireless AirPort technology, if your iMac is so equipped. Connecting to a remote server enables you to retrieve and store files on that computer.*

If you'd like to change the behavior of the Recent menus, you can do so through the Apple Menu Options control panel (Apple menu | Control Panels | Apple Menu Options). In the control panel, you can decide if you want to use the Recent menus; if not, click to make sure there's no check mark in the check box next to the Remember Recently Used Items option. If you are using Recent menus, you can select how many items your iMac remembers—the default is 10. If you want to change that number, just click in the entry box and edit the number. When you're done, click the Close box in the Apple Menu Options control panel. Your changes are noted and put into action.

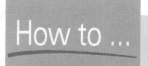 **Delete Entries from the Recent Menus**

Open the Apple Menu Items folder that's stored in your System Folder. Now, open the folder that corresponds to the Recent menu you want to clean out. In that folder, each alias corresponds to an entry on that Recent menu; drag any of the aliases to the Trash. Check the Recent menu in the Apple menu; those trashed items should be gone from the menu.

5

The Classic Application Menu

Up in the top-right corner of the Classic and Mac OS 9 screen you'll always find the Application menu, a menu dedicated to switching between your open applications. Which menu is it? It's the one with the name and icon of whatever applications you're currently running. Point to that icon and name, then click the mouse button to open the menu.

Switch Between Applications

If you have an application other than the Finder open, you can head up there right now, pull down the Application menu, and see all of your open applications. Choose one of those applications and it'll move to the *foreground*—you'll suddenly see that new application's menus and windows in front of you, ready to be worked on. While this is most useful when you're working directly within Mac OS 9, it also works in the Classic environment of Mac OS X, giving you an alternative to the Dock for switching applications.

 *You can switch between applications with a keystroke, too. Press ⌘-TAB to switch from application to application. You can press ⌘-SHIFT-TAB to switch back in the opposite order. Again, this works in both Mac OS 9 and Mac OS X.*

Hide and Show Applications

The Application menu has some other useful commands that help you when you switch between applications. If you've switched applications, and windows from another application are getting in your way or cluttering up the screen, you can pull down the Application menu and choose Hide Others, which hides all applications except the one you're currently working in. The applications are still running and you can still switch to them using the Application menu—only their windows are currently hidden.

You can also hide the application that you're working in—perhaps so you can see an open window in a background application. To do that, pull down the Application menu and choose Hide ... (the ellipse represents the name of the current application).

The Show All command does exactly what you think it would—it reveals the windows of all hidden applications. You can also reveal individual applications by switching to them using the Application menu.

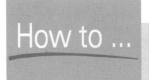

Want to hide an application as you switch away from it? Just hold down the OPTION key as you switch between applications. The application you're switching from gets hidden as you switch to the new application.

 Float the Application Menu

If you select the Application menu and hold down the mouse button, then drag straight down the menu right off the bottom edge, you'll "tear away" the menu. Suddenly it becomes a floating window that includes the icons and names of the currently running applications. (Note that this only works when you've started up in Mac OS 9, not from within the Classic environment.)

The window will always float *on top* of all your other applications, so you'll always be able to see it. To switch to a different application, all you have to do is click once on that application's icon.

You can also customize the window somewhat. Do you want just icons and no words? Click the maximize box and the menu shrinks down to small icons. If you'd like the icons bigger, hold down OPTION and click the maximize box. If you'd like to change from vertical to horizontal, hold down SHIFT-OPTION and click the maximize box.

Need to get rid of the floating menu window? Click its Close box and it's gone. You can still, as always, use the Application menu the next time you need to switch applications.

Classic Finder Tricks

While the Finder in Mac OS X and Mac OS 9 are similar in most respects, they have some significant differences. What's odd about the differences, though, is that they aren't all in Mac OS X's favor—Mac OS 9 has some great features that haven't yet been (and may never be) incorporated into Mac OS X. If you're opting to stick with Mac OS 9 for the time being, you may want to know about those features, covered in this section.

Drag to Spring-Loaded Folders

The Mac OS 9 Finder offers some interesting ways to accomplish your dragging and dropping. Consider this: What if you have a file on the desktop that needs to go into a subfolder—say, a folder named Memos inside the folder named Documents? You could double-click through tons of folders, but there's a better way, using spring-loaded folders.

   Pick up the icon you want to move (point the mouse pointer at it and hold down the mouse button) and drag it over to the Macintosh HD icon. Now, leave it on top of the icon (so that the Macintosh HD icon is highlighted) for a few seconds. Keep holding down the mouse button— don't drop the file yet. Suddenly, the Macintosh HD window springs open! Now, locate the Documents folder icon and do the same thing—keep holding down the mouse button while hovering over the Documents icon. It'll spring open, too. You can keep doing that until you reach the folder you want to drop the icon in. When you get there, release the mouse button and you've successfully moved the icon. In fact, this feature is so cool that the other windows will close as you open the next window, just to keep things neat and tidy. And it works with any folder—simply drag an item (or items) to a folder, then hover for a second and it pops open.

Quickly Access Pop-Up Windows

Here's another fun feature of Mac OS 9 Finder windows. If you have a window open that you use a lot—like the window showing your Documents folder—you can keep it open all the time, but out of the way. Just grab the window by its title bar and drag it to the bottom of the screen. Get far enough down and suddenly the window becomes anchored to the bottom and the title bar becomes a little tab (see Figure 5-4).

5

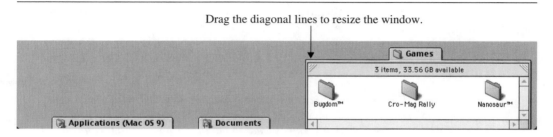

FIGURE 5-4   Tabbed windows are a great way to store often-used windows accessibly, yet out of the way.

NOTE *You can select any open window in the Finder and choose View | As Pop-up Window from the Finder's menu to change it into a pop-up window.*

To open the window and see its contents, just click the tab once. The window pops up. If you want to drag an item to a pop-up window, just hover over the tab itself (with the dragged item in tow) and the window pops up to reveal its contents. You can also resize the window using the little resize tools (the diagonal lines) on the side of each pop-up window.

To turn a pop-up window back into a regular window, just drag the tab up until the outline turns into a normal window. Release the mouse button and the window is back to normal. You can also select the pop-up window and choose View | As Window to change it into a regular window.

Create and Use Favorites

Mac OS X has a Favorites feature, but it isn't quite as useful as Mac OS 9's version. A Favorite enables you to choose parts of the Mac OS and sort of *bookmark* them for future use. When you create a Favorite, you're adding an alias to that item to the Favorites menu that appears in the Apple menu. At the same time, you're also creating an alias that shows up elsewhere in the Mac OS—particularly in the Classic Open and Save dialog boxes discussed in Chapter 7. So, it's a double-whammy, making it easier for you to get at the files and folders you use a lot.

Speaking of folders, when you create a Favorite of a folder, you can actually access it as a hierarchical menu from within the Apple menu. Choose Apple menu | Favorites, then the folder's name, and you'll see a menu of its contents.

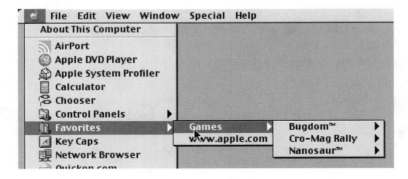

Before all this magic can happen for you, though, you're going to need to create a Favorite. Follow these steps:

1. Select an item in the Finder—it can be a file, a folder, or even a disk. It's probably best that it's a folder, though. (Select the folder icon, not an open folder window.)

NOTE *You can select a disk icon and make it a Favorite, but that will likely slow down your iMac when you access the Apple menu. The iMac is forced to check all of those subfolders (at least, four levels deep) so that it knows what to put on the menus. That can cause a little delay while the Apple menu is opening up.*

2. Then choose File | Add to Favorites.

This creates an alias to that item and places it in the Favorites folder that's stored in the Apple Menu Items folder, which, in turn, is in the System Folder on your iMac's hard drive. Once you've got the Favorite created, you can access it immediately by selecting it in the Favorites submenu of the Apple menu.

Want to delete a Favorite? Simply select the Favorite command itself from the Apple menu. That opens the Favorites folder, which is stored inside the System Folder. Drag to the Trash any aliases you no longer want to see on the Favorites menu.

Use Labels to Organize

The Mac OS 9 Finder is capable of giving individual folders or items a special label that marks the folder with a particular priority and changes the color of the folder or icon. That may not seem immediately important, but it has some sophisticated implications.

To change the label on an item, choose the item in the Finder, then choose File | Label. A number of label options pop up in the Label menu. Choose one of those color labels and it's assigned to the selected icon, as shown in Figure 5-5.

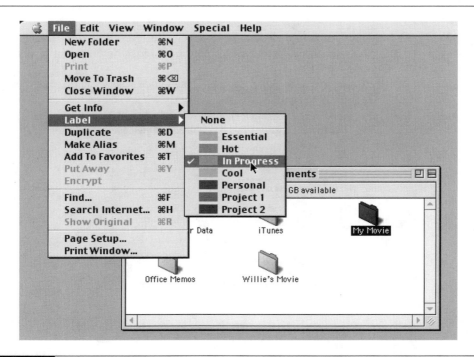

FIGURE 5-5   Assign a label to icons you want specifically flagged.

Why do this? First, a folder with a certain color may come to mean important things to you—that it needs immediate attention, that it's a project folder holding a bunch of aliases, or something along those lines. Perhaps more importantly, though, you'll often encounter applications and utilities that can read the label and do something accordingly—for instance, you might label a particular folder as "Hot" and have an automatic backup program choose to back up all Hot folders. You can even search your hard drive using Sherlock 2 (discussed in Chapter 3) to find all the Hot folders or a similar label.

You can change the label names. Choose Edit | Preferences in the Finder and click the Labels tab. Now, click in the box where you see the name of each label and edit it to suit your needs. You could label things according to backup priority, according to the names of everyone who uses your iMac (Little Billy's file folders are all in Purple), or for whatever other reasons strike your fancy.

Get Help in Classic and Mac OS 9

Need a little help? If you're dealing with Classic Mac applications, you may encounter a system similar to the Help Viewer discussed in Chapter 2, which Apple had moved toward in earlier Mac versions. But you may also encounter a few others—holdovers from a time when Apple used to like cute, friendly help systems (and before people were as familiar with the hyperlink metaphor). Those include Apple Guide and Balloon Help.

Apple Guide

In some ways, Apple Guide is similar to the Apple Help system—it offers both topic listings and a search to help you find what you need to know. (It also offers an index of terms that is more extensive than what's found in Apple Help.)

Once you find the Help topic you're looking for, the Apple Guide walks you through the process in small steps, often telling you and showing you exactly what to do on the screen. You may notice, for instance, that some Apple Guide lessons will circle menus or highlight menu commands in red to help you find the correct command. More than just Help documents, Apple Guide offers something akin to electronic lessons on different topics:

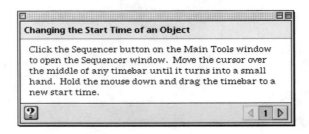

You start up Apple Guide the way you start up the Help Viewer—select Help | *Application* Help or Help | *Application* Guide from the application's menus.

Balloon Help

Balloon Help's simple role is to tell you what something is when you point to it. Unfortunately, Balloon Help isn't universally implemented by all Classic applications (and it's non-existent in Mac OS X applications). It's useful when it is, though, so it's always worth checking for Balloon Help when you have a question about a Classic application's interface.

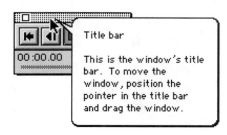

To turn on Balloon Help, choose Help | Show Balloons. Now, aim the mouse pointer at anything onscreen that you'd like to learn more about. If Balloon Help has been implemented for that application and that item, a small cartoon-like balloon appears at the mouse pointer, offering information.

To turn off Balloon Help, choose Help | Hide Balloons.

Chapter 6

Get a Quick Start on the Internet

How to...

- Sign on to the Internet
- Get your Mail
- Browse the Web
- Manage Web history and Favorites
- Search the Internet

Clearly the Internet is a big part of the iMac experience—after all, it's what the "i" in iMac stands for. So, getting signed onto the Internet and walking through the basics of e-mail and Web browsing are important enough that I'd like to cover them here. In this chapter you'll see how to connect and disconnect a modem connection to the Internet. You'll also see the basics of reading and sending e-mail messages and surfing the World Wide Web. Throughout I'll cover both Mac OS 9 and Mac OS X issues, including getting and reading your e-mail in either the Mail application that's part of Mac OS X or Microsoft Outlook Express, which is included with all iMacs.

Connect to the Internet

If you've already stepped through the instructions for plugging in your modem and creating your Internet account in the Setup Assistant as discussed in Chapter 1, then you're ready to connect to the Internet via your iMac's modem. All you need to do is launch the appropriate Internet *dialer* application, either Internet Connect (Mac OS X) or Remote Access (Mac OS 9). Then, you tell the dialer to connect and it goes through the process of dialing your ISP and beginning the Internet session.

 If you have another type of connection—or if you need to configure your modem connection manually—see Chapter 23 first, then proceed with this chapter.

Sign On (and Off) in Mac OS X

In Mac OS X, you'll connect to the Internet using the Internet Connect application, which is located in the Utilities folder inside the main Applications folder. Launch Internet Connect by double-clicking its icon. At the top of the Internet Connect window, you'll see the Configuration menu, which should say Internal Modem. Now, all you have to do is make sure nobody else is using the phone line (just yell really loud there in your home, if necessary) and click Connect. The Connect button immediately changes to a Cancel button, and you'll see messages on the Status line, indicating whether the connection is being completed or not.

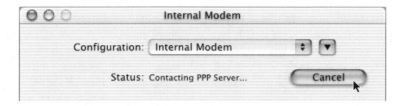

Once the connection is open, the Internet Connect application will display your current connection status, including how long you've been connected, whether data is being sent and received, and what your IP (Internet Protocol) address is currently.

At this point, you're ready to fire up your e-mail application or Web browser and start enjoying the Internet. While you're connected to the Internet and Internet Connect is active, the Internet Connect icon in the Dock shows a small lightning bolt. When you're ready to disconnect, click the Disconnect button.

NOTE *You can actually quit Internet Connect and your Internet connection will remain active as long as you're using the Internet. Eventually, it may "time out" and disconnect after a period of inactivity, according to the settings discussed in Chapter 23. To sign off manually, launch Internet Connect again.*

Sign On (and Off) in Mac OS 9

In Mac OS 9, you have two different ways to sign onto the Internet, assuming you've configured a modem-based account using the Setup Assistant. (Again, for other types of Internet access, see Chapter 23.) For more control and feedback, you can launch Remote Access (Apple menu | Control Panels | Remote Access), enter a password (if necessary), and click Connect. As with Internet Connect in Mac OS X, Remote Access will display the status of your connection as well as Send and Receive indicators.

The easier way, though, is via the Control Strip that appears at the bottom of the screen. Open the Control Strip and you should see the Remote Access control strip module—it looks like a little Mac and a telephone pole. This is the control you'll use to sign onto the Internet. Click once on the control strip module and the Remote Access control strip menu will appear.

Make sure your iMac's modem is connected to the phone line and make sure the phone line isn't currently in use. Click Connect. You should hear your iMac pick up the phone and start dialing. Now iMac goes through the Internet sign-on phase. If things don't work out, you'll see an error message telling you why Remote Access can't sign on. If all goes well, the Apple menu in the top-left corner will blink to show a connected icon.

Now you're ready to work with Internet applications. When you're done with this session and you want to sign off, choose the control strip again and click Disconnect. Your session will be terminated and the modem will hang up.

Get, Read, and Reply to E-mail

If you use Mac OS X with your iMac, you may also opt to use Mail, the built-in e-mail application, for sending and receiving messages. You also have the option of using Microsoft Outlook Express 5, a very popular e-mail application that comes with your iMac and can run either in Mac OS 9 or as a Classic application. In either case, the basics of reading, sending, and receiving e-mail are very similar.

Get Your Mail

If you've used the Setup Assistant in either operating system to create an Internet account, then your e-mail programs should already have all the information they need for you to get started. Once your Internet connection is active, launch Mail (click its tile on the Dock) or Outlook Express (located in the Internet folder inside the "Applications (Mac OS 9)" folder on your hard disk).

 With OE, you'll need to step through the Account Setup Assistant the first time you launch it. However, it already has the information it needs for your e-mail account if you've walked through the Internet Setup Assistant in Mac OS 9.

When you open Mail or Outlook Express (OE for short), you are immediately greeted by the main viewer window in each application. By default, Mail automatically checks for new e-mail. (If your Internet connection isn't active, you'll receive an error message.) In OE (see Figure 6-1), you click the Send and Receive button to check for new messages; in Mail (see Figure 6-2), you can check manually by clicking the Get Mail icon in Mail's toolbar.

 *In Mail, select Window | Activity Viewer to display a small window that shows activity as e-mail is being retrieved; in OE, choose Window | Progress to display a similar window.*

Check for new mail.

Message list

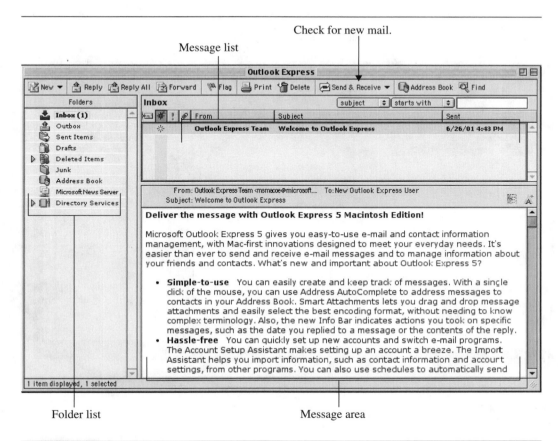

Folder list   Message area

FIGURE 6-1   Outlook Express's main viewer window

Once your mail has been downloaded, the messages will appear in the message list. If you don't see any new messages, but you think you've received some, make sure you have the Inbox selected. Click the Inbox icon in OE's Folder List or in Mail's Mailboxes drawer to view your Inbox, where new messages are routed automatically. Now you're ready to read messages.

NOTE   *If you don't see the Mailboxes drawer in Mail, click the Mailbox icon in the toolbar to reveal the Mailboxes drawer.*

Check for new mail.

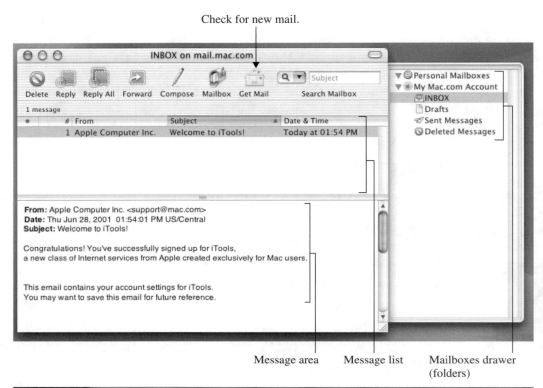

Message area   Message list   Mailboxes drawer
(folders)

FIGURE 6-2   Mail's main viewer window

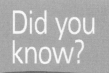

E-mail Addresses

The key to sending and receiving e-mail is the e-mail address. In order to receive e-mail, you have to tell others your e-mail address. To send messages to others, you'll need to know their addresses. The e-mail address can be broken up into three or four parts:

■ **Account Name**   The name that identifies you or your e-mail account (if more than one person is using it) is unique among the accounts on your ISP's e-mail server computer. That's the "myusername" part of *myusername@myisp.net*.

■ **Server Computer**   Some, but not all, e-mail addresses will include the actual name of the e-mail server computer in the address. An example might be *todd@mail.mycompany.com* where "mail" is the actual e-mail server computer.

■ **Domain Name**   The domain name is a name given to a group of computers at a particular organization. If you work for Apple, for instance, your address might be *todd@apple.com*. The "apple" part suggests the domain for that company.

■ **Domain Name Extension**   The domain name extension suggests the type of organization you're dealing with. A commercial entity gets a .com, while an ISP (like Earthlink) generally gets a .net extension, as in earthlink.net. Other extensions include .edu (educational), .mil (military), .org (organization), and country codes like .uk (United Kingdom), .fr (France), and .au (Australia).

It's not terribly important to remember what each part of an e-mail address is intended to signify. What's more important is remembering that whenever you enter an e-mail address, you need to enter the entire address as you've been given it, so that it can reach its destination account.

Read Your Mail

Messages you haven't yet read appear in the Mail message list with a dot in the left column of the list; in OE, unread messages are bolded and show a blue asterisk in the message list. To read a message, just click once on its topic—the message's text appears in the message area, where you can scroll to read the message. If you prefer, you can also double-click a message subject, which causes a new window to appear with the message.

Once a message has been read, it stays in the Inbox message list but the small dot disappears (and in OE, it's no longer bold) to indicate that it's already been read.

Sort Your E-mail

Want to switch the view around a bit? Each message in the message list takes up a full row—the columns represent the read or unread status (the small dot in the far-left column), From, Subject, the date the message was sent, and other information. In both Mail and OE, you might notice that these columns work a little like the columns in Finder window List views. You can click the column heading in each case to change the organization of the Inbox.

Once you have the message list sorted according to one of the column headings, you'll notice that it's in either ascending or descending order. You can change that order by clicking the heading again in both Mail and OE. The little triangle flips sides to indicate that you've switched from ascending to descending order or vice-versa.

 *You can turn on and off some additional columns. In OE, choose View | Columns and choose a column name from the menu to turn it on or off. In Mail, choose View | Show Message Numbers to see a serial number assigned to each message as it appears in the Inbox, or choose View | Show Message Sizes to see the size, in kilobytes, of each message.*

Search Your Mail

Have quite a bit of e-mail in your Inbox? You can search through the Inbox or any other folder so that the list shows only messages that are *focused* on a particular person or topic.

In Mail's toolbar, open the Search Mailbox menu, which looks like a small magnifying glass. In that menu, select the part of the messages you'd like to focus on: Any, Subject, To, or From. Then, enter a keyword in the Search Mailbox entry box, such as the name of the sender (if you've chosen From) or part of the subject (if you've chosen Subject). As you type, you'll notice that the message list gets smaller. It's focusing on messages that match your keyword.

Search Mailbox

In OE, you'll see two menus in the toolbar—one for the part of the message (From, To, Subject) and one where you select either Starts With or Contains. Then, start typing your keyword—again, messages are focused as you type.

In fact, in both programs, you don't have to type the whole keyword at all—often typing just a few letters will work. Once you've found the message or messages you're interested in, you can read, reply to, file in another folder, or delete the message(s). When you're done working with the focused messages, delete the text from the search entry box and you'll remove the focus, once again revealing all your e-mail. (In Mail, you can also choose View | Show All Messages to remove the focus.)

 Focusing works in any folder or mailbox that you select, not just the Inbox—see Chapter 18 for details on creating and using additional folders for storing messages.

Reply to a Message

If a message that you're reading deserves a reply, then click the Reply button in the toolbar (or select Message | Reply to Sender) and a new window appears, ready for your reply.

You should see that the original message has already been "quoted" for you—that just means that the original message has been included in your reply so that the person you're replying to can have his or her memory jogged about what, exactly, you're replying to. Now you can just begin typing, creating a message that probably looks something like one of the two shown in Figure 6-3.

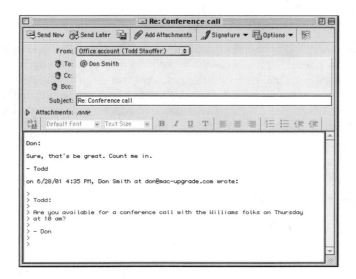

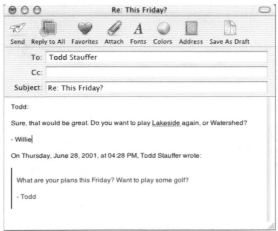

FIGURE 6-3   A reply (top: OE, bottom: Mail) complete with the original message quoted below it

Notice in Figure 6-3 that the quoted part appears at the bottom of the message window with the new reply (the part I wrote) at the top of the message. This is both OE and Mail's default treatment of quotes. You can tell the quoted text by the fact that it appears in a different color. (In fact, each "level" of quoted text appears in a different color, so you can easily follow an entire back-and-forth conversation.)

When you're done composing the reply, you're ready to click buttons in the Reply window (OE's command name, when different, is shown in parentheses):

- **Send (Send Now)** This button sends the message immediately if you're still online. If you're not connected, OE will put the message in the Outbox folder and wait until the next time you send and receive messages. Mail will display a dialog sheet asking if you'd like to save the message for later delivery. If you choose OK, the message is stored in a mailbox called To Be Delivered. It's then delivered the next time you successfully send another reply or new message.

- **Send Later** (This one is in OE only.) Click this button if you want to place the message directly in the Outbox and not send it until the next time you click Send and Receive or the next automated connection.

- **Save as Draft** Select this button and the message isn't sent at all—it's saved in the Drafts folder. Drafts are just that—rough versions of e-mail messages you don't yet want to send. You can select the Drafts folder to view those saved messages, then double-click a draft to re-edit it and, if desired, send it at that point.

TIP *Don't forget to check the Drafts folder every once in a while so you don't leave a message languishing, unsent, because you still need to edit it. (I do it all the time, then I kick myself for not sending an important message.)*

- **Attach (Add Attachments)** Click this button to send another file or files as *attachment(s)* to this message. Attachments are discussed in Chapter 18.

How to ... Reply to All Senders

This is a special case—if you're reading a message that was sent to more people than just you, you can send your reply to all recipients. If Mindy sends a message to you, Jack, and Tina, the question is whether or not you want to send a reply just to Mindy, or if you want everyone to see the reply. If you want to send it just to the original sender, select the message in the main viewer window and click Reply; if you want to send it to all recipients to keep the group conversation alive, click Reply All.

In Mail, if you've already clicked Reply and you're viewing the Reply window, you still have another chance to add those additional recipients. Click the Reply to All button in the toolbar of the Reply window.

Delete a Message

In both OE and Mail, you can highlight a message in the message window and click the Delete button in the toolbar to delete it from the message list. It's not gone forever, though; it's simply moved to the Deleted Messages mailbox in Mail or the Deleted Items folder in OE.

> **NOTE**   *Deleted Mac.com messages appear crossed out in OE. To remove them from the Inbox, select Edit | Purge.*

In Mail, if you'd like to immediately delete all messages in your Deleted Messages mailbox, choose Mailbox | Empty Deleted Messages. You'll see an alert box confirming your decision—click OK to delete those messages. In OE, you can simply select all messages (Edit | Select All) in the Deleted Items folder and click the Delete button in the toolbar to delete them, or you can select Tools | Run Schedule | Empty Deleted Items Folder.

You can set Mail to empty the Deleted Items folder when you quit the program or after a certain number of days in the Deleted Messages mailbox. To alter this setting, choose Mail | Preferences and click the Viewing button. In the Erase Deleted Mail When menu, choose how long Mail should wait before permanently deleting a message after it's been moved to the Deleted Messages mailbox.

> **TIP**   *To automate message deletion in OE, you'll need to create a new schedule. Choose Tools | Schedules and click New to begin creating a new schedule. In the When section of the Schedule window, choose Repeating Schedule. In the Action section, choose Delete Mail and set the other options that appear. Click OK to close the Schedule window and put the schedule into effect.*

Compose a New Message

If you're interested in sending a new message, it's even a little easier to do than replying. The only difference is that you need to know the e-mail address of the person you want to send the message to and you'll need to enter a subject for the message.

>  **SHORTCUT**   *By default, Mail checks the spelling of your message as you type. (Outlook Express will also check spelling, but only if you have Microsoft Word or Microsoft Office installed.) In both, a word that appears underlined as you type is an unrecognized word. Hold down the CONTROL key and click that word to reveal a pop-up menu that includes suggested spellings. If you see the correct spelling, select it; if the word is correctly spelled, you can choose Ignore Spelling or Learn Spelling (Add in OE) to add that word to your dictionary.*

6

Compose in Mail

Here's how to compose a new message in Mail:

1. Click the Compose button in the toolbar or select File | New Compose Window.

2. In the New Message window, enter an e-mail address for the To: box. If you have more than one To: recipient in Mail, you can type a comma (,) between each e-mail address.

3. Now, press TAB to move to the Cc entry box and type an e-mail address if you'd like to send a "courtesy copy" to anyone.

4. Next, press TAB to move to the Subject line. Enter a subject that's informative without being terribly long. Press TAB.

> **TIP** *If you want to send a Bcc (Blind courtesy copy), select Message | Add Bcc Header from the menu. A blind courtesy copy is sent to the specified recipient without the other recipients' knowledge.*

5. Type your message in the body of the message window, then select a signature from the Signature menu if you're set up to add a signature to your messages (discussed in Chapter 18).

> **NOTE** *If you have more than one e-mail account, a small menu appears above the message body. Here you can choose the account from which you want to send your message.*

After you've typed the body of your message, it's pretty much like a reply—click the Send or Save as Draft buttons in the toolbar.

Compose in Outlook Express

Here's how to compose a message in OE:

1. Click the New button in the toolbar or select File | New | Mail Message.

> **NOTE** *If you have more than one account set up in Outlook Express, you should choose the account from which you want to send the message in the Account menu.*

2. In the window, enter an e-mail address for the To box. If you like, you can press TAB to enter another To recipient.

3. Now, select the CC tab to type an e-mail address if you'd like to send a "courtesy copy" to anyone.

4. Next, you can select the Bcc tab and type an e-mail address in the BCC box (blind courtesy copy). If you do so, this person's e-mail address won't appear to any other recipients. Only you and the BCC recipient will know that you sent a copy to that person.

5. Now you'll click in the subject area to type a subject for your message. When you're done, press TAB.

6. Type the message in the body of the message window, then click the Signature button if you're set up to add a personalized signature to your messages (see Chapter 18).

From here it's like a reply—click Send Now, Send Later, or Save as Draft according to your preference.

Web Browser Basics

The World Wide Web is really a *protocol*—a set of computer-coded rules for transmitting information—more than it is a place or program. While it may seem that you're connecting to some monolithic mechanism that broadcasts information like a TV network, the fact is that Web server computers are distributed all over the Internet and, therefore, all over the world. Since each individual server has its own address and each one speaks the same HyperText Transport Protocol (HTTP), it's possible for you to connect to and read documents from computers all over the globe.

Did you know?

E-mail Formats

By default, Mail sends messages formatted in Rich Text Format, which enables you to add different font effects, styles, and colors to messages using the controls in the composition window. This works great when you're sending to and from other Mac OS X users and many Microsoft Windows users, but can fall down a bit when sent to other computer users and platforms. (OE defaults to plain text, but selecting Format | HTML enables you to send formatted e-mail messages.)

If you find that your recipients are complaining of odd character codes in your messages, you should instead send them plain text messages; when you're composing a message in Mail, you can choose Format | Make Plain Text to send a particular message without codes and formatting. To make Plain Text the permanent default, select Mail | Preferences, then click the Composing icon. In the Default Message Format menu, choose Plain Text.

If you do send Rich Text e-mail and you opt to use special fonts in your e-mail messages, note that they should be very common fonts—Arial, Helvetica, Times New Roman—particularly if you're sending this message to users of non-Mac OS X computers. The message will be more likely to look the way you intended.

The Web Browser

You may be surprised to learn that the Web browser is a fairly simple program. It's designed to read Web documents and format them to fit on your screen. The documents have instructions—things like "make this text bold" and "place an image here on the page"—that the Web browser interprets. Those instructions are in the HyperText Markup Language (HTML), which is actually simple to learn.

Your Web browser is able to translate those commands into a coherent page, while offering you built-in features that help you organize, search, and approach the Web in a structured way. We'll take a look at some of those basic features here, while more advanced Web browsing topics are covered in Chapter 19.

> **NOTE** *This chapter focuses on Internet Explorer, the version included with iMacs that are preloaded with both Mac OS X and Mac OS 9. If you have another browser, such as Netscape Communicator—located in the Internet folder inside the "Applications (Mac OS 9) folder"—or Omni Development's OmniWeb (**www.omnigroup.com**) you'll find that browsing, bookmarks, and history are similar.*

The Internet Address

The basis of locating pages on the Web is the Uniform Resource Locator (URL), which serves as the primary mechanism for addresses on the Web. The idea of the URL is simple—every Web document has its own address on the Internet. That way, if you want to view a particular document on a particular computer in a particular country, you simply enter the address.

Consider these sample URLs:

```
http://www.apple.com/
http://www.mac-upgrade.com/imac_book/index.html
```

URLs are made up of three basic components—the protocol, the Web server address, and the path to the document. The protocol tells the browser what sort of Internet server you're trying to access. Enter **http://** for Web servers, **https://** for Web servers that have security enabled, and **ftp://** if you're accessing a File Transfer Protocol (FTP) server (FTP allows you to download files).

The server computer address is simply the address to a particular computer or group of computers running a Web server application. Note that this can sometimes be a numbered address like *206.100.129.49* instead of a named address like *www.apple.com*. (In fact, as far as the Internet is concerned, all computer addresses are numbers, not names. The names are just for human convenience.)

The path statement tells the server computer what folders and subfolders a particular document is stored in on the Web server computer. Something like */imac_book/index.html* tells the server computer to "look in the *imac_book* folder and get me the *index.html* file." The server computer complies and sends a copy of that document, which is then displayed in your Web browser.

 *Most browsers allow you to enter Web addresses without the full URL. If you prefer, type **www.apple.com** or **206.100.129.49** without the protocol. It's a little quicker.*

Surf the Web

It's called "surfing" because, just like riding waves in the ocean, you never know exactly how you're going to get somewhere or how far down the beach you'll end up. In a Web browser, though, you surf by clicking a *hyperlink* (see Figure 6-4).

What you'll most often do on the Internet is read documents and click links to new documents. Sometimes you'll do other things, such as filling in forms and downloading files, which we'll discuss in depth in Chapter 19.

If you want to get a quick start, though, here are the basics:

■ *Hyperlinks* are the basic method for "browsing" on the Web—click a link you think is interesting to see the associated document. A hyperlink may appear as text that is underlined and in blue, or as an image or a button. Click a hyperlink once with the mouse to open a new Web page.

When you pass over a hyperlink using Internet Explorer, your pointer icon will turn into a hand with an index finger sticking up—that means the pointer is over a hyperlink that can be clicked. To select it, just click the mouse once.

■ The *Back* and *Forward* buttons are used to move to a previous page, then forward again (if desired). If you click a hyperlink, for instance, read the page, and then decide to go back to the previous page, click the Back button.

■ The *address box* is used to directly enter URLs, as discussed in the previous section. It's in the address box that you'll type URLs (like **http://www.apple.com/**), then press RETURN to visit that address. You should enter addresses as precisely as possible including all the dots (.) and slashes (/).

To quit Internet Explorer, choose File | Quit from the menu. Once you've quit the browser, you might also want to sign off of the Internet via Internet Connect or Remote Access so you don't keep the phone line tied up.

Don't be surprised if some links open a new Web document in a new window. There's a special code Web authors use to make a link open a new window. It's harmless enough, but if you don't like it, click the Close box or button in the new window. In fact, you can open a new window yourself by holding down the ⌘ key whenever you click a link.

6

Back   Forward   Go to Home page   Address box

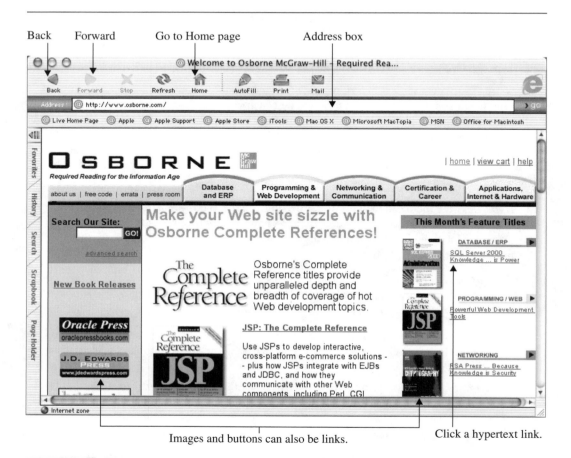

Images and buttons can also be links.   Click a hypertext link.

FIGURE 6-4   The main browser window in Internet Explorer

Sign Up for iTools

If you're working primarily in Mac OS X, you may have already signed up for an iTools account—Apple's online suite of applications discussed in Chapters 18, 20, and 21. If you didn't sign up while using the Assistant, however, you can do so by visiting **http://www.apple.com/itools/** and walking through the Sign Up process. You'll then have a Mac.com e-mail account, an iDisk (for remote file storage), and access to the HomePage tool for creating Web sites.

In Mac OS X, you can sign up another way—open the Internet pane of the System Preferences application and select the iTools tab. Click the Sign Up button and you'll be sent to the iTools Web page to sign up for an account.

Manage Bookmarks, Favorites, and History

Eventually, you'll come across a site that's worth remembering, and at that point you'll want to create what Internet Explorer calls a Favorite and what most other browsers call a *bookmark*. Favorites and bookmarks do the same thing—save a URL for future reference. To set a Favorite, open the page in the browser window. In Internet Explorer, choose Favorites | Add Page to Favorites.

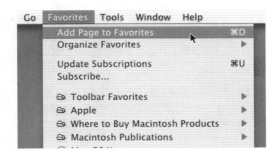

When you do this, the browser stores the URL to the open page and places the title of that page on the Favorites menu. Now, whenever you want to return to that page, simply choose the Favorites or Bookmarks menu in your Web browser, then select the site. Your Web browser will find that page again and display it.

Edit Favorites

In Internet Explorer you can edit your Favorites list in one of two ways—either clicking the Favorites tab that appears on the left side of the browser window (to reveal the Favorites *pane*), or by selecting Favorites | Organize Favorites. In the Favorites pane or window, you can drag-and-drop Favorites to move them into folders or to change their order. When you're dragging a Favorite around, notice that a thin black line moves along the window with you to show you where it will appear when you drop it.

In the Favorites window, you can rename a favorite by clicking once on its name—similar to renaming an item in the Finder. You can also highlight an item and choose File | Get Info to edit the Favorite or even change its URL.

You can also create folders and dividing lines by choosing New Folder or New Divider from the Favorites | Organize Favorites menu. If you want to create a Favorite from scratch, choose Favorites | Organize Favorites | New Favorite. You'll then need to manually enter a name and URL for this Favorite.

To delete a Favorite, select it in the Favorites pane or window and press the DELETE key on your keyboard, or drag the Favorite from the Favorites window to the Trash can.

> **TIP** *You can edit the Toolbar Favorites to change the favorite items that appear on the toolbar just below the Address entry box. You can also drag Favorites directly off of the Toolbar to a Finder window or to the desktop, if desired, thus creating an Internet shortcut.*

Follow Your History

All browsers, including Internet Explorer, maintain a *history* of the sites. How they maintain that history varies—Internet Explorer tends to remember every site that you've visited in the past five sessions or so, according to a setting in the Preferences. Some other browsers (notably Netscape Navigator and Communicator) only remember the sites that have been visited during a given browsing session. The history is simply a list of recently visited URLs that you can revisit from the Go menu.

> **TIP** *In any Web browser, you can open a new window by selecting File | New Window. In fact, you can browse simultaneously in two, three, four, or more browser windows. Internet Explorer tracks them all and remembers visited sites even if you subsequently close those windows and open others.*

You can edit the history in IE if you'd like to delete items or if, perhaps, you'd like to drag-and-drop between the History pane and the Toolbar Favorites. Click the History tab on the left side of the browser window to open your history, where you can drag the links from the History window to the Toolbar Favorites area, to the browser window (to view that Favorite), or to the Trash (to delete that link from the History).

> **NOTE** *You can delete your entire stored history by selecting Explorer | Preferences, selecting the Advanced icon, and clicking the Clear History button in the History section. Note that you can also determine how many sites are stored in your History by entering a number in the Remember the Last ___ Places Visited option.*

Search the Internet

To search the Internet, you can turn to Apple's built-in search tool, Sherlock, introduced in Chapter 3. Sherlock (or Sherlock 2, as it's called in Mac OS 9) has the ability to search the

Internet from within the Mac OS—you don't have to open up Internet Explorer or another Web browser. It can also search more than one Internet search engine at once, meaning you don't have to jump around from search engine to search engine on the Web—Sherlock does all of this for you.

Want to search the entire Web for a particular keyword or phrase? Launch Sherlock or Sherlock 2 (in the Finder, you can press ⌘-F, or you can select Sherlock in the Dock or Sherlock 2 in the Apple menu). Begin by clicking the Internet channel icon—it looks like Earth from space. Now, type words in the entry box. You can simply separate the words with spaces; if you want to search for a phrase, put the phrase in quotation marks.

NOTE   *If you use your iMac's modem to connect to the Internet, remember that you need to have established the Internet connection before searching the Internet with Sherlock.*

Now, put a check mark next to the Internet search sites you want to use in Sherlock's list area. You can choose as few or as many search engines as you'd like. With your Internet search sites selected, click the magnifying glass icon. Sherlock performs a search using all of the different search engines and returns a list of items that it has found (see Figure 6-5). Each listing is a different Web page. Notice that you see three things about each page—the name, the site, and the *relevance* of that result. Relevance just tells you how likely a match Sherlock believes that page is for your criteria. It's based on how many of your keywords appear in the Web page and how often they appear.

To see a summary of the Web page that's been found, click the Web page's entry once. The summary appears in the information area. You can now double-click the item to launch it in your Web browser. If you'd prefer to simply save the found site as a Web link, you can drag the item from the list area to your desktop, an open Finder window, or the Dock. It will become a Web link document.

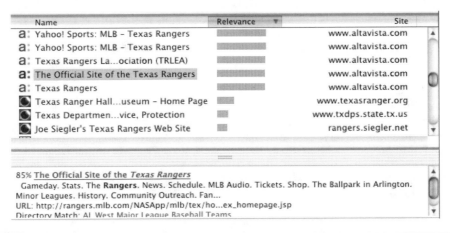

FIGURE 6-5   After an Internet search, Sherlock returns a list of Web pages (retrieved from different Web search engines) ranked by relevance.

Changing Channels

The Internet channel isn't the only way to search the Internet. Sherlock's channels enable you to click and select different groupings of Internet search sites. Click the shopping cart icon, for instance, and you'll see a different list than when you click the earth icon.

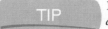 *You can drag the little bar between the channels icons and the keyword box. Drag it downward and you'll see more spaces for channels; drag it upward to cover all but the first row again.*

Sherlock actually offers different *types* of channels, which allow you to search for different types of information and see results listed in different ways. Depending on the type of channel you're using for a search, the results will be formatted differently. As you've seen, regular Web searches are relevance-ranked. But if you clicked the shopping cart icon and did a search, you'd see results ranked by price and availability. (For auction sites, *availability* usually represents the closing date and time of the auction.)

There are four different types of channels in Sherlock:

- **Searching**   These channels return relevance-ranked results.
- **People**   People channels return information about the person, like e-mail address and phone number.
- **Shopping**   Shopping channels return information that includes a description, price, and availability date.
- **News**   News channels show results very similar to Internet channels, but they tend to show the date of an article as well as relevance and title.

Try it. Select a channel and you'll see the different Internet search sites for each channel. Try a search in each one and you'll see different types of results in the different channels.

Add New Search Sites

The other thing you might like to do is add third-party search sites to your Sherlock window. That means you can use Sherlock to search all kinds of sites, including those that don't have a special Search Site plug-in installed by Apple, such as some third-party retailers and government Web sites. Apple keeps track of some plug-ins being offered by other companies. Visit **http://www.apple.com/sherlock/** on the Web to see what they have available. Another great source is the Dr. Watson database of Sherlock plug-ins at **http://watson.online.co.ma/**.

 Actually, Sherlock will add search sites on its own, sometimes, without even telling you—it just downloads and adds them.

When you find a Sherlock plug-in you want, download it to your iMac using Internet Explorer or an FTP program (see Part III of this book for much more on Internet tools). Once you have the plug-in downloaded, here's how it's installed in Mac OS X:

1. Select the channel in Sherlock (by clicking that channel's icon at the top of the Sherlock window) where you'd like to add the search site.

2. Choose Channels | Add Search Site.

3. In the dialog box, locate the search site that you just downloaded and click Add.

You'll see the search site appear in the channel that you'd selected. Note that you can now delete the search site file if it was on your desktop or in a download folder; it's been added to your personal Library folder.

You can also add search sites by dragging them to the particular channel folder (such as Entertainment or Reference) inside your Internet Search Sites folder, located inside the Library folder inside your home folder in Mac OS X. Drag-and-drop is the main way to install search sites in Mac OS 9. Once you've downloaded the search site plug-in, drag it to a particular channel folder inside the Internet Search Sites folder within the main System Folder. Now it's installed for Sherlock 2 to access.

Want to move a search site from one channel to another? Simply drag the search site from the list area to the target channel's icon at the top of the window. (Note that this will sometimes cause Sherlock to download a second version of that search site.)

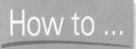 **Create a New Channel in Sherlock**

You can do more than simply add search sites—you can actually create a whole different channel to Sherlock, if you like. Then, you can drag Internet search sites from other channels to your new channel. Here's how to create a channel:

1. Choose Channels | New Channel.

2. In the New Channel dialog box, enter a name for the channel in the Name the Channel entry box.

3. In the Channel Type menu, choose the type of channel you want to create.

4. Now, click the up and down arrows in the Icon section to choose an icon for this channel.

5. Enter a description if you want to, then click OK.

Now you've got a new channel. You can drag Internet search sites from other channels to your channel or you can select the new channel and use the Channels | Add Search Site command to add search sites to the channel.

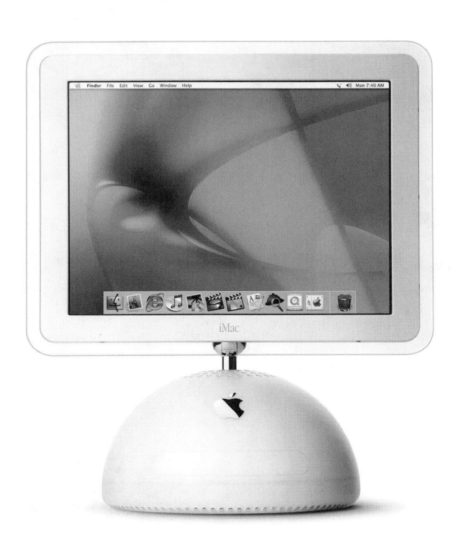

Chapter 7

Common Application Commands

How to...

- ■ Launch documents
- ■ Create, open, and save documents
- ■ Use commands to perform basic tasks like selecting text, cutting, copying, and pasting
- ■ Undo mistakes, close documents, and quit applications
- ■ Dig into the Preferences settings of your applications

In the first part of this book you've seen the tools—the Finder, the Dock, the Apple menu—that Mac OS 9 and Mac OS X make available for launching and managing applications. At the same time, those tools can be used to manage documents that you create—after all, documents comprise those icons that you're duplicating, creating aliases of, and sometimes throwing away. But you need to create some documents before you can manage them, right?

That's what this chapter is about—opening, saving, and invoking common application commands within documents. Fortunately, you'll find that most Macintosh applications have a lot of things in common, including the commands discussed in this chapter. If you haven't used Macintosh applications in the past, get ready to learn a little bit about all of them.

Launch, Open, and Create Documents

You've already seen that there are myriad ways to launch an application to begin using it—double-clicking application icons, choosing applications in Recent menus or launching them from the Dock (Mac OS X) or Apple menu. In this section, let's move on to how, exactly, you begin working with documents in applications—you can launch documents directly, open them from within applications, or create new documents.

Launch a Document

If you want to work with a particular document that you've already created (or one that's been downloaded or copied from a CD or another disk), you can launch that document directly. That causes the document's associated application to launch as well, enabling you to begin working with the document immediately.

The easy way to launch a document is simply to double-click its icon in a Finder window or on the desktop. Doing this launches the document's associated application and tells the application to load the document you double-clicked. This works great when you're loading a document that has been saved by that same application previously. For instance, when you double-click an AppleWorks document, the AppleWorks application will be launched. Note that the document's icon can be a clue that tells you what application it's associated with.

TIP   *You can also launch a document by selecting it in the Recent Items menu in the Mac OS X Apple menu or the Recent Documents menu in the Mac OS 9 Apple menu, or by single-clicking a document on the Dock (Mac OS X).*

The other way to launch a document is to drag-and-drop the document onto an application's icon—whether that application icon is on the desktop, in another Finder window, or on the Dock in Mac OS X. This method is particularly effective when you're trying to launch a document that was not originally saved by the application. In many cases, the application will launch and attempt to translate the document if necessary, so that you can work with it.

Resolve Start-Up Trouble

If you double-click a document that your iMac hasn't properly associated with an application (maybe you copied the document over the Internet or over a network connection), then you'll see an alert box. In Mac OS X, the alert warns you that an application isn't associated with this document.

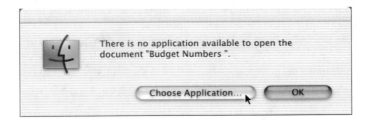

When you see this, click the Choose Application button. In the Choose Application window that appears, you can locate an application to use with this document, highlight that application, then click Open.

In Mac OS 9, you'll see a special alert box that enables you to select the application immediately. In the list, select an application that can successfully load or translate the file. If it's a graphics file, you'll probably have success loading it into a program that includes QuickTime translation; a text document may be successfully translated by AppleWorks or, if you have it, Microsoft Word.

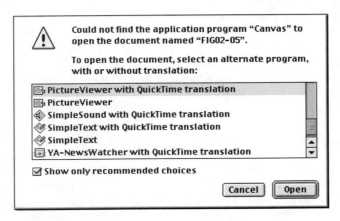

Once you've found the right application, select it in the window and click the Open button. Nothing bad happens if you select the wrong application, by the way, so feel free to make a guess. If it doesn't work out, you'll just have to try again.

> TIP
> *If you don't see an application that you know could open the document, uncheck the box that says Show Only Recommended Choices. Then you'll see nearly every application on your iMac—hopefully, the one you want will show up now.*

Create a New Document

When you first launch an application, sometimes it will create a blank document for you as it opens. Other times, it just launches and sits there. If that's the case (or if you're already working in the application and you want a new document), you can create a new document by choosing File | New. This works in *any* application that creates documents.

What happens next can vary. In some cases, a document window just pops up. (That's what happens in a program like Mac OS X's TextEdit.) In other cases, you may be greeted by a dialog box that requires you to make choices as to what sort of document you want to create, whether or not you want special help creating the document, and so on.

> TIP
> *You can also use ⌘-N to create a new document in nearly all applications.*

Open a Document

If you've already created a document you want to work on, the first thing you'll do after the application has started up is head to the File menu and choose Open. That brings up the Open dialog box, which may look something like Figure 7-1 for a native Mac OS X application. If you're working with a Classic application, the Open dialog box may look more like Figure 7-2. If it still doesn't look like either of these, then you're probably working with either a much older Mac application (or a Microsoft application—they like to be different).

The native Mac OS X Open dialog box tends to open directly to your home folder, which usually makes it a little easier to find your documents. The dialog box works like the Column view in the Mac OS X Finder—select a folder to peer into and its contents appear in the right-hand column. To move back, use the scrollbar at the bottom of the columns. (You can also use the From menu at the top of the Open dialog box to change the folder you want to view.) Once you find the document you want to open, select it and click Open, or simply double-click the item.

Not all programs' Open dialog boxes have a File Format or Document Type menu, but when they do, you can use those menus to narrow down the number of files you'll see in the dialog box. The application will offer suggestions like "AppleWorks Document" or "HTML" that you can choose if that's the sort of file you're looking for. If you choose something other than "All Documents" or "All Readable Documents," then be aware that you're not seeing every file in the folder. You're seeing a subset that matches the Document Type menu criteria.

FIGURE 7-1 The Mac OS X Open dialog box appears in applications that have been updated to use it.

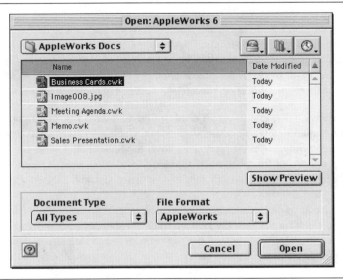

FIGURE 7-2 The older Open dialog box still shows up in applications you run in Mac OS 9 or the Classic environment.

TIP

In AppleWorks 6.1.2 and higher, you'll find Microsoft Word and Microsoft Excel entries in the File Format menu, which enable you to import Microsoft documents into AppleWorks for editing. Likewise, the Save dialog box offers the option of exporting in those formats.

In the Classic Open dialog box, things work a little differently. In this one, you dig into a folder by selecting that folder and clicking Open, or by double-clicking a folder. If you need to move "up" in the folder hierarchy, do that using the pop-up menu at the top of the dialog box. When you see the document you want to open, highlight it and click the Open button.

NOTE

Unlike native Open dialog boxes, Classic dialog boxes aren't quite as aware of the home folder structure of Mac OS X, so they may open automatically to some odd folders. Remember, if you're using Mac OS X, your home folder is located inside the Users folder (on the main level of your hard disk). If you're using Mac OS 9 exclusively, then you can probably just save your files in the Documents folder on the main level of the hard disk.

Save Your Document

Save quickly and save often. This is some of the best advice I can give you. When I'm writing a typical book chapter, I save that document just about every three sentences or so. That's right— every three *sentences.* Why? Because I don't want to type them again.

Whenever you're working in an application there's always a chance that the application could run into an error, something could go wrong in the Mac OS, or something could go wrong with your iMac. Whatever happens, losing a lot of data because you forgot to save regularly is no fun. So, learn to save.

TIP

Some applications have an auto-save feature that you can use to automatically save your documents at regular intervals. For instance, AppleWorks has such an option; choose Edit | Preferences (in Mac OS 9) or AppleWorks | Preferences (in Mac OS X) and choose General. In the Topic menu, choose Files; you'll see the Auto-Save option, which you can turn on and off or change the number of minutes between saves.

The first time you save a document, you'll need to find a place to put it and you'll need to name it. To do that, become acquainted with another dialog box. Choose File | Save to bring up the Save dialog box and start the saving process. Figure 7-3 shows the Save dialog *sheet* (as opposed to a dialog box, it actually pops out from under the title bar in your document's window) that appears in native Mac OS X applications. This can be helpful—it lets you know exactly which document is to be saved.

Most of the time, the Save dialog sheet will be a bit simpler than is shown in Figure 7-3. Using the pop-up menu at the top, you can quickly select a folder, if it appears. If it doesn't, though, then you'll want to click the disclosure triangle at the top right of the dialog sheet. That will reveal the full Columns-style interface. Here's how to save:

1. Select the folder you want to use to save the file. You can create a new folder for the file by clicking the New Folder button if you need to.

2. Type a name for the file in the Save As entry box, then choose the file format from the Format or File Type menu (if necessary).

3. Click Save. The document is saved and you're returned to the document to continue working.

The Classic Save dialog box (see Figure 7-4) works in a similar way. The only difference is the absence of the Columns interface; instead, you'll select a folder and click the Open button to dig through subfolders until you find the folder you want to use for saving.

Once you have the document saved, you can choose File | Save to save any changes to that same document—you won't see the Save dialog box, since the application already knows where to save the file and what to call it. In fact, for even faster saving you can just press ⌘-S to instantly save what you're working on. (That's what I do every three sentences.)

7

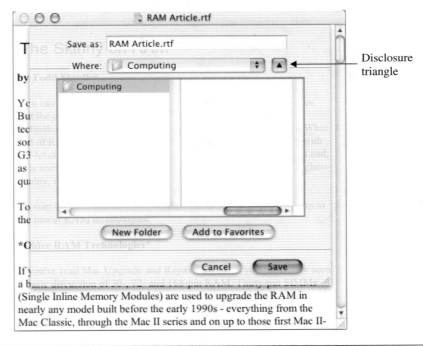

Disclosure triangle

FIGURE 7-3   The Mac OS X Save dialog sheet is similar to the Open dialog box, except it pops out from under the document's title bar.

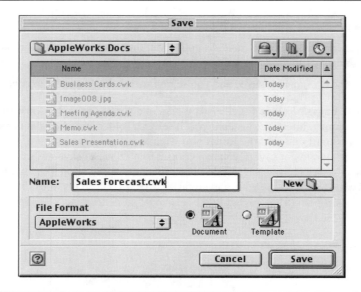

FIGURE 7-4   The Classic Save dialog box

What if you want to save this file in a new place and/or with a new name? In that case, you use the Save As command in the File menu. That brings the Save dialog box (or dialog sheet) back up, allowing you to save the document (and any changes you've made since your last Save operation) to a new document located in a new folder. This is sort of like invoking the Duplicate command in the Finder—you create an entirely new copy of the document, which you can give a different name and put in a different folder, if you like.

Plus, after you've invoked the Save As command, the document file on your screen is the new document you just created. This can be useful if you want to keep the original file as it was, but you want to alter a copy of it to use for some other reason. Perhaps you're creating an invoice—you open last month's invoice, choose File | Save As to create a new copy with a new name, then edit the new copy for this month's invoice.

Basic Application Commands

Now that you've seen how to create, open, or save documents, you're ready to actually do something within those documents. Obviously, what you do depends somewhat on the application in question (I wouldn't try writing a novel in the Palm calendar software, for instance), but there are some common commands that you'll find in nearly every application you encounter. Let's look at some of them.

Select and Select All

You're familiar with selecting icons in the Finder with the mouse. Selecting text (or objects like spreadsheet numbers or graphical images) in a document is similar, although it can vary a bit. For instance, if you're typing text in a text editor or word processor, you can't just point and click the mouse once to select a word in that document. You can, however, point and *double-click* to select a word.

To select more than one word, hold down the mouse button and drag the mouse pointer across the words you want to select. The words (or parts of words) become highlighted, just as if you were selecting multiple icons in the Finder. You can drag the mouse pointer (which will look like a capital letter "I") from left to right and/or up and down the page to select multiple words or lines of text.

> You may also have to watch the SO-DIMMs on revision /A iMac, which is only certified by Apple to handle 64 MB SO-DIMMs. Apple support admits that the revision /A iMac might work with larger SO-DIMMs, but it's a good idea to check with your retailer, too, and make sure they warranty the DIMM as compatible.

There are a couple of tricks, too. In most text programs, triple-clicking will select an entire paragraph or a continuous line of text. In applications where triple-clicking doesn't select the entire paragraph, try clicking four times rapidly.

If you'd like to select everything in a given document, there's a command for that, too. From the Edit menu, choose Select All. All the text (or objects) in the document will be highlighted. You can also invoke this command from the keyboard by pressing ⌘-A in nearly any application, including the Finder.

Cut, Copy, and Paste

These three are present in nearly every application ever written. The Cut, Copy, and Paste commands allow you to move text and objects around within documents or from one document to another. In fact, you can cut and paste between applications in most cases.

The Cut and Copy commands are similar. Highlight text or objects in your document and select the Edit menu. Choose Cut if you'd like to delete the text or objects from the current document or current spot in the document; if you just want to copy the selection to use elsewhere, choose Copy. You can also use the keyboard: ⌘-C invokes Copy and ⌘-X invokes Cut.

Your selection is moved to something called the Clipboard. Now, the contents of the Clipboard can be pasted into another section of the document or another document altogether. (Realize, though, that the Clipboard is just a portion of system memory—if you turn your iMac off or invoke the Copy or Cut command a second time, the original contents of the Clipboard are erased or overwritten.)

NOTE *You can switch to the Finder and choose Edit | Show Clipboard to see the contents of the Clipboard at any time.*

To paste, place the insertion point in the document where you'd like the text or objects to appear. (In some documents you don't place the insertion point; you just click the document window to make sure it's active.) Then, pull down the Edit menu and choose Paste. (Or press ⌘-V on the keyboard.) The text or objects will appear in the document. Note that if you highlight something before pasting, the highlighted objects will be replaced with the Clipboard contents. Want to do it another way? In many applications you can drag-and-drop text to different parts of the document, to a new document, or even to the Finder. Try this:

1. Using the mouse pointer, highlight some text you've typed into a document—for instance, an AppleWorks document.

2. Now, point the mouse pointer at the highlighted text, click the mouse button, and hold it.

3. Drag the text to another part of the document or to another document entirely.

4. Release the mouse button.

When you're finished you've effectively cut and pasted the text, even though you didn't use the commands.

TIP *Also, as a neat trick, some applications will let you drag text or images from the document to your desktop, creating a "clipping" file. That file can then be used to store the text or to drag it into another document at a later date.*

You can copy and paste much more than just text and objects like drawings and images. If you can select it in an application, there's a good chance you'll be able to copy and paste it. When in doubt, try the commands and see if they work.

Undo

Here's another perennial favorite of application programmers—the Undo command. This command is designed to immediately countermand the most recent action or command you've performed. For instance, if you just deleted an entire paragraph in AppleWorks, choose Edit | Undo to get that paragraph back. It usually works for formatting text or objects, pasting, deleting, typing, and so on. Most any activity can be taken back. You can usually undo immediately by pressing ⌘-Z on the keyboard.

Many programs will also have a Redo or similar command that is designed to undo an Undo command. If you undo something you didn't actually want to undo, head back to the Edit menu and look for the Redo command.

NOTE
Some applications, such as Microsoft Word or Apple's iMovie, have multiple undo capabilities. Basically, that means you can undo more than one command—keep choosing the Undo command and the program will keep working backward through your most recent actions.

Quit the Application

About done with that application? All applications have a Quit command that closes the application, hands the RAM memory space back to the Mac OS, and cleans up any open files. In a native Mac OS X application, that command is in the application menu (the one named for the application, such as TextEdit or AppleWorks) under Quit. You can also press ⌘-Q in almost any Mac application to quit. In Classic applications, you'll find Quit in the File menu.

When you quit a program, it should ask you to save any unsaved documents and may ask you to make other decisions—like hanging up the modem or waiting until a particular activity is finished. Of course, it depends on the program.

NOTE
Most of the time, closing a document window in a program does not actually quit the program. Many beginning Mac users make the mistake of closing a document window and believing the application is also closed. You can close a window by clicking its Close box or button, choosing File | Close Window, or pressing ⌘-W. But that rarely quits the program—it just closes the current window or document. You need to invoke the Quit command in applications; otherwise, they remain open, take up RAM, and make it more difficult for you to run other programs.

Set Preferences

Most applications offer a dialog box that allows you to set your preferences for how the program behaves, what values it defaults to, and so on. The preferences are completely up to the individual application—there really isn't too much in the way of standardization, except for the location of the Preferences command. I'll talk about the Preferences settings in AppleWorks, iMovie, Mail, Internet Explorer, and your other iMac applications throughout the book.

To open the Preferences dialog box you'll generally invoke a Preferences command. In most native Mac OS X applications it's under the application menu, such as AppleWorks | Preferences or TextEdit | Preferences. In Classic applications, you'll often find it under Edit | Preferences. If you don't find it there, look under the File menu. If you don't see it in either of those two menus, then chances are good that you're using a Microsoft application. Look in the Tools menu for a command called Options or Preferences.

7

The Application Menu

All Mac OS X native applications have a special menu, called the application menu, that appears just to the right of the Apple menu when the application is active. You can tell it's the application menu, because it's named after the application! For instance, if you're working in TextEdit, you'll see the TextEdit menu; if you're working in AppleWorks, you'll see the AppleWorks menu.

The application menu is basically designed to do two things. First, it reminds you instantly of what application you're working in, which can come in handy if you're having a long, hard day. Second, it holds application-specific commands, such as Quit and Preferences. While Classic applications often have these commands in the File menu, Apple's Mac OS X engineers decided that didn't make much sense—you're not quitting the file, you're quitting the *application*. Thus, the application menu was born.

Other Interface Elements

You already know a lot about what to expect from applications. You'll see windows, menus, icons, pointers, and other little tidbits. But let's focus for a few moments on some elements you're likely to see pop up in various parts of the different applications you'll be working with. You'll want to be familiar with these parts of the interface so you can get your work done.

Click Buttons, Check Boxes, and Sliders

You'll find that many preferences settings, dialog boxes, and other components that make up applications—and even parts of Mac OS 9 and Mac OS X—rely on some typical controls to help you make decisions. You've already seen some of these, but let me go ahead and define them formally. Here's what they do:

- ■ **Radio Buttons**   This type of control allows you to make one selection among two or more different choices. Click the button next to the item you want to choose.

- ■ **Check Boxes**   A check box allows you to choose each item individually—if you want the item active, you'll click in the box next to the item and a check mark (sometimes it's an "X") will appear in the box.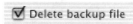

■ **Sliders**   A slider bar allows you to choose a range of values from low to high just as you might for a volume control on a home stereo system. In

fact, slider bars are used most often for changing the volume level, brightness level, and so on. The volume control in Mac OS 9's Control Strip (discussed in Chapter 5) is a slider control. You just drag the slider back and forth on the control to change the value.

Use Toolbars

While not required of Macintosh applications, toolbars are a popular addition. Toolbars put small *iconic* buttons in a special bar below the menu bar in an application, giving you quick access to the most popular commands in that program. An example is the following illustration, which shows the toolbar from AppleWorks.

Many such toolbars allow you to quickly access fonts, font styling, and many other commands that you might use frequently in the program. But often, at least for me, the little icon buttons on toolbars make no sense whatsoever. In that case, the solution is usually to point at an icon with the mouse pointer and wait a few seconds. Most applications have a little pop-up window or other way of showing you what a particular icon is for.

More and more native Mac OS X applications offer a toolbar that's similar to the Finder window's toolbar, which can often be customized in the same way. Look for a Customize Toolbar command in such applications, which enables you to drag icons to and from the toolbar easily.

Check Out the About Box

Want to know more about an application? All applications are required to have an About box, which you can access while the application is active. If you're currently working with a Mac OS X native application, pull down that application's named menu (such as TextEdit, AppleWorks, etc.). You'll see that the first menu item is About…, followed by the name of the application. (In a Classic application, you'll find About… in the Apple menu.) Choose that item and you'll see a little something about the application. Some applications will place help, tips, and other buttons in the About window that will, occasionally, give you help when using the application.

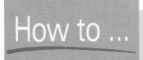 **Get Help in Applications**

Many Apple-written applications use the standard Help Viewer discussed in Chapter 2, while others use the other Classic and Mac OS 9 Help systems discussed in Chapter 5. If you encounter an application that doesn't offer either, that doesn't necessarily mean you're out of luck. Choose the Help option on the Help menu, and start by looking for hyperlinks to click, topics to explore, or a search box that lets you enter keywords. You'll find that most alternative help systems will likely offer something along the lines of hypertext links within explanatory documents. Most of them will be similar enough to the Apple Help system that you should be able to figure them out with relative ease. If your application doesn't have a help system, look in the application's original folder for a Users Guide or a Read Me file, which may give you some indication as to how to use it. Many such files are in PDF format, meaning they can be viewed in the Preview application (in your main Applications folder in Mac OS X) or Adobe Acrobat Reader, which is installed on all iMacs.

Chapter 8

Type and Format Documents in AppleWorks

How to...

- Create a word processing document
- Type your document and format the text
- Format paragraphs, align elements, and create headers and footers
- Format the entire document, including margins, sections, and tabs
- Spell-check and find and replace automatically
- Create style sheets and paragraph styles
- Use pre-built templates and create your own document templates

As you know, a computer makes you a better writer. My ramblings, for instance, are almost instantly translated into readable, friendly, and useful text, thanks to my iMac. Otherwise, not only would my text be misspelled, grammatically unapproachable, and improperly formatted, it would also be completely unintelligible and morally reprehensible.

OK, so that's a bit of an exaggeration. A computer isn't about writing better—it's about typing a little better, formatting documents more effectively, and being able to edit, cut, paste, and shape your document without scissors and glue.

In this chapter, you'll get a brief introduction to AppleWorks, the iMac's built-in productivity application. As you'll see, AppleWorks is great for creating written documents, offering all the tricks that a computer brings to bear on the task. And AppleWorks is so much more, as well, which is why Chapters 9 through 13 are also dedicated to this unique application.

 *AppleWorks (**http://www.apple.com/appleworks/**) is a Carbon application, meaning it can run both natively in Mac OS X, and it can be launched and run in Mac OS 9 or higher. The commands are the same, with the exception of the Preferences menu, which appears in the AppleWorks menu in Mac OS X and the Edit menu when running in Mac OS 9.*

Get to Know AppleWorks

AppleWorks is what's referred to as a "works" application, because it's designed to perform more than one major document-creation function. While a program like Microsoft Word is designed solely for word processing, AppleWorks offers a number of different modules, allowing you to create word processing documents, spreadsheets, databases, images, drawings, and other types of documents. So why would you choose anything else?

In most cases, you probably won't have to. AppleWorks is a very good program that allows you to do some rather unique things—including putting its parts together to create layouts that feature word processing, images, spreadsheet tables, and database data in the same documents. In that respect, it's a very powerful and very enjoyable program to work with.

But you may need more specialized capabilities or you may need to use a particular program—like Microsoft Word—because the rest of your office, school, organization, or secret-handshake society requires it. That's okay, but you'll need to spend more money and install that application yourself.

In exchange, you'll get a program that's specifically tailored to the task at hand. Microsoft Word, for instance, offers a lot of tools for collaborating on important word processing documents—you can embed comments, track changes, and even give different human editors a different color to use within the document so it's easy to see who is making what changes. We used Microsoft Word to create this book, for instance, largely because of its collaborative capabilities.

So, you'll want to use a tool that's designed for the job. Sometimes that's Microsoft Word, but AppleWorks is truly an impressive application, and you'll be able to accomplish a lot with it. If your tasks are personal, educational, or even for a small business, you'll likely find it completely adequate for your needs.

But even if it doesn't fit all of your needs, in nearly all cases, documents created in AppleWorks can be translated into documents that can be read by other applications like Word, Excel, QuarkXPress, and others when the times comes. So, feel free to try things in AppleWorks first, then move on to something else if you need more power.

NOTE *Actually, AppleWorks 6.1 and higher now has Microsoft Word (and Excel) translators built into it, so you can actually load and save documents in Word's .doc format. See Chapter 7 for details.*

8

Write with Your iMac

If you need to write documents with your iMac, you'll likely turn to a word processing application—an application designed to accept typed input and allow you to manipulate it on the page. Unless you've chosen to install a different word processing application, your best bet is to launch AppleWorks, which came with your iMac and includes a full-featured word processing module.

A word processing program is designed to do a number of things. It's designed to accept text and images that you type or add through menu commands, then allow you to format the text and images in many different ways. It's worth saying that word processors are designed to help you format entire documents—from memos and letters to longer documents like reports, pamphlets, and books. Word processors allow you to do many things to long and short documents:

- Change the document size, margins, and spacing
- Insert headers and footnotes
- Change the font, style, and formatting of text
- Create documents in outline form
- Format text in tabular form
- Format text with bullets, numbers, or special tabs and indents
- Check spelling
- Change formatting for paragraphs, sections, or the entire document

In most cases, however, a word processor is not designed for creating a particular *page*. That's what layout applications like QuarkXPress and Adobe PageMaker are designed for.

Such applications have highly sophisticated tools that allow a page designer to drop text, images, effects, lines, and shapes onto a page and manipulate them freely to create the most stunning advertisement, pamphlet, or publication. Even within AppleWorks we'll use a different module to create newsletters and similar layouts.

So, word processing really is a little closer to the typewriter than it is to the layout table. But there is a difference between a typewriter—even most electronic, computerized typewriters—and a word processing application. Word processing applications allow you to change your mind. You can experiment with documents after the fact. That means you can create the document first, then worry about how it will be formatted.

Start Your Document

To begin, launch AppleWorks or choose File | New if AppleWorks is already open. The Starting Points window appears, allowing you to choose the type of document you'd like to begin.

In AppleWorks, the type of document you choose helps determine what sort of tools and menu commands you see. In this case, you're interested in creating a word processing document, so click the word processing icon. Now you'll see the word processing commands and a blank document window.

Next step: Start typing. There are actually a couple of rules you should follow when typing in a word processor, especially if you're used to a typewriter. Some of these rules are

- *Don't press TAB to indent the first line of a paragraph.* You can format paragraphs so that they are indented automatically, either before or after you type them.

- *Don't press RETURN at the end of a line.* You only need to press RETURN at the end of a paragraph. Whenever you type to the right margin of the page, the next thing you type will automatically *wrap* to the next line.

- *Don't put two spaces after a period.* Many typists get used to pressing the SPACEBAR twice after the end of a sentence, but that throws off the automatic spacing capabilities of a word processing program and it just looks bad with many standard Mac fonts.

- *Don't worry about double-spacing while you type.* You'll be able to set line spacing for your document at 1.5, double-, or triple-space after you've typed it (or, as you'll see, before you begin).

- *Don't press RETURN many times to get to a new page.* You can easily insert a page break if you're done on one page and want to begin on another one.

- *Don't enter asterisks, dashes, or numbers for lists.* You can do all that automatically. If you need to create a list like the one you're reading right now, you can do that with commands—just enter each line and press RETURN. You'll be able to go back and format the bulleted or numbered list later.

- *Don't do anything weird to change the margins.* You don't need to insert many spaces, add tabs, or press RETURN in order to create special margin spacing—for instance, if you want to have a block of quoted text that's squeezed onto the page. Again, you can do that with special document formatting commands, covered later in this chapter. For now, just type the paragraph normally.

- *Don't uses spaces to create columns or table layouts.* At the very least, you should use tabs and the document ruler to set up the spacing in your document. That's covered later in this chapter, too.

Most of these issues are addressed in the section "Format your Document," which appears later in this chapter. You'll find that what you need to do while typing is pretty simple:

1. Type words.

2. When you get to the end of a sentence, type a period, then press the SPACEBAR once.

3. When you get to the end of a paragraph, press RETURN.

That's all you do while you're typing your document. Remember, you'll be able to change just about anything once you have the words on the page. For now, typing is the primary goal.

Fonts, Styles, and Sizes

Aside from the typing basics, there are two other precepts for the accomplished word processing typist. (That's you.) The first is to *save often,* which is covered in the next section. The second is to format your text as you're typing. It's not mandatory, but learning to format as you type makes creating your documents easier.

By text formatting I mean three things: the font, the style, and the size of the text. These things can be changed easily before or while you're typing a line of text, so I'll include them here while you're getting started with your word processor.

Fonts

The word "font" is used in most Macintosh applications to mean "typeface," which is defined as a general design for a set of characters. Popular typefaces are Courier, Times New Roman, Helvetica, and so forth.

If you'd like your typed text to appear in something other than the default font, you can head up to the Font menu, choose a new font, and begin typing. Your text appears in that new font.

Similarly, you can select existing text and change it to a new font. Select text by moving the mouse pointer to the left of the first word you want to highlight, press the mouse button, and drag the mouse pointer to the right of the last word you want to choose, then release the mouse button. If you want to choose all the words in your document, choose Edit | Select All. Then select Text | Font and click the font you want to use for the highlighted text. Your text should change immediately (see Figure 8-1).

You can also select a font from the Font menu that appears at the top of the document window in the ruler area.

TIP *You can opt to have the Font menu in AppleWorks show you the shape and style of the fonts as you select them. (It slows down the menu's rendering, but it's pretty useful.) Select AppleWorks | Preferences | General in Mac OS X, or Edit | Preferences | General in Mac OS 9. In the Preferences dialog box, choose General from the Topic menu. Then, turn on the Font Menus in Actual Fonts option and click OK. Now whenever you select the Font menu, you'll see actual examples of the fonts instead of just their names.*

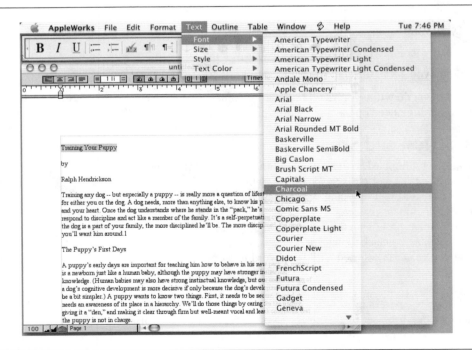

FIGURE 8-1 Highlight text, and then select a new font from the font menu.

Styles

The text styles represent different effects you apply to the fonts for emphasis—things like italics and boldfacing. You can change the style of your text in either of the two ways that you change the font—either before you type, or by selecting text that's already been typed.

To change the style, select the Text | Style menu in AppleWorks, then click on the style you want to use. Begin typing and your text appears in that style.

To change the style of text that already appears, select that text in the document window and then pull down the Style menu. Choose the style you want to use and the highlighted text changes immediately to that style. Note that you can also select styles from the default button bar that appears above your document window. "B" is for bold, "I" for italics, and "U" for underline. (For plain text, make sure all three are deselected.)

Often you'll want a more convenient way to change styles, especially with the four major styles: Plain, Italic, Bold, and Underlined. In these special cases, you'll find it's most efficient to learn the keyboard commands for changing text styles. Except for the Plain command, these commands are common not just in AppleWorks, but in almost any application where you can create style text:

⌘-B	Boldface	⌘-U	Underline
⌘-I	Italic	⌘-T	Plain, unstyled text

Now you can quickly switch styles while typing. Press ⌘-I, type a word in italics, then press ⌘-T to return to plain text. (You can also press ⌘-I to turn italics off again—you'll find that some applications don't support ⌘-T.) Press ⌘-U and ⌘-B and you'll be typing bold, underlined text; press ⌘-T and you're back to plain text again.

> TIP
>
> *Most fonts also include a few special characters that you might want to enter as you're typing. OPTION-8, for instance, will type a bullet point character; OPTION-DASH (the "-" sign) will create an en dash; OPTION-SHIFT-DASH will create an em dash. To learn other special characters, use the Key Caps application found in the Apple menu (Mac OS 9) or the Applications folder (Mac OS X).*

Sizes

You can change the size of text in your document by highlighting the text and using the Text | Size menu to choose the point size. Points are a traditional way of sizing fonts in publishing terms—72 points equals about one inch, so 12 points equals about one-sixth of an inch in height. Traditionally, 72-point text was reserved for newspaper headlines that declared war or the surprise winner of a presidential election—these days the biggest headline on the front page on any given morning is probably about 72 points.

Readable body type is typically about 12 points; 14 points looks like "big" type you find in some of those movie novelizations. Try 18 points for a subhead in your report—24 or so can look good for the title of your report. As with fonts, you can also use the special Size pop-up menu that appears in the document window's ruler area (see Figure 8-2).

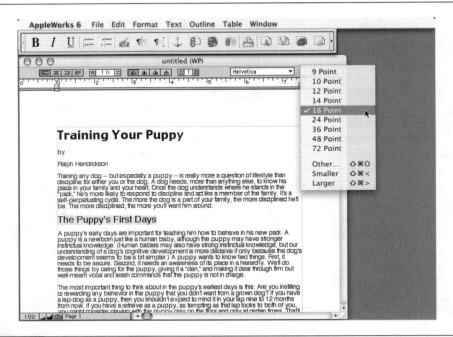

Different point sizes clearly define the parts of your document.

You can also change text sizes as you type. Pull down the Text | Size menu and choose the new size from the menu, then type in that new size. If you want to use the keyboard commands for changing font sizes, they might take some memorizing: ⌘-SHIFT-< makes text smaller and ⌘-SHIFT-> makes it bigger. (Note, by the way, that these are specific AppleWorks keyboard commands and don't work in all applications.)

Save Often

If you've been following so far, you might see from the figures in this chapter something terribly wrong is going on. The document I'm working on is still untitled, which means it hasn't been saved!

My rule: Save every three sentences. It usually doesn't take long for each save (once the initial save is complete) and it'll sure make you happy if and when your iMac or your application crashes. (It does happen. That fashionable iMac encourages you to put it in high-traffic areas where you're bound to trip over the power cord.) Having saved very recently, you won't be as upset when you only have to retype a few sentences to catch up. If you have to retype an entire page or two, you won't be nearly as pleased.

To save the document the first time, choose File | Save once you've typed something. Use the Save dialog box to find the folder where you want to store the file, and then give it a name and click Save.

From then on, you can just press ⌘-S to save as you're typing. Every three sentences, remember? (For more on saving, see Chapter 7.)

NOTE *AppleWorks 6 includes an Auto-Save function that automatically saves your document every few minutes. Choose Appleworks | Preferences | General or Edit | Preferences | General, then choose Files from the Topic menu. If it isn't already, check the box next to Auto-Save. You can also use the entry box to enter the number of minutes (or hours or seconds) you want AppleWorks to wait between saves. Click OK to put your preference into action.*

Format Your Document

I know it seems that creating a document should be so much more complicated than the "just type it" mantra I've repeated so far. And it's true that you can do some complicated things in a word processing document—the sort of stuff that would make a Ph.D. thesis advisor proud. But "just type it" is still great advice, because it's easier to format the document before or after you type—not during. Let me show you what I mean. This sections covers a lot of stuff in a little space, including:

8

- Formatting paragraphs: indenting, spacing, alignment
- Inserting elements: page breaks, headers, footers
- Formatting whole documents: margins, page numbers
- Formatting sections: book-type formatting
- Using tabs and the ruler: making changes visually

Whether you're writing reports, documentation, thesis papers, research, legislation, contracts, or books, you'll find you're able to get pretty deep into document formatting without filling too much of the space in your head. After all, you've got important things to store in your brain, including birthdays, phone numbers, where your aunt hid her will, and how to tie a double-Windsor knot.

Format Paragraphs

There are four basic formatting tasks you'll be managing when it comes to your paragraphs—indenting, line spacing, bullets, and alignment—and all four are controlled from within the Paragraph dialog box. To start formatting a paragraph, place the insertion point in that paragraph (you don't have to highlight the whole paragraph, but you can if you like). To format more than one paragraph at once, select them. (Remember that quadruple-clicking usually selects paragraphs.) With that out of the way, choose Format | Paragraph. That causes the Paragraph dialog box to appear:

Paragraph		
Left Indent: 0 in	Line Spacing: 1	li
First Line: 0 in	Space Before: 0	li
Right Indent: 0 in	Space After: 0	li
Label: None	Alignment: Left	

Apply Cancel OK

Indenting

Now, in the Paragraph dialog box you can make some choices about how that paragraph is going to look. On the left side of the dialog box, you have three margin choices. All three are entered in the entry boxes in inches—a standard indent is about 0.5 inches. You can indent the left, right, or both margins (both is usually for block quotes, programming code listings, or movie script dialog) or you can indent just the first line of the paragraph.

Click in the entry box next to Left Indent, First Line, or Right Indent, then type the number of inches you want for the indent. You can press TAB to move to the next box or press RETURN to accept the value and close the dialog box. If you'd like to see how your settings look before you close the dialog box, click the Apply button. That makes your changes but leaves the dialog box open for further changes or experimentation. (You can also drag this dialog box around if it's hiding the paragraph you need to see after the change is applied.)

 *You don't need to type the "in" for inches when entering your own number—just the number will suffice.*

Line Spacing

In the Line Spacing entry box enter a number, then choose the units for that number in the little pull-down menu next to it. If you want to double-space, you can just keep the units set at "lines."

You can also fine-tune your spacing to give yourself more or less space between lines as necessary. For instance, you'll sometimes want a document to look like it's double-spaced, but it's actually squeezed a bit less than double to fit more words on a page. (For instance, you might do this in the unlikely event that you actually wrote too *much* for your mid-term paper.) In that case, you should choose Points as the units for Line Spacing and select a point size that's a little less than twice the point size of your text. If your text is 12 points, for instance, you could choose 20 points to get a slightly squeezed double-spacing effect.

NOTE *You'd think you could just choose 1.75 lines for the Line Spacing, but AppleWorks rounds it up to 2 lines. It will only accept whole and half values, so 1.5 is acceptable, but 1.25 gets rounded up to 1.5.*

The other spacing options allow you to add additional space above and below a paragraph—this can often be useful if you choose a more contemporary style for your document in which you don't indent the first line of your paragraphs. In that case, a little extra space before and after a paragraph will make it clear where one ends and the next paragraph begins.

Make a List

When you type a list in AppleWorks, you simply type each item or sentence, then press RETURN after each. So, technically, you're creating a number of different paragraphs, even if they're really short. In order to turn them into a list, you can select each item and give it a Label in the Paragraph dialog box. The labels vary from bullet points to numbers to roman numerals.

There's a slightly more efficient way to make a list:

1. In the document window, type each list item and press RETURN after each.

2. Drag the mouse pointer to select every item in the list.

3. Select Format | Paragraph.

4. Choose the Label menu from the Paragraph dialog box and select Bullet.

5. Click Apply or OK.

That's it—the list is created. Every item you've highlighted becomes its own list item. If you clicked Apply and you're still in the Paragraph dialog box, you can change the item's left and right indent as desired—sometimes you'll want a list indented from the left margin to help it stand out.

If you want to change a bulleted paragraph back to a regular paragraph, select it and choose None from the Label menu in the Paragraph dialog box. That will return the paragraph to normal, non-bullet mode.

Alignment

The last little task for the Paragraph dialog box is aligning the paragraph. You can align the paragraph in four different ways:

- **Left** Paragraph is flush with the left margin and ragged on the right margin.
- **Right** Paragraph is ragged on the left margin and flush with the right margin.
- **Center** Both left and right margins are ragged, but the entire paragraph is balanced toward the center.
- **Justify** The paragraph is spaced so that the text is flush with both the left and right margins, like most columns of text in a newspaper.

To choose one of the alignments, just pull down the Alignment menu and make your choice. Click Apply and you'll see the paragraph's alignment change.

8

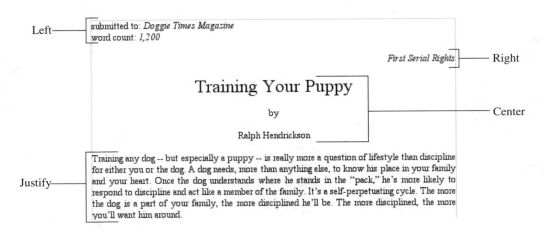

Format Multiple Paragraphs

Clearly, it could get a bit tedious to format every paragraph of a document manually like this. Fortunately, that's not mandatory. If you like, you can select as many paragraphs as you like—or even choose Edit | Select All (⌘-A) to highlight the entire document—and perform the same Paragraph dialog box changes to them all at once.

You can also copy one paragraph's traits and apply them to another paragraph. To do that, place the insertion point in the paragraph you want to use as a model, then choose Format | Rulers | Copy Ruler (⌘-SHIFT-C). This copies the paragraph settings. Now, place the cursor in the paragraph you want to change to the copied settings (or highlight multiple paragraphs). Choose Format | Rulers | Apply Ruler (⌘-SHIFT-V). The selected paragraph(s) change to reflect the model paragraph's settings.

 *Why are these commands called Copy Ruler and Apply Ruler? Because the ruler in the document window reflects all of the settings you can make in the Paragraph dialog box. See the next section for information about using it to quickly format paragraphs.*

Shortcut: Use the Ruler

For some of the paragraph formatting options, you don't have to go to the Paragraph dialog box. Instead, you can access them (along with font and font size commands) right in the document window, in the ruler. (If you don't see the ruler area, choose Format | Rulers | Show Rulers. To hide rulers, choose Format | Rulers | Hide Rulers.)

For instance, if you'd like to align a paragraph, place the insertion point somewhere in that paragraph and click one of the alignment buttons in the ruler. You can tell by looking at the buttons how they align—left, center, right, and justify (see the following illustration). If you don't like how the paragraph looks, click another alignment button. The changes are made instantly.

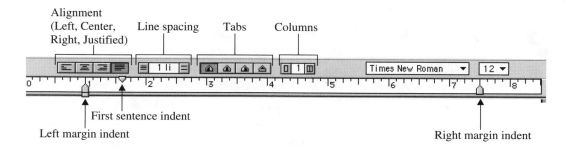

For line spacing, the button on the left pushes lines together while the button on the right spreads them apart. Select the paragraph(s) you want to alter the line spacing of, then click on the line spacing button of your choice.

SHORTCUT   *Here's a cool trick—if you double-click the line-spacing number box where it says something like 1 li or 2 li, you'll immediately open the Paragraph dialog box.*

The ruler can also be used to quickly format the indenting of paragraphs. Select the paragraph(s) you want to indent, then drag the little indent sliders. (Point at a slider with the mouse pointer, hold down the button and drag it to the right or left. Let go of the mouse button to place the slider.)

The sliders determine how things are indented—on the left side, the top slider determines the first line indent and the bottom slider determines the left side indent of the rest of the paragraph. Notice what this lets you do—if you indent *only* the bottom slider, then you'll end up with a paragraph whose first line is flush with the left margin and the rest of the lines are indented, just like in academic bibliography entries.

The right margin indent slider just controls the right-side indent of the entire paragraph. Using a combination of the three you can quickly and visually accomplish anything you can do with indents in the Paragraph dialog box. Of course, you'll have to eyeball the measurements—in the control panel you can be exact to a fraction of an inch.

Insert Elements

Once you have your paragraphs nice and neat you may start to get the feeling that there are still some things missing—elements you'll usually find at the edges of your document. Here are some of the special elements you can insert into your document:

■ **Headers**   Need something at the top of every page? Add a header and it'll automatically be put at the top of all your pages.

■ **Footers**   Create a footer and the same thing appears at the bottom of your pages.

- ◼ **Page Numbers**   Add page numbers that automatically count up for you.
- ◼ **Date and Time**   Choose a quick menu item to add these to your documents in the header, footer, or wherever you like.
- ◼ **Section Breaks**   Dividing your document into sections—for new chapters, for instance—makes it easier to renumber and manage things.
- ◼ **Page Breaks**   When you're ready for a new page, but not finished with the last one, you can break immediately and start a fresh page.
- ◼ **Footnotes**   Writing a scientific, academic, or commercial report that needs footnotes? You've got 'em.

Headers and Footers

These small sections appear at the top and bottom of the page and allow you to add your name, the document's name, a page number, the date and time, or just about anything else required.

To create a header, select Format | Insert Header. A small section appears at the top of the current page in your document window. Now, you can type anything you need in that section—you can even adjust what you type using the paragraph formatting tools.

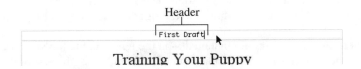

Footers work the same way—choose Format | Insert Footer and a small section appears at the bottom of the page. While editing a header or footer, you can press the RETURN key to add additional lines. Doing so will take away space from the document, not from the margins, which will always stay the same as their setting in the Document dialog box (discussed in the section "Format the Whole Document," later in this chapter).

Now all you need is something to put in the header and footer.

Page Number, Date, and Time

Over in the Edit menu, AppleWorks makes it easy to add the page number, current date, and current time into your document. You can add them anywhere, but the best plan is to put them in the header or footer of your document. And the best part is that the date, time, and page numbers will be updated automatically. The Date and Time commands are a great way to get an automatic record of when documents are modified.

To insert a date, time, or page number, place the insertion point in the header or footer where you want the date to appear. (Note that you can type your own text as well, such as "Modified:"

and "Page Number:") Then, choose the appropriate Insert command from the Edit menu. Whatever element you're inserting appears, as shown here:

```
First Draft Modified: 6/1/02 -- 5:19 PM  |  Page Number: 1
```

TIP *Want to enter a date, time, or page number that never changes automatically? Hold down the OPTION key as you select one of the Insert commands in the Edit menu.*

When you select the Insert Page Number command, you'll get a small dialog box that allows you to choose which page-related number you want to enter. Here's the breakdown:

- **Page Number**   Inserts the current page number for that page in the document or section.
- **Section Number**   Inserts the current section's number. You can create different sections of a document—for instance, for chapters—and number them. (We'll cover the "sections" concept next in this chapter.)
- **Section Page Count**   Enters the number of total pages in the current section.
- **Document Page Count**   Enters the total number of pages in the document. This would be useful for something at the top of the page that said "Page 4 of 15"—you'd get the "15" to automatically update by inserting the Document Page Count command.

Beyond these, there's a Representation menu you can use to choose how the page numbers will be shown. If you want something that says "Section C, Page 4," you can have those numbers automatically updated, too.

NOTE *The point of having all of these different page numbering options is to give you the opportunity to choose different combinations of page numbering schemes and have them automatically updated. Plus, you can add your own text in the header to help explain your scheme.*

Section Breaks

While we're on the topic of all this numbering, let's quickly look into section breaks. You can create a section break anywhere in your document—a section is simply an internal label for a part of your AppleWorks document. Sections allow you to divide a large document up into chapters, lessons, segments or, well, sections. You can then number the sections separately, start over with new page numbering, and so on, as discussed earlier.

To create a section break, place the insertion point where you'd like the new section to begin within your document, then select Format | Insert Section. Now, a line appears dividing the two sections of the document. (This line will not print in the final document.) If you've used the automatic section numbers with the Insert Page Number command, then the section numbers on subsequent pages will reflect the new section.

8

You can do a whole lot more with sections, too. That's discussed in "Format the Section" later in this chapter.

Page Breaks

If you're typing along in your document and you decide you want a new page, you can choose Format | Insert Page Break. That automatically moves you to the top of a new page. Plus, new text below a page break will always appear at the top of a fresh page when printed, even if you add text before the page break occurs. If you just pressed RETURN a bunch of times to get to a fresh page, you'd have to go back and fix the Returns every time you reformatted, added text, or otherwise messed with the text in the document.

Footnotes and Endnotes

If you need footnotes in your document, they're pretty easy to add. Place the insertion point at the end of the word or sentence you want to footnote. Then, choose Format | Insert Blank Footnote. A superscript footnote number appears next to the selected word, and you are magically transported to the bottom of the page (or the end of the document) where you can type the footnote text.

> Some dogs that are bred as guard or alert dogs might have a suddenly heightened sense of awareness or urgency when a stranger appears on the premises. But that isn't the simplest explanation in most cases. The simplest explanation is that some dogs think that the front door
> _____
> [1] "Basic Dog Psychology," Dog Universe Journal, vol. 4, issue 3, p. 45

You can choose where footnotes are added—at the bottom of the page or the end of the document—using the Document dialog box, which is covered later in this chapter in the section, "Format the Whole Document." If you're currently set up to place footnotes at the end of your document, the command will be Insert Endnote instead of Insert Blank Footnote.

To get rid of a footnote, delete the footnote number in the body of the document. The footnote itself will automatically disappear.

Format the Whole Document

After you're done formatting individual paragraphs, you may have reason to make choices of a more global scale—in that case, you'll want to get into the Document formatting preferences. Select Format | Document and the Document dialog box appears.

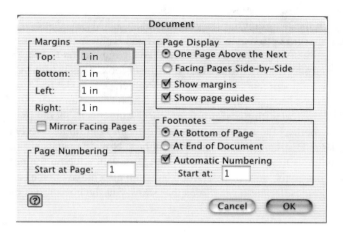

Here's a look at the different options in this dialog box:

- ■ **Margins**   Your first Document options focus on the margins for your document. You can select the top, left, right, and bottom margins for the entire document from this dialog box. Just enter the value for each margin, in inches. The larger the margin numbers, the more white space will appear around the text in your document.

- ■ **Page Numbering**   In the entry box, you can enter a number other than 1 if this document should start its page numbering from a different value.

- ■ **Page Display**   In this section, you can choose how pages are displayed on screen (discussed next) as well as whether or not margins and page guides (lines around the text that show margins) are displayed on the screen.

- ■ **Footnotes**   The last little section in the Document dialog box allows you to choose how footnotes will appear—if space is left for them at the bottom of every page or if they all appear, as endnotes, at the end of the document. You can also have footnotes automatically numbered, if you desire—just check the check box and enter the number the footnotes should start with in the entry box.

So what's this about facing pages? Think about a typical letter or memo—usually, pages come right after one another and no one really expects you to print on the back side of pages. When you finish one page you move it out of the way and read the next page.

If you're writing a book, report, pamphlet, or similar document, though, you may be creating facing pages. That is, readers expect to turn the page in a book and read the backside of that same page, then move over to the right side page and read that one. Those are facing pages, and you can set up AppleWorks to create facing pages in the Document dialog box.

8

While working with the margin numbers you can select the Mirror Facing Pages check box in order to change the margin options slightly. The Left and Right margin options change to Outside and Inside margins. Why? Because once you have pages set up to face one another, you can adjust the inside margins together to provide a uniform look. This is important if you plan to bind and distribute your documents in a booklet, pamphlet, or newsletter form—you'll want facing pages to have mirror-image margins when placed next to one another (see Figure 8-3).

Of course, if you'll be formatting and printing your documents as facing pages, you'll probably want to view them as facing pages, so select the radio button next to Facing Pages Side-By-Side in the Page Display section of the dialog box. Now the pages are moved so that the document window looks more like Figure 8-3. (Likewise, click the button next to One Page Above The Next to return to the default behavior.) You can also make choices as to whether or not margins and page guides, the light gray lines that show you the boundaries of the page, should be displayed.

Format the Section

You saw earlier in the section "Insert Elements" how to create section breaks. Now, with your document broken out into sections, you can choose Format | Section to format each individual

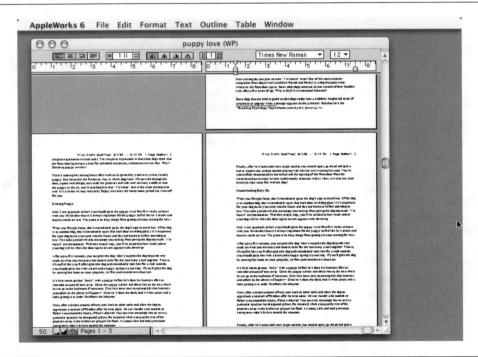

FIGURE 8-3   Facing pages need mirror-image margins to look right once they're in book or booklet form.

section. In fact, even if you don't break your document into different sections, you can still format it as one, big section. There are options in here you might want to check out, including the ability to make the first page of your document a "title page" (meaning it has no headers or footers) and the opportunity to choose different headers and footers for left- and right-facing pages.

To begin, place the insertion point somewhere in the section you want to format (or anywhere in the document if you haven't added any section breaks). Now select Format | Section. The Section dialog box appears, as shown in Figure 8-4.

NOTE   *You may have noticed that I'm ignoring most things that have to do with columns in this chapter. We'll discuss them in more depth in Chapter 12, which covers creating brochures, newsletters, and similar page layouts that use multiple columns.*

Your first decision is how this new section should manifest itself. Choose one of the following from the Start Section menu:

- ■ **New Line**   Choose this option and the section really is pretty much invisible—it'll be for your reference, but readers won't necessarily notice it.

- ■ **New Page**   If the section is to be a new chapter or a major section in a pamphlet, for instance, you'd choose New Page to insert a page break along with the new section.

- ■ **Left Page or Right Page**   If you've formatted your document with facing pages (read about it in the earlier section "Format the Whole Document"), then you can choose if this new section begins with a left or right page. If the new section represents a new chapter, for instance, you'd likely choose to start it as a right page.

In the Page Numbers portion of the dialog box, you have some housekeeping options. If you've chosen to have your new section begin on a new page, you can now choose to have it

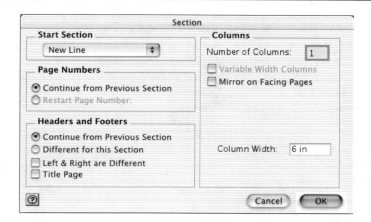

FIGURE 8-4   The Section dialog box gives you even more formatting options.

begin a new page counting scheme. You can have the page count start over at 1, for instance, so you can keep track of the count in the section or chapter instead of in the whole document. (You'll find that many pamphlets and booklets will number with a section number and a page number, like "C-3" or "3-3." You can do the same thing by inserting section and page numbers into the header or footer of your document.)

Finally, you can choose to have the headers and footers the same as they were in previous parts of the document, or choose to build all new headers and footers for this section. (Choose between Continue From Previous Section or Different For This Section by clicking the appropriate radio button.) If you will have new headers and footers, you can click the Left & Right Are Different option to have different headers and footers on the left and right pages. Click the Title Page option to have the first page of the section appear without headers or footers.

Got it all set? Click the OK button and you're returned to the document, complete with its new section formatting. Now, if you chose to have new headers and footers in this section, you'll want to insert and edit them as discussed earlier in the section "Insert Elements."

Tabs and the Ruler

The TAB key on your iMac keyboard can be a powerful tool in the fight against chaos in your documents. By default, a standard document offers tab points every half-inch or so. But you might want more specialized tabs than that—tabs that help you align text, for instance.

There are four different types of tabs you can add to your document: left-aligned, right-aligned, centered, and aligned to a particular character, usually a decimal. What these tabs do, in most cases, is give you the freedom to align things for impromptu tables and arrangements of columns of text in your documents.

Say, for instance, that you wanted to create a table of contents. In that case you'll need two things: a right-aligned column of chapter descriptions and a column that's aligned to the dash that separates a document's section and page number. (OK, so maybe this example is an overly regimented military-type report. Just bear with me.) It'd look something like Figure 8-5.

How does this work? Before you type any text, click the button that corresponds to the type of tab you want to create. Now, click on the ruler itself to place that tab on the ruler. You can then drag it back and forth to get it lined up exactly how you want it.

If you want a right-aligned column to end on the two-inch mark, drag it there. If you want to align a column of currency figures, put the decimal-aligned tab on the six-inch mark and that's where the dollars will line up.

Need to switch some things around? Three rules:

- *Highlight all rows.* If you need to change a tab that affects more than one row of text, select *every* row first, then change the tab in the ruler. Otherwise, you'll only change it for the row where the insertion point is. This will happen to you a lot by accident, so be wary.

- *Double-click the tab.* If you need to change a tab that you've already dragged to the ruler, double-click it. The Tab dialog box appears, allowing you to make changes. For instance, you can change the alignment of the tab, add a fill (automatically fill in

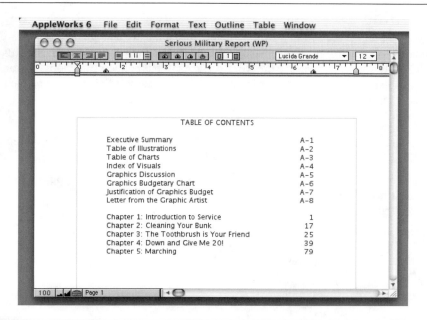

FIGURE 8-5   This table uses a left-justified tab for the titles and a right-justified tab so that the numbers line up nicely.

behind the tab with dots or dashes, which nicely completes the Table of Contents effect), or tweak the location of the tab by entering the inch mark where it should appear.

- *Drag tab off ruler to remove.* To get rid of a tab, select *all* rows that are affected by the tab—they need to all be highlighted—then pick up the tab and drag it back up to the top of the ruler. It'll disappear.

NOTE   *It's worth emphasizing that if you can't find a tab, if a tab is still there even though you moved it, or if only part of your document is lined up to tabs correctly, there's a good reason. It's because you didn't select every line in your document affected by that tab. Go back, select all the lines, and make your change once more.*

Spell, Find, Change, and Count

You've finally gotten through most of your document creation. You've formatted the text, cleaned it up with tabs and saved after every three lines. Now that you've seen what a computer can do to help you format an important report or document, how about seeing what it can do to help you clean up and edit the words themselves? Here's where some of that computerized speed and savvy comes into play.

Check Spelling

By brute force your word processor can jump quickly through a document and check every word against an internal dictionary. If it finds one it's not familiar with, it'll suggest other words that seem to be similarly spelled. If you see the word you meant to type, you can choose it from the list. Otherwise, you can either add the word that AppleWorks doesn't recognize, type the correct spelling yourself, or just skip the suggestion.

Here's how it works:

1. When you're ready to check spelling, select Edit | Writing Tools | Check Document Spelling.

2. AppleWorks begins checking. When it finds a word it doesn't like, it pops up in a dialog box like the one here:

3. If AppleWorks offers the correct spelling, select it in the box and click Replace (or press the keyboard command ⌘-*number* where *number* is the number of the suggestion in the list). If you don't see the correct spelling, you can type it into the entry box. If you type something you want to check against AppleWorks' dictionary, click the Check button. If the word is spelled correctly, click Learn so that AppleWorks won't flag it again in the future. If the word isn't worth worrying about (it's an odd abbreviation or something), then click Skip.

4. AppleWorks moves on to the next word it finds misspelled.

If you don't need to check the entire document, you can check just a selection of text—highlight the text you want to check, then select Edit | Writing Tools | Check Selection Spelling.

Find and Change

The Find and Change features use some of the same technology as spell-checking, but instead of checking the document against an internal dictionary, it checks the file against whatever text you enter in the Find dialog box. It can then change the found text to whatever text you choose.

Need an example? In earlier editions of this book, the discussion in this chapter centered on ClarisWorks, which was the original name for AppleWorks up until late 1998 or so. So, in subsequent editions, I've been able to use the Find dialog box to hunt down occurrences of "ClarisWorks" and automatically change them to "AppleWorks."

Here's how to do a Find and Change:

1. Select Edit | Find/Change. In the submenu that comes up, select the Find/Change command.

2. In the Find/Change dialog box, enter a word you'd like to search for in the Find entry box. If you plan to replace that word with something else, enter it in the Change entry box.

3. Click the Find Next button. The first instance of the word is found (if there are any instances of that word).

4. If you want to change this instance of the word, click Change. You can also click Change, Find, if you want to change the word and move instantly to the next instance of the word. If you don't want to change this instance, click Find Next.

5. Rinse and repeat. If you want to stop finding, click the Close box on the Find window.

If you just want AppleWorks to find and change every instance of a word, you can click the Change All button instead of going through the entire document by hand. Think carefully before doing that, though, since you could accidentally change words you don't mean to change. Consider my example, where I've used Find to change nearly every instance of ClarisWorks in this chapter to AppleWorks. If I'd performed a Change All during that Find search, I would have changed the sentence right before this one you're reading. The sentence would then read: "Consider my example, where I found and changed nearly every instance of AppleWorks in this chapter to AppleWorks."

In the Find/Change window you'll find two check box options:

- **Find Whole Word**   Check this option to find instances where the word in the Find entry box matches only a whole word in the document. If you search for the word "pup" without this option checked, it'll find the letters "pup" within the word "puppy." If you check the Find Whole Word check box, it will only find the word "pup," not parts of words that include the letters "pup."

- **Case Sensitive**   Check this option and Find will pay attention to the upper- and lowercase letters you type in the Find entry box. If you search for "Puppy" with the Case Sensitive option checked, Find will not stop on the words "puppy" or "puppY."

SHORTCUT   *You can change words to simple spaces or nothing at all. That's a great way to delete every instance of a particular word. You can also find just about anything you can cut and paste into the Find entry box, including spaces and line returns. Get creative—use ⌘-V to paste things into the Find entry box for more advanced searches.*

8

Standardize with the Styles Palette

If you're serious about word processing, you should get to know the Styles palette window. What does it do? When you create a paragraph style you really like, you can give it a name and save it. Then, you can invoke that style anytime by simply selecting it in the Styles palette. Instant high-end formatting—perfect if you do a lot of the same sort of documents and you want to stop re-inventing the wheel.

To open the Styles window, select Format | Show Styles. The Styles palette appears.

To select a style, just click it once in the Styles palette and click the Apply button. (You can also double-click the style in the Styles palette to apply it.) The currently selected paragraph in your document will instantly change to that style. If you select more than one paragraph and then select a style in the Styles palette and click Apply, all of the paragraphs will change to that paragraph style. If you don't like the style you've changed it to, click the Unapply button.

To add your own style, format a paragraph just the way you want it. Make sure the insertion point is in that paragraph. Then, in the Styles palette, click the New button. In the New Style dialog box, give your style a name and choose the Paragraph radio button. Make sure the Inherit Document Selection Format option is turned on, then click OK. The style is created. You can now double-click the new style in the Styles palette to format other paragraphs.

NOTE　*The Styles can be used for other types of formatting, too, including table and outline styles.*

Use Templates for Automatic Documents

AppleWorks has built into it Assistants (little programs that walk you through a task) and Templates (sample documents) that can help you create a number of different types of documents. We'll focus on some of the Assistants—those that create business documents like newsletters, business cards, brochures, and such—in Chapter 12. For now, let's see some templates that can help you with memos and letters.

Templates in AppleWorks are pre-formatted, often by professional designers, to make you look good. When you create a new document using a template, you get a new document that already has some attractive elements created for you. Then, you enter your own information to finish the document. In the Teacher Letterhead templates, for instance, you can select the sections of the document that are currently generic looking and change them into something you can use. For example, you can change the name section and address to your own, as shown here:

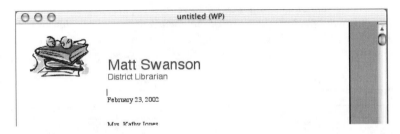

Create a Document from Templates

To use a template, you'll begin by creating a new document by selecting File | Show Starting Points or pressing ⌘-1. (Or, if you are just starting up AppleWorks, the Starting Points window will automatically appear.) In the Starting Points window, click the Templates tab. The icons in the window change to reflect the templates you can use. Scroll through the window until you see the template you'd like to use. When you see an interesting one, click it. AppleWorks creates a new, styled document in the template's image.

You'll find that some templates are more involved than others. Some feature special Styles, for instance, that allow you to continue to format the paragraphs according to the template's theme. In any case, all you have to do to work with the template is start editing, adding your own text, images, and other objects, as desired.

At some point you'll want to save the document—just save it like any other document using the File | Save command. This doesn't alter the original template—you can always go back to the Templates tab in the Starting Points window to create another document that looks like it.

> **TIP** *If you have Internet access, you can click the Web tab in the Starting Points window. Now, click the Templates icon to launch a special AppleWorks document with Web links. Now you can click through the available templates, then click the Download link next to an interesting looking template to retrieve the template to AppleWorks and work with it.*

Save a Document as a Template

If you have a particular document design that you like a lot, you can save it as a template of your own, adding it to the Templates tab in the Starting Points window. That way you can use it to automatically create new documents that look like it.

With the document created, choose File | Save As. Give your template a name, then click the Template icon down in the corner of the Save As dialog box. You'll be automatically transported to AppleWorks' Templates folder in the Where menu. Click the Save button and your template is saved. Now, the next time you want to create a document in that style, you can choose your template from the Templates tab in the Starting Points window (see Figure 8-6).

NOTE *If you've created a document you need to save as an actual document, do that first. Then you may want to clear out parts of the document—like the salutation and the body, if you're creating a letterhead template—that are specific to that document so you have a more generic document to use as a template.*

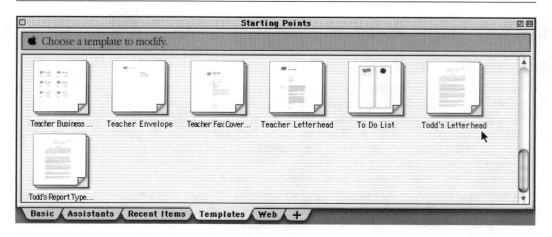

FIGURE 8-6   Choose your new template just as if it were one of AppleWorks' built-in templates.

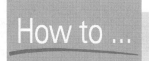 **Customize the Button Bar**

The Button Bar that appears by default above your documents offers quick access to some common style commands (when you're working in a word processing document) as well as quick access to buttons that let you create other types of documents. But you can also customize the Button Bar with your own command buttons, if you like. Hold down the CONTROL key and click the button bar, then choose Customize Button Bar from the pop-up menu. In the Customize Button Bar dialog box, scroll through the list to find the command you want to add. (Note that Word Processing has a whole subtopic about halfway down the list.) When you see a command you want to add, just drag that command from the list up to the Button Bar. It's added as a new button.

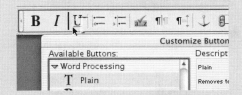

When you're finished customizing, click Done. To delete a button you've added, CONTROL-click that button and select Remove Button from the contextual menu.

8

Chapter 9

Work with Numbers and Build Charts

How to...

- Recognize when to use spreadsheets
- See the basics of spreadsheets
- Enter and format text and numbers in your spreadsheet
- Cut, copy, paste, and sort your data
- Build formulas that work with your data
- Use advanced formulas for "what-if" scenarios
- Chart your data to see it visually

The computing industry likes to think in terms of something called "killer applications" (or "killer apps" in a hip shorthand). Basically, the killer app is a reason to use a computer that's so new and so compelling that it drives millions to buy new machines and software to join the revolution. In the mid-to-late 1980s, for instance, the Mac's early ability to offer desktop publishing capabilities—allowing you to format text, add images, and arrange pages completely onscreen, then print it all to laser or color printers—was its killer application. In some ways, the Mac is still superior for that sort of work.

Before this happened, though, there was another time in Apple's history when it saw its computer sales spike—the killer app that prompted that spike was the spreadsheet. At the time (the late 1970s), the spreadsheet was called VisiCalc, the concept was completely new, and the computer that sold like gangbusters as a result was the Apple II.

We've come a long way. With the iMac, computers have become cute and with AppleWorks spreadsheets have become easy to use. Just you wait and see.

The Spreadsheet Defined

A spreadsheet application is one that allows you to create what amounts to a digital ledger book. Ebenezer Scrooge, for instance, might have tracked his accounts in one of those cool-looking, lined, leather-bound ledger books. But times have changed. These days we have electronic spreadsheets instead of ledger books. And it's the iMac that looks cool.

Why Use Spreadsheets?

So, this is like a ledger book, but better. Why? A spreadsheet allows you to do three major things well:

- **Math**   You can concoct all sorts of formulas and impose them upon the numbers you've entered into your spreadsheet. Do loan calculations, find the average or standard deviation, figure the net present value—tons of things that no human should try without computerized help. By getting your numbers into the spreadsheet—where every cell has a name—you can perform many different mathematical functions.

- ■ **What-If**   Once you have a spreadsheet full of data and calculations, the spreadsheet allows you to change numbers quickly and see how that affects the whole. Say you've laid out an entire budget for the next six months. What if you decide to take a job that pays less but allows you to perform that invaluable human service (not to mention the ego boost)? Edit up that income number in your budget and see how things shake out.

- ■ **Charts**   Once you have the data entered and represented the way you like it, you can create graphics from the numbers that allow you to more clearly make your case at the next board, team, faculty, or family meeting. AppleWorks is capable of creating all sorts of charts, including exciting 3-D charts that will wow them for weeks.

So, all you have to do is enter the data, format it correctly, then get working on your calculations, what-if scenarios, and charts. Before you do that, though, you're going to have to know how to enter the data into the spreadsheet.

The Cell

The building block of any spreadsheet document is the *cell*—the conjunction of a column and a row that is given a unique name in the two dimensions of a spreadsheet. In that cell you can put text, numbers, formulas—even images, although there's less reason to do that. As shown next, those cells, because they're uniquely named (with names like "A2" and "F18"), can be added together, subtracted from one another, even cosined and tangented, if those are words. (I never did terribly well in trigonometry.)

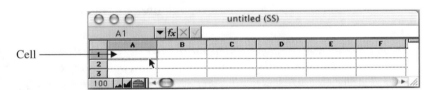

In working with spreadsheets, you'll need to get to know cell notation—the cell's name acts as a *variable* in formulas you build to work with the numbers in those cells. It's basic algebra—you'll create a formula that says "add C3 to C4," which tells the spreadsheet to sum the values it finds in cells C3 and C4. So how does it know which cells those are?

In the typical spreadsheet (AppleWorks included), the columns are lettered from left to right across the top of the document and the rows are numbered from top to bottom. So, the first cell at the top-left corner is A1. The cell C3, then, is the cell at the conjunction of column C and row 3.

Sound exciting yet? Let's run through how to create your own spreadsheets, doctor them up, and make them look nice.

NOTE   *By default, a spreadsheet in AppleWorks is 40 columns wide (reaching cell "AN") and 500 rows long. You can add to them both—the limit is 256 columns and 16,384 rows.*

9

Get the Spreadsheet Started

Spreadsheet documents start the same way any other documents begin—with the New command. In AppleWorks, choose File | New | Spreadsheet. Or, if you have the Starting Points window showing, select the Spreadsheet icon on the Basic tab.

 Want to password-protect your spreadsheet? Actually, this works for any AppleWorks document. Choose File | Properties, and then click the Set Password button. Enter a password and click OK. Now, any time you attempt to open this document in the future, a password dialog box will appear, and you'll have to know the password to access the document.

Move in the Spreadsheet

The first thing you'll want to do is learn how to get around. It's pretty basic. You'll start out in the top-left cell, but you can click anywhere on a cell and instantly be transported there. Once you have a cell selected, you can enter something in that cell by simply typing. Notice, when you start typing, that nothing actually appears in the cell.

You edit in the Entry Bar at the top of the document window. You won't see the results in the cell until you move on from the cell—you do *that* by pressing TAB or RETURN.

Table 9-1 shows you how to move around in a spreadsheet document.

It won't take too long before these keys will become second nature to you. You just need to remember that if you want to edit something that's already in a cell, move to that cell (with the keys or the mouse) and edit it in the Entry Bar, not in the cell itself (the program won't let you edit in the cell).

NOTE *The arrow keys don't allow you to leave a cell if you're currently editing data in that cell, because then you can't use those keys to move the insertion point around in the Entry Bar. If you'd prefer that arrow keys allow you to immediately leave a cell, select AppleWorks | Preferences | General. From the pull-down menu, choose Spreadsheet, if it isn't already selected. Now, select Always Selects Another Cell in the Pressing Arrow Keys section. Notice you can also change the behavior of the ENTER key in this dialog box. Click OK to exit Preferences.*

Press This	To Do This
RETURN, DOWN ARROW	Move down one cell
TAB, RIGHT ARROW	Move right one cell
SHIFT-RETURN, UP ARROW	Move up one cell
SHIFT-TAB, LEFT ARROW	Move left one cell
ENTER (under number pad)	Accept data in cell without moving to a new cell

TABLE 9-1 Moving Around in a Spreadsheet Document

You can enter either text or numbers in a spreadsheet, although it's best to have a plan before you jump in and start entering things randomly. In general, you'll want a series of numbers—budget numbers for every month of the year, for instance—to be in a row or a column, unbroken by other text or numbers. Figure 9-1 shows an example of a nice, neat spreadsheet that will be easy to deal with when it comes to building formulas and creating "what-if" scenarios.

Select Cells

There are three basic ways to select cells in the spreadsheet window:

- If you're selecting a single cell, click it once. Its frame becomes outlined.

- To select more than one cell, click and hold the mouse button on the first cell you want to select, then drag the mouse across the other cells you'd like to select. When you've highlighted all the cells you need, release the mouse button. (Note that the first cell in your selection will not be highlighted—the frame will be outlined. It's still selected, though.)

9

	January	February	March	April	May	June	July	August	September
Annual Household Budget									
Work Income	3000	3000	3000	3000	3000	3000	3000	3000	3000
Investment Income	200	200	200	200	200	200	200	200	200
Savings Interest	25	25	25	25	25	25	25	25	25
Other Income	0	0	350	0	0	350	0	0	350
Total Income	**3225**	**3225**	**3575**	**3225**	**3225**	**3575**	**3225**	**3225**	**3575**
Rent	800	800	800	800	800	800	800	800	800
Car	225	225	225	225	225	225	225	225	225
Insurance	75	75	75	150	75	75	140	75	75
Medical Insurance	150	150	150	150	150	150	150	150	150
Groceries	240	240	240	240	240	240	240	240	240
Dining	200	200	200	200	200	200	200	200	200
Entertainment	250	250	250	250	250	250	250	250	250
Clothing	500	100	100	500	100	100	500	100	100
Household	150	150	150	150	150	150	150	150	150
Misc.	75	75	75	75	75	75	75	75	75
Cash Expenses	**2665**	**2265**	**2265**	**2740**	**2265**	**2265**	**2730**	**2265**	**2265**
Mastercard	50	50	50	50	50	50	50	50	50
Discover	25	25	25	0	0	0	0	0	0
Amex	100	100	100	100	100	100	100	100	100
Credit Expenses	**175**	**175**	**175**	**150**	**150**	**150**	**150**	**150**	**150**
Over/Under	385	785	1135	335	810	1160	345	810	1160

FIGURE 9-1   The best spreadsheets are arranged logically in a table format.

- To select an entire row or column, click its letter or number once. In the "F" column, for instance, you can click the "F" at the top of the screen to highlight the entire column. If you want to select more than one column or row at a time, hold down the SHIFT key and click once for each column or row that you want to add. Notice that multiple columns or rows must be adjacent in order to be selected and you can't select both rows and columns at once.

Save the Spreadsheet

To save a spreadsheet, just select File | Save or File | Save As. The Save As dialog box appears, allowing you to name the document and find a folder to save it in. When you've made those choices, click Save. From there on, you can quickly save the spreadsheet every few minutes by selecting the Save command again or pressing ⌘-S on your keyboard.

Enter and Format Data

In most spreadsheets, you'll enter text to label the rows and columns that will be filled with numbers. With both the text and the numbers, it's possible to do some rather intricate formatting, including the basics like font, size, style, and alignment. You'll also find some formatting options that are different from those in word processing—options like formatting numbers as currency, dates, or times.

TIP   *Actually, it's possible to perform calculations on text as well—you can do a number of things with text, including comparisons for word length, changing the case of text, sorting the text, adding text strings together ("concatenating" them), and so on. I'll discuss some of that in the section "Add Formulas to your Spreadsheets."*

Format Text and Cells

Let's begin with text, since you'll likely begin with text in your spreadsheet. (You'll need to create labels for the columns and rows of numbers you plan to enter.) You might want to begin by typing a title into the first cell of the spreadsheet—cell A1. You can type text that's longer than the cell, and all of the text will actually appear just fine—as long as you haven't typed text into the adjoining cells. If you're creating the title line for your spreadsheet, that should be no problem.

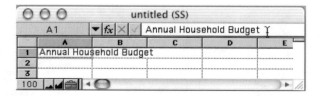

TIP   *Want text to wrap within the cell instead of continuing off the edge? Highlight the cell and choose Format | Alignment | Wrap. Now text will wrap within the cell.*

You can also format text using the same settings that you use in a word processor—font, size, styles, and alignment. The major difference is that, for spreadsheets in AppleWorks, all of those commands appear in the Format menu. You can't format selected text differently within the same cell—formatting for text in the cell applies to all text in that cell.

Here's how to format:

1. Select the cell(s) that have text you want to format.

2. Select the Format menu and point the mouse at the type of formatting you'd like to change—Font, Size, Style, Font Color, or Alignment.

3. In the menu that appears to the right, make your formatting selection.

All the text in the cell will be affected, although the cell itself won't change. That can be a problem if you've changed the size of the text in the cell, for instance, and can no longer read it clearly. The solution: Resize the cell.

Actually, you can't really change the size of an *individual* cell—you either change the size of its row or its column. To change the size of a row, point the mouse all the way over at the numbers that label each row. If you place the mouse pointer on the line that appears between any two rows, the mouse pointer changes to a pair of arrows. That's your cue that holding down the mouse button and dragging will change the size of the row, as shown in the following illustration. A column can be resized in the same way—just drag the line between the numbers.

9

Text is important in most spreadsheets, especially if you want other people to understand what the heck your spreadsheet is for. Text is also very useful for charting data, which we'll get into later in this chapter. AppleWorks likes to find text on the top and left borders of your numbers; it can use that text for labels in charts, for instance. So, think in terms of labeling your data in rows and columns—the more structured the data now, the more easily it will be viewed and manipulated later.

One special case is alignment—you'll probably want to format your columns and rows so the values in them line up together nicely. Select an entire range of cells or an entire column or row and use the Format | Alignment menu command to align every cell in the range to the left, right, centered, or justified. You may also find it helps the readability of your spreadsheet to choose the row or column where your "label" cells are, then format them as bold, larger text, or what-have-you to make them stand out.

Want to delete text? Just select the cell and press DELETE. (You can also choose Edit | Clear to delete cell contents.) Likewise, you can highlight more than one cell and press DELETE to clear many cells of text (or numbers and formulas, for that matter) at once.

Enter and Format Numbers

AppleWorks automatically recognizes a number as a number (not as text) when you type a number into a cell. In fact, in order to type a number as text, if you need to, you must enter a sort of mini-function that looks like this: ="5467". Using this formula, the number is treated as a *string* of text characters. This might be useful if you needed to label a column or row with a number—for instance, if you wanted your columns to represent years. If you enter **2002**, that's seen as two thousand and two. Enter ="2002" and it's treated as text, so you can use it as a label representing the year.

Otherwise, numbers are numbers. If you need to enter a negative number, enter a minus sign (–) before it, such as **–5467**. And, as is true with text, you can copy and paste numbers from one cell into another if you like.

Number Formats

Numbers can be formatted in the same way as text—font, size, style, color, and alignment—by selecting the cell or cells and using the Format menu. Numbers also have their own formatting schemes that can be used specifically to make them more meaningful, easier to read, or both. Those formatting options appear when you select a cell or group of cells, then choose Format | Number. You can also access the Format Number, Date, and Time dialog box (shown in Figure 9-2) by double-clicking a cell.

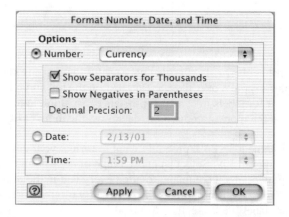

FIGURE 9-2   Format numbers using this dialog box.

In the dialog box, you start by selecting the radio button next to the type of number (Number, Date, or Time) you want in that cell or range of cells. Then select further choices from the pop-up menus:

- **Number**   In the Number pop-up menu, you can make choices that allow you to change the appearance of your numbers—they can be regular numbers, currency, percentages, scientific notation, or fixed decimal numbers (with a certain number of decimal places shown). Using the check boxes, you can also decide if there will be a separator for thousands and whether or not negative values will appear in parentheses, which is common in accounting and financial notation. In the Decimal Precision entry box, enter the number of decimal places you want to show for the numbers.

- **Date**   Choose one of the date formats from the pop-up menu.

- **Time**   Choose one of the time formats from the pop-up menu.

You'll probably often want to format an entire row or column with a certain type of number formatting—Currency, for instance. Go ahead and select an entire range of cells or even a complete column or row. In fact, you can select an entire column or row that already has text labels in it and the text won't be affected by what you do with the number formatting, only the numbers will.

Cut, Paste, Fill

In spreadsheets, you can cut and paste either text or numbers very easily. In the sample budget document I've created for this chapter's figures, a lot of numbers repeat. It's possible to select an entire range of numbers—part of a column, for instance—then copy and paste it into the next column.

Another way to quickly enter numbers is to use the Fill Right or Fill Down commands in the Calculate menu. Enter a value for one cell, then highlight that cell and a number of cells to the right or down from that cell. Now, choose the appropriate command—Calculate | Fill Right (⌘-R) or Calculate | Fill Down (⌘-D)—and all those cells are filled with the first cell's value.

Add Formulas to the Spreadsheet

Here's where the real power of the spreadsheet shines through—creating formulas that allow you to manipulate the data. So far, you've entered text that labels data and you've entered numbers that represent data. Now it's time to put some of that algebraic knowledge swimming around in your head to the task of creating formulas that work with your data. In this section, I'll show you the anatomy of a formula, then we'll move on to some of the formulas included in AppleWorks.

Anatomy of a Formula

You've already seen that by simply typing text and numbers into the cell, AppleWorks can differentiate between the two for formatting purposes. It can immediately tell the difference between a number and text.

It can't, however, tell the difference between the cell reference "A3" and the text "A3." In order to differentiate a formula, AppleWorks needs a little code. That code comes in the form of an equals (=) sign. If you begin your typing in a cell with an equals sign, AppleWorks will interpret what follows that sign as a formula.

After you exit the cell, if you've typed the formula correctly you won't see the formula again in the cell. Instead, you'll see the result of that formula. (If you highlight the cell, you'll again see the formula up in the Entry Bar.)

Formula Types

Beyond the equals sign, there are two basic types of formulas you'll create. The first is a straight mathematical formula with addition (+), subtraction (–), multiplication (*), division (/), or exponential (^) operators. A typical mathematical formula could easily be =34+45 or =34^2, although that'd be reasonably useless in a spreadsheet (you'll see why in a moment).

The other type of formula uses a built-in function from AppleWorks. These functions range from financial to trigonometric to logical. An example might be =AVERAGE (34, 45, 56), which would return the average of those three numbers.

As you might guess, it's also possible to use these two types of formulas together in the same cell, so that =34+45+(AVERAGE (34, 45, 56)) is a legal formula, too. Notice, by the way, that parentheses are used pretty liberally in these formulas to separate one operation from another. Again, it's like algebra—functions and math inside parentheses get done first, then the result gets entered into the larger equation.

Build with Cell Addresses

What's missing in this discussion of formulas, of course, is the cell address. By using cell addresses as *variables*, you're suddenly able to do amazing things with formulas. For instance, while =34+45 isn't terribly useful in a spreadsheet (since you could just enter **79** and be done with it), the formula =B3+B4 could be *very* useful. Why? Because if you change the value in B3 or in B4—or in both—the result changes as well. And getting results is what spreadsheets are all about.

Now you're able to create a cell whose value is based on values in other cells. You could take this even further. How about a cell whose value is the sum of many different cells—something along the lines of =B4+B5+B6+B7? That's shown in Figure 9-3.

Notice that the cell addresses are starting to get a little out of hand, even with just four—what if you were adding together four hundred? In your spreadsheet, you can use a special notation to denote a range of cells to be acted on. The range is separated by two periods, as in =SUM(B4..B7), which gives the same result as =B4+B5+B6+B7.

*Once a formula is evaluated, you can use that formula's cell address in another formula. If you put SUM(B4..B7) in cell B8, you can type **B8** in another formula, where it will represent the result of that sum.*

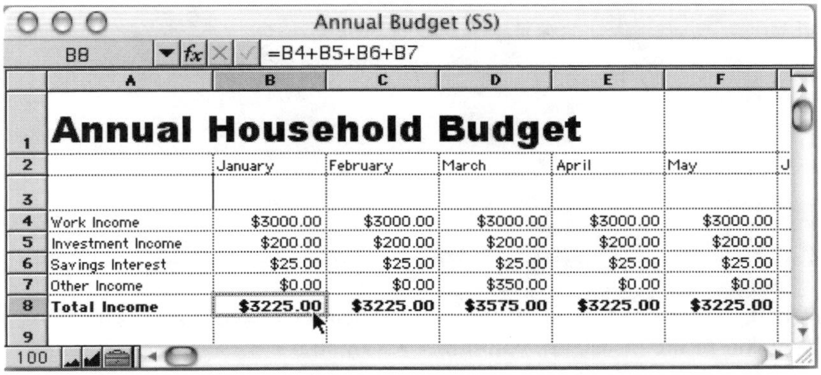

FIGURE 9-3   A basic formula for adding cell values together

Relative vs. Absolute

The cell addresses we've been talking about are called *relative* addresses. What does that mean? Say you wanted to use the Copy and Paste or Fill Right/Fill Down commands with a formula you've created. With relative addressing, the addresses within that formula will change relative to the cell you paste it into. For example, if cell B29 had the formula =SUM(B10..B27) in it, you could copy that formula from cell B29 and paste it into cell C29. The formula in C29 is changed slightly, though, to =SUM(C10..C27). AppleWorks is just assuming that's how you want it.

You can circumvent this by creating an absolute address using dollar signs ($). The address $B$10 is an absolute address that always points to cell B10. If I create a formula in cell B29 that looks like =$B$10+B11, then copy that formula to cell C29, the result will be =$B$10+C11. Since the second address was relative, it changed. But the first address is still B10.

NOTE   *You should note that absolute addresses aren't updated automatically if you add rows or columns to your spreadsheet. In the above example, if I add a column between A and B, I'll need to change all the absolute references to $B$10 so that they read $C$10. Otherwise, the values will be incorrect.*

More Operators

Want a little more confusion? In dealing with cell addresses, you can use two additional operators to change the way numbers are evaluated—the percent operator (%) turns a number into a decimal percentage (for example, =C3%) while the minus sign (–) can be used in front of a cell address to make it negative (for example =–C3).

Other operators besides the numeric ones can be used in your formulas—they're called relational and text operators. The relational operators offer comparisons between two values.

9

They are

=	Equal to
<>	Not equal to
>	Greater than
>=	Greater than or equal to
<	Less than
<=	Less than or equal to

Using a formula like =A3>A4 will return a value of either True or False, which will appear in the cell. If you don't find this useful, you'll likely want to use these operators within logical functions like the IF function. (IF is discussed later in this chapter, with examples.)

There's also one text operator, the ampersand (&), which allows you to concatenate text. The formula =B5&" "&B6 would create one long string of text with a space between the two cell's text entries.

 What happens when you concatenate numbers? They're turned into text. It works fine, but you won't be able to perform any math on the text-ified numbers until you turn them back into numbers with the TEXTTONUM function, discussed a little later in this chapter.

Operator Precedence

Before you can build formulas you need to know one last little thing about them—operator precedence. We used to call this "order of operations" back in algebra class. Say you have the formula =40+10*3. What's the answer? It depends on what you do first. If you evaluate from left to right, then 40 plus 10 is 50; 50 times 3 is 150. If you evaluate the multiplication first, then 10 times 3 is 30 and 40 plus 30 is 70. You get two different answers.

One way to manage this is to rely on parentheses. Since operations inside parenthesis are always evaluated first, you could create the formula =(40+10)*3 to get 150 or =40+(10*3) to get 70.

Or, you could rely on the operator precedence. In this case, multiplication has higher precedence than addition. Without parentheses, the formula =40+10*3, by rule of precedence, equals 70. Multiplication is done first, then addition. Table 9-2 shows the order of precedence for all operators—the higher in the table, the sooner the operation is performed.

Whenever a precedence level is the same for two operations, the formula is evaluated from left to right. So, if a subtraction is further left than an addition, the subtraction is done first.

When in doubt, use parentheses. That way you'll be able to decide exactly how a formula is evaluated.

()	Parentheses (done first)
%	Percentages
^	Exponentials
+, −	Positive or negative numbers (sign is before a cell address)
*, /	Multiply, divide
+, −	Add, subtract
&	Concatenate text
=, >, <, >=, <=, <>	All comparisons (done last)

TABLE 9-2   Order of Precedence for Spreadsheet Formulas

Add Functions to Your Formulas

You'll soon come up with a reason to do more than just basic mathematics between a few different cells. You've already seen that the SUM function can be used with a range of cells to add them all together and get a total. But what if you need to do something more sophisticated in your formulas?

In that case, it's time to call in a function. Here's how you add one:

1. Select the cell where you want the function to appear.

2. Next to the Entry Bar on your spreadsheet document window is the Function (Fx) button. Click it and the Insert Function dialog box appears (see Figure 9-4).

3. Choose one of those functions and it's added to the Entry Bar, where you can edit it. (Note that you can filter the type of functions shown in the dialog box by selecting a category from the Category pop-up menu. The categories are discussed below.)

4. Edit the function to taste (usually, you'll add cell addresses and values) and exit the cell.

AppleWorks offers a number of different categories of functions:

■ **Business and Financial**   These are functions like PV (present value), NPV (net present value), RATE (tells you the interest rate of a payment schedule), and PMT (figures the payment required to satisfy a particular type of loan or payment scheme).

■ **Date and Time**   These functions allow you to perform various calculations regarding time. The date, day of the week, and time can all be stored as numeric values, allowing you to easily do math using them. That's discussed in more detail later in this section.

■ **Information**   These functions are used to send information, such as alert boxes and error tones, to your user.

9

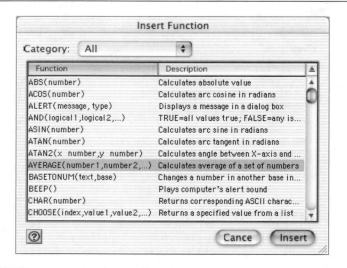

FIGURE 9-4 The Insert Function dialog box helps you enter functions into your spreadsheet.

- ■ **Logical** These programming-like functions can be used to determine if a number of values are true (AND) or if any values are true (OR), or it can evaluate values and perform other calculations based on whether they're true or not (IF). Other functions determine whether a value is present or if there's an error.

- ■ **Numeric** These functions allow you to work with numbers and ranges of numbers. They include SUM (sum of numbers), RAND (generates a random number), ROUND (rounds a number), and SQRT (returns the square root of the number).

- ■ **Statistical** These functions take the MEAN, find the MODE, determine standard deviation, and more.

- ■ **Text** Text operators allow you to find certain words programmatically, change words to upper- or lowercase, get the length of a word, and perform similar functions.

- ■ **Trigonometric** Here are those crazy functions all about angles. You can figure the cosine, sine, and tangent and convert between radians and degrees, among other things.

Some Cool Functions

Okay, I'm well over my allotted pages for this chapter, but I just had to show you some cool functions available for your spreadsheet. I'll try to get through these very quickly so you can get back to your regularly scheduled tutorial.

Autosum

This is a shortcut from the AppleWorks button bar. It allows you to quickly generate a SUM formula in a spreadsheet of numbers like a budget or financials. I used it for the sample budget shown in this chapter. Here's how it works:

1. Highlight the range of numbers you want to total *plus* an additional cell at the end of the list.

2. Click the Autosum button.

That's it. The sum automatically appears in that blank cell (see Figure 9-5).

Now you can do it again for the next row, or just use the Fill Right command for all the other total cells in that row of your budget. Since the Autosum button creates a SUM function with relative addresses, the function will copy just fine for the rest of the row.

Although they all don't have their own "auto" buttons on the button bar, some other formulas work just like SUM. They include AVERAGE, MIN, and MAX, all of which can accept a range of cells such as AVERAGE (B2..B10).

Text to Date, Date to Text

In the spreadsheet, AppleWorks allows you to deal with dates in an interesting way—you can add and subtract them, if you like. How? AppleWorks turns a typical date into a *serial number*,

9

Autosum button

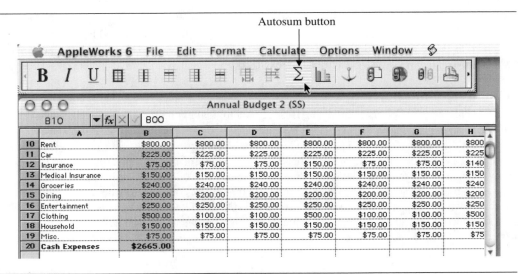

FIGURE 9-5   Quickly create a total of an entire selection of cells.

which is a regular integer that represents how many days the entered date is since January 1, 1904. Pretty weird, huh?

The TEXTTODATE function accepts a text entry of the current date. (The year should be in four digits to avoid those pesky Y2K issues.) For instance, you could enter the date in cell B2, in the format 00/00/0000. In cell B4, enter the formula **=TEXTTODATE (B2)**. Now, you have a serial number.

What can you do with that? You can add or subtract from it. For example, I'll figure out what date is seven days past the date entered by adding 7 to the serial number in cell B5 (**=B4+7**). Now, I'll use the DATETOTEXT function to turn the serial date back into one read by humans. The formula typed into cell B7 is **=DATETOTEXT (B5, 1)**. The 1 represents the date format I want to use—the numbers are explained in AppleWorks help for the DATETOTEXT function. The result? A readable date that's seven days after the one entered above:

If you'd like to work with time, too, it works much the same way, except that time's serial number is a decimal—it's the percentage of 24 hours. The time 6:00 p.m. (18:00 hours) is represented as 0.75. You could figure that out with the formula TEXTTOTIME ("18:00") or TEXTTOTIME (B2) if cell B2 contained the text 18:00.

IF Function

Here's a great one for all sorts of analysis. IF accepts a logical expression, followed by what it should do if an expression is true and what it should do if an expression is false. For instance, let's say that the value of cell B27 in my budget spreadsheet represents my over/under value for the month. If I come out more than $400 ahead on my budget for that month, then I'll put half of it in my retirement account. If I have less than $400, then I'll put $0 in my retirement account.

So, with that in mind, I can create an IF function that checks out my over/under balance and decides what to do. It'll look like this: =IF (B27>400, B27/2, 0). That is, if B27 is greater than 400, return B27 divided by 2 as the value. If B27 isn't greater than 400, return 0. Here it is in action:

Amex	$100.00	$100.00	$100.00
Credit Expenses	**$175.00**	**$175.00**	**$175.00**
Over/Under	**$385.00**	**$785.00**	**$1135.00**
Retirement	$0.00	$392.50	$567.50

Chart Your Data

Once you've got the data in your spreadsheet arranged, calculated, and accounted for, you may find the best way to communicate the data is to create a chart. Charts go a long way toward making numbers in rows and columns much more bearable—plus, it's possible to see the relationships between data more clearly when you're looking at a chart. Here are a few suggestions about charts:

- *Make sure your data is chart-able.* You should have data sets in your spreadsheet that have an obvious relationship that makes a comparison worthwhile. Sales figures among different regions, budget categories, and demographic numbers are all very chart-able. (If your rent doesn't change month to month, it won't be very effective in a graph.)

- *Charts should convey one comparison.* If I take all of my expenses and chart them over six months, the graph will be unreadable. Instead, I should either chart *one* expense over *multiple* months or *multiple* expenses in *one* month, but not both. (In some cases, you might convey two related comparisons, such as total expense and total revenue over six months.)

- *Don't include totals.* If you graph all of your expenses in one month—including the *total* of all those expenses, you'll throw your graph way off. Make sure you're not accidentally including totals when you're comparing data.

- *Totals (by themselves!) look great in graphs.* If you graph *only* totals, that's another story. In a budget, for instance, you might graph total monthly income over six months. That'll make a great graph—especially if income has been going up.

Create the Chart

Creating a chart is more about choosing the right data than it is about using odd commands. In fact, you may need to replicate your data in another part of the spreadsheet before you can chart it. When necessary, you can always re-create a part of your chart somewhere else on the sheet. You can simply have formulas that point to another cell, like =B20, to allow you to copy a new table of values to a part of your document that you can chart more easily:

		Annual Budget (SS)						
A30								
	A	**B**	**C**	**D**	**E**	**F**	**G**	**H**
28								
29	TOTALS SECTION							
30		January	February	March	April	May	June	July
31	Total Income	$3225.00	$3225.00	$3575.00	$3225.00	$3225.00	$3575.00	$3225.00
32	Total Expenses	$2840.00	$2440.00	$2440.00	$2890.00	$2415.00	$2415.00	$2880.00
33								
34								
35								
100								

Here's how to create your chart:

1. Choose a range of data you want to chart.

2. Select Options | Make Chart. The Chart Options dialog box appears:

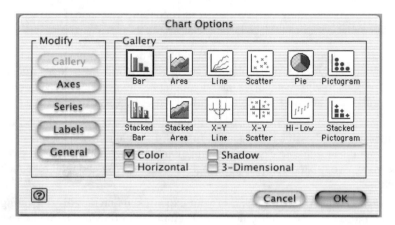

3. In the Gallery, choose the type of chart you want to use. Use the check boxes at the bottom of the window to add options.

4. Click the Axes button. Here's where you label each axis of the chart. Choose the X-Axis radio button, enter a label in the Axis Label entry box, then make other choices for how you want the axis to appear in the final chart. (If you don't customize the tick marks, min/max values, and step values, they'll be done automatically.) Choose the Y-Axis value and make the same choices.

5. Click the Series button. Most of this you won't need to worry about. You can, however, click the Label Data check box, then place the label, if you'd like each individual part of the chart (each column, pie piece, and so on) to include a label that gives the exact data amount it represents.

6. Click the Labels button. Here you can decide if you're going to have a title (click the Title check box) and what that title will be. You can also decide if you'll have a legend (check or uncheck the Legend check box) and how it will be arranged.

7. Click the General button. Now you get to choose the series that is listed in the legend. You can change this by clicking the Rows or Columns radio button. This is significant—the series you choose is what each colored bar or area will represent. (If your chart comes out backward from what you expected, create another one and change the series you graph.)

8. Click OK. A chart appears in the document window (see Figure 9-6).

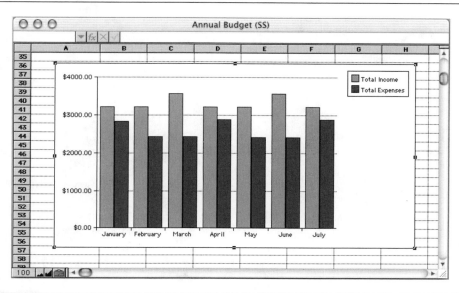

FIGURE 9-6 The final chart—looks pretty spiffy.

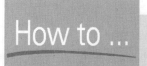

Make the Chart Look Great

Need to move the chart around? It's a graphical object—it's not in a cell or attached to the spreadsheet. If you like, just click somewhere in the chart and hold down the mouse button, then drag the mouse to move the chart to another part of the spreadsheet document window. In fact, you can even move it into a different AppleWorks document if you'd like, to add it to a slide show or word processing document, for instance.

Want to make it prettier? You can double-click the chart to revisit the Chart Options; make changes and click OK to update the chart instantly. You can use the Show Tools command in the Window menu to view the drawing tools, which allow you to change the way the chart looks with new colors, backgrounds, text, and other elements. We'll talk more about using the drawing tools in Chapter 11.

Chapter 10

File Information and Ideas with Databases

How to...

■ Learn about databases

■ Create the fields for your database

■ Enter data in Browse mode

■ Sort the database

■ Create a new layout

■ Build a quick report

The database module in AppleWorks is probably the most misunderstood of the components. So many people instantly associate the idea of a database with, well, computer programming or something. It seems like too much work to create a database, too much effort to be *that* organized.

But the fact is, the database module in AppleWorks is very easy to work with—and there are a lot of things you can track in a database. The basic rule is this: If you have something you need to store, sort, or search through, then it's probably a good idea to consider creating a database.

What's a Database?

A database is a document that stores many different *records,* each of which is composed of several *fields* in which data is stored. Databases and spreadsheets have a lot in common—in fact, you can view databases in rows and columns just like you can spreadsheets (see the following illustration). But databases are really designed to do something quite different from spreadsheets—they're designed to track data and help you create reports based on that data.

Client Name	Address	City	State	Zip	Phone	Fax	Email
Rachel Wise	1234 Main	New York	NY	10009	212-555-	212-555-	rachel@wis
Wes Wills	463 E 94th	New York	NY	10023	212-555-	212-555-	wes@hotm
Roger Smith	345 W 12th	New York	NY	10012	212-555-	212-555-	roger@mail.
Mike Richards	425 E 59th	New York	NY	10023	646-555-	646-555-	mike@phot
Anthony Tikes	345 Marble	Greatneck	NY	12340	646-555-	646-555-	anthony@gr

The best metaphor for a computer database is probably a card catalog at the local library. Each record is a card; each field is a line item on one of those cards. The author's name is a field, the title of the book is a field, even whether or not someone currently has the book on loan is a field. As you know, electronic databases of books are popular these days in libraries. A well-made library database offers many advantages, including reports on loaned books, searches based on author's names, searches based on titles, and so on.

How Databases Work

You'll begin by creating a database file and defining the fields that will be used by the database to create each record. Once the fields are defined, you're ready to create your first record. It's shown to you using a default *layout*—the data entry screen. If desired, you can edit this layout, or you can create other layouts for your database.

Different layouts can be composed of different fields, if you like, allowing you to look at the same record in different ways. Or you can use alternate layouts for different methods of data entry and/or searching.

Layouts also allow you to create different reports based on the data. For instance, you could create a layout that shows all of the books in your classroom that haven't been returned (and who checked them out) or all of the invoices in your small business that are 30 days past due. Layouts can be very complex, if desired, since you're offered most of the same drawing and formatting tools you'll find in AppleWorks' drawing module (see Chapter 11 to learn about the drawing tools).

And a big part of using a database is generating useful reports. The fact that layouts support the drawing tools also means you can create reports that will look good (and be useful) when printed.

Create Your Database

Creating your database is really pretty simple. In AppleWorks, choose File | New, then choose to create a Database document and click OK in the New dialog box. (From the Starting Points window, click the Database icon.) Things get complicated in a hurry, however. Immediately, you're confronted with the need to create fields for your database. And in order to do that, you'll need to think a little about your database.

Plan Your Database

With AppleWorks you'll begin by creating a new database file into which you will eventually store records. After you've launched the new document, you're asked to create fields for that database—each record will be composed of these fields. It's important to know ahead of time what sort of data you'll be tracking, since you need to define your fields before you can begin to use the database.

The key to planning your database is getting a good feel for what information you'd like to store in each record. Begin with what will be unique about each record—if you had to give each record a title, what would it be? Would it be a customer, student, or contact ID number? Would it be an invoice number? Would it be a recipe name, a CD title, the name of the photographer, or a room in your house? Once you know why each record will be unique, you may have a better idea of what you'll want to store in that record and what fields will be necessary.

For instance, I might have a database that stores information about my students in a particular class I teach. Before the semester begins, I'll want to seriously consider all of the information about each student that needs to be recorded over the next four or five months. I'll want names, addresses, phone numbers, and other contact information. I also know I'll be giving five major tests and twenty graded homework assignments. I'll need to have fields available to record all of that information, too.

But what about teacher conferences? Should I include parental contact information and a check box to show that each of the three conferences has been completed? How about a special section for storing notes so I can remember what to discuss with the parents?

Field Types

AppleWorks offers a number of different types of fields you can define for your database. Some are general in purpose—text fields are designed to hold pretty much any combination of text and number characters like addresses or zip codes; number fields are designed to hold numbers you plan to use in calculations. Other fields hold more specific types of formatted numbers, such as dates and times.

Still others do very specific, techie kinds of things like offer you a pull-down menu of options or allow you to click a radio button or check box. Table 10-1 shows you all the different fields.

By the way, the fact that there are a lot of field types doesn't mean that database building is hard. It can be a little intimidating, but usually only in the beginning. Once you have the correct fields set up, you'll definitely like having the database available when you need to find, search, or sort something important.

Most of the fields you create will be text fields—they're the catchall for personal and small business databases. You're more likely to use menus, radio buttons, and check boxes—fields called *controls*—if you're designing a database for someone else to do the data entry. (Controls are a good way of limiting typos by offering multiple choices.) You'll also likely use name and date fields in most any database you create, especially for business, organizational, or social databases.

Other fields that are very interesting are serial fields (where numbers are incremented automatically, which is important for invoices and inventory), calculation fields, and record info fields. All of these can be used to automate your database in a way that can make it much more valuable to use. Later in the chapter, you'll see how calculations can be used to automate important database functions.

Type of Field	What It Can Contain	Examples
Text	Any combination of letters, numbers, and symbols up to 1,000 characters	Courtesy titles, personal titles, addresses, notes, phone numbers, product names, product numbers, customer ID codes, zip codes, social security numbers
Number	A negative or positive integer or decimal up to 255 characters	Dollar amounts, student grade percentages, number of children, quantity of purchased items
Date	Date, month, and year (offers different formats)	Current date, shipping date, date order received, date of birth, wedding date, party date
Time	Hours, minutes, and seconds (in 12- or 24-hour formats)	Current time, time of order, time shipped, time of birth
Name	Full, proper names	People's names, company names, organization names
Pop-up menu	A menu of values; use anytime you want a limited response from many options	Compass direction, city names, U.S. states, demographic groups
Radio buttons	Multiple choice; similar to a pop-up menu but designed for fewer choices	People's titles (Mr., Ms.), name suffixes (Jr., III), computing platform (Mac, Windows, Unix), housing payments (rent, own), marital status (single, divorced, married, widowed)
Check box	Yes or no answer	U.S. citizen? Self-employed? Product shipped? Checked zip code? Turned in form? Talked to parents?
Serial number	AppleWorks assigns a new, ordered number for each record; good for giving each record a unique value	Customer ID, product ID, invoice ID
Value list	Choose from a list of values or enter your own	Local restaurants, election candidates, favorite computer games, magazines subscribed to
Multimedia	An image or movie file	Photo of employee, photo of household item, movie walkthrough of property for sale
Record info	Time, date, or name of person who created/modified data	Record creation date, date/time modified, name of entry clerk
Calculation	Result from a formula using other fields	Total of invoice, sales tax, final student grade, days since shipped
Summary	Calculation from fields in this and other records	Total receivables, total of unshipped items, class average, number of items due

TABLE 10-1 Database Fields

10

Add Your Fields

Once you know the field types, you can add them to your database. The process for that is simple. If you've already chosen File | New | Database to create a new database document, you're presented with the Define Database Fields dialog box.

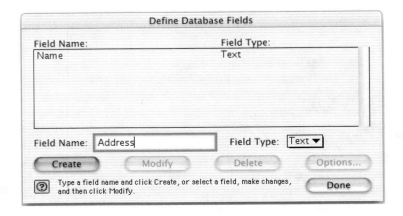

Here's the process for creating a new field:

1. In the Field Name entry box, enter a unique name for your field. It should be reasonably short and avoid additional non-text characters, especially if you think you might one day export this database to another database program.

2. In the Field Type menu, choose the type of field you want to create.

3. Click the Create button to create the field.

4. If desired, click the Options button to make specific choices about the field's behavior. The Options dialog box allows you to make basic choices about your field, such as setting default values, a range of accepted values, and so on.

5. Done with all your fields? When you're ready to create your first record, click OK in the Define Database Fields dialog box. (Don't worry, you can still add fields later if necessary.) The dialog box disappears and you're presented with the entry screen for your database. Enjoy!

NOTE   *You can always add fields to your database later by selecting Layout | Define Fields to pop up the Define Database Fields dialog box and add fields. Note that when you add fields after you've created some records, you'll have a new blank field on each existing record (in Browse mode) that you may want to go back and fill in. Also, you may need to add the field to any custom layouts that you've created.*

Control Fields

Certain control fields—menus, radio buttons, value lists, and record info fields—will require additional information from you before the field can be added to the database. If the field contains radio buttons, a value list, or a menu, you'll need to enter values for those lists. A dialog box will appear right after you click the Create or Modify button in the Define Database Fields dialog box.

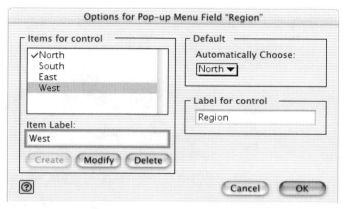

Here's what you can do in this dialog box:

- To enter a value, type a name in the Item Label entry box and click the Create button (or press RETURN).

- To create another value, type a different name and click the Create button.

- To modify an existing value, highlight the value in the Items For Control list, then type a new name for it and click the Modify button.

- To choose the default value for the control, pull down the menu in the Default section of the dialog box and choose the default value. This is the value that the control will be set to until the user changes it. (With some field types, such as a value list, you'll need to type the default value instead of choosing it from a list.)

Click OK when you're done creating the control. If you've chosen to create a record info field, you'll see a different dialog box.

This one is more straightforward—just click the corresponding radio button to create the field you want in your database.

Calculation Fields

Here's another instance where you won't get away with a quick swipe of the Create or Modify button. A *calculation* field is one that requires you to enter a formula, somewhat akin to a formula in a spreadsheet.

If you're creating a calculation field, you'll be asked to create the calculation before the field is complete. To do that, you'll work with the Enter Formula dialog box, which appears when you first create a calculation field.

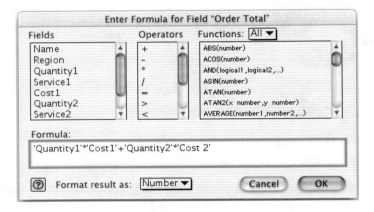

If you read Chapter 9 closely, you might notice something familiar here in the Enter Formula dialog box—the functions. In fact, most of them are exactly the same as those functions found in the spreadsheet module, although some are more limited in the database module. Still, you'll find that many of the same calculations are possible. (Refer to Chapter 9 to learn about some of the special ones.)

In database formulas, you'll find that field names are your variables—they replace the cell names in a spreadsheet when you create mathematical formulas or build functions. Most of the time you'll want to use number fields in your calculations, although you can use the built-in text functions to work with text fields, if necessary, and the date and time functions to deal with date, time, or record info fields.

There are a couple of different ways to create a formula:

- To create a basic formula, you can click a field name, click an operator, and then click another field name. (Perfect for adding together the cost of each item in an invoice, for instance.)

- If you want to use a function, you'll usually choose the function first, then choose the field name(s) it should operate on.

- Just type it—if you already know the exact field names, operators, and/or functions you want to use.

At the bottom of the Enter Formula dialog box, choose how the result should be formatted from the Format Result As menu. (Remember, when you're entering data, this field will show the *result* of the calculation in each record, not the calculation. So, you've got to decide what sort of value that's going to be, just as with other fields.)

Then, click OK to save your formula. If AppleWorks thinks you've formatted things correctly, the dialog box goes away and the field appears in your field list. If not, you'll see an alert box telling you something is wrong. Fix the problem and click OK again.

> TIP
>
> *Since a calculation field stores the result according to the field type you specify in the Format Result As menu, you can use the field name as a variable in other calculations. For instance, you can have a calculation field called Total, then a calculation field called Sales Tax (which might be Total * .075), and a Final Total calculation field that calculates Total + Sales Tax. Just make sure all the results are formatted as numbers if you're going to be adding and multiplying them together.*

Enter and Find Records

Once you've defined your fields, you're ready to enter your first record. AppleWorks immediately drops you into Browse mode, the mode used to create records and move between them manually (see Figure 10-1). The mode is chosen from the Layout menu in the menu bar.

In Browse mode, you can click near a field name to begin entering data in that record. Press TAB to move to the next field after you've entered data; press SHIFT-TAB if you need to move back up to a previous field. Once you've entered all the data you need to enter, you can quickly

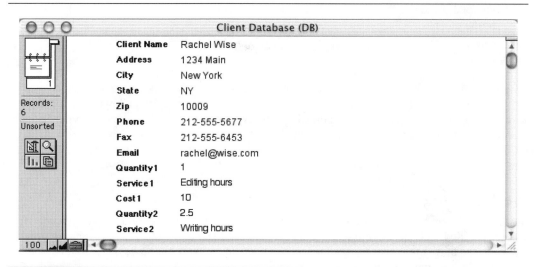

FIGURE 10-1   Browse mode is where you move through records and enter new data.

choose File | Save or press ⌘-S to Save, then choose Edit | New Record or press ⌘-R to begin entering a new record.

List View

If you prefer, you can also do your data entry in List view, which makes it a little easier to see more than one record at a time. If you have many fields, however, the window will need to scroll quite a bit. To switch to List view, choose Layout | List. (The List view was shown back in the section "What's a Database?")

> **TIP**   *You can drag the line that separates columns to make them wider or narrower, just as in the spreadsheet module.*

Find Records

If you only have a few records in your database, it won't be that tough to click around in Browse mode and find a particular one. But if you have quite a few records, or you're interested in looking at only certain ones, then you need to instigate a Find.

It's actually really easy to find records. Just follow these steps:

1. Choose Layout | Find.

2. You'll see a blank version of the Browse screen. Enter data in one or more of the fields that you'd like to match with your Find.

3. Click the Find button in the left margin.

4. If any records are found, they'll be displayed. The found records are now a subset of the total database. You can scroll back and forth through the records and see only the found records.

5. Choose Organize | Show All Records when you're ready to deal with the entire database again.

By the way, it might be helpful to know that number fields in the Find layout (and calculated fields with number results) can accept basic comparisons. For instance, if you have a field that calculates a testing average, you can enter **<65** to see every record that has an average under 65. The same goes for a number field that's holding a dollar amount—use <, >, <>, <, >=, or = to see which records match up. And it's the same for dates and times. You can enter **<10/10/02** in a date field to find records with dates before October 10, 2002, for instance.

Save Your Search

Want to create a Find that lasts for a while? You can do it with the Search button that appears on the Tools palette in the left margin of the database window. The Search button is the magnifying glass; click the button to see its menu. Choose New Search and you can name the search before you enter criteria in the Find layout view.

Now, when you want to perform that search again, it appears right there on the Search button menu. Just click the button to see all your named searches.

Print Records

If you choose Print while viewing records in your database, the Print command automatically defaults to printing *all* visible records. (This doesn't mean the records you can see with your eye—it means records that are visible within the database after a Find command has been done. If you want to print records numbered 1-5, for instance, perform a Find to find records with record numbers less than 6.)

If you just want to print one record, you'll do that from the Print dialog box. Locate the untitled pull-down menu in the Print dialog box that defaults to General or Copies & Pages; select it and choose AppleWorks. Now you'll see the Print Current Record option.

Give It a New Layout

Whenever you create a new database, AppleWorks designs a very basic layout, called Layout 1, which offers only the rudiments of design. Fortunately, you can do something about that by editing the layout.

Layouts are used for more than just the data entry screen—they're also used for creating and printing reports. As you'll see, a report is simply a sorted, searched database that uses a particular layout to make it look good. A layout doesn't even have to include every field in your database, so you'll often create different layouts to correspond to different reports you want to build (see Figure 10-2).

10

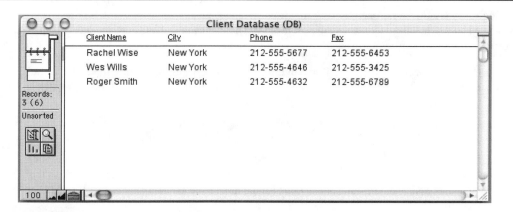

Client Name	City	Phone	Fax
Rachel Wise	New York	212-555-5677	212-555-6453
Wes Wills	New York	212-555-4646	212-555-3425
Roger Smith	New York	212-555-4632	212-555-6789

Client Database (DB)

Records: 3 (6)
Unsorted

100

FIGURE 10-2   Here's a report layout I've created specifically to show me basic contact information. Notice that it uses very few of the fields in my inventory database.

Because a database can have more than one layout, you might decide it's best to have different layouts for data entry and reports. It's up to you, but even if you don't, you can jazz up your layout so that it looks good for both a report and data entry.

Choose a Layout or Start a New One

To begin, you should figure out which layout you're currently using. Click the Layout menu to open it and look toward the bottom. The current layout is the entry with a check mark next to its name. If you want to use a different layout (assuming you have others), choose it in the Layout menu. If you want to create a new layout, choose Layout | New Layout.

If you choose to create a new layout, you'll see the New Layout dialog box. Give the layout a meaningful name, then choose whether you want the standard layout (like Layout 1), a duplicate of an existing layout, or a blank layout. You can also choose a Columnar Report, which helps you build a simple report layout that will place information about each record on its own line, as was shown in Figure 10-2.

 *The New Layout dialog box also has a Labels option, which you can use to create a layout suitable for printing to a variety of different Avery-compatible label sheets for inkjet or laser printers. Select Labels, then choose the corresponding Avery code from the pop-up menu.*

Edit the Layout

The fun is just beginning, because you can edit as you please. You edit in Layout mode. To get into Layout mode, pull down the Layout menu and choose the layout to edit. Now, go back to the Layout menu and choose the Layout command.

What can you do? You can move your text and fields around, you can draw boxes around parts of your layout, or you can add graphics and text. For the most part, the drawing and painting tools are the same ones used in the drawing and painting modules, so I'll point you to Chapter 11 to learn things like drawing and moving shapes around. But there are a few things specific to the database layout process you should know:

- Don't forget the SHIFT key. You can click a database field, then click the field's label while holding down SHIFT. Now you can click and drag one field and the other will follow along.

- You can also use the SHIFT key to select all of the field labels at once, then you can use the Format menu to change the font, size, style, or color of the field labels.

- If you want to add something that appears at the top of every record, choose Layout | Insert Part, then choose to add a Header. You can drag the Header line around on the layout to resize it, then add the text or image above the Header line and it'll appear at the top of every page in your layout.

■ If you want more than one record on a page, you'll need to edit the layout so that more than one will fit, then drag the Body line up under the abbreviated layout. If you only have a few fields and want each record to appear on one page, do the opposite and drag the Body line down to the bottom of the page.

■ To change the appearance of a field, you can select it (or more than one field) and use the text formatting options in the Format menu. For both text and number fields, you can also double-click the field to quickly format it. (This includes things like formatting for currency and setting the precision of decimals.)

■ Switch to Browse mode to test things (assuming you have more than a few records in your database). That'll give you a good idea how things look. You can switch back to Layout mode to keep editing.

After a while you'll have a nice, edited layout designed for data entry or for a report, depending on your needs. Figure 10-3 shows the report in Layout mode; Figure 10-4 shows that same report in Browse mode.

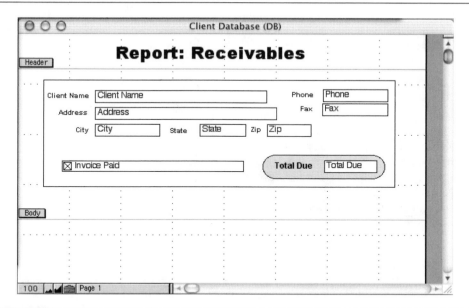

FIGURE 10-3   A new layout, still in Layout mode

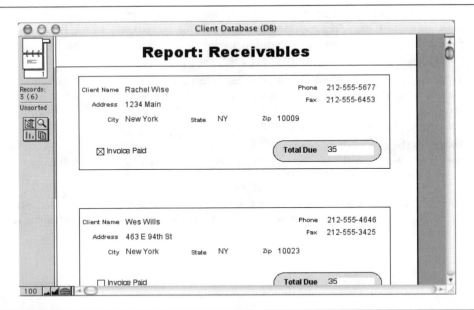

FIGURE 10-4 Here's how the new layout looks in Browse mode.

Sort and Report

The slash-and-burn report works like this—create the layout that you want to use for the report. Perform a Find and create a subset of matching records you want to report on. Switch to the report layout in the Layout menu, then change to Browse mode. If the report looks good, print it.

You can even get more sophisticated. If you're going to be creating the same report over and over again, you can go ahead and save the whole thing—the search, the sort, and so on. You might also want to perform a quick sort before you run the report—that way you can find whose grades in the database are below 65, for example, and you can organize the report alphabetically or based on some other criteria.

Sort

Once you get a number of records in your layout you may find, for many different reasons, that it's useful to have them sorted. This isn't always a priority while you're entering data, but it can be very important when you're ready to generate a report.

Here's how to sort:

1. To begin a sort, choose Organize | Sort Records.

2. In the Sort dialog box, select the Field name you want to sort, then click the Move button.

3. Click the Ascending or Descending button in the bottom-right corner of the dialog box.

4. Next, choose the secondary field you want to sort on. This is the "sort-within-the-sort" field. If your first-level sort is on the State field, for instance, and you have more than one record within a given state, then the records could be secondarily sorted based on, say, the Phone Number field.

5. Continue until you have enough sort fields, then click OK. Your database is now sorted.

So, things are sorted. If you add records and want to sort them again, just choose Organize | Sort Records again. The criteria should still be there in the dialog box and you can just click OK again.

Save a Sort

Want to save a sort for posterity? You might find reason to work with more than one sort. If that's the case, you'll need to head down to the Sort button on the Tools palette in the left margin of the database window. Select the Sort button (it's the one with the three bars) and choose New Sort.

You'll get the same dialog box as with a regular Sort, except there's an entry box at the bottom to name the sort. Do so, then set up the sort criteria. Click OK and the sort is created. Now you can return to the Sort button to perform the sort or edit it. Any new sorts you create show up on the Sort button's menu.

Build a Report

I'm not trying to rhyme the titles of these last two sections, I promise. It's appropriate, though, because the processes are so similar. If you're ready, it's time to head to the Report button and create a new report. The Report button is the one with an image of two sheets of paper on it.

Pull down the Report button menu and choose New Report. The New Report dialog box appears. Here's the crazy part—all you do is give the report a name, then choose a saved Layout, a saved Search, and a saved Sort from the menus in the New Report dialog box. If you want the report automatically printed when you choose the item in the Report button menu, then check the Print The Report check box.

That's all it takes—you've just built and saved a report. Pretty easy, huh?

Chapter 11

Paint and Draw

How to...

- Decide whether to create a painting or a drawing
- Create a painting
- Add text to your painting
- Save the painting
- Create a drawing
- Add AppleWorks elements (charts, paintings, text) to your drawing

People seem to love to play with the Painting and Drawing modules in AppleWorks, which allow you to create some of the great graphics that Macs are known for. If you're quite the artist, especially with a computer mouse, then you'll want to head directly for the Painting module, which puts both your free-form and shape-driven ideas on a virtual canvas.

If you're a little less abstract in your thinking, you'll prefer the drawing tools, which can be used to create diagrams, drawings, signs, labels, and even desktop layouts with precision. Drawing documents are about creating straight lines, curves, boxes, circles, and shapes, and adding text when necessary.

The drawing and painting tools overlap somewhat, enabling you to create shapes, lines, colors, text, and objects from other AppleWorks modules. As you'll see in Chapters 12 and 13, these tools make it possible to extend AppleWorks into other realms, too—layouts and presentations, for instance. For now, though, it's all about getting something on your virtual canvas.

Start Your Painting

To create a new Painting document in AppleWorks, select File | New, then choose to start a Painting document. (If you're already viewing the Starting Points window, simply click the Painting icon on the Basic tab.) Your untouched document "canvas" appears onscreen along with the tools you'll need to get started. If you'd like to immediately save, choose File | Save As to give this document a name and find a folder to store it in.

Set the Document Size

Depending on your reason for creating this painting, the first thing you might want to do is create a document that's a certain size. If, for example, you're building an image for use in a newsletter page or a page on the World Wide Web, you may want to create a painting that's less than the standard document size. You can then place it in the larger document, wrap text around it, and create an interesting layout.

NOTE *Layouts are covered in more detail in Chapter 12.*

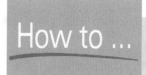 **Decide on Painting vs. Drawing**

You may be wondering why AppleWorks offers two different modules—Drawing and Painting—for what seem to be very related tasks. The answer is simple: *objects*. The drawing tools in AppleWorks allow you to create objects—shapes, lines, text—that can be moved around, grouped together, and placed relative to one another on the Drawing document. This is different from the Painting module, which treats the document window more like an actual artist's canvas. Once you put a shape, line, brushstroke, or text on the canvas, that's it—it can't be moved again as an individual shape.

You *can* cut and paste portions of a Painting document, and you can erase parts, too, but you can't pick up an individual shape or text object and drag it around—you can only cut, copy, paste, or erase sections of the canvas. The difference is a little like watercolor painting versus collage art. In a collage, you can lay down elements on your canvas, and then pick them up and move them around. In watercolor painting, once you paint something on the canvas, you have to either wipe it off (if you can) or paint over it to change it. But once you've blended colors and shapes together, you can't move them again.

Of course, the AppleWorks painting tools offer a little more freedom than that. After all, you can select square chunks of your Painting document and drag them around. And the Magic Wand tool can be used to grab shapes from within the painting and drag them around. But, if you want to create boxes and lines that can be moved around and organized on the page, you're better off using the Drawing module.

11

Choose Format | Document and you can determine exactly how many pixels wide and high you want your document. In the Document dialog box, use the entry boxes under Size to determine the width and height of your painting in *pixels*. (Pixels are *picture elements* or individual dots on the screen.) When you close the Document dialog box, your canvas will change to reflect your sizing.

This is another distinction between the Painting and Drawing modules—the painting tools can be used for editing individual pixels if you zoom in close enough. The drawing tools can't be used on individual pixels.

Use the Tools

With document size set, you're ready to begin work with the painting tools. There are quite a few of them, but they fall into basically three different categories: shapes, pickers, and brushes. Before you can see any of them, though, you may need to make sure that Window | Show Tools has been chosen. (If you see Hide Tools when you choose the Window menu, that means that the tools are currently being shown. See 'em?)

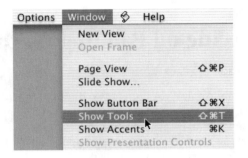

Shape Tools

If you want to create a shape, simply select a Shape tool by clicking it in the Tools palette. Then, move the mouse pointer to the window and choose a starting place for your shape. Now, click and hold the mouse button, and then drag out to create the shape. When you release the mouse button, the shape is committed to the document canvas.

> TIP *Double-click the Rounded Rectangle, Curve, or Triangle tools' icons to change some options that govern how the shapes look.*

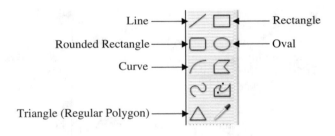

Six of the shape tools—Line, Rectangle, Rounded Rectangle, Oval, Curve, and Triangle (Regular Polygon)—all work in the same way: Just select the tools, then drag to place that shape in your painting. Be aware that many of the tools have options that you can see by double-clicking the tool. For instance, the Triangle tool can be used to create other-sided polygons by double-clicking the tool in the Tools palette and entering a number in the dialog box that appears.

The other three shape tools work a little differently. Each requires a little extra input before you can draw the shapes. Here's how to use each of them:

■ **Freehand Tool** Select this tool, then click and hold down the mouse button in the document window. Drag around the screen to create a curvy shape. When you release the mouse button, a line is drawn straight back to the starting point and the shape is filled in. (If you're trying to create a particular shape, draw it so that you end up as close to the starting point as possible.)

■ **Bezigon Tool**   Choose the tool, click the mouse button in the document window, and then move to the next place you want to create a point. Click the mouse button to create the point. To close the shape, double-click the mouse on your last point or click very close to the original point.

 ■ **Polygon Tool**   Choose this tool, and then click once in the document to begin your polygon. Move the mouse to the next point in the shape and click again. Continue to click for each point on the shape until the next to last one—you can double-click that point to automatically draw a line back to the original point. (The lines of your polygon can be curved, if you like—just hold down the option key while you move the mouse.)

Selection Tools

The next set of tools are the Selection tools, which allow you to select different parts of your painting in order to copy, paste, clear, or drag the part to some other section of the canvas. Here's how they work:

 ■ **Eyedropper**   This tool does one thing—it picks up the color that you're pointing to when you click the mouse button. Choose the Eyedropper, point at a particular color, and click the mouse button. That color then becomes the Fill color (you'll see the Fill color change in the colors section of the toolbar as well as in the Accents window, which is discussed later in the section "Color Tools.")

 ■ **Rectangular Selection Tool**   This tool is designed to select a rectangular section of the document. Choose the tool, and then click and hold the mouse button in the top-left corner of the part of the document you want to select. Now, drag down toward the bottom-right corner of the portion you want to select. Let go of the mouse button and it's highlighted. (Double-clicking the tool icon selects the entire window.)

 ■ **Lasso**   The Lasso allows you to be a little more cavalier in your selection. Select the Lasso's icon, and then click and hold the mouse button in the document window while you draw, freehand, the shape you want to select. Release the mouse button and your selection is highlighted.

 ■ **Magic Wand Tool**   With this tool, you won't need to drag and release—the Magic Wand is designed to "magically" select shapes in the document window. Select the tool, and then head over to a shape and click it. All or part of the shape will be highlighted. If you don't get what you want, try clicking a different part of the shape. (You can also hold down the SHIFT key while selecting in order to select more of a shape or more shapes.)

What do you do once something is selected? Hit the DELETE key and everything in the selection area will disappear. Or pull down the Edit menu and choose any of those commands—Cut, Copy, Paste, Duplicate—to perform such functions on the selection.

11

Brushes

With each of the Brush tools, you hold down the mouse button and move around on the document window when you want to draw or paint. When you don't want to draw or paint, release the mouse button. Brushes come in different shapes and purposes:

 ■ **Paint Brush**   Use this tool to paint brushstrokes of color onto your document. You can change the shape and size of the brush by double-clicking the Paint Brush icon. Select a new size and/or shape and click OK. Also, notice the Effects menu, which allows you to change the way the Paint Brush works, offering more sophisticated special effects like blending and tinting.

 ■ **Pencil**   Use this tool to draw thin lines or to fill in a drawing at the pixel level. The Pencil can be used at high magnification to fill in individual pixels with color. Double-click the Pencil to switch instantly to 800 percent magnification.

 ■ **Paint Can**   This is the fill tool—choose the Paint Can and click in your document and any shape or form is filled in with color. You can draw a closed shape, and then fill it with this tool, or click outside of a closed shape to fill the entire screen with color.

 ■ **Spray Can**   The Spray Can creates a spray-painting effect, making it look as if some paint is scattered on your electronic canvas. The more you spray on one particular area, the thicker the coverage of paint in that area. Double-click the Spray Can to change the size of the dots and the amount of coverage the Spray Can shows. You can also test the settings in the testing area in this window.

 ■ **Eraser**   The last brush tool is actually an "anti-brush" of sorts—the Eraser. It erases all layers of shapes and color on your document, taking it back to the original white background.

Options for most of these brushes can be found in the Options menu, where you'll also find options to change the Paint Mode from the standard Opaque to Transparent Pattern, and Tint, which mixes your paint color with any colors you paint over.

Color Tools

Want to change the colors? To see the color tools, you'll need to select Window | Show Accents if the Accents window isn't already on your screen. Now you'll see the Accents window, shown in Figure 11-1. This is a powerful little window that's chock full of controls, which I'll try to cover here quickly. In essence, you're able to select the characteristics for three different tools: the Fill color, the Pen color, and the Text color.

 The Accents window's color tools are duplicated at the bottom of the toolbar in AppleWorks 6.1 and above. The color tools on the toolbar are a bit confusing at first blush, but once you get used to the options presented in the Accents window, you can quickly make most of those same choices on the toolbar without opening the Accents window.

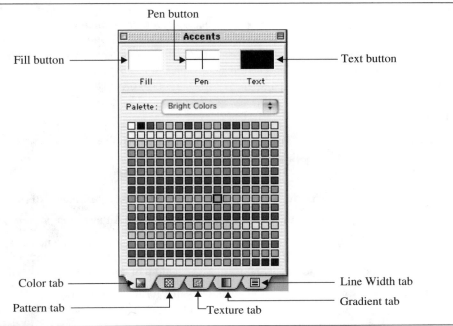

Pen button

Fill button ——————→

Text button ←——————

Color tab ——————

Line Width tab

Pattern tab ——————

Gradient tab

Texture tab

FIGURE 11-1   The Accents palette window is where you'll find all your color and line controls.

11

Here's how the Accents palette works in a nutshell. Select the tool—Fill, Pen, or Text—that you need to alter. Then, click the tab that corresponds to the characteristics you want to alter. For instance, if you'd like to change the Fill color—the color that fills a particular shape, for instance—click the Fill button at the top of the Accents palette, and then click the Color tab at the bottom. Now you'll see a window full of color options. Click one of the colors to make it the Fill color. (Note also that you can select options in the Palette menu to change the colors that are shown in the window.) You can change the Pen (for the outline of shapes and lines) or Text color in the same way: click the Pen or Text button at the top, click a tab at the bottom, and then make your selection. If you want the Pen tool to have a pattern, for instance, you can select the Pen button at the top of the window, click the Pattern tab, and then select a pattern.

You'll get used to the Accents palette window after some practice. Be aware that not every tool is active when you click a particular tab—for instance, the gradients and patterns only work with the Fill tool, not Pen or Text. The Line Width options only work with the Pen tool, not with the others. (Inactive tools are "grayed out" and can't be clicked.) Once you've selected your color, pattern, width, or other options, return to the drawing and enjoy the new settings!

TIP *Want my limited artistic tips? When painting an object or landscape, remember your light source. Figure out where the light is coming from, then use darker versions of your colors on the farther side and use lighter versions of your colors on the side closer to the light. Also, a nicely placed shadow goes a long way toward making a painting look more realistic, if that's your goal. You can use the Tint and Transparency options (Options | Paint Mode) to create distance and perspective effects, too.*

Add Text

Here's the last thing I'll show you in the Painting module—you're going to have to figure out the artistic part yourself. Adding text to a Painting document actually involves switching to the Word processing tools and creating a text *frame*. Here's how:

1. At the top of the Tools palette, choose the Word Processing frame tool (the letter "A").

2. Click in the document where you want the text to be. An insertion point appears.

3. Head up to the menu bar and format the text (using the cleverly named Text menu) just as you would text in the Word Processing module. You may also want to use the text color tools in the Accents window or at the bottom of the toolbar to change the text color.

4. Type the text you want. If you need to change formatting, quickly type ⌘-A to invoke the Select All command, and then format the text using the Text menu.

When you're done entering and editing the text, click the Pointer tool just above the shape tools on the toolbar to switch back from the word processing tools to the painting tools. Once you've placed the text, it's there for good. It can't be moved (unless you also move the background behind the text using the selection tool) or edited. It has become part of the painting, like a brush stroke or a shape. (Sometimes, but not always, you can manage to select text with the Magic Wand, especially if you zoom in close. Zooming is discussed in Chapter 12.)

TIP *Fonts in Paint documents don't always print as well as fonts in Draw documents. If you want smooth printed fonts, you should select your Paint image, choose Edit | Copy, and then use Edit | Paste to add the image to a Draw document. Now, create your text with the Draw tools (discussed later in this chapter) and print from there for best results.*

Save Your Image

You know that File | Save allows you to save your Paint image in AppleWorks document format. But if you'd like to use the Paint image in other programs—to use the image in an iMovie or add it to a professional layout or World Wide Web page, for instance—you'll need to save it as a more common file format. To do so, you can choose File | Save As. In the dialog box, give the file a name, and then choose the file type from the File Format pop-up menu. There you'll find options such as JPEG, PICT, TIFF, and other common image formats. (If you're not sure which to use, choose PICT for working with other Macintosh programs and JPEG if you plan to use the image on the Web or as an e-mail attachment.)

If you plan to use the document in an earlier version of AppleWorks, called ClarisWorks, or in ClarisWorks for Kids, select one of those options. Once you've chosen how to save it, click OK to save the file.

NOTE   *Need to know more about image file types? They're discussed in Chapter 14.*

Draw Objects and Text

The drawing tools can be used much the same way the painting tools are used—for fun, for artistic creation, or for logos and images you'll use elsewhere. The Drawing module can be used for more business-like reasons than the Painting module. As I've said, the drawing tools are a good way to present information graphically. Using these tools, you'll be able to create signs, posters, certificates, and more. In Chapter 12, we'll take a close look at some of the different ways you can use the Drawing module for layout tasks, such as creating interesting printed materials.

Draw in Databases and Spreadsheets

By the way, the drawing tools are also found elsewhere in the AppleWorks suite, including the Database module and the Spreadsheet module when you're dealing with charts. You'll notice that a lot of the object-manipulation commands (as well as some of the drawing tools) are found in those parts. If you're trying to create a database layout or improve the appearance of a chart, what you'll learn in this section on the drawing tools will help.

Create Objects

To begin, open a Drawing document by choosing File | New, and then select Drawing and click OK. (From the Starting Points window, simply click the Drawing icon on the Basics tab.) A new Drawing document appears.

You can place text, graphics, shapes, other multimedia objects, and even spreadsheet objects in your Drawing document. When you're in the Drawing module, everything is an object, meaning that everything you add to your Drawing document remains its own entity. You can pick objects up, move them around, and even stack objects on top of one another (see Figure 11-2).

There are three basic types of objects you'll create in the Drawing module: shapes, text, and objects from other modules. That includes spreadsheet objects, charts, painted images, scanned photos, QuickTime movies, and other multimedia objects you can bring in from other applications.

Shapes

The shapes you find in the Drawing module are a subset of those found in the Painting module, and they work pretty much the same. One important thing to remember is that most objects in the Drawing module can easily be reshaped or resized after they've been created, so your dimensions don't have to be as perfect as they do in the Painting module.

11

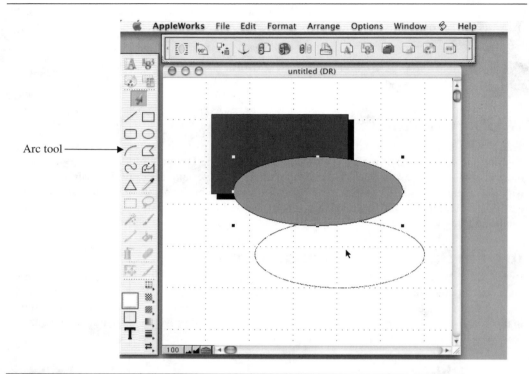

Arc tool

FIGURE 11-2   In the Drawing module, you create objects that can be moved around.

Here are the tools you can use to draw different shapes:

- **Line Tool**   Click the Line tool, and then click once in the document window. Move the mouse pointer and click again to create a line between the original point and the final location.

- **Rectangle Tool**   Choose the Rectangle tool, and then click and hold the mouse button in the document window. Drag the mouse to create your rectangle, and then release the mouse button when the rectangle is the size and shape you want it.

- **Rounded Rectangle Tool**   Choose this tool, and then click and drag in the document window to create the oval. Release the mouse button when you've got it the right size. To shape the corners of the rounded rectangle, make sure the tool is selected, and then choose Edit | Corner Info.

- **Oval Tool**   Select the Oval tool in the toolbar, and then click and drag to create the oval. Release the mouse button when it's the correct dimensions and circumference.

- **Freeform Tool**   Select the tool, and then click and drag in the document window. Drag out the shape you want to create, ending as close to the starting point as possible. In the Draw module, this shape isn't forced closed—it can just be a squiggly line, if you prefer.

- **Bezigon Tool**   Select this tool, and then click in the document to create the first point. Now, move the mouse and click to create additional points for the shape. End as near the first point as possible, and then double-click to complete the shape.

- **Triangle (Regular Polygon) Tool**   Select this tool, and then click and drag in the document window to create a triangle (by default). To change the number of sides, make sure the tool is selected, and then choose Edit | Polygon Sides. In the Number of Sides dialog box, you can enter as many sides as you'd like the polygon to have.

- **Polygon Tool**   Select the Polygon tool, and then click in the document window to place the first point. Move the mouse pointer and click to place a second point; repeat until all the points for the shape have been laid out, and then double-click to draw a line between the last point and the first point, closing the polygon.

- **Arc Tool**   Select the Arc tool (shown in Figure 11-2); then click and drag in the document window until the arc is the correct size. To change the arc's characteristics, make sure the Arc tool is selected, and then choose Edit | Arc Info.

TIP   *The SHIFT key can be used to constrain many of these tools. Hold down the SHIFT key while you draw a line (or draw the side of a shape) and the line will be perfectly straight. Hold it while using the Rectangle tool to draw a square. Hold it down while using the Oval tool to draw a circle. Hold it down while drawing an arc to keep the arc symmetrical.*

11

The Drawing module also includes an Eyedropper tool and the same Color tools (in the Accents palette) described in the Paint section. The Accent tools work slightly differently, though. To change colors and textures in a drawing, first select a shape that's already been created. Then choose a color, texture, or pattern from the Accents palette. Same with lines—even if they've already been created, just select them in the document window and choose a new color, pattern, or size, or add arrows. You can always change them back later, if desired.

TIP   *To change the Polygon tool's behavior, choose Edit | Preferences | General and make sure the Topic menu shows Graphics. Now, click to change the shape-closing behavior in the Polygon Closing section. With the Manual option, you need to click to place the last point pretty much right on top of the first point in a shape.*

Text

To create a text object, click the Text tool in the top of the Tools palette. It's the tool that looks like a capital "A"; it allows you to click and drag in the document window to create a text box.

This is similar to working with the painting tools. You've actually created a word processing *frame* within the Drawing document here—it's like you opened up a little window into the word processing module. Watch carefully and you'll notice that the button bar and menus change when you're editing inside the text box. The insertion point appears and you're ready to type.

TASTY CAKES

Type your text, then format it using the menus. When you're pleased with your text, click the Pointer tool in the Tools palette or click outside the text box to switch back to the drawing tools.

Unlike the painting tools, you can edit text that you create in the Drawing module. If you want to edit the text, just double-click it if the Pointer tool is selected, or select the Text tool and single-click the text. The text box appears, the menus change, and you're ready to edit the text.

Other Frames

We'll get into this topic in much more detail in Chapter 12, but I want to touch on it here. You can create spreadsheet and painting frame objects right here within the Drawing module. Just as you can create a text frame that switches around your menus and button bars, you can create spreadsheet and paint frames that let you use the tools from those modules.

To add frames from other modules, click one of the frame tools at the top of the toolbar—you'll see icons that represent word processing, spreadsheet data, painting, and a table frame. To add a spreadsheet frame, select the Spreadsheet icon (it looks like a small spreadsheet with numbers on it), and then click and drag in your document window to create the spreadsheet object. A table of cells appears and the insertion point is ready to edit. Now you can type away to add spreadsheet data in your Drawing document. You can enter anything you might enter in a typical AppleWorks spreadsheet.

You can even create a chart. Enter spreadsheet data that works for a chart, then choose Options | Make Chart. (If you don't see that option, double-click the spreadsheet to make sure it's selected for editing.) Now, create a chart as discussed in Chapter 9. When you click OK, the chart appears in your document. Best of all—it's an object, just like everything else (see Figure 11-3).

Creating a paint frame within your Drawing document is a similar process. Select the Painting icon (it looks like a painter's palette board); then drag out a paint object in the document window. You'll notice that the tools and menu commands change to those of the Painting module. Paint all you want inside the paint object; then click outside it when you're done.

Manipulate Objects

Once you've got your objects created, you're ready to arrange them. The key is to figure out how to select and drag them around—that part's pretty easy. With the Pointer tool selected in the toolbar, point to an object, and then click and hold down the mouse button while you drag the object around the screen. Drop the object when you're done moving it by releasing the mouse button.

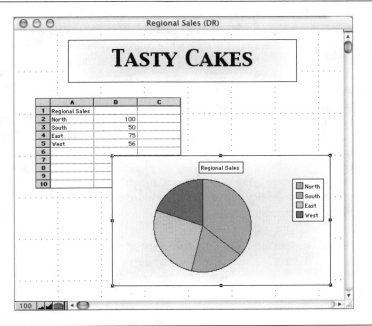

FIGURE 11-3   A chart from spreadsheet data can easily be added to your Drawing document.

Don't forget Undo! Most of these manipulations can be immediately undone by choosing Edit | Undo right after you perform the change.

Select Objects

If you want to change an object's size, just click once on it to select it. You'll see the *resizing handles*—little black rectangles—appear.

You can click and drag one of the handles to make the object larger. This includes text boxes, spreadsheet objects, and paint objects, all of which can be stretched to offer you more space to work in.

But that's not all you can do. With an object selected, you can hit the DELETE key to delete it from the document, or choose any of the Edit menu commands like Cut, Copy, or Paste. You can paste an object from any AppleWorks module into any other module. (The major exception is the Painting module, which will accept the Paste command, but won't store the object as an object—it just turns it into dots, or pixels, that become part of the Painting document. That's even true of spreadsheet objects, which can be painted right into a Painting document.)

Arrange Objects Front and Back

Sometimes you'll find you have one object that's "on top of" another object—it's obscuring part of the second object. This often happens, for instance, if you decide to create the background for a text object after you've created the text object. Drag the background to the text and it'll obscure the text.

If you really want that background in the background, then make sure it's selected and choose Arrange | Move Backward or go for the gold and choose Arrange | Move to Back. In either case, the selected object is moved behind other objects. The Arrange | Move Backward command is designed to move objects back one layer at a time (just in case you have three or four objects stacked on one another). Move to Back immediately moves the selected object to the back of all objects on the screen.

As you might guess, you can bring objects to the foreground just as easily. Select an object, and then choose Arrange | Move Forward or Arrange | Move to Front.

Align Objects

There are two different ways to align objects. You can select a particular object and choose Arrange | Align to Grid. This only does something if you've previously selected the Options | Turn Autogrid Off command. Autogrid is what forces objects to "snap" to a particular position on the page whenever you drop them. It keeps you from making precise little movements, but helps you by aligning everything to the grid. If you've turned it off, but you now want an object aligned to the grid again, choose the Align to Grid command.

The Align Objects command is even cooler. Select two or more objects that you want to align relative to one another. Now, choose the Arrange | Align Objects command. You'll see the Align Objects dialog box.

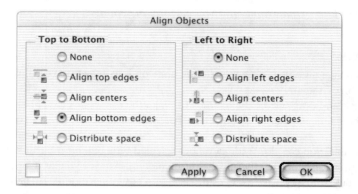

See the options? Decide how you want objects aligned, asking yourself some questions like:

■   If your objects are in a vertical column, do you want them aligned on the right or left edge? Should the vertical distance between the objects be distributed evenly?

- If it's a horizontal row of objects, should the bottom or top be aligned? Should the horizontal distance between the objects be distributed evenly?

- In either case, should the centers of the objects be aligned?

Make your choices and click OK.

Reshape Objects

As mentioned, objects in the Drawing module are unique because they can be changed and reworked after they've been created. One way to do that is to change the way the shape is made with the Reshape command. This works with objects created using the Arc, Polygon, Freehand, Bezigon, and Regular Polygon tools. Choose Arrange | Reshape and you'll see resize handles that let you change the shape of the object.

After you've changed the shape, you'll still be in Reshape mode until you select Arrange | Reshape again. So, click another object and reshape again. Or choose the menu command to return to normalcy.

Free Rotate

The Free Rotate command works much the same way that the Reshape command does:

1. Choose Arrange | Free Rotate from the menu and you're in Free Rotate mode.

2. In the document window, select an object to rotate.

3. Now, click and grab one of the image's handles, and then move the mouse. You'll see the object rotate along with your mouse movement.

4. Release the mouse button when you have the object where you want it.

Don't forget to choose Arrange | Free Rotate again when you're done rotating to leave Free Rotate mode.

Flip and Rotate

These are more precise controls that allow you to do exactly as much rotation and flipping of an object as you'd like. For these, you'll select the object in the document window first, and then choose the command from the Arrange menu. Here are the commands:

- **Flip Horizontally**   Quickly flips an object from left to right.
- **Flip Vertically**   Flips the top and bottom of an object.
- **Rotate**   Brings up a dialog box that allows you to enter how many degrees the object should rotate. Rotation works counterclockwise (entering **90** causes the object to rotate counterclockwise 90 degrees), but you can enter a negative number to rotate clockwise. Note that **–90** and **270** give the same results, since rotation covers the total 360 degrees in a circle.)

11

■   **Scale by Percent**   Brings up a dialog box that allows you to reduce or enlarge your object vertically or horizontally. Enter a percentage for each to stretch or enlarge the object.

Group and Lock

With the Lock command, you fix an object so that it can't be moved, reshaped, or rotated. Locking is simple—just select the object and select Arrange | Lock (⌘-H) from the menu. The object becomes locked—it can't be moved or shaped. (You can edit text and make changes in spreadsheets and similar objects, though.) To unlock the object, select it and choose Arrange | Unlock (SHIFT-⌘-H).

The Group command allows you to take two or more objects and cause them to function as a group—move one and you'll move them all. They become, in essence, one object. To group objects, select them all (hold down the SHIFT key as you click additional objects in order to select more than one). Choose Arrange | Group (⌘-G) and the different objects become one object. You'll notice that the object handles change so that the entire group can be selected, moved, resized, shaped, or rotated as one object.

To ungroup, select the object and choose Arrange | Ungroup (SHIFT-⌘-G). Once you've created a grouping, you can also group that grouping with other objects (and so on, and so on) although that can get a touch complicated.

Obviously, it's best to group related elements, especially things that always need to be together as one object or together but a certain distance apart. (It can be annoying to get everything set up correctly and then accidentally move one of the related objects. Just group them and that can't happen.) It's also easy and recommended that you group objects temporarily when you want to move them, together, across the screen. Select, group, move, ungroup—you can do it very quickly and it keeps all those objects the same relative distance from one another.

Chapter 12

Use AppleWorks for Layout

How to...

- Work with page layouts
- Use Assistants for common documents
- Create a layout using Drawing tools and text frames
- Add images and wrap text around them
- Draw shapes and create floating text for your layout
- Create layouts quickly using the word processing tools
- Merge data from your databases with your layout documents.

You've seen text layout and management in Chapter 8, numbers and calculations in Chapter 9, data management in Chapter 10, and artistic creation and communication in Chapter 11.

Now, what if you could put all this stuff together?

AppleWorks is a special sort of program. Although we've taken a reasonably thorough look at the individual parts and what they can do for you, in this chapter we'll look at AppleWorks as a whole. If you're interested in creating dynamic, professional-looking, and creative documents, you're going to enjoy this chapter.

How Layouts Work

These days, the desktop publishing revolution has made it so that most of the *page layout* process—the steps used to create a newsletter, newspaper, or magazine page—happens on a computer screen. You type and edit your story in a word processor, then you simply cut and paste it (or some close equivalent) into *frames* that are laid down in a special desktop publishing program. With the text laid down in columns, you can change fonts, sizes, spacing, and alignment. Then you can drop digital images right into the document itself and move them around on the page.

Popular programs for this sort of layout include Adobe PageMaker and QuarkXPress. They usually cost hundreds of dollars apiece and can take a little training to master.

Or, you can use AppleWorks and get somewhat similar results. The tools aren't all as advanced as those in the layout programs, but AppleWorks does offer you the ability to format documents in columns, create text frames, add images, and even create graphic elements in the Painting and Drawing modules. The best part is how all the modules work together.

The AppleWorks Frame

You already know that you can create different types of documents—word processing, spreadsheet, Paint documents, and so on—in the different AppleWorks modules. And you've even seen—in the Drawing and Presentation modules, for instance, how it's possible to add individual frames of data, text, and graphics using different modules' tools in the same document. Using that same principle, you can create a word processing frame or a spreadsheet frame and place it on the Draw document, the same way you might lay out a strip of typeset text on a paste-up board to create a newspaper. Figure 12-1 shows an AppleWorks document with multiple frames.

FIGURE 12-1   Using multiple frames in an AppleWorks document makes sophisticated layouts possible.

12

A frame is just a window into another part of AppleWorks—when you double-click in the frame, the AppleWorks menus and tools change to the tools that are available in that module. Double-click a spreadsheet frame and you'll see the spreadsheet tools and commands; double-click a text frame and you'll see all the word processing tools. With frames, you can create a sophisticated document that communicates very effectively.

What Can You Lay Out?

So, you'll be able to use AppleWorks to lay out many different sorts of documents using all the different frames and tools at your disposal. What sort of things can you create? You can use just a few frames in a document to spice it up, or you can create entire documents out of nothing but frames that work together to create a whole. Here are some ideas:

- Add charts and graphs to your word processing reports.

- Create text frames in spreadsheet documents that explain the spreadsheet or help the novice user enter data in the spreadsheet form. You can similarly use a text frame in a database layout to offer instructions.

- Add Paint or Draw images to your spreadsheet, database, presentation, or word processing document.

- Create text frames within text documents in order to create headlines, pull quotes, or other special elements (like the Tips and Notes you see in this book) on the page.

- Create spreadsheet charts within other types of documents, like Draw or word processing documents.

- Create text and image frames within a database to create a presentation, slide show, or flash cards that can be used for teaching or lecturing.

- Create a merge, in which data from a database can be merged into a word processing document or a text frame. This is great for mail merges (personalizing form letters and addressing envelopes) and it works for other things, too.

And there's much more—you can use layouts to create brochures, holiday letters, reports, and newsletters; you'll likely use all the different permutations. Want to create a newsletter that features text, graphics, painted objects, drawn objects, charts, and spreadsheet data? How about a newsletter that does all that, then allows you to print multiple copies and automatically address them from a database of names and addresses?

Don't ever let anyone tell you AppleWorks isn't a powerful program.

Consult Assistant

In fact, AppleWorks is so powerful that you don't even have to create your own layouts—you can start with help from the Assistants. There are six Assistants to help you create different layouts:

- **Address List**   This Assistant walks you through the process of creating an address list database, where you can track the names, addresses, phone numbers, and other information of your personal, business, or other contacts.

- **Business Cards**   This Assistant walks you through adding the company name, address, title, and phone number to create a business card, which it then generates as a database document. Using the database tools, you can modify the card in Layout mode, then switch to Browse mode, which automatically fills a page with eight instances of the card. The cards can then be printed to plain paper and taken to your print shop, or printed on card stock and cut at home. You can also get perforated card stock at most office supply stores, which can be used to create business cards.

- **Calendar**   Using the spreadsheet tools, this Assistant quickly creates a monthly calendar, automatically placing the dates correctly, based on the month(s) you choose. There's really only one choice—a single month per sheet of paper.

- **Certificate**   This Assistant quickly tosses together a certificate, award, diploma, or something similar. The result is a Draw document that can easily be edited.

- **Envelope**   This Assistant walks you through the process of setting the alignment and printing path for the envelope. Envelopes can be tough to print—you'll need to read your printer's manual carefully to figure out how to orient and feed the envelope to your printer. Then you can make an informed decision on how to set up this Assistant, which generates a word processing document that's easily edited.

■ **Home Finance** This Assistant automates the process of creating a variety of different "What If" spreadsheets that you can use to decide how to manage debt, calculate net worth, and even determine how much you can afford to put into a home.

To use an Assistant, select the Assistants tab in the Starting Points window. Double-click one of the Assistant icons to begin. Assistants work by asking you a series of questions about your document. You enter information in the Assistant dialog box, then click the Next button to move on to the next series of questions.

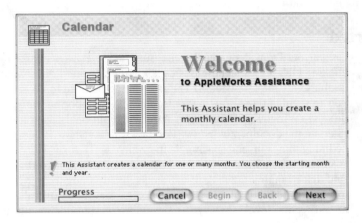

When you get to the end of the Assistant, you'll see a Create button, which causes the Assistant to take all the information you've input and create the document based on that information. You can also click the Cancel button to leave the Assistant, click the Back button to go back to the previous questions, or click the Begin button to return to the beginning of the Assistant.

Layout Basics: Text Frames

One of the options missing from AppleWork's Assistants is a Newsletter Assistant. (It's been there in past versions, but Apple has taken it out of this one.) Newsletters are useful for any variety of reasons, including sales, school functions, or even a regular holiday newsletter you can drop into your holiday cards to update friends and family on your year. You'll find that Apple has at least one Assistant template available on the Web tab of the Starting Points, if you want to use it to begin.

In this section, though, I want to focus on creating a newsletter from scratch that incorporates all the different sorts of frames you can create in AppleWorks. We'll create text frames in columns, drop in images, add headlines—it'll be fun. Plus, what you learn by creating a newsletter can be applied to any sort of layout, from brochures to letterhead to mail merge documents. We'll get to those other things later in this chapter, but right now let's cover the general instructions for dealing with frames on a page.

With a newsletter, there's actually a more fundamental problem to broach before you can start typing and framing things. You need to choose which type of AppleWorks document—word processing or Draw—to use as the foundation for your newsletter. Here's the basic rule—if you're more interested in the text than you are in the layout, then choose the word processing module for creating the basic document. Your newsletter may come out looking a little more like a pamphlet or brochure, but you'll have a more structured document with headers, columns, and other tools for automating the layout.

If your primary focus is the appearance of the newsletter—you want it to be visually pleasing, creative, and incorporate a lot of different framed elements—then you'll want to create a Draw document. Draw documents give you the most flexibility, since they're specifically designed for creating and moving objects around in the document window.

Getting Started

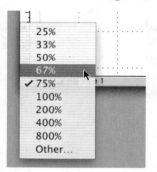

Create your Draw document by choosing File | New, selecting Draw, and clicking OK. (Or, select the Basics tab in the Starting Points window and double-click the Draw icon.) The first thing you need to do is make sure you're seeing all the drawing tools—they'll be important throughout this process (Window | Show Tools). You'll also probably want to view the rulers in the document window (Format | Rulers | Show Rulers), since you'll be lining things up and spacing them evenly.

Next up is a little tool we've ignored until now: magnification. You'll find that changing the magnification is a handy thing to do when you're trying see the whole page at once and get a feel for its overall design. The magnification level allows you to see more of your document (decrease magnification) or to see a smaller portion of your document up close (increase magnification). It's helpful to drop back to 75 or 67 percent sometimes, because then you'll be able to see the whole page. Then, return to 100 percent so you can actually see the text and detail in the images. While you're at it, you can also zoom in up to 800 percent to get a very close look at part of an image, text layout, or other feature of the page.

To change the magnification, select the percentage in the bottom-left corner of any AppleWorks document. It's actually a menu—you can simply choose the percentage to change the size of the document.

> **TIP** *You can use multiple "views" to open different windows showing the same document at different magnifications. To create a new view, choose Window | New View. Notice that the title bar of the new view has ":2" in it. It's still the same document—this is just a convenient way to look at the same document in two different magnifications so you can switch quickly between the two.*

Next, you'll probably need to set up the document's margins and pages. This works the same as with any other Draw document. Choose Format | Document, then enter numbers for the margins on the page and the number of Pages Down and Pages Across you'd like the document to have.

(I prefer to place all my pages horizontally, since that just looks more like a newsletter to me. Your approach is up to you, though.)

> **NOTE** *Most inkjet printers and many laser printers can't print all the way to the edges of a page, so you'll probably want a minimal margin even if you plan to use most of the page for your layout. If you're using a typical letter-sized page, a margin of .25 inches on each side gives you 8 inches for your document's width and 10.5 inches for the height; 0.5 inches for each margin leaves you 7.5 by 10 inches to work with. Later in the chapter you'll be measuring things pretty closely, so keep these numbers in mind.*

Now you're ready to create the frames that will hold the different parts of your newsletter. If you're serious about creating a newsletter *right now,* remember that you can pre-type your stories in the word processing module to get them nicely spell-checked and formatted, and you might want to have some graphics or images on hand to drop into the layout. (Chapter 14 discusses manipulating digital images, while Chapter 26 discusses scanners and digital cameras.)

You can also type directly into the layout, as you'll see, but sometimes it's easier to have written the story beforehand so it can be spell-checked and edited.

Create Text Frames

Much of your layout will likely be composed of text, so you'll be working with text frames a lot. Fortunately, they're pretty flexible. After all, a text frame is sort of a window into the word processing module of AppleWorks. Draw your text frame on the page and you'll have all the text tools at your disposal.

In Drawing projects you'll create a text frame, type text, and then the text will become an object. Unfortunately for our newsletter, AppleWorks, by default, collapses the text frame around the typed text so that only that text becomes the text frame, regardless of the size of the frame you draw.

That won't quite work for us in the newsletter, since we want the column to stay a fixed size. That way we can move text around within the columns and the column won't change sizes just because we don't have enough text to fill it. It can be convenient to have the frame grow around your text in certain cases. But in order to build a newsletter-type document, you'll want to create frames that are a fixed size.

To do that, you must create a *linked* frame (this might be a good time to drop back to 67 percent magnification, by the way).

1. With the Pointer tool selected, choose Options | Frame Links.

2. Now, select the word processing frame tool (the letter "A" icon) and drag out a frame on the page.

3. Release the mouse button and the insertion point appears—you can type in the frame if you want.

4. To see the entire linked frame, click once outside of the frame. Its handles appear to show you the entire frame object.

12

The text frame is an object in the same way that a drawn rectangle or line is an object—it can be rotated, resized, moved, or even sent to back or sent forward (see Figure 12-2).

> **TIP** *If you already have a regular non-linked frame of text, you can select it and choose Options | Frame Links to turn that frame into a linked frame.*

So why is it called a "linked" frame? Well, it'll take some explaining, which I'll do later in this chapter in the section called "Link Text Frames." For now, suffice it to say that linked frames allow text to flow from one frame to another, like text flows from column to column on a newspaper page.

> **TIP** *The frame borders keep disappearing after you select other objects! To see your frames at all times, select them and choose to surround them with a line (choose Hairline from the Line Width button menu in the toolbar). Just don't forget to remove the lines before you print the document.*

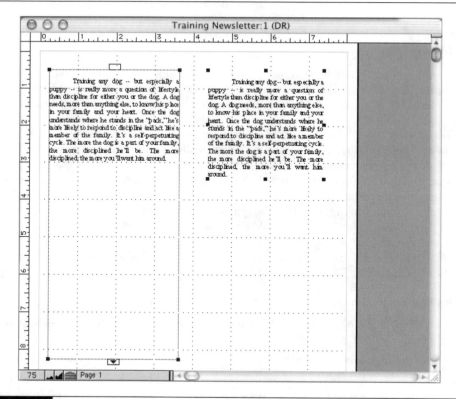

FIGURE 12-2   On the left, a linked text frame; on the right, a typical text frame—it collapses around the text instead of maintaining its shape.

Add Text

There are three basic ways you can add text to a linked frame. They all start with creating a linked frame, dragging it to about the right size for a column, and then clicking in the frame to make sure it's selected for input—the insertion point appears and you can type, if desired. In fact, that's the first way to add text:

- ■ **Type**   You'll notice that, when you're in insertion mode in the text frame, your tools (menus and the button bar) are all the same as they are in the word processing module. That should make it easy to type, format, and even clean up your newsletter story.

- ■ **Cut and Paste**   If you have parts of an existing word processing document that you'd like to drop into this frame, you can open that document, select the text you want in your frame, then use the Edit | Copy and Edit | Paste commands to copy the text from the word processing document into your frame.

- ■ **Insert command**   You've already created your story in the word processing module, you've edited it, and you're ready to simply drop it into your layout. Select the text frame, then choose File | Insert. Find the word processing document you want to insert, then click OK. If you subsequently want to change the inserted document, you can select all the text by choosing ⌘-A, then insert a different document. (Or you can delete all the existing text first and then insert the new document.) Note that changing the text once it's been inserted doesn't affect the original word processing document's text at all. And if you change your mind about an insertion, simply select Edit | Undo to remove it.

> **TIP**   *If your column is resized so that it reaches way off the bottom of the page, head down to the section "Resize Frames," and then resize the height of the frame so that it fits on the page—10 inches or so.*

If you insert text into a frame from another document—or if you simply have a lot to type—then you may run into a little problem, because you may end up with a frame that's too big after it has been resized to fit your text. You can use the frame's handles to move the frame around and try to make things fit, but that probably won't work if you're creating a newsletter, report, or similar document. Instead, you'll probably want to move the additional text to a new frame and have it flow nicely so the story continues onto the next column. Almost as if, say, those frames were *linked*. Hey now!

Link Text Frames

If you've created one text frame that's overflowing with text, you can create another one to link to it so that it takes up the slack. Here's how:

1. Select the first frame to see its frame handles.

2. At the bottom of the frame, locate the continue indicator. (You may need to drag the bottom of the frame up so that it fits on the page.) Click it once.

3. Now you're ready to draw the linked frame. Drag to draw the frame onto your page. (Don't worry—you can resize it later.)

4. When you release the mouse button, text flows into the frame from the original frame. They're linked. When selected, the new frame will show a linked indicator (a little chain link icon) at the top and, if the story is long enough to overflow the frame, it'll show a Continue indicator at the bottom, as shown in Figure 12-3.

What's important to realize about linked frames is that they flow just like different pages in a word processing document flow. So, if you go back to the original frame and add or delete text,

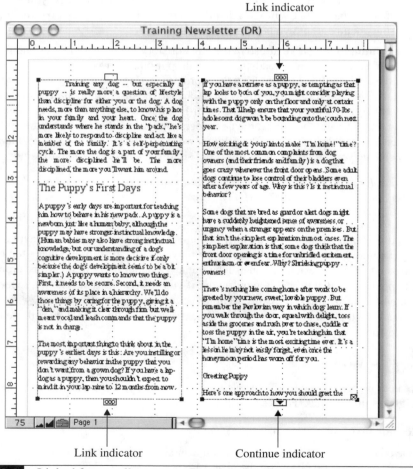

the linked frame will change to reflect the added or subtracted text. If you simply had two frames into which you'd cut and pasted text, you'd be in for quite an experience if you added text to or subtracted text from either of them, because you'd need to do some crazy cutting and pasting to make the columns look right again.

If you're used to expensive desktop publishing programs, you'll find these linked frames useful but limited. You can't re-order the links or link to an existing frame. You can only create linked frames by clicking the Continue indicator and drawing the frame. Also, cutting or copying the frame breaks the link—a pasted frame can create its own linked frames, but it's no longer linked to the original.

Frames don't have to be the same sizes or shapes to be linked, so you can link a narrow column of text to a large rectangle of text and it will still flow fine. In fact, you can create a linked frame on a new page, if you like.

Resize Frames

Once you've got a couple of text frames on your page you'll probably realize that it's nearly impossible to get them to look like perfect columns on the page—after all, you're drawing and arranging them by hand. This can be frustrating, to say the least.

Fortunately, there are some tools to help you. The first is the Object Size window, which allows you to make some very precise decisions about how each frame will appear. Choose Options | Object Size and the Size window appears.

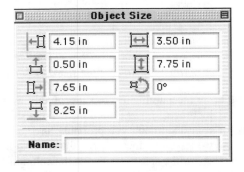

This is a great little window, because it gives you amazing precision in placing and aligning your frames as columns. From top to bottom in the left column, the measurements are:

- ■ **Left Location**   The point, in inches, where the left side of the frame appears.
- ■ **Top Location**   The point, in inches, where the top of the frame appears.
- ■ **Right Location**   The point, in inches, where the right side of the frame appears.
- ■ **Bottom Location**   The point, in inches, where the bottom of the frame appears.

Now from top to bottom in the right column:

- ■ **Object Width**   The width, in inches, of the frame.
- ■ **Object Height**   The height, in inches, of the frame.
- ■ **Rotation**   Amount of rotation, in degrees, of the frame.

While you're creating your layout, you should keep in mind how useful these measurements are. For instance, if you want all of your frames to be aligned at their tops, you can choose a Top Location measurement and enter it for each. Similarly, you can check all your columns to make sure their bottoms align exactly. This will also help to keep the text aligned across columns so the column layout doesn't look jagged. An example of what you *don't* want is shown here:

> Training any dog -- but especially a puppy -- is really more a question of lifestyle than discipline for either you or the dog. A dog needs, more than anything else, to know his place in your family and your heart. Once the dog understands where he stands in the "pack," he's

> If you have a retrieve as a puppy, as tempting as that lap looks to both of you, you might consider playing with the puppy only on the floor and only at certain times. That'll help ensure that your youthful 70-lbs. adolescent dog won't be bounding onto the couch next year.

Probably the best tools here are column width and height—two measurements that are almost impossible to eyeball. Select one of your columns and check its width—if you've got three columns, it's probably about 2.5 inches or so wide, right? Go ahead and make it a nice, round 2.5 inches exactly. Now, select another column and make it 2.5 inches wide. Do it for the last one, and your columns will all be a uniform width.

 *Align the bottoms of your frames, then give them all the same height measurement if you want them to align at the tops, too. Columns of different heights simply can't align at both the top and bottom. It goes against the laws of physics...or something.*

While you're working with these measurements, you'll probably want to keep in mind a little mathematics. By default, a Draw document shows all 8.5 inches of a standard letter-sized sheet of paper. If you have margins for your document, you probably have 8 or 7.5 inches for your document's width. If you have an 8-inch wide document with three 2.5 inch columns, that will leave you 0.25 inches for the *gutters*—white space—between the columns. (There are two gutters for three frames, remember.) That's a good size. If you only have 7.5 inches to work with, though, you'll need to pare back those column widths a bit to get a decent gutter—say, about 2.333 inches for each column, which would give you back 0.25 inches per gutter.

You can select more than one column (or another frame) at one time by holding down the SHIFT key as you select them. Then you can apply uniform sizing to them all at once.

Align Frames

Keep repeating to yourself that frames are objects and objects can be manipulated, as we saw in Chapter 11. You're using the Draw tools, so all of the same tools for shapes can be used to manipulate frames. That includes the alignment tools.

Here's a neat trick to align frames as columns and get that gutter just perfect:

1. On your layout, place your left- and right-most columns where you want them on the page relative to the edges.

2. Now, select all three frames by holding down the SHIFT key while you click them.

3. Choose Arrange | Align Objects.

4. In the Align Objects dialog box, choose Distribute Space in the Left To Right section.

5. Click Apply.

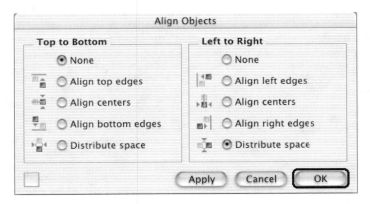

See what happened? Your columns snapped into place, distributing the remaining space equally between the two gutters. Perfect. If you like what you see, click OK to get out of the Align dialog to change other alignment issues regarding your columns.

Lock Frames

When you've finally got your frames in place the way they need to be, go ahead and lock them down. That'll keep you from accidentally moving the columns around once they've been carefully arranged. Select the frames to lock (hold down the SHIFT key as you select more than one frame), then choose Arrange | Lock. You can still select the frames and edit text within them, but you can't move them on the page until you unlock them.

12

Graphics, Floating Text, and Shapes

Once you have your main column frames created and locked down, you're ready to start adding text and images around the columns in order to create a more vibrant layout. The basic concept is simple—you create frames that can be placed near or even over the existing frames that you've created. Then, using a special command, you can force text to wrap around the floating frames, creating the effect that an image or block of text is diverting the columns around it, drawing attention to the visual element. Fortunately, it's very easy to do.

Add Graphic Frames

Let's begin by adding images to your layout. The graphics can be from a variety of sources, including graphics you create or one of the many images that comes with AppleWorks, which you can find by selecting File | Show Clippings. And, you can just as easily scan graphics or digital-camera images into your computer and store them as image files. Any of these are easily added to your layout.

There are four basic ways to add graphic images to your layout:

- **Build the Graphic** Using either the tools in the Draw module, a Paint frame, or a spreadsheet frame, you can add images (or spreadsheet cells) you've created in AppleWorks.

- **Insert from File** If you don't have a frame selected and you choose File | Insert, you can search your hard drive (or connected network drives) for image files that can be added to your document as their own frames.

- **Insert Clipart** AppleWorks offers libraries of *clipart*—small images, royalty-free, that you can add to your documents—which can be used to augment your layout from the Clippings window.

- **Cut and Paste** In most cases, you can select images or parts of other documents, then copy and paste them into your Draw document using the Edit | Copy and Edit | Paste commands. They'll show up in their own frames that can then be moved, stretched, rotated, and so on.

You already know from Chapter 11 how to create and manipulate AppleWorks graphics, and you know how to cut and paste. Let's look at adding a graphic from a file or the Clippings window.

To add a graphic from a file, make sure no frames are selected in the document (so that AppleWorks doesn't try to add the graphic into that frame), then choose File | Insert. The Insert dialog box appears. Find the file you want to add and click OK. The graphic appears in your document in its own frame. Note that the file *format* of your graphic is important—you'll need to have it in PICT, TIFF, JPG, GIF, BMP, or a similar format. (You can see them all by pulling down the Show menu in the Insert dialog box.) Graphic file formats are discussed in detail in Chapter 14.

If you're adding from a library, choose File | Show Clippings, then select the type of clipart you'd like to look at. The topics appear on small tabs at the bottom of the Clippings window. If you don't see any topics, you should click the Search button in the Clippings window to retrieve clippings from Apple's server computers over the Internet. (Remember that you'll need to activate your Internet connection if you have a dial-up or certain DSL connections. See Chapter 23 for details.)

To search for a graphic, enter a keyword in the search box and click the Search button. Now, scroll through the results. Once you find the graphic you like, simply drag it from the Clippings window to your document (see Figure 12-4). It becomes an object in your layout. If you're done with the Clippings window, click its Close box.

Notice your floating graphic and your text co-mingling in an uncomfortable way? We'll cover that in the section "Wrap Text," coming up shortly.

Create Floating Text

You've already seen quite a bit on adding text in frames—this really isn't much different. You may find that creating a linked frame is the best approach here, if only because a linked frame

Graphic created using draw tools

Floating graphic from the Clippings window

FIGURE 12-4   Drag the image from the Clippings window to your document, where it becomes an object.

Add Inline Graphics

You can also add graphics in another way—as inline graphics (or other objects) that become embedded in the text. Instead of floating freely in their own frames, embedded images are placed at a specific point in the text. You accomplish this by inserting, pasting, or dragging an image from the Clippings window while you have the Text tool selected and the insertion point placed somewhere in the selected text frame. The image appears as part of the text instead of in its own frame, meaning it will move around if you alter the text that comes before it. (In fact, you may notice this happening accidentally if you have the Text tool selected when you're dragging and/or pasting images into your layout.) You can learn more about this in "The Word Processing Layout," later in this chapter.

doesn't collapse around the text. You likely won't actually be linking it to anything—you just want the additional control the linked frame gives you. Here's how to create floating text:

1. Make sure Frame Links is selected (with a check mark next to it) in the Options menu.

2. Click the Text tool and drag to create a text frame on the page.

3. Enter the text (a pull-quote, headline, and so on) for this floating text frame. Format the text.

4. Click outside the text frame. The text frame should be selected, with handles showing. (If it's not, click it once to select it.)

5. Click and drag the text frame to its final destination. It's OK if the frame obscures the text beneath it—you'll fix that momentarily.

Note that not all of your floating text will necessarily have other text wrapped around it. You can use this same approach to create two-column headlines over three-column stories—the "Training Your Puppy" headline in the examples in this chapter (for instance, in Figure 12-5) is floating text, too.

Wrap Text

Whether it's a text frame or a graphic, if you've created a frame that you want to float among the columns of your layout, then you'll want to wrap text around it. This is a great way to add visual appeal and a hint of professionalism to your document. It's also simple to do:

1. Select a graphic or text frame (such as the pull quote example in the previous section) that's currently overlapping text. It may be a little tough to select—try to make sure the underlying columns aren't also selected. If they are, SHIFT-clicking one of the selected frames will de-select it while leaving others highlighted.

2. Choose Options | Text Wrap.

3. In the Text Wrap dialog box, choose the type of wrap you want. Regular wraps text around the frame, while Irregular will wrap the text around the actual image or shape within the frame. None, of course, eliminates the text wrap if it was there.

4. Enter a number for the gutter, if desired. This determines the number of points to keep between the frame (Regular) or graphic (Irregular) and the wrapped text. The typical text size of typed output is 12 points, so something like 6 points might be good for each side (6 points is 1/12 of an inch).

5. Click OK.

That's it, the text is wrapped either regularly or irregularly. An image with regular wrap is shown in Figure 12-5.

This gives your layout a great look, although you'll still need to look at it carefully to make sure everything is lined up nicely. If things aren't working out, you may need to resize the graphics frame or choose Regular instead of Irregular wrap, for instance.

Shape and Lines

In Chapter 11, you saw how to create various shapes and add them to a drawing. Your layout is also a drawing, meaning it can just as easily accept lines, shapes, and curves if you'd like to use them. Just draw them right on the document, then arrange them—back to front, text-wrapped, and so on—as you like.

A couple of ideas stand out. First, you can take an odd shape—a curve, oval, jagged shape, or something similar—and group it with an image or text frame, putting the shape behind the text or image.

12

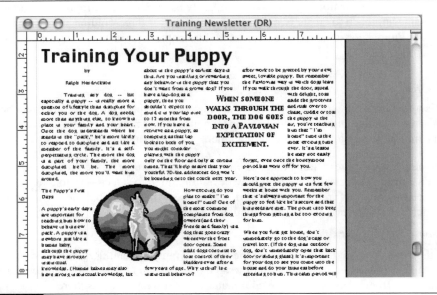

FIGURE 12-5   Text wrapped around frames and graphics

Now, if you choose to make the border of the shape invisible and wrap text around it, you can create some very interesting text wrap shapes that will give your layout even more artistic flair. Similarly, you can create a shaded or patterned background for your floating images or text, if you like.

You can also use shapes around individual stories in your layouts—surround shorter stories with boxes (or boxes with light-colored backgrounds in them) to separate them from the surrounding text. And, of course, you can use shapes combined with text and use other Draw tools to create special elements like a table of contents for your newsletter.

Lines are also a great addition to layouts, especially since they no longer require the special "border tape" that was required in the days of yore. (That same tape still decorates the drafting table I have my iMac situated on at this very moment. It was certainly a big part of the journalist's life at one time.)

You know how to draw the lines. My only suggestions are:

- *Remember the different sizes and shapes available.* If you like, you can pattern lines so that they're dashed, broken, or otherwise more interesting.

- *Arrange your lines To Back.* Traditionally, gutter lines go behind other elements, including images and shaded background. You can get this effect by selecting the lines, then choosing Arrange | Send to Back.

- *Lock your lines!* Put the lines in the gutters of your document, then select Arrange | Lock to keep them there. Nothing gets more annoying than replacing your lines every few mouse movements because you've accidentally selected and moved them.

- *Copy and paste.* Want lines that are the same size, width, and orientation? Copy an existing line, then immediately paste it into the layout. It shows up as an object, ready to be added to the layout.

Figure 12-6 shows some of these line suggestions in action.

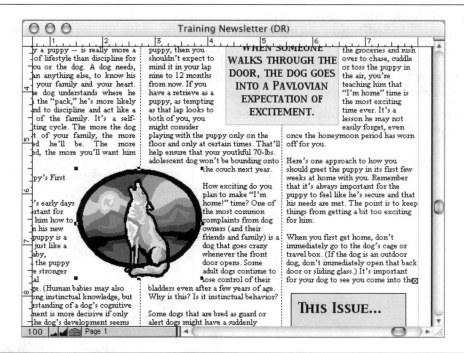

FIGURE 12-6   The dotted lines help break up the text, giving the newsletter a professional look.

Build Layouts Quickly

The Draw tools, as we've seen, are exceptional for creating dramatic layouts. You can use many different elements to design a few pages and create complex newsletters and other documents. But you can also see why people have full-time jobs as graphic designers and layout artists. It can take quite a while to get each page right.

What if, instead, you're trying to create a good-looking layout that takes a little less time to create? There are a number of templates and assistants in AppleWorks to help you do just that— you can create business cards, brochures, flyers, invitations, signs, birthday cards, posters, and many other publications. If you're creating a more serious report or similar document, you can also get it done more quickly by sticking with the word processing module. You'll get a less graphical, more formal publication, but it can be accomplished much more quickly.

The Word Processing Layout

Say you've already typed a long document as a word processing document and you'd prefer not to format it using drawing tools. And yet, you're interested in adding some graphical elements to the text—in fact, you might even want to format the document as a newsletter. It can be done.

Columns

To begin, you can place the document in columns. This is much easier than creating columns in the Drawing module, although it gives you less flexibility. You can create the columns in two ways:

- *Click the More Columns button.* In the ruler bar of the word processing document, click the more (or less) columns button to add (or remove) columns for the document. The columns are added immediately.

- *Add columns to the section.* Choose Format | Section. In the Section dialog box, enter the number of columns for that section in the Number of Columns entry box.

The Section dialog box also allows you to choose the width of the columns and/or the width of the gutters (choosing one affects the other, by necessity). Note that if you have more than one section defined in your document, you'll need to define columns for each section.

Graphic and Spreadsheet Frames

You can use any of the four previously discussed methods to add graphics or spreadsheet frames to your word processing document: draw them, use the File | Insert command, copy them from a library, or paste them in. (See the section "Add Graphic Frames," earlier in this chapter.) You can also move them around, wrap text, and generally have the same sort of rollicking good time you can have in the Drawing module.

If you're inserting or pasting an object into your word processing document, you must have the Pointer tool selected in the word processing document. That allows you to add an item as a frame. If you have the Text tool selected, the pasted, inserted, or library graphic (or other object) will appear *inline*. In this case, the image appears as part of the text, not as a floating object. An inline image is useful for those little graphics newsletter editors like to put in newspapers and newsletters that show you when a story has ended.

you walk through the door, squeal with delight, toss aside the groceries and rush over to chase, cuddle or toss the puppy in the air. **END**

12

NOTE *This book is using the same inline vs. floating concept. The graphic just shown is inline—it flows with the text so I can talk about the image and ensure that it's in the same place as the text that discusses it. This book also features "floating" images—they're the ones with Figure numbers.*

Draw and Text Frames

You can't create a text frame in the word processing module, supposedly because a word processing document is sort of one big text frame. This can be a little annoying, though, since it's tough to create pull quotes and multicolumn headlines without using text frames. (You can create paint frames with text in them, but it's not the same since paint frames won't allow you to re-edit the text.)

The trick is to create a text frame in a Draw document, then copy and paste it into your word processing document. It's convoluted, but it works:

1. Create (or switch to) a Draw document and create your text frame.

2. Select it and choose Edit | Copy.

3. Switch to the word processing document.

4. Make sure the Pointer tool is selected in the word processing document (you may need to choose Window | Show Tools first) to verify that you're placing the frame as an object and not as inline text.

5. Choose Edit | Paste. The text should show up in a text frame.

Now you can move the text frame around, use Options | Text Wrap, and generally do the same things that are possible in the Draw module. It's just a little more of a pain. You'll probably want to keep a Draw document open just as a sort of "scratch" document to allow you to create these objects and paste (or drag-and-drop) them into your word processing layout.

This is actually the process used to get any complex, drawn object into the document. You can draw basic shapes—rectangles and circles—directly on the word processing document. But if you have a more complex drawn object, you'll want to create it in a Draw document and transfer it to the word processing document as an object. Then you can manipulate it just like any other frame, making things look good.

At least you saved a lot of time by not having to worry about creating columns!

Use Other Layout Templates

AppleWorks includes a number of templates that you can use for other types of layouts, ranging from fax cover sheets to memos to letterhead to "Car for Sale" fliers you can post on bulletin boards. And, of course, there are other templates available for other types of documents, like spreadsheets, databases, and drawings.

You saw how to create templates in Chapter 8—select the Templates tab in the Starting Points window, then double-click the template you'd like to work with. It will launch automatically in the Draw module (assuming it's a layout of some kind) and then you can go to work customizing it.

You should also explore the options on the Web tab of the Starting Points window, particularly if you aren't seeing a good template option on the Templates tab. Click the Templates icon, and AppleWorks will connect over the Internet to Apple's server computers. Some template documents will be downloaded to AppleWorks, showing you other optional templates you can download in different categories such as For Home, For Business, For Everyone, and so on. These dynamic links enable Apple (and third parties, like the AppleWorks User Group) to post interesting, optional templates that you can download and explore whenever you're looking for layout (not to mention database, spreadsheet, and presentation) ideas.

Mail Merge

The ultimate meeting point for automating documents and generating layouts is the concept of mail merge. Mail merge allows you to take data elements that are stored in a database document and automatically create new layouts that fold the information into the document automatically.

It's called a "mail merge" because the most obvious use for this scheme is to take names and addresses out of a database file and drop them into a letter or newsletter so that they can be mailed. You're creating a form letter. While it's possible to create a form letter as a layout in the database module, a mail merge allows you to use all of the sophistication of the word processing part— spell checking, sections, footnotes, and headers—to create more advanced form letters. In fact, any form letter more than a page long is best created in the word processing module.

A mail merge is created in three different steps: setting up the database, altering the document, then generating the merge.

12

Set Up the Database

First, you need to make sure your data is well arranged for a merge. AppleWorks' Help offers this example: If you want to use a salutation in your merged letter that includes a first name, then you're going to need a field in your database that stores that first name. You're also going to need logical address fields—address lines, city, state, ZIP—if you want to add addresses.

Remember that you can create any sort of merge you want using database fields. If you need to add fields that correspond to invoice numbers, products ordered, hair color, registration number, or whatever you have stored, you can put those fields in your database.

Now, before you create the merge document, find and sort the database as if you were creating a new report. If you only want certain records (people in a particular ZIP code, unpaid invoices) included in the merge, you should use Find to pare them down now. Similarly, you should sort to put the database in the order in which you want the merged documents generated. After doing this, leave the database open in the background.

Add Field Variables to Your Document

Now you're ready to edit the document. What you're going to do is add *field variables* to your document. The field variables tell the mail merge which field's data should be inserted into the document and where.

Here's how to add field variables to a document:

1. Open the document you're going to merge with your database.

2. Choose File | Mail Merge.

3. In the Open dialog box, find the database you want to use for the merge. Select it and click OK. (You need to perform this step even if the database document is already opened in AppleWorks.)

4. The Mail Merge palette window appears. Choose the field you want to add as a field variable, then click the Insert Field button.

5. Meanwhile you can still edit the document, adding text around the fields being merged, punctuating them, and so on (see Figure 12-7). You can add the same field variable more than once, if desired.

> **TIP** *Creating a mailing label for your newsletter or brochure in the Drawing module? You can make a text frame that includes your field variables and use the Arrange | Rotate command to rotate the text 180 degrees, so you can fold the newsletter over and have the address printed correctly. The merge still works, even upside-down!*

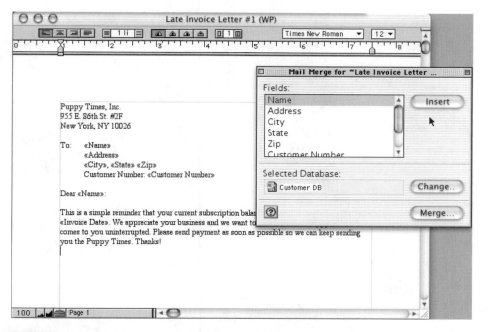

FIGURE 12-7   The field variables fit right in with any sort of text, formatting, or punctuation. If you're building a form letter, for instance, you can even have field variables within paragraphs of text.

Print the Merge

When you're done adding field variables, you're ready to print the merged documents. This part is simple. Click the Merge button in the Mail Merge palette window. The Mail Merge Destination dialog box appears. Select the option for where you'd like the merged documents sent (either directly to the printer, to a single large document, or to multiple documents). Click Continue and the merge begins.

TIP   *Scared? If your large mail merge has typos, you could waste a lot of paper. Instead of sending the merge directly to the printer, choose the Save in a New Document option in the Mail Merge Destination dialog box. Now you can page through that document and make sure all of the merged documents—or, as many as you can stand to check—look good before you commit to printing hundreds of pages.*

12

Chapter 13

Create AppleWorks Presentations

How to...

- Create the presentation
- Build master slides
- Create and edit slides
- Arrange and organize slides
- Present the show

AppleWorks 6 includes a module that's specifically designed to help you create presentations, although you'll find that the tools are very similar to the drawing tools. In essence, the tools enable you to create a number of *slides* (often based on a template) that are really just 640 × 480 Drawing documents that can then be displayed, full-screen, one at a time. You can use the special slide show controls to automatically advance the presentation, or you can press a key to move from one slide to the next.

Because the Presentation module relies heavily on the drawing tools, you'll find the discussion of those tools in Chapter 11 helpful. Then, you can move on to creating and editing slides, placing transitions between them and even adding information from other AppleWorks modules or imported items like QuickTime movies and sounds. Finally, you'll display the image, full-screen, so others can witness your handiwork.

Create the Presentation

You've got two options for building a slide show—the easy way and the hard way. The easy way is to use a pre-existing template to create your slides, complete with a few sample slides and a full-fledged design. This is easier because, with such a template, all you really need to do is focus on your text and bullet-point ideas, not how the overall slide will look. To build a slide show from a template, open the Starting Points window (File | Show Starting Points) and click the Templates tab. Now, locate a presentation style that looks good to you and click its icon. After a moment, the Presentation module loads and you'll be looking at your first sample slide (see Figure 13-1). If you're working directly from the template, all you have to do is create new slides as desired and edit the text and/or add images or other frames, all of which we'll discuss later in this chapter.

The other way to create a presentation is completely from scratch. You begin by selecting File | New | Presentation or by clicking the Presentation icon from the Basics tab in the Starting Points window. That will launch a blank presentation with no elements designed into it. From there, you'll build and edit the master slides for your presentation. First, you'll need to access those master slides using the Controls window, discussed next.

The Controls Window

To create or edit your presentation, you'll dig into the Controls window, which appears whenever you launch a new presentation or presentation template. (If you don't see the controls, select Window | Show Presentation Controls.)

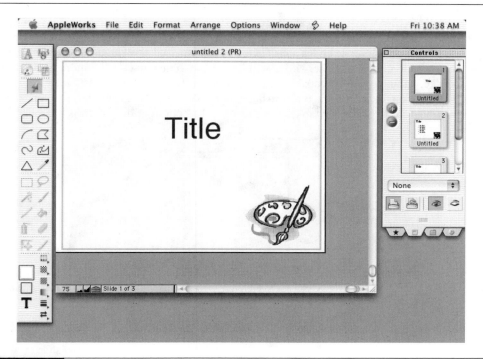

FIGURE 13-1   Select a Presentation template and you can immediately begin editing your slides.

The Controls window includes four tabs across the bottom—Master, Slides, Organize, and Slide Show. You'll work through each of the tabs as you edit both the look and the content of your presentation until finally, you're displaying your presentation onscreen.

TIP   *You can click and drag on the Drag lines at the bottom of the Controls window if you'd like to make the Controls window larger to reveal more slides or other items.*

Drag lines

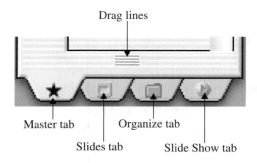

Master tab   Organize tab

Slides tab   Slide Show tab

13

Build Master Slides

Whether you've used a template or started from scratch, the first step you may want to take is editing your *master slides*. These slides aren't actually used in your presentation—they're design masters, from which all of your other slides will be created. You can create hundreds of master slides if you like, although you'll probably find that you don't need more than between three and five master slides, one for each basic type of slide you'd like in your presentation. To work with your master slides, click the Master tab (the star icon) at the bottom of the Controls window.

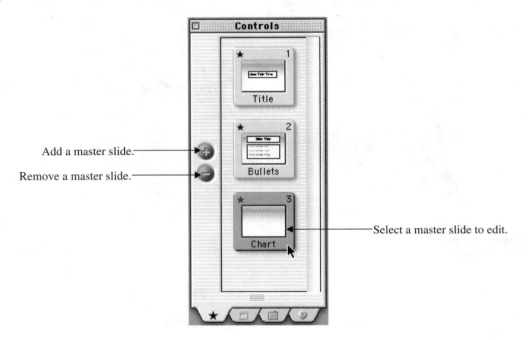

Add a master slide.

Remove a master slide.

Select a master slide to edit.

If you're creating a presentation from scratch, you'll note that you have only one untitled master slide to start with. You might want to create a few more at the outset, depending on your presentation. For instance, you may want one master slide for section titles, another for slides that are primarily bullet-point slides, and another master for slides that include a special area for images or QuickTime movies, and so on.

> **TIP**   *You can click the name of a master slide once to highlight it, then type to give the master slide a more unique name, such as "Title slide" or "Bullets slide" or something to remind you of its purpose. Also, the bullet character—which you may find useful when creating your slides—is typed by pressing OPTION-8 in most fonts.*

Now, whether or not you're working from a template, you can select a master slide in the Controls window and edit its general appearance in the main presentation window (see Figure 13-2). You can use all of the drawing tools to create the slide—lines, shapes, colors, and even text. In fact, you'll particularly want to work with text because you'll need to create the places on your master

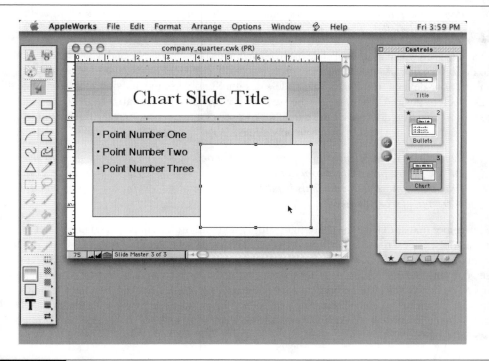

FIGURE 13-2   Editing a master slide from scratch

slide where you'll later be able to edit the text for each individual slide of your presentation. Note, however, that once you're editing the actual slide, you won't be forced to use every text area or bullet point that you create—you'll have full control over each individual slide. The master slides are simply starting points.

Once you have your master slides edited to taste, you can move on to creating and editing the actual sides for your presentation.

Create and Edit Slides

The next step in building your presentation is to create some slides. You can begin by creating all the slides you think you'll need for your presentation at once, or you can create them one at a time, go in and add the text and images for that slide, then move on to the next one. In either case, actually creating the slide is simple:

1. In the Controls window, make sure the Master tab is selected, then click once on the master slide you'd like to use to create your new slide.

2. Click the Slide tab in the Controls window.

3. Click the Add button (+) on the Slide tab. The new slide is added and automatically appears in the main window for editing.

If you select an existing slide first, the new slide will be added immediately after the selected slide.

That's it. Now you can edit the slide itself, changing its title, bullet text, and whatever else you'd like to do to the slide. As noted earlier, you can actually edit right on each individual slide, if you think it needs to deviate from the master slide's design. Simply use the drawing tools to change the slide as much as desired. Then, repeat the steps above for each additional slide that you want to create, noting that you don't need to switch back to select a master slide every time if you'd like to use the same master slide for multiple new slides.

Remember, when attempting to edit text on the new slide, you may first need to select the text (word processing) tool at the top-left of the toolbar. Then, click the text on the slide that you want to edit. This is particularly true if the text is part of a grouped (Arrange | Group) object.

Remember that slides can be more than simply text and drawn shapes. You can select one of the frame tools, as described in the "Draw Objects and Text" section of Chapter 11, if you'd like to add data or images from another AppleWorks module. This enables you to add spreadsheet data, graphs, painting frames, tables, or other frames, using the tools from other AppleWorks modules.

If you have a QuickTime movie, an external image file, or some other external file that you'd like to add to a slide, you can do that, too. Select File | Insert, then locate the multimedia file you'd like to add in the Insert dialog box. (For more on the Insert command, see the section "Add Graphic Frames" in Chapter 12.)

AppleWorks can import AIFF and MP3 files and song tracks directly off of audio CDs. It can also import QuickTime movies, Macromedia Flash animations, and a variety of others. As you'll see later in the section "Present the Show," AppleWorks has special options that enable you to play back audio and video files automatically on each slide.

As you're adding and editing your slides, you can also arrange and re-arrange them on the Slides tab of the Controls window. Each slide is an icon that you can drag-and-drop before or after other slides. Click and drag one slide and you'll see a small line appear in between slides. Release the mouse button when the line appears in the new location where you'd like the slide to be and the slide will be placed there, as well as renumbered.

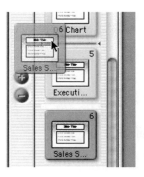

At the bottom of the Controls window, you'll find a menu and some buttons that help you make choices about each slide. Select a slide and use the pop-up menu to select a *transition* for that slide. Each transition represents a special effect that is used to transition from the previous slide into this slide. (That is, the transition that you select for the slide will be used when the slide appears on screen, not when it's leaving the screen.) Special transition effects are a fun way to spice up the presentation and make it a bit more professional—as long as you don't go overboard. I suggest you pick a few basic transition types and stick to them.

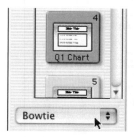

You can also select a slide and click one of the four buttons along the bottom of the Controls window to determine whether or not the slide should be printed and whether or not it should be shown as part of a slide show. If you'd like to leave a slide in your presentation, but not print it, select that slide and click the printer icon with the circle and a line through it. If you'd like the slide to be in the presentation, but not show the next time you display the slide show, select that slide and click the closed-eye icon.

Add Notes to Slides

The Presentation module has a neat little feature that you may find useful if you're serious about your presentations—the Notes view. In Notes view, a small text area appears beneath each slide, where you can type a little information about the slide, such as notes to yourself, a script of what to say about that slide, and so on. To enter Notes view, choose Window | Notes View. You'll see the main Presentation window change to show you a small view of the slide and a text area underneath where you can begin typing your notes (see Figure 13-3).

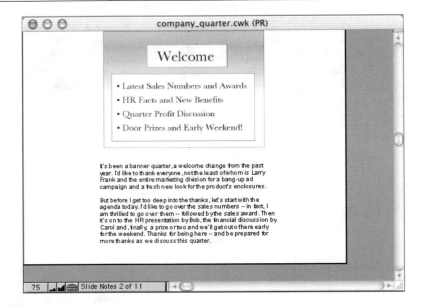

FIGURE 13-3   In Notes view, you'll find a small area below the slide for typing your notes.

Once you have notes associated with your slides, you may find it handy to print those notes separately, perhaps to use while you're actually giving the presentation. To print your notes, choose File | Print. In the Print dialog box, choose AppleWorks from the pull-down menu.

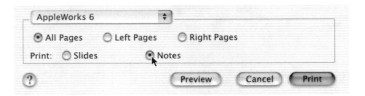

Now you'll see a radio button that enables you to print the Notes instead of the Slides—turn on that option and click Print to begin printing. What comes out of your printer are pages that include a representation of the slide at the top of the page and the notes below them, making it easy for you to see, at a glance, which notes are related to which slides.

Arrange and Organize

On the Organize tab of the Controls window, you can drag slides around more quickly than you can on the Slides tab. You'll find, however, that the Organize tab is best used when you've already named your slides on the Slides tab. Otherwise, you'll see a listing of "Untitled" slides that are impossible to do much with.

If you have named your slides, then you can use the Organize tab to drag individual slides around and change their position in the slide show. You can also use the Add (+) button to add a folder, which you can then name. The folders you create are for your benefit only—they won't affect the order or presentation of slides. You can, however, drag slides into the folders to create different logical breaks in your presentation, which may help you see and organize the presentation better. You can then click the disclosure triangles to hide and reveal the slides in each folder, making it a bit easier to work on one section of your presentation at a time.

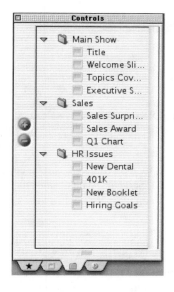

Note that the Organize tab gives you one other interesting capability—when you select a folder and click the Delete (–) button, you'll delete not only that folder, but also the slides in that folder. This is an easy way to quickly delete slides, but be careful—it's also an easy way to delete slides you didn't mean to delete, thus ruining an afternoon's worth of work!

Present the Show

Once you've created and arranged your slides, you're ready to present the show. To begin, you should set the options for how the slide show will be presented by clicking the Slide Show tab in the Controls window. There you'll see a number of settings you can select and alter to determine whether the show will run automatically, whether the cursor will be visible, and how movies and sounds will be played.

13

Here are the options:

- Under Slide Options, you can turn on the Auto Advance Every option to have the slide show run on its own. In the Seconds entry box, enter the number of seconds each slide should appear on the screen. You can also enable the Play Show Continuously option if you'd like the show to loop onscreen.

- Turn on or off the Show Cursor option depending on whether or not you'd like to be able to move the mouse cursor around on the screen while the slide show is being displayed.

- Under Movies & Sounds, turn on the Show Controls option if you'd like the QuickTime player controls to appear. This will enable someone watching a self-running presentation to stop and start the QuickTime movies or sound playback.

- Select Play Automatically if you'd like any inserted QuickTime movies or sounds to play; select Finish Before Advancing if you'd like the slide show to wait until the movie or sound has fully played before going to the next slide.

- Select Play All Movies & Sounds in a Slide at Once if you'd like all multimedia to play simultaneously in slides that have more than one movie and/or sound inserted.

Once you've made your selections, you can click the large Play button (with the right-pointing triangle) to play the slide show onscreen. (You can also select Window | Slide Show to begin the show at any time.) Once the slide show is playing (if it isn't set to advance automatically), you can either press the SPACEBAR or the RETURN key, or click the mouse button to advance to the next slide. To stop the presentation and return to AppleWorks, press the ESC key.

TIP

As noted in Chapter 1, many iMacs have a VGA-out port that can be used to display your presentation on a larger monitor or on a compatible presentation system. Hook your iMac up to an external display and you can use AppleWorks for presentations to large groups!

Create a Self-Running Presentation

You may have noticed that the AppleWorks Presentation module gives you all the tools you need to create a self-running presentation, good for a "kiosk" presentation or a multimedia brochure for your company or organization. The key to a good self-running presentation, though, is to create QuickTime audio files and/or video movies that accompany each slide. (See Chapters 14 and 15 for hints on how to create audio and video files.) For each slide, you'll want to record some narration or display a QuickTime movie, which you add to the slide using the File | Insert command. Then, use the Slide Show tab in the Controls window to set the show to auto-advance, play continuously, and play movies and sounds automatically so that the media files finish before advancing to the next slide.

The result: As people watch the slide show, each slide will advance automatically either after a set number of seconds, or after the narration audio (or video) is finished. Your viewers can then concentrate on watching as much of the show as they want—it will continue to loop. What's this good for? How about setting up an iMac in the front of your real estate office, chamber of commerce, school, organization, or company and have that iMac play back a presentation complete with audio and video of your group's highlights, sales materials, or interesting educational tidbits?

13

Chapter 14

Work with Movies, Music, and Images

How to...

■ View a QuickTime movie

■ Display image files on the screen

■ Rip, mix, and burn with iTunes

■ Watch a DVD movie

Apple markets the iMac and other Mac models as *digital hubs,* suggesting that they can be the center of your creative world, enabling you to create and edit quite a bit of digital, audio, and visual material. In this chapter, you'll be introduced to QuickTime, the technology behind the iMac's *multimedia* capabilities—the ability to integrate sound, video, and images.

So what can you do with QuickTime? With both QuickTime and other technologies, you can play digital movies and movie clips, create and edit digital sounds, and work with images to incorporate them more easily into your documents. In this chapter, you'll meet the QuickTime Player, the iMac's image viewers, iTunes, and the DVD Player.

Understand QuickTime Technology

Just as your iMac requires underlying technologies to allow it to print—you may have noticed that nearly every application offers almost identical Print dialog boxes—it also benefits from underlying technology to play digital movies and digital sound. That technology, developed by Apple, is QuickTime.

What QuickTime Is to You

QuickTime is a rather advanced digital technology that, in a way, mimics an animation flipbook. It stores images in the form of ones and zeros, then displays them in rapid order, usually between 10 and 30 frames per second. (For comparison, a film is generally shown at 24 frames per second, while television is displayed at about 30 frames per second. Any more than about 10 frames per second gives a reasonable sensation of movement to the viewer.)

QuickTime is also capable of recording audio and layering it in with the video so that it can be synchronized with the video or complementary to it. Audio can also stand alone within a QuickTime "movie" file, then be played back at any time using the QuickTime Player application or many others that support QuickTime technology.

NOTE   *QuickTime is also a translation technology—built into it is the ability to translate between different audio, video, and image file formats. Different applications and computer platforms (like those from Microsoft, Sun Microsystems, Silicon Graphics, and other computing companies) save files in different formats. QuickTime, and applications that take advantage of QuickTime, offer the capability to translate to and from Macintosh file formats. In that way, it's easy to play or display nearly any movie, sound, or image file you find on the Internet or elsewhere.*

Want QuickTime to do more? It can. QuickTime *streaming* is a technology that makes it possible to view QuickTime movies as they are transferred over a network connection—generally, this is done over the Internet. In most cases, you'll open a movie document that is stored on your iMac's hard drive. With streaming, it's possible to view a movie as it arrives, instantaneously, over long distances. This has many applications, not the least of which is the possibility that you can watch live events via *Webcasts* or "narrowcasts." This can be a very interesting technology, especially if the event wouldn't otherwise be broadcast for television.

Finally, QuickTime is multimedia. You've probably heard that catchphrase before and wondered why it's significant. *Multimedia* is defined as the bringing together of many different media—audio, video, still imagery, text, virtual reality—to communicate ideas, educate, or entertain. Obviously, QuickTime fits the bill quite nicely.

The QuickTime Software

The manifestation of QuickTime on your iMac comes in the form of Mac OS Extension files that are stored in the System Folder on your iMac's hard drive in Mac OS 9. In Mac OS X, the technology is built into the operating system. There's also a QuickTime Settings control panel stored in the Control Panels folder in the System Folder in Mac OS 9; and a QuickTime pane of the System Preferences application in Mac OS X.

While those QuickTime components are interesting, they're not as relevant to us as users as is the QuickTime Player software and, in Mac OS 9, the PictureViewer application. Both of these can be found in the Apple Extras folder on your main hard drive. You also probably have an alias to the QuickTime Player on your Mac OS 9 desktop if you haven't deleted it (it's installed there automatically), or as a tile in Mac OS X's Dock. You can just launch that alias anytime you want to launch the QuickTime Player.

At the time of writing, the latest version of QuickTime is QuickTime 5. If you have an iMac made before the summer of 2001, however, it may include an earlier version of QuickTime. I recommend that you upgrade to QuickTime 5, as it offers new features and faster performance. QuickTime 5 for Mac OS 9 is a free download from **http://www.apple.com/quicktime/** on the Web. (QuickTime 5 is built into Mac OS X, and can be updated via Software Update, discussed in Chapter 29.)

NOTE   *Plan to work a lot with movies and multimedia? Then I recommend you upgrade to QuickTime Pro. To get QuickTime Pro, you must register with Apple and pay a small fee (about $30 at the time of this writing) via the QuickTime Web site. In exchange, you'll get a registration code that upgrades the capabilities of the QuickTime Player and the QuickTime Web browser plug-in.*

Use the QuickTime Player Application

If you have a QuickTime movie that you've downloaded over the Internet or copied from a CD-ROM, you can double-click it to launch the movie file. When you do, most likely the QuickTime Player application will launch (see Figure 14-1).

Playhead and slider bar
Volume control
Reverse
Forward
To beginning
Play button
To end
QuickTime TV
Size control

FIGURE 14-1   The QuickTime Player interface is a little like a VCR, but with a bunch of other little features.

The QuickTime Player, in both Mac OS 9 and Mac OS X, offers controls that look a lot like a cassette recorder or VCR's controls. When you have a digital movie file loaded, you'll find Play, Stop, and Fast Forward buttons. You'll also find a slider bar that shows the progress of the movie as it's playing. Grab the playhead on that slider and drag it back, and you can play part or all of your movie again. You'll also find you have control over the volume by dragging the little volume slider back and forth with the mouse.

Select the Movie menu (from the menu bar) and you can choose the size at which your movie will display. Movies generally open at their optimum size for quality viewing. If you'd like to see the movie a little larger, you can choose Movie | Double Size. The quality of the video won't be as good (it'll most likely appear more "pixelated" or jagged) but it'll be larger. The further back you sit from your monitor, the better it will look.

You can also get some information about the movie—choose Movie | Get Movie Properties to see the Properties window. Here, you can find out about the different audio and video tracks in the movie and view other relevant information.

NOTE   *There are three kinds of tracks that a QuickTime movie can have: video, audio, and text. Each track is a separate line of data in the movie document that is synchronized with the others. The digital data stored in the video and audio tracks is compressed because video and audio, without compression, require huge amounts of storage. These compression schemes are called codecs, which stands for "compressor/decompressor." The better the codecs, the better the quality of a QuickTime movie file and the smaller and more transportable the movie will be.*

The QuickTime Player has some sound controls, as well, that are hidden by default. Select Movie | Show Sound Controls to change the balance, bass, and treble settings for QuickTime playback.

Explore QuickTime TV and Favorites

With the push toward QuickTime streaming technology, Apple has made it possible to view things like newscasts, music videos, and live events over the Internet, just using the QuickTime Player. To see these options, choose QTV | QuickTime TV | Show QuickTime TV Channels. (You can also click the TV button on the front of the QuickTime window, near the other controls.) That causes the QuickTime TV tab to appear, complete with a series of icons that represent channels you can watch. You'll also notice the Favorites tab (with the heart icon) immediately behind the QTV tab.

With the QTV window open, you can single-click one of the channels to load it into the QuickTime Player. You'll probably need to have your Internet connection active (or set to automatically connect) before the movie can be played in the viewer. Eventually, depending on the speed of your connection, you'll see a new movie appear in the window. It may be a streaming video, or it may be a special screen that incorporates Macromedia Flash technology. In this case, you can actually click in the movie window to view different types of content.

You can save your own movies as Favorites, if you like. Usually, you open movies using the File | Open command or by double-clicking a movie in the Finder. If you'd like to open a movie from the Favorites tab, you'll need to add it first. With the movie open in QuickTime Player, choose QTV | Favorites | Add Movie as Favorite. Now, a small icon appears on the Favorites tab that represents your newly added movie file. In the future, you can select QTV | Favorites | Show Favorites, then click the movie's icon to play it again.

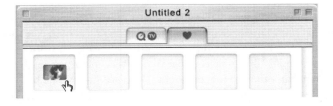

14

 *You can also drag movie icons from the Finder to an open slot in the Favorites drawer to add them as Favorites.*

To remove a Favorite from the Favorites tab, simply drag it from the window to the Trash.

View a Streaming Movie

You've already seen one way to view a streaming movie—by selecting one of the channels that appears on the QuickTime TV tab, you'll be connected over your Internet connection to a streaming movie site, then the movie will appear in your QuickTime Player window.

> *Again, don't forget that a streaming movie doesn't necessarily have video. You can listen to National Public Radio (NPR), for instance, using one of the QuickTime Player's Favorites. The live broadcast is sent as a streaming "movie" (since that's what all QuickTime media is called) but it only has an audio component. You'll just hear it—you won't see any video in the Player.*

There are other ways to viewing streaming movies, though. The most common way is to locate a streaming QuickTime *feed* somewhere on the Web using your Web browser application. You'll click a link or a button on a Web page that begins the streaming movie. When you do that, your QuickTime Player is often automatically launched (or switched to if it's already running) and the streaming movie appears. You might see indications of the streaming process before the movie actually starts—QuickTime Player gives you messages to show what's happening, like "Connecting," "Negotiating," and "Buffering." Those are all indications that your streaming movie is being loaded over the Internet and preparing to play.

Your streaming movie experience may be a little different than playing a movie from your hard disk or from a CD. First, you'll probably notice that your streaming movie is lower quality than a typical QuickTime movie you play from your hard disk or a CD-ROM. Why is that? Because the data has to be sent in real time over the Internet. *Real time* means it's played almost as it arrives, to give you a seamless viewing experience. Good quality QuickTime movies need a lot of data to flash up a pretty picture 15-30 times per second, and many Internet connections can't handle that sort of demand. So, picture size and quality are compromised in order to allow you to see *something* in your QuickTime Player. The slower your Internet connection (and the slower the Internet server computer that's sending the movie data) the worse the picture quality. That's one good reason to get a cable modem or special DSL access! (See Chapter 23 for more on high-speed access.)

The second thing that's a little weird about streaming video is the way fast forward and rewind work. Usually, a QuickTime movie played from a regular hard disk, CD-ROM, or DVD-ROM allows you to flip through each frame or use the Fast Forward/Rewind buttons to shuttle through the movie just like a VCR does. With a streaming movie, though, things don't work that way. You can often go to a different section of the movie, but you generally do this by moving the slider bar in the QuickTime Player. Then the connection has to be renegotiated (you'll see those messages again) before the movie can begin playing in its new spot.

If the streaming movie you're watching is a *live event* or *live broadcast* then you obviously can't fast forward or move to a later part of the movie, since it hasn't happened yet! With live broadcasts you also generally can't pause the movie and return to the same spot—when you click Play again, you'll see the connection negotiated and you'll start at the current spot in the live broadcast. In other streaming movies, you can pause and play again at the same spot.

Use the QuickTime Web Browser Plug-in

Along with the QuickTime Player comes the QuickTime plug-in, an addition to Web browsers that allows them to display QuickTime movies directly within the Web browser's document window. You'll notice that the controls are pretty much the same whether you're viewing a movie with QuickTime Player (playing from your hard disk) or with a Web browser (playing across the Internet).

QuickTime movies must be embedded in the Web page for them to appear in the browser— otherwise they're downloaded to your iMac first, and you view them in the QuickTime Player. If they're embedded in the page with special HTML codes, the movie, QuickTime VR, or QuickTime audio movie plays from within the browser screen itself. This works great for streaming QuickTime, which allows you to watch a movie *while* it is being transmitted over the Internet.

> **NOTE** *If QuickTime movies aren't displaying correctly, the QuickTime plug-in may not be in the right place. In Mac OS X, it should be stored in the Internet Plug-ins folder inside the main Library folder on your hard disk. In Mac OS 9, it should be stored in the Plug-ins subfolder found in your Web browser's folder. If it's not there, do a quick Sherlock search for **QuickTime Plug-in**, then copy a version of the file to the Plug-ins folder.*

If you've upgraded to QuickTime Pro, you'll be given a few other options with the plug-in, including the ability to save movies directly from Web pages. Click and hold the mouse button on an embedded QuickTime movie (or CONTROL-click the movie) and a pop-up menu appears. Choose Save as QuickTime Movie to save the movie to your iMac's hard drive. Then you're free to view it in the QuickTime Player.

Work with Images

PictureViewer is a small utility program that displays image files in Mac OS 9. Preview is a similar application in Mac OS X. Both applications can handle the basic Mac file formats (PICT and QuickTime Image) as well as TIFF (for high-resolution photos), JPEG (for Web photos), GIF and PNG (for non-photo Web graphics), and others.

NOTE   *PictureViewer is found in the QuickTime folder inside the Applications (Mac OS 9) folder. Preview is found inside the main Applications folder in Mac OS X.*

Load Images

To load an image into PictureViewer or Preview, you can double-click the image file, drag-and-drop the image document on the application's icon, or choose File | Open from within the application.

Once you have the image open in PictureViewer, you can change the size at which the image is displayed by selecting one of these commands: Image | Half Size, Image | Normal Size, Image | Double Size, or Image | Fill Screen. You can also rotate the image by choosing Image | Rotate Left or Image | Rotate Right, and you can flip the image by choosing Image | Flip Horizontal or Image | Flip Vertical.

The options in Preview are a little more basic. Select Display | Zoom In or Display | Zoom Out to change the magnification of the image, and choose Display | Actual Size to see the image at its original dimensions.

If you've upgraded to QuickTime Pro, PictureViewer Pro is capable of saving files to a number of different formats, effectively working as a file format translator. Once you have an image loaded in PictureViewer, you can save it as a BMP (Windows Bitmap), PICT, PCX, QuickTime image, or Photoshop image file. Choose File | Export and a Save dialog box will appear.

Preview can save images even if you haven't upgraded to QuickTime Pro, but only in TIFF format. To save an image as a TIFF, select File | Save As. In the Save As dialog box, give the image a name and click Save.

Use iPhoto

Apple includes iPhoto, which works only in Mac OS X, with its latest iMac models. (You can also download it from http://www.apple.com/downloads/macosx/apple/.) iPhoto enables you to easily import images from a digital camera, then use it's tools to improve and output those images in various ways.

To begin, plug your camera into your iMac (usually via a USB port). If your camera is recognized, iPhoto should launch automatically; if it doesn't, then launch iPhoto (double-click its icon in the Applications folder) and see if your camera is recognized (it appears at the bottom of the iPhoto window). If it is, click Import to import the image from your camera into iPhoto.

Once your images are in iPhoto, they're stored in the Photo Library. To export an image as a regular image file, select it and click File | Export. Make your selections in the Export dialog box and click Save.

Double-click an image to edit it (or select an image and click Edit in the toolbar at the bottom of the screen). The image will appear full size, and you can use the tools in the tools area at the bottom of the window—Rotate, Constrain, and Black & White—to change the image's qualities. You can also use the Crop tool to trim the image and the Red Eye tool to fix the red-eye issue created by some camera's flashes, but you first need to drag a box directly on to the photo (click at the upper-left corner of the area of the photo you want to affect, then drag down to the lower-right corner). With the box onscreen, choose Crop to trim the image to the box's contents or Red Eye to fix a problem with red eye.

With your images edited, you can create an "album" that you'll use to share the images by printing them or translating them to the Web. Here's how:

1. Select File | New Album and type a name for the album in the New Album dialog box.

2. Next, click the Organize button at the bottom of the screen. In the Photo Library, you can drag photos to your newly created album.

3. Finally, click the album's entry in the Album list, and now you can drag the photos around to arrange their order in the album.

What you do next depends on the type of output you want. Click Book if you'd like to format your photo album as a book. You'll be able to rearrange pages, choose different Themes, and even edit the text. Once you've created the book's format, click Share, then click Print or Order Book if you'd like to order a printed version of the book from Apple (you'll need an active Internet connection).

14

For other types of output, just click Share. In the tools area, you can select HomePage to use your photos with the iTools HomePage tool (discussed in Chapter 21). Click Slide Show to see your images onscreen in a slide show format, complete with music.

Click Export, and you'll see a dialog box that lets you export an album in different ways. Click the File Export tab to export each image as a separate image file. Click the Web Page tab and you can automatically generate a Web page of images, including thumbnail images (smaller images you click to see the bigger images). Choose the QuickTime tab and you can export your images as a short QuickTime movie, displaying each image for a certain number of seconds. When you've made your choices, click Export to export your album's photos in whatever format you've chosen.

Mix, Rip, and Burn Audio

Today's iMacs come with a fair amount of free software, care of Apple, designed to make using an iMac quite a bit more fun. Not the least of these offerings is iTunes, a great little application that enables you to work with CDs and MP3 audio files. *MP3* files are special, high-quality music files that are generally only a few megabytes in size, meaning they can be easily transported over the Internet. (That's what all the Napster hype was about a little while back.)

With iTunes, you can turn CD audio tracks into MP3s, and store that music on your hard disk. And you can create your own playlists, then use those playlists to burn CDs using the built-in CD-RW drive that many iMacs feature. In Apple's marketing materials, they call it *Rip, Mix, Burn.*

> **NOTE** *Apple has both Mac OS X and Classic versions of iTunes available. If you're having trouble with any features (particularly CD burning), don't forget to use the Software Update feature to update iTunes to the latest version available. Also, note that Mac OS 9 still has the Apple CD Player in the Applications (Mac OS 9) folder, which you can use simply for CD playback if desired.*

On new iMacs, you'll find iTunes in the Applications (Mac OS 9) folder for the Mac OS 9 version, or the main Applications folder for the Mac OS X version. If you don't have iTunes, it's a free download from **http://www.apple.com/itunes/** on the Web. When iTunes is launched, you'll see the main interface, shown in Figure 14-2.

> **NOTE** *The first time you launch iTunes, you'll be greeted by the iTunes Setup Assistant. After you've answered the Assistant's questions, you'll see the main iTunes screen.*

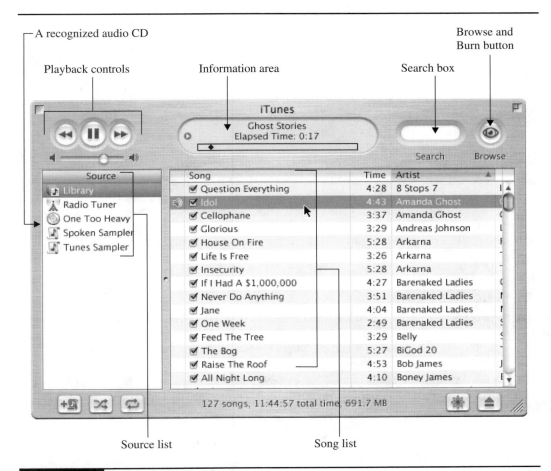

A recognized audio CD

Browse and Burn button

Playback controls

Information area

Search box

FIGURE 14-2   The iTunes interface

Source list

Song list

On some iMac models, you'll immediately be greeted by a listing of MP3 songs—these are songs that Apple has pre-loaded on your iMac's hard disk for you. To play one of the songs, select it in the list and click the Play button in the top-left corner of the iTunes window; it becomes a Pause button you can click to pause playback. The small slider bar underneath the

Play button can be used to adjust volume. The Forward and Reverse buttons can be used to move between songs, while the small slider in the information area can be used to move around within a song.

> TIP
>
> *iTunes has a special feature, called Visuals, which can be fun to watch while you're playing back songs. Click the eight-sided star button in the bottom-right of the iTunes window, or select Visuals | Turn Visuals On to see this effect in action. Also, if you see the option, try Visuals | Full Screen.*

If you look at the Source list, you'll notice that you're seeing the Library; the Library is where all imported MP3 songs are stored in iTunes. To search for songs in the Library, you can begin typing in the Search box; as you type, matching songs and artists appear in the song list. If you'd like to take a different look at your Library, click the Browse button. Now you can peruse your songs by artist and album as well as by title.

Need to delete a song? Select it in the Library and press the DELETE key or chose Edit | Clear. In the dialog box that appears, click Yes if you really want to delete the song.

Play (and Rip) CDs

One of the most basic reasons you'll launch iTunes is to play audio CDs. Insert an audio CD and that CD will appear in the Source list. Select the CD and the song list changes to show you that CD's songs. To play a song, select it and click the Play button, just as you would with an MP3.

> NOTE
>
> *If you have Internet access, iTunes can check a special database for the names of your commercial CDs and the songs on it. If you don't see those names, choose Advanced | Get CD Track Names.*

As with a home CD player, you can opt to have the songs shuffle or repeat during playback. Choose Controls | Shuffle if you'd like songs to play back randomly; choose Controls | Repeat One or Repeat All if you'd like the songs on the CD to repeat.

> TIP
>
> *You can drag the CD's songs around in the song list if you'd like to hear the tracks in a particular order.*

The real power of iTunes, however, is the fact that it lets you import songs from your CDs into the iTunes Library. (That's the "ripping" part.) Importing songs turns them into MP3 files, which can then be played back directly off your iMac's hard disk without the CD. As you'll see, you can then place the songs on a playlist (for custom mixes of your favorite songs) and, if desired, you can burn those songs onto a recordable CD, if you have a compatible CD-RW drive.

To import a song from a CD, insert the CD in your iMac's CD drive. Now, when the CD appears in the Source list, select it. Next, drag the song you want to import from the song list to the Library icon in the Source list. The song will be imported. You'll see a small orange icon appear next to the track number of the CD song and "Importing" will appear in the information area. (iTunes imports songs more quickly than it plays them, so you'll see the import process end before the song stops playing.)

To import all the songs on that CD, simply click the Import button in the top-right corner of the iTunes window. All of the songs on that CD will be imported. When it's done, you can switch back to the Library by selecting it in the Source list. The songs from the CD have been added to your song Library; they can be selected and played at any time, regardless of whether the CD is in your iMac's drive.

> TIP
>
> *Want to automate this process? Choose iTunes | Preferences (in Mac OS X) or Edit | Preferences (in Mac OS 9) and choose the General tab. In the CD Insert menu, you can choose Import Songs and Eject if you'd like songs automatically imported as MP3s the moment you insert the CD.*

To eject the CD, you can press the EJECT key on the keyboard (if you have one), press ⌘-E, or choose Controls | Eject CD.

> TIP
>
> *Click the minimize button (in Mac OS X) or the minimize box (in Mac OS 9) and iTunes turns into a tiny window that shows only the basic playback controls, the volume slider, and a truncated information window. Perfect for playing songs in the background while you work, study, or surf the Web.*

Mix Songs and Burn CDs

The "Mix" part of iTunes' features refers to the *playlists* that you can create and manage in the Source list. A playlist is simply an arrangement of songs in your Library; you drag songs from the Library to a playlist and the songs are played in that order. Playlists can be created and deleted at any time without affecting the songs on the playlist—the MP3 files aren't deleted when you delete a playlist, and they aren't duplicated when you create more than one playlist. They're always there, safe in the Library, until you decide to delete them from the Library itself.

To create a playlist, choose File | New Playlist. Now, type a name for the playlist and press RETURN. (If you need to rename the playlist, it works just like a list item in the Finder; click once

14

on the name and wait a second, then you'll be able to type a new name.) To add songs to the playlist, simply switch back to the Library and drag songs to that playlist's entry in the Source list.

SHORTCUT *You can select the songs first in the Library and choose File | New Playlist from Selection.*

Now, with the playlist itself selected, you can pick up songs and drag them around to change their order; to remove a song from the playlist, select it and press DELETE. (It isn't deleted from the Library, just from the playlist.) To add more songs, switch back to the Library and drag more songs to the playlist.

You'll notice that the number of songs and the amount of time those songs take up is shown at the bottom of the iTunes window when you're viewing a playlist—this is to help you if you plan to burn a CD using this playlist. Once you have all of the songs on the playlist you want to burn to CD (and the total length doesn't exceed the rated length of the CD-R, which is usually 74 minutes), you're ready to burn.

NOTE *Actually, total length can exceed the CD, if you like, but only the songs that fit will be burned onto the CD.*

Burning a CD in iTunes requires either an internal Apple CD-RW drive or a compatible third-party drive that's supported by iTunes. (See **http://www.apple.com/itunes/compatibility/** for a list of compatible CD-RW drives.) If you've got that, and you've created your playlist, here's how to create the CD:

1. Click the Burn CD button in the top-right corner of the iTunes window.

2. You'll be prompted to insert a blank CD-R disc. Do so. (Remember that CD-R discs tend to be a little more reliable than CD-RW discs if you plan to play your CD in standard CD audio players.)

3. When iTunes has recognized the disc, you'll see "Click Burn CD to Start" in the information window, along with the number of tracks and the total time for the disc. If it all looks good, click Burn CD. (iTunes doesn't warn you if the total time for your playlist is longer than your CD can support, so do the math yourself before clicking the Burn CD button.)

Now, iTunes will step through the process of burning the CD. Depending on the speed of your CD-RW mechanism, this could take quite a while—somewhere between five and fifteen minutes. It's also pretty important not to do anything else on your iMac while the CD is burning—an application or system crash could cause problems, as could a system slowdown. (You'll have fewer problems in Mac OS X with crashes and slowdowns.)

When iTunes is finished, you should see the new CD there in the Source list, with the same name as the playlist you used to create it. Now you can play the songs directly off the CD, if desired, or you can eject the CD and take it with you to play in other CD audio equipment.

Play a DVD Movie

If you have an iMac DV or later model with an internal DVD drive, you have the special ability to play DVD movies using the DVD-ROM drive and some special software included with your iMac. All you have to do is insert a DVD movie title in your iMac's DVD-ROM drive and launch the Apple DVD Player application, which you'll find in the Applications (Mac OS 9) folder on your iMac's hard disk.

NOTE   *If you want to play DVDs in Mac OS X, version 10.1 or higher is required. If your iMac has a DVD drive and you're using Mac OS X 10.1 or higher, you'll find the DVD Player application in the main Applications folder.*

Once you've got the player up and running, you'll see the Viewer window and the DVD controller, a small, slick interface that offers some controls that should be familiar if you've ever used a VCR or even a tape recorder (shown is the Mac OS 9 version).

14

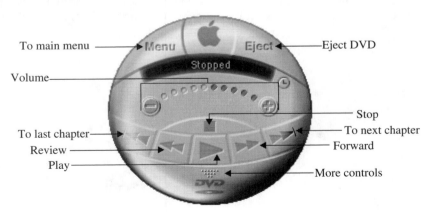

To main menu ──── Menu   Eject ──── Eject DVD

Volume ────

To last chapter ────   ──── Stop
Review ────   ──── To next chapter
Play ────   ──── Forward
     ──── More controls

NOTE   *Mac OS X's DVD Player controller offers the same basic functionality, but with a slightly different look, which we weren't able to screen shot in time for publication.*

To begin playing the DVD movie, click the Play button. You should see the movie's opening sequence and then, in most cases, you'll see the movie's main menu. You can then click in the Viewer window itself to select what you'd like to do next—view the movie, see additional features, and so on.

While you're viewing the movie, you can use the different controls to move forward or back within the film. Most DVD movies are divided into chapters, so you can use the Previous Chapter and Next Chapter buttons to move back and forth between different chunks of the movie. And, at any time, you can click the Menu button on the Controller to return to the DVD's main menu.

You can change the size of the movie fairly easily. Choose the Video menu and choose the size you'd like, or choose Present Video on Screen if you'd like to watch the movie without seeing window controls or the menu bar. To bring the menu bar back, simply move the mouse up to the top of the Mac's screen and the menu reappears.

TIP   *While you're watching the movie you may also want to get that controller out of the way. You can do that by selecting Window | Hide Controller. To get the controller back, choose Window | Show Controller.*

Many DVD movies include significant additional features, including multiple sound tracks (often in different languages), the ability to display subtitles, and even wackier features like the ability to change the camera angle while you're viewing a movie. To access these controls in Mac OS 9, click the DVD logo at the bottom of the controller. This causes the bottom part of the controller to "open up," revealing more controls. (Once revealed, there is a small control at the bottom-center of the controller that you can click to close the DVD controller back up.)

Point the mouse at one of these buttons and leave it there for a moment—you'll see a small label appear, showing you what the purpose of the button is. Click the button to activate that option—you'll likely see a response in the small indicator in the Controller.

When you click the Stop button, your place in the movie is saved; you can click Play again to resume from that point. If you're done with the movie, you can click Eject to eject the DVD from your iMac.

Chapter 15

Edit Your Own Movies

How to...

- Get your movie into your iMac
- Edit the clips
- Add transitions, sounds, and titles
- Lay in your soundtrack
- View, save, and export the movie

It's happening again. We've talked about killer apps in other chapters in this book. Killer apps are those applications that introduce an entirely new capability to computing, drawing in new people, creating new careers, and altering the technological landscape. In the past, killer apps have included spreadsheet computing, desktop publishing, and Web publishing, all of which are covered in this book, because the iMac is capable of all those killer apps.

If you have an iMac that includes FireWire ports, then you're ready for the next killer app for personal computers: desktop video. Using a digital camcorder, the FireWire port on your iMac, and a wonderful little program called iMovie 2, you can turn your iMac into the most inexpensive non-linear video editing bay that the world has yet seen. The funny part is that iMovie 2 is incredibly easy to use and gives really good results.

Digital Video Explained

Digital video (DV) camcorders have hit a magical price point, now coming in well under $1,000 for a consumer model. That's made them very popular among the folks who like to buy camcorders. But they're becoming even more popular for the folks who like the idea of *editing* videos, not just shooting them.

Instead of recording analog information (electronic signal information) to a VHS or Betamax tape, digital camcorders work sort of like computer scanners with a lens. They immediately translate what you see in the viewfinder into digital data—ones and zeros. Most of them then store that data on magnetic tape, just as some computers write backup files to magnetic tape.

The advantage to this is two-fold. First, the image can be corrected digitally as it's brought into the camera. If you shop for them, you'll notice that digital cameras have a lot of interesting features—built-in effects, image stabilizers, digital zoom—that aren't available on most analog cameras.

Second, digital data doesn't lose quality from copy to copy (in the biz, they say "from generation to generation"). This *generational* loss is more than evident whenever you copy from one VHS video to another; the copy is always worse than the original. With digital data, there's nothing to degrade over multiple copies (unless the tape starts falling apart). Just like a word processing document or a PICT image file, the quality of a digital video recording doesn't fade as you copy it.

In fact, a digital camera is basically just creating a computer file that's stored on that digital tape. And, since it's already a computer file, that means it's also easier to work with on your iMac. Since the latest iMac models have FireWire ports—and nearly all DV camcorders have FireWire ports—you can connect your camera to your iMac. Now, with iMovie, you can actually control your camera (at least, many models) and copy the video from the camera to your iMac.

Then, since the video is already a computer file, it's a simple matter to cut, paste, add in transitions, and lay down a soundtrack from CD or MP3. You'll also find that iMovie can add special digital effects and scrolling titles and credits, and it even offers you the ability to edit the sound separately from the video.

Finally, you can save the digital video as a QuickTime movie and put it on the Web, send it in e-mail (if you have a nice, fast connection), or save it on your hard disk. Or, you can copy the video back to your camcorder, then use your camcorder as a VCR to play the movie on your TV (or transfer it to typical VHS tape.)

> **NOTE** *In this chapter, I'll be discussing iMovie 2, which has versions that work in both Mac OS 9 and Mac OS X. If you didn't receive it with your iMac, iMovie 2 for Mac OS X is available as a free download (at the time of writing) from **http://www.apple.com/downloads/macosx/apple/** on the Internet. Earlier versions of iMovie are similar, but you'll find that some of the controls and commands have changed. Those earlier versions are also incompatible with Mac OS X—in fact, they don't even work correctly in the Classic environment.*

Get Video into Your iMac

Before you can edit your movie, you'll need to connect your camcorder to your iMac and launch iMovie. Then you'll copy the video *clips* into the program so you can edit them.

> **TIP** *If you don't have a DV camcorder, iMovie versions that came on CD or bundled with your iMac include a sample project that you can use to practice your editing. In fact, iMovie has an Apple Help-based tutorial that's pretty good for learning the basics of iMovie.*

Hook Up Your Camera

You can hook up your camera at any point—FireWire is hot-pluggable and iMovie will recognize the camera once the camera is plugged in. So, I'd recommend launching iMovie first, just so you can see the status of things. (iMovie 2 for Mac OS X is in the Applications folder on your iMac's hard disk; iMovie 2 for Mac OS 9 is in the Applications (Mac OS 9) folder.) Once launched, you'll see a dialog box with three options (and catchy music): New Project, Open Project, or Quit. Click New Project, then give the project a name in the Save dialog box that appears. In the future, you won't see this dialog box, because iMovie automatically opens your most recent project. (To open a different project, you'll need to select File | New Project or File | Open Project.)

> **NOTE** *If iMovie hasn't been used before, it may ask you if it can change your screen resolution; iMovie prefers to run at 1,024 × 768.*

15

Now, use a FireWire cable to connect your DV camcorder to one of the FireWire ports on the side of your iMac. Both of the connectors are designed to fit only in the correct direction. The longer, flatter connector plugs into the FireWire port on your iMac; the smaller, square connector connects to the camera.

Once you've got the camera connected, turn it on. If all goes well, iMovie will recognize the camera, as shown in Figure 15-1.

Depending on the camera, you may need to be in Playback or VCR mode in order for iMovie to control the camera. Then, click the small Camera mode icon (it looks like a camcorder and says "DV") to put iMovie in Camera mode so it can control the camera. If the camera is in its recording mode, point it around the room and you'll see the image play through the iMovie viewer (called the *monitor* window) in real-time.

> NOTE   *Apple maintains a list of compatible cameras and manufacturers at* **http://www.apple.com/imovie** *on the Web.*

Import the Clips

Once you have iMovie connected to your camcorder and iMovie is in Camera mode, you're ready to import clips. Place your camcorder in VCR or Playback mode, then click the Import

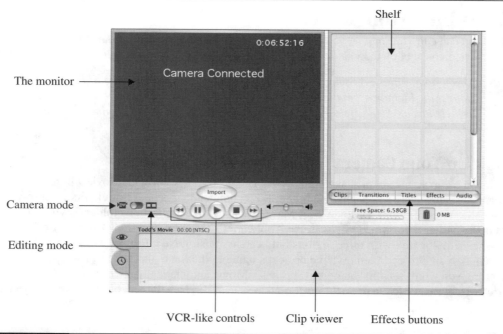

FIGURE 15-1   iMovie has recognized my camera and is ready to import video clips.

button on the iMovie interface and iMovie will fire up your camcorder and start importing clips from the camera.

NOTE
If you want every clip on your camcorder, make sure you've rewound the tape. You can do so using iMovie, if you like, by clicking the rewind button in the monitor window while you're in Camera mode.

iMovie moves through the tape and finds clips to import, then it places them on the "shelf" on the upper-right side of the iMovie screen. Each clip is a distinct segment of video; once you're in iMovie, you'll be able to drag-and-drop movie clips to change the order of the segments in your video.

TIP
iMovie ends the current clip whenever it encounters a point on the tape where you pressed Pause or Stop. If you'd prefer to have your clips imported as one long clip, choose Edit | Preferences and, on the Import tab, turn off the Automatically Start New Clip at Scene Break option.

Let iMovie continue to import clips until you've got all the clips you need. When you're done importing, you can click the Import button again to stop the process. Note that you can also use the VCR-like controls (when Import is not selected) to move around on the tape if you need to find additional clips you want.

You should be aware that digital video clips take up *tons* of hard disk space. In the iMovie window, you can see a Free Space indicator that shows you how much hard disk space is left on your iMac. You'll have to watch this carefully. In raw DV format, video takes around 3MB per *second* of video being created. That means every five minutes of video takes up about 1GB of hard disk space. You should watch the Free Space gauge to make sure you're not running out.

NOTE
If you're planning to save the video in QuickTime format, it will be compressed and take up much less space, but your raw clips still require a lot of disk space while you're working with them in iMovie.

Preview Your Clips

Once your clips are imported, you can preview them if you like. Click a clip on the shelf and it appears in the monitor. Now, click Play to see that clip, or use the other VCR-like controls to fast forward, rewind, stop, or pause. There's also a volume control in the monitor window if you need to change the volume.

Toss a Clip

Do you have a clip on the shelf that you don't want? You can toss those clips into iMovie's special Trash receptacle. Just drag the clip from the shelf to the small Trash icon. (This is not the same as the iMac's Trash can.) You can empty the Trash by selecting File | Empty Trash.

 *Parts of clips that get cropped or otherwise trimmed are put in this Trash as well. And emptying the Trash will reset the Undo function, so you won't be able to undo anything you've done prior to emptying the Trash. So, make sure you're happy with all the edits you've made recently before emptying.*

Edit Your Video

Once you have your clips imported into iMovie, you're ready to start editing. You'll do this in two steps—first, you clean up your imported clips, if necessary. Then, you'll lay the clips down in the clip viewer and arrange them to please.

Crop Your Clips

Although you're free to edit your clips once you've placed them in the *clip viewer* (the area at the bottom of the screen where you'll arrange the order of your clips), I think it's best to clean them up while they're still on the shelf. Then you can organize the clips a little more easily.

Select a clip on the shelf by clicking it once. It will appear in the monitor window. Now, you can do some basic cropping to the clip to get it to the rough length you want it to be. To crop a clip, you'll need to get to know the monitor's controls a little more intimately.

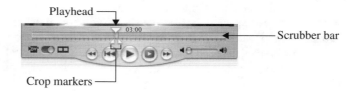

The scrubber bar is a bar that shows you the length of the clip. As the clip plays, you'll see the playhead move along the scrubber bar to show you where you are in the clip. You can drag the playhead to any point in the clip to start at that point. Once you have the playhead in about the right place, you can use the arrow keys on the keyboard to get it to exactly the frame of video you need.

The crop markers appear when you hold down the SHIFT key and click the mouse just below the scrubber bar. These markers can be used to select the area of a movie that you'd like to crop. Just drag the crop markers to the beginning and end of the section of the clip that you'd like to *keep*.

Once you have that portion selected, choose Edit | Crop from the menu. Only the portion of the original clip that was between the two markers will remain.

If you'd like to undo the cropping, you can do that. In fact, iMovie is capable of multiple Undo commands, so you can undo a series of edits or changes if you're not pleased with them. Just select Edit | Undo to undo a change.

Split Your Clips

If you need to split a single clip into two different clips, you can do that, too. Use the playhead to choose the exact point where you'd like to split the clip into two, then choose Edit | Split Clip at Playhead to split the clip. The clip now becomes two clips on the shelf.

TIP   *iMovie 2 has a neat trick—select a clip on the shelf and then choose Advanced | Reverse Clip Direction. The clip will now play backwards!*

Rename Clips

If Clip 01 and Clip 02 aren't creative enough for you, you can give your clips new names. Click the mouse button on the name of a clip that's on the shelf. Wait a second and the name becomes highlighted, just as if you were renaming an icon in the Finder. Now you can edit the name of the clip; press RETURN when you're finished.

Arrange the Clips

With your clips cropped down to the parts you want, you're ready to drag them from the shelf to the clip viewer. Make sure the clip viewer tab (the one with the eye icon on it) is selected, then drag clips down to the viewer. You can drag them in any order—in fact, you're using the clip viewer to create the order for your video.

Once you have clips on the clip viewer you can still move them around all you want. Just drag-and-drop a clip to its new location. And once you've got everything arranged on the clip viewer, you can play the whole movie through if you'd like. Make sure you don't have any of the clips selected (you can use the Edit | Select None command to make doubly sure), then click the Play button in the monitor window. You'll see the video from start to finish.

TIP   *You can also select one, two, or more clips in the clip viewer and play them back in the monitor window. To select more than one clip, hold down the SHIFT key while you select them. Then, click Play in the monitor window to view the series of clips you've selected.*

15

To remove a clip, drag it back to the shelf. If you're absolutely sure you don't need it any more, you can drag it to iMovie's Trash icon or you can select the clip and press DELETE.

Transitions, Sounds, and Titles

If you've been reading along so far, you're probably impressed with how easy iMovie is. You've already got an edited video! Well, it's not going to get much harder. Instead, you're just going to easily lay in some transitions and sounds, and add titles to your movie using a little more drag-and-drop.

Transition Between Clips

Transitions are just the fades and wipes between clips in your video. You don't have to use transitions; often, a clean cut between two clips looks fine. But you'll find that transitions are useful in many cases, either to suggest the passage of time, to help the viewer change thoughts along with you, or just to make things a little smoother between two different scenes. Plus, adding a transition is a great way to make your video look like it was edited on expensive professional equipment.

Before you can add a transition, you'll need two clips between which you can create a transition. Or, with some types of transitions (such as Fade In or Fade Out) you can create a transition at the beginning or the end of your video. In either case, you need to consider where the transition will look good.

Once you've got that location locked in your head, click the Transitions button. The transition list pops up, along with the preview screen that shows you how your transition will look. Select the transition you'd like to use from the list. Whenever you click a transition, you'll see a small preview in the preview window. Likewise, you can click the Preview button to see the transition previewed in the monitor window.

TIP *If I'm planning a transition between two clips, I like to select the two clips in the clip viewer (hold down* SHIFT *while you're selecting the second clip), then I select one of the transitions from the list. The preview shows a sample of the transition between the two selected clips.*

Once you've found the transition you like, drag it from the transition list down between the two clips (or in front of the first clip or behind the last clip) where the transition should take place. A small box appears, representing the transition. You'll also see a small red line as the transition is rendered. (You'll need to wait for this to complete before you can view the video in the monitor. You can do some other dragging and dropping if you like, though.)

Add Titles to the Video

Another pro-level touch is to add titles to your video. You can add titles anywhere in your movie if you'd like to introduce the video, roll some credits, or just have a little fun with written commentary on the screen.

To superimpose titles on a particular clip, select the clip in the clip viewer and click the Titles button. The Title controls appear, showing you a list of title styles and some options for those titles.

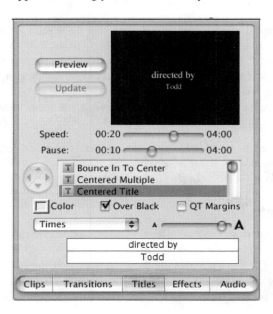

15

To get started, select one of the title styles, then enter text for the title. You can also choose the font, font size, and color for the title text from the pop-up menus, if desired. (Note that if you want to create a new, self-contained title clip, you can turn on the Over Black option, as discussed in the "How To…" sidebar later in this section.) Whenever you make a change, you'll see what your title looks like in the small preview window, or you can click the Preview button to see the titling in the big monitor window.

There are a number of different types of titles. As you click through them, you'll notice that they offer different ways you can type information, too. For instance, some titling schemes will support scrolling or centered credits, and they offer you multiple lines for those credits. Other options will enable you to create just a single title line. Still others allow for an entire block of text, which can be scrolled, centered, and so on. You can experiment with the different types to see which works best with the type of titling you're trying to do.

Also, notice the Pause slider and the Speed slider in the Title controller. The Speed slider allows you to determine how quickly the title effect will appear and disappear, while the Pause slider determines how long the title will appear, unchanged, on screen. These may be important if you'd like the title effect to fill the clip that its overlaying—you'll need to use the sliders to make the length of the titling sequence the same as the length of the clip it's overlaying. If it's longer, the titling will overlap two clips. (You'll notice that the shortest amount of time the title sequence can span is dictated by the effects that are being performed. After all, the title can only scroll so fast, for instance.)

NOTE   *If your titling sequence is shorter than the clip it overlays, then a split is created when you drag in the title style. The titled portion of the clip is followed by the new second clip that represents the rest of the original clip's video.*

Once you've got the length of the title the way you want it (again, you can test by clicking Preview), you can drag the title style from the style list down to the clip viewer. Place the title style in *front* of the clip that the title should overlay. The titled clip appears in the clip viewer. The titling needs to be rendered, so you'll see a small red progress indicator on the clip. You can't play the clip until it's done rendering.

Once the titled clip is rendered, you can view the movie again to see how your new title fits into the scheme of things.

TIP   *You can add a transition to a titled clip, but you need to render the titled clip first, then render the transition. For instance, if you want to fade into a titled clip, create the titled clip first, then place the Fade In transition in front of the titled clip.*

Add Special Effects

New in iMovie 2 are some optional special effects that you can see via the Effects button. They range from effects to change the colors of your image (including an Old West-style Sepia Tone or Black-and-White effect) to those that change the sharpness, brightness, or focus settings of the image. Using an effect is easy—select the clip in the clip viewer, then select the effect. Now, a few settings slider bars or other controls will appear in the Effects controller area; change them

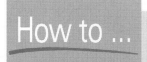

Add "Over Black" Titles and Credits

If you'd like to create titles or credits on a standard black background, you can do that easily.
In the titling window, select a title style that's designed for credits (Centered Title, Centered
Multiple, Rolling Credits, Rolling Centered Credits, and Centered Multiple are good choices),
then turn on the Over Black option. Choose White (or a slightly more gray-white color,
particularly for TV playback) as the text color. In the text area, you'll likely find a number
of text boxes for typing your credits; you can click the Add button to add more. (Click the
Preview button to see how the credits line up—you may need to type different parts of each
credit line in different text areas to make the credits looks right.)

When you're done building your credits, just drag the title style to the clip viewer and
drop it where you want the credits. (You'll probably place this title clip at the end of all your
other clips, since it's being used for credits.) The black-screen credits are rendered and, once
they're ready, you can play your video to see them.

to taste. (Not all effects have sliders.) When you like what you see, click the Apply button to
apply that effect to the clip.

Once you've applied the effect, you'll see a small red bar appear on the clip in the clip viewer
and a frame counter will slowly count out each frame as the effect is rendered. Note that you

15

can't change the effect of a clip that already has a transition attached to it (you'd have to remove the transition first) but you can place an effect on a titled clip.

 The Effects controls offer another interesting twist, however. You can choose an Effect In and an Effect Out time for the clip. This causes the effect to take place over time, meaning that, for instance, the frames of the clip will become Sepia Tone or Black and White as they play back, instead of the entire clip taking the effect. You'll find this fun to play with—set different Effect In and Effect Out times and preview the results to see what might work for your clips.

Drop in Sound Effects

You can create an entire soundtrack for your movie, but before you do that, you might want to add some simple sound effects. Click the Audio button and you'll see some sample sounds you can add to your video.

You can add more sounds by dragging them to the Sound Effects folder inside the Resources folder in the iMovie folder on your hard disk. Sound clips need to be AIFF files. (In Mac OS X, you may need to have an administrator's account to add files to this folder; see Chapter 27 for details on administrator accounts.) Note that adding sound effects slows down the launch time for iMovie.

To view the sound portions of your movie, click the timeline tab (the one beneath the clip viewer tab that looks like a clock face). Now you'll see three different tracks; each looks a little like a bar graph. The top track is the video track—you'll see bars that represent the video clips you've added to the movie. The second track is your first audio track; you can add the sound effects by dragging them to this track. The third track is the second audio track, which you'll generally use for adding underlying music if you'd like it in your movie.

To add sounds, simply drag them from the sound list in the Audio panel to the timeline. Place them on the audio track where you'd like them to occur relative to the video clips—the sound effects show up as small blue boxes with a line between them to indicate the duration of the sound. (Note that sound effects can be placed over other audio clips on either audio track, if necessary.) You can then play the video to see how the sounds are matched up with the video. If the sound isn't in the right place, just drag-and-drop it to a new location in the sound effects track.

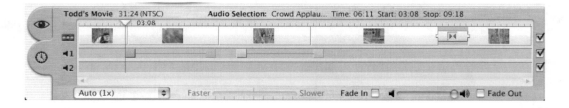

To remove a sound from the sound effects track, select it with the mouse and press DELETE.

Edit Your Audio

Another of the advantages of iMovie 2 over the original iMovie is the ability to edit the audio that is *part* of your original DV clip. You can actually extract the audio, making it separate from the video. Then you can change or even delete the audio, if desired. Some of that is beyond the scope of this chapter, but it's worth experimenting with.

First, note that you can simply change the volume level for a particular clip from the timeline. Select the clip on the top track, then use the volume slider at the bottom of the timeline to change the audio level for that clip's audio. You can also use the Fade In and/or Fade Out check boxes to add those effects to the audio associated with the selected clip.

Next, you can extract the audio from your clip. Select the video clip and choose Advanced | Extract Audio. After iMovie has had time to think about things a bit, the extracted audio clip will appear as an orange bar—it's now separate from its associated video clip.

Another neat trick with iMovie 2 is its ability to paste video *over* other video, leaving the audio of the clip intact. This is useful for something called *intercutting*, where you edit in different video scenes while the same audio continues to play. For instance, if you have a long video clip of a park ranger talking about a nature hike, you could intercut with clips of the trailhead, the flowers discussed, and the group as it hikes.

To create this intercut, you need an *original* clip and one (or more) intercut clips. Then, you select an intercut clip that's still on the shelf and highlight a short portion of the clip using the crop markers in the monitor window. Choose Edit | Copy. Now, on the timeline, you place the playhead at the point in the original clip where you'd like the copied video to appear instead of the original video. (When the aforementioned park ranger is talking about flowers, that's when you'd add the flower intercut clip.) With the playhead placed, select Advanced | Paste Over at Pastehead. Now the intercut clip will appear in the place of that portion of the original clip. When you play back that portion of the video, you'll see and hear the park ranger, then you'll hear the park ranger and see the intercut (flowers) footage, then you'll see and hear the park ranger again. Just like a roving reporter on the nightly news!

Lay in Some Music

The last editing step is to lay in your background music. With iMovie, you'll need to have either an audio file (in AIFF or MP3 format) or a CD handy for adding music.

Here's how to add music from an AIFF or MP3 file:

1. Place the playhead at the point in your movie where you'd like the music to begin. (This is probably easiest if you've got the timeline showing.)

2. Select File | Import File.

3. In the Open dialog box, find the AIFF or MP3 file you want to import. Click Import.

That's it. The audio is imported into the program and placed on the second audio track. When you play back the movie, you'll hear the music in the background.

To add music from a CD, do the following:

1. Place the playhead where you'd like the music to begin. (Again, this is probably easiest if the timeline is active.)

2. Click the Audio button in the Effects controller.

3. Insert an audio CD in the your CD or DVD drive.

4. You'll see the tracks for the CD appear in the Effects controller. Select a track and you can use the little Play, Pause, and other buttons to hear the music. If you decide to record music from that track, click the Record Music button.

5. Now, as the music records, you'll see your video in the monitor window. When you get to the point where you'd like the music to stop, click the Stop button.

TIP *If you record at least a few extra seconds of music after your video ends, you can have it fade out nicely.*

Once you have your music clip on the timeline, you can drag the music clip around to place it perfectly. You can also drag the small triangle at the end of the music clip toward the beginning of it to shorten the music clip. The additional recorded music isn't played, but it isn't actually deleted—you can drag the triangle back out again to recover it.

You can delete the music clip by selecting it and pressing DELETE. It's placed in iMovie's Trash.

NOTE *At the bottom of the audio viewer, you'll see controls that let you set the volume for the background music or select the fade options. Select the music clip, then turn on Fade In if you want the music to fade in as it begins; turn on Fade Out if you want the music to fade out as it ends.*

View and Export Your Movie

If you've gotten this far, hopefully you've pulled through the editing phase and you're ready to do something with your masterpiece. You can view it full screen to make sure everything looks good, then you can export the movie either back to your camcorder or as a QuickTime movie.

View the Movie

There's a special button that enables you to preview the movie full screen. It's just to the right of the Play button in the monitor's VCR-like controls.

To stop viewing the movie while it's full screen, simply click the mouse button or press any key.

TIP *If you choose Edit | Preferences and click the Playback tab, you can choose whether the movie playback in iMovie is Smoother Motion or Better Image quality. If the former, you'll see a more pixelated image on screen, but you'll see more frames of video per second. If you choose Better Quality, the images will look good, but the video may appear to jump a bit. This only affects playback onscreen. Once you get the movie back out to your digital camera, it should be smooth and as high quality as your camera is capable of producing.*

Export to Your Camera

If you plan to view the video on your television or transfer to standard VHS videotape, your best plan is to export it to your camcorder (unless you have a DV video deck, in which case I envy you.) Your camcorder is designed to hook up to all that analog equipment quite nicely, so it's the perfect place to put your finished video.

NOTE *Don't forget that the length of the cassette in your camcorder may limit the length of the movie it can store from your iMac. (Your iMac has the potential to edit a one- to two-hour movie, depending on hard disk space, and some mini-DV cassettes have only a 30-minute capacity.)*

Here's how to export to your camera:

1. Make sure the camera is connected via FireWire and, if necessary, put the camera in VCR or Playback mode.

2. In iMovie, choose File | Export Movie.

3. In the Export Movie dialog box, choose To Camera from the Export menu.

4. Enter the number of seconds iMovie should wait while the camera gets ready to record. (This is often at least five seconds.) Then enter the number of seconds of black video you want recorded to the tape before and after the movie itself.

5. Click Export.

A progress slider will appear onscreen and you'll see the video in the background. You'll also likely see the video on your camera's viewfinder or LCD display.

15

That's it. iMovie will stop your camera when the video is done recording. Now you can hook up the camcorder to the TV and show the in-laws, or hook the camera up to your VCR and make a videotape for mailing off to friends.

Export to QuickTime

Want to distribute your masterpiece via the Internet or place it on removable media to hand out? You'll need to export it to QuickTime.

 Before distributing any videos you create publicly, you should take pains to make sure you aren't violating copyright laws. If you used music from CDs or downloaded images in your video, for instance, it may not be a good idea to distribute your video publicly over the Internet.

This process can be time-consuming, because the QuickTime movie needs to be compressed well beyond the minor compression that happens for the DV format. This compression is sophisticated and processor-intensive. Its end result is a much smaller QuickTime movie that can play back with good quality. To create that compressed movie file, though, takes time.

Here's how to export to QuickTime:

1. Choose File | Export Movie from the menu.

2. In the Export Movie dialog box, choose To QuickTime from the Export menu.

3. Now, select the type of video you want to create in the Formats menu. You can choose from different recommended compression schemes based on the type of movie you're creating. (Despite its name, the CD-ROM setting is a good choice if you plan to store the movie on your hard disk or place the movie on removable media disks.)

TIP *If you know a little something about compression schemes, you might want to select Expert from the Formats menu. You'll then be presented with a dialog box that enables you to specify the compression settings for your QuickTime movie. Also, if you'll be using this QuickTime movie in another movie editing or compression application, choose Full Quality, Large to export in full, DV quality.*

4. In the Export QuickTime Movie dialog box, select the location to save the movie to, give the movie a name, and click Save.

Now, give yourself a pedicure, go for a bike ride, or hit the phones and see if you can find some friends who'll go bowling with you. You'll be waiting a while, depending on the length of your video and the compression scheme you chose. In the meantime, you can't really use your iMac for much of anything—the whole processor is given over to the complex task of rendering the movie. (You will, however, see the video's progress in the monitor window, so at least you can check in every once in a while and see how things are going.)

When it's done, you'll have a new QuickTime movie that you can view in the QuickTime Player or distribute to your heart's content.

Chapter 16 Play Games

How to...

- Play Nanosaur
- Play Bugdom
- Play Cro-Mag Rally
- Check out your iMac's 3-D capabilities
- Add game controllers

Well over five million iMacs have been shipped, comprising a sizeable market of consumers who might be willing to play a few games with their iMac. Plus, the iMac continues to be improved to the point that the latest models offer very impressive graphics capabilities for gaming, often surpassing other desktop models. The result has been something of an explosion in the Mac gaming market—a market once left for dead only a few years ago.

Even better, your iMac comes with some free games! In this chapter we'll take a specific look at the games that come with the iMac, and you'll learn how to install, optimize, and use other games. Plus, you'll learn about the iMac's graphical capabilities as well as how to add gaming hardware.

Play Nanosaur

Nanosaur, shown in Figure 16-1, has gotten something of a cult following since the release of the iMac. Millions of copies of Nanosaur have been distributed with the machines, leading to quite a bit of Nanosaur fever. It's pretty well deserved, since the game's theme makes it appropriate for reasonably young kids, even if it is what's called a "first-person shooter" (meaning that you follow just behind your character and shoot at the enemies, although, in this case, there's no blood or gore).

NOTE   *Nanosaur is not a "Carbon," or native, Mac OS X application, so you'll be running it in Classic if you launch it from within Mac OS X. It is playable from within the Classic environment, although you'll have better luck booting in Mac OS 9 to play it.*

In this game, you're a Nanosaur—a type of genetically altered dinosaur brought back to life by humans in the future. Unfortunately, the humans die out, but the Nanosaurs thrive and create a technological civilization. You've been elected to head back in time to recover the eggs of different species of dinosaurs from the pre-extinction days. That'll give the Nanosaurs more genetic material to work with to ensure their survival.

So, the point is to run around the screen and find the colorful eggs. You then go back to a certain place where you toss the eggs into a time portal and they are sent back to the future. You only have a limited amount of time before a meteor crashes into the Earth and drives the dinosaurs to extinction. (Too bad you didn't set that time machine back a few months more.)

The eggs of different species are different colors—the first egg is worth 20,000 points and subsequent eggs of that same color are worth 5,000 points. The ultimate goal is to find the eggs

FIGURE 16-1   Nanosaur is a first-person "shooter" where you play the dinosaur.

of all five species and send them through the time portal so that life can be wonderful back in the future. (You get a bonus of 150,000 points for accomplishing such a feat.)

Get Started

Once Nanosaur is installed on your iMac, open the Applications (Mac OS 9) folder and look for the Games folder. Inside Games, you'll find the Nanosaur folder; open it, then double-click the Nanosaur icon to start the game. You'll see the Nanosaur opening screen—press the SPACEBAR. You'll see the opening animation; when you see the dinosaur running, you're ready to access the game's controls—press the SPACEBAR again.

You move between the game's control commands by pressing the LEFT and RIGHT ARROW keys—you'll see that the ring rotates and a new picture will be in your view. To select that particular option, press the SPACEBAR.

Here's what each command does:

- **The Dinosaur**   This allows you to start playing the game.
- **The Check Box**   Press the SPACEBAR to see some options you can change. The fewer options selected, the faster the game can be played.

16

- ■ **The Question Mark**   This is the Help screen—it shows you the keys used for commands during the game.
- ■ **The Exit Sign**   This allows you to quit the game.
- ■ **The Medal**   This shows you the high scores and scorers.

When you're ready to play the game, put the dinosaur to the front, and press the SPACEBAR. The game begins.

Play the Game

As the game starts, your Nanosaur is dropped to the ground, ready to start running around the screen. You move with the ARROW keys, which allow you to run in all four directions. Immediately, you'll see a *power-up*—gamers' lingo for something that you're supposed to run directly into and which gives you extra powers or some other goodies. In this case, the power-ups you initially see are to give you more ammunition for your laser gun, which is the weapon you have at the start of the game.

Move and Jump

There are a number of different controls you'll want to master right away. These commands enable you to move the dinosaur and play the game:

Press This	To Do This
ARROW keys	Move the dinosaur
SPACEBAR	Fire weapon
⌘	Jump
OPTION	Pick up (egg)
SHIFT	Change to next weapon
A, Z	Move up and down with the jetpack

You'll move using the ARROW keys, then press the SPACEBAR to fire at any hostile dinosaurs. Your typical T-Rex takes about two shots before he disappears—other dinosaurs can take more or less.

Jumping can be very useful—in fact, you should get used to both jumping and double-jumping. If you press the ⌘ key once, you'll jump; press it twice in succession (or anytime while the Nanosaur is still in the air) and you'll jump again, doing a flip in the process.

Gather Eggs

When you find an egg, move up close to it and stand still, then press the OPTION key. The Nanosaur bends down and attempts to pick up the egg in its mouth. If you've got it, it's time to return to a time portal, since you can only carry one egg at a time. Check the temporal compass and head off in the direction it points.

Once you arrive at the time portal, you need to toss the egg into its time stream. Press the OPTION key again. You'll see the egg leave the Nanosaur's mouth and fly straight forward—hopefully it encounters the time stream before it hits anything else or lands on the ground. Try not to hit OPTION accidentally while you're running with an egg, since that could cause you to toss the egg into water, lava, a crevice, or under a dinosaur you don't feel like getting close to. (Fortunately, those sturdy dinosaur eggs don't break.)

Change the Camera and Options

Aside from the commands for controlling your Nanosaur, other keyboard commands enable you to change the gaming environment:

Press This	To Do This
< > (brackets)	Spin the camera around
1 2	Zoom the camera in and out
CTRL-M	Toggle music on and off
CTRL-B	Toggle sounds on and off
+/-	Raise or lower volume
F8	Show the current frame rate (performance of the game)
ESC	Pause the game
TAB	Change the camera mode (look from behind the Nanosaur or look through the Nanosaur's eyes)
G	Toggle the GPS map on and off (which gives you an overview of your current position and the surroundings)

The Quit command is the same in Nanosaur as in other applications—press ⌘-Q to quit the game. There are no Save and Load commands—you simply have to play a new game straight through or quit.

Get More Help and Update Nanosaur

You've learned enough here to start playing quickly, but you'll want to consult the Nanosaur manual, an Adobe PDF document, to learn more about weapons, power-ups, and the creatures you'll encounter. You'll find the manual in the Nanosaur folder in a file called Nanosaur Instructions.

You should also check **http://www.pangeasoft.net/** for updates and information about Nanosaur.

Play Bugdom

Bugdom, by the same Pangea folks who brought you Nanosaur, is a painfully cute game. Ideal for kids but addicting for adults (at least, this one), this is a nice game to have included on your iMac.

16

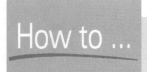 **Win at Nanosaur**

Here are some hints for playing the game:

- *Move quickly.* If you want to win the game, you've got to get eggs back through time, fast.

- *Don't gather all the eggs.* You get 5,000 points for each egg gathered, but each species of egg (that is, each different color) is located on a different "section" of the map. For instance, the first egg color is found in the marshes where you begin the game; the next egg color is found in the lava flow portion of the world. Keep moving along. There are five different-colored eggs you need to gather.

- *Learn to use the jetpack.* You can fill the jetpack by standing over a gas vent that's shooting up out of the ground. Then, use the jetpack, but spend as little time in the air as possible—it uses up fuel fast.

- *Pick your weapons.* The SHIFT key lets you toggle between weapons. Some weapons—like the "nuke"—are only appropriate when you need to hit many enemies at far range. Make sure you've selected the best weapon for the job.

- *Try new things.* There are a few different "tricks" that will help you get more points or additional bonuses. For instance, you can jump on the backs of pterosaurs (the flying ones) if you do a double-jump at the right moment. That'll result in some interesting bonuses.

NOTE *If don't have Bugdom, you may have Otto Matic, a new game (Mac OS X native) from PangeaSoft that is very similar to Bugdom. Skim this section, then read the on-screen intro to learn the differences in Otto Matic.*

The story is simple: After years of benevolent rule by the Rollie Pollies and the Lady Bugs, Bugdom has been swarmed by hostile forces—the Fire Ants and the bugs they've recruited to perform their evil. The kingdom is now ruled by King Thorax, who holes up at the anthill. You, Rollie McFly, have to get to the anthill, defeat Thorax, and crown yourself king, hopefully returning the kingdom to the peaceful paradise it once was.

The point of the game is to kick walnuts to get power-ups, keys, and other special powers, like buddy bugs. (You can use buddy bugs, who follow you around, to dive-bomb your enemies.) You also seek out Lady Bugs who are trapped in cages and kick their cages to free them. As you proceed through gates and tunnel between levels, your ultimate goal is to come up against King Thorax and defeat him.

Get Started

When you first launch Bugdom you'll see the main menu, which allows you to view the high scores, change settings, load saved games, read the credits, or begin the game. Here are some things you can do from the main menu:

- To load a saved game, double-click the Saved Games icon. You'll see an Open dialog box that allows you to locate a saved game.

- Double-click the High Scores icon to see who has done the best at the game.

- Double-click the "?" walnut to see the credits for the game.

- Double-click the Start icon to begin the game.

To change settings, double-click the Settings icon. This brings up a dialog box where you can choose a few different settings for the game:

- **Easy Mode**   Select this option if you'd like Rollie to sustain less damage when attacked.

- **Configure Input Sprocket**   Click this button to bring up the Input Sprocket dialog box, where you can alter settings for your input device (joystick or gamepad) if you have one that supports the Input Sprocket. (See "Configure Input Sprocket," later in this chapter.)

- **Keyboard Controls Are Player-Relative**   Select this option if you'd like controls to be player-relative instead of camera-relative. (This is discussed in the "Control Rollie" section.)

- **Rage II Mode**   This option allows you to downgrade the quality of graphics for the original iMac or other early Power Macintosh G3 computers. It's not necessary on recent slot-loading iMac models, but should be turned on for Bondi-blue tray-loading iMacs.

- **Clear High Scores**   Clear out the names and scores when you're sick of seeing your sibling's or children's embarrassingly superior scores.

Once you're done setting options, click OK to return to the main menu.

Play the Game

As the game begins, Rollie appears on the ground, ready to run around the screen. You move with the ARROW keys, which allow you to run in all four directions. Immediately, you'll see a walnut that likely contains a power-up. Go and kick it by pressing the OPTION key. In this case, the early power-ups you kick to reveal are likely to be clovers, which add bonus points to your score.

Control Rollie

Rollie has two basic modes—bug mode and ball mode. (Remember, he's a Rollie Pollie.) Press the SPACEBAR to switch between modes. While he's a bug, Rollie can jump, kick, and walk. While he's a ball, he can either roll or roll *faster*. As a ball, he can also roll into enemies, walnuts, and Lady Bug cages instead of kicking them.

16

There are a few different ways you can control Rollie:

- **Mouse**   You can use the mouse to move Rollie in any direction, and click its button to kick. If he's in ball mode, clicking the button gives him a turbo boost while rolling.

- **Mouse and Keyboard**   Using the mouse while holding down the SHIFT key, you can control Rollie's direction while he walks forward. This is the recommended mode of play, if you have enough dexterity for it.

- **Keyboard**   Using only the keyboard, you can use arrow keys to get Rollie to move just as you would with the trackpad. In this case, the OPTION key is used to kick or boost speed, depending on Rollie's mode.

 You can switch to what Pangea calls player-relative controls, which allow you to use the UP ARROW to move him forward, the DOWN ARROW to move him backward, and the LEFT and RIGHT ARROWS to turn him without moving him. Used in concert, the arrow keys give you more controls, but they can also be tough to get used to.

You can also use the keyboard to accomplish a few other things, including jumping, changing modes, or launching a buddy bug. Table 16-1 shows the controls.

 *You can also freeze the screen (and the game) in a special pause mode that allows you to take a screenshot. Press F12, then press ⌘-SHIFT-3 to take a picture of the entire screen.*

Scoring Points and Tracking Health

You score points in two ways, by gathering clovers (within walnuts that you kick open) or rescuing Lady Bugs. Each is registered in the status bar at the top of the screen.

At the far left of the status bar you'll see the number of lives Rollie has left. Next to it, you'll see the two types of clover you'll encounter—each new clover you discover in a walnut and walk over to pick up is added to its respective four-leaf clover in the status bar. In the middle, you'll see Rollie holding up any special items he's found, like keys or money. Next, you'll see the Lady Bug gauge. If the image of the Lady Bug has wings, then you've freed all Lady Bugs on this level. If not, you still have work to do. On the far right you'll see a tally of how many Lady Bugs you've freed.

There are two indicators near the picture of Rollie in the middle of the status bar. The green curved indicator tells you how much more "ball time" you have—Rollie can only stay in ball mode for so long. If you've depleted your ball time, you'll have to find a power-up that gives you more. The red straight line is a health indicator. Run out of health and you'll lose a life.

A third indicator appears whenever you're fighting a level "boss" (a meaner bug that you have to defeat to end some levels). That indicator, which appears on the bottom of the screen, tells you how much health the boss has left.

Key	What It Does
OPTION	Kick in bug mode, turbo boost in ball mode
SPACEBAR	Switch between bug and ball mode
⌘	Jump (in bug mode only)
TAB	Launch your buddy bug at an enemy
+/-	Raise or lower the volume
⌘-Q	Quit the game
ESC	Pause the game
M	Toggle music on and off
1/2	Zoom in/Zoom out
</>	Swivel camera

TABLE 16-1   Controlling Rollie and Setting Options in Bugdom

TIP   *Whenever you see a large candy cane-colored pipe with a bubble of water coming out of it, you've reached a checkpoint. Jump up to pop the bubble and register at the checkpoint. Now, if you lose a life while playing, you'll return to this checkpoint instead of the beginning of the level.*

Fight Bad Bugs

One of Rollie's strengths seems to be running away and since you don't score additional points for beating up an enemy, you can run away with impunity. That said, sometimes you've got to stop, clinch your feet into fists, and take on the bad bugs.

Some bugs can't be beat, like the snails. Instead, avoid those. Others have to be kicked (or rolled into) more than once before they're knocked out. It's easier to roll into bad bugs than kick them, especially if they have weapons. Remember that you only have a certain amount of ball time before you have to stand up and take it like a, uh, bug.

You've got another trick up your sleeve—the buddy bug. If you've got a small bug following you around that you can't get rid of (after kicking a walnut where he was hiding) it might be because he's your buddy. While you're in a fight, press the TAB key to launch the buddy bug at an enemy. He can knock most of them silly with one punch.

Play Cro-Mag Rally

Pangea Software's third game, Cro-Mag Rally, is included with the latest round of iMacs, including those that run Mac OS X. Cro-Mag Rally is a "Carbon" application that can run in either Mac OS 9 or Mac OS X, although Mac OS X support is a work in progress.

16

If you don't have the full version of Cro-Mag 2.0 for Mac OS X, you may want to check ***http://www.pangeasoft.net*** *to download an updated version.*

Cro-Mag Rally is easy to play, appropriate for the whole family, and it doesn't have too much plot to set you back. It's a racing game where caveman cars and drivers race to the finish line. Along the way you'll encounter different terrain (desert, jungle, glaciers) and various obstacles such as tornadoes, oil slicks, tossed bombs, and the occasional ice monster.

Get Started

When you first launch Cro-Mag Rally, you'll see a small dialog box asking you what resolution and color depth you'd like to use for the game. Choose a resolution from the pop-up menu, then click the radio buttons to determine whether you want to see 16-bit or 32-bit color. (If you notice the game seems slow on your iMac, using a lower resolution or fewer colors may speed things up a bit.) With your selections made, click Set.

You'll see the opening screens—press any key to move past them. On the main menu, use the ARROW keys to select an option, then press the SPACEBAR to select that option. Choose Play to begin playing, Saved Game to load a previously saved game, Options to change game settings, or Quit to leave the game. (You can use the ESC key to move "up" to a previous menu.)

If you select Options, you'll encounter another menu, from which you can choose Help; Credits, where you can see the credits for the game; or Physics Editor, where you can experiment with different characteristics for the various cars. You can also select Settings, where you can set the following:

- **Split-Screen Mode**   Choose how you'd like the screen split for two-person play.

- **Difficulty**   How hard do you want the computerized opponents to play?

- **Tag Duration**   If you're playing a multi-player game, you can play Keep-Away Tag, where one person is "it" until she manages to tag another player or time expires. How long the tag lasts is determined by this setting.

- **Language**   Choose your default language.

Click the Configure Controls button and you'll see the standard Input Sprocket interface (described later in the section "Configure Input Sprocket") for re-configuring the controls.

Play Cro-Mag Rally

With the game configured, you're ready to move on to gameplay. From the main menu, select Play. Next, you'll be asked if you'd like to play 1 Player, 2 Player, or Net Game. Make your choice and press the SPACEBAR.

If you've selected 1 Player, you have two choices: Practice and Tournament. In Practice, you simply choose a track and race against computer player; in Tournament, you begin at the first track in the Stone Age, then work your way up by winning each race and advancing to the next track. There's another difference in Tournament mode—you have to pick up (drive into) all eight of the arrowheads on the track, and be first in the race, before you can advance to the next level.

In either case, driving is simple. For a one-player game, you drive using the ARROW keys on the keyboard—as you drive, you can pick up weapons that are used to slow down other drivers. To throw a weapon forward, press ⌘; to throw a weapon behind you, press OPTION. Table 16-2 shows many of the keyboard controls.

> TIP
>
> *Learn to use the brake in Cro-Mag Rally—you'll find that it's more important to stay pointed in the right direction than it is to be going top speed all of the time. Also, get used to the idea of throwing weapons behind you—oil slicks and bombs tossed over your shoulder can slow down the computer racers breathing down your neck!*

In two-player games, the screen is split so that each player can see his or her own car; likewise, Player 2 has keys on the keyboard to use for controlling the car. A, D, W, and S are used for driving, TAB is used for brakes, SHIFT for forward weapon, and 3 for backward weapon. In Mac OS 9, you can change those keys in the Settings area by clicking Configure Controls.

Two-player and net games have other options once you've selected them—different types of races, including:

- **Keep-Away Tag**   All other players try to avoid the player who is "it."
- **Stampede Tag**   The "it" player tries to stay away from other players.
- **Survival**   Weapons and crashes permanently damage players until their "health" runs out.
- **Quest for Fire**   Players try to capture a flag.

Check Your 3-D Specifications

Your iMac features an ATI graphics chip that's designed to accelerate the drawing of 3-D images. With the correct ATI drivers installed, your iMac should take advantage of the 3-D acceleration code built into popular games, especially those that support QuickDraw RAVE or ATI Rage

Key	What It Does
ARROW keys	Drive direction (left, right, forward, reverse)
OPTION	Throw weapon behind you
SPACEBAR	Hit the brakes
⌘	Throw weapon forward
+/-	Raise or lower the volume
⌘-Q	Quit the game
ESC	Pause the game
~	Change camera angle

TABLE 16-2   Keyboard Controls in Cro-Mag Rally

16

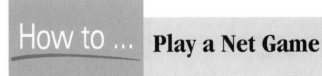

How to ... Play a Net Game

At the time of writing, only the Mac OS 9 version of Cro-Mag Rally supports network play. (In my experience, it's a bit buggy, so save changed documents in other applications and proceed at your own risk.) You can play Cro-Mag Rally against up to five other players on a local LAN that uses AppleTalk or TCP/IP protocols. To set up the game, you'll need to either *host* or *join*. You'll need one host per networked game and you'll need to already have your LAN configured, as discussed in Chapter 28. Here's how a Net Game works:

1. The host player selects Play from the main menu, then Net Game.

2. Choose Host Net Game. On the next screens, choose the type of game to play and the desired track.

3. Now you'll see the NetSprockets dialog box. Choose a protocol at the top of the dialog box (either AppleTalk or TCP/IP), enter a name for this session in the Game Name entry, and a password (if desired). If you'll be playing on the host machine, check the Play on This Machine option and enter a name. Click OK.

4. Now, on other machines, choose Play | Net Game | Join Net Game.

5. Once all players have joined the game, the game is started on the host computer. Now, you're off to the races!

acceleration. You should look for this sort of support when you're buying a game—check the side of the box.

Similarly, games may require a minimum processor speed. Your iMac has at least a 233 MHz PowerPC G3 processor and at least 32MB of system RAM, just in case the game asks. The original iMac also has a 4GB hard disk. Table 16-3 shows the gaming-related specifications for different iMac models.

Mac Model	Processor Speed	RAM (Base)	Hard Disk	Video Card	Video RAM
Rev. A/Rev. B (Bondi)	233 MHz	32MB	4GB	ATI II	2MB/6MB
Rev. B (Bondi)	233 MHz	32MB	4GB	ATI II	6MB
iMac 266 (Colors)	266 MHz	32MB	6GB	ATI Pro	6MB

TABLE 16-3   iMac Models and Their Gaming Specifications

Mac Model	Processor Speed	RAM (Base)	Hard Disk	Video Card	Video RAM
iMac 333	333 MHz	32MB	6GB	ATI Pro	6MB
iMac (slot loading)	350 MHz	64MB	6GB	ATI Rage 128 VR	8MB
iMac DV	400-500 MHz	64MB (128MB SE model only)	10GB-30GB (varies per model)	ATI Rage 128 VR	8MB
iMac (early 2001)	400-600 MHz	64MB (128MB on high-end models)	10-40GB (varies per model)	ATI Rage 128 VR	8MB (16MB on high-end models)
iMac (summer 2001)	500-700 MHz	128MB (256MB on high-end models)	20-60GB (varies per model)	ATI Rage 128 VR	16MB
iMac 64 (early 2002)	700-800 MHz (G4)	128MB (256MB on high-end)	40-60GB	NVIDIA GeForce2 MX	32MB

TABLE 16-3   iMac Models and Their Gaming Specifications *(continued)*

These are just specifications for gaming reference. To learn more about screen resolutions, see Chapter 24. To learn more about upgrading RAM, see Chapter 26.

Add Game Controllers

One other variable when you're playing games on your iMac is the controller. In many cases, you'll play the game using the keyboard—a lot of games are designed to allow you to do that. Others will specifically encourage the use of a joystick or gamepad. (Joysticks work like flight sticks in fighter planes; a gamepad is usually similar to the controllers that come with Nintendo or Sony Playstation game boxes.)

On the iMac, nearly all controllers connect via USB. In most cases, these joysticks require driver software to allow them to operate correctly. That driver software can come in three forms:

- It can be a generic driver that allows the controller to be a substitute for the mouse with a particular game.
- It can be a specific driver that works with certain games.
- It can use the Input Sprocket driver software created and installed by Apple for easy gaming.

The easiest way for this to work is with the Input Sprocket driver software, but then the game must specifically support Game Sprockets, a special technology that Apple has created to make gaming easier. Unfortunately, not all games use this, so sometimes you have to get creative.

16

Likewise, Mac OS X doesn't yet include Input Sprocket support, so you'll likely need to configure Mac OS X games using routines developed by the game programmers—in other words, it'll be different for each game.

NOTE   *USB Overdrive, shareware written by Alessandro Levi Montalcini, is a universal USB driver that enables you to configure nearly any controller to work with nearly any game or application. Montalcini is also working (at the time of writing) on a Mac OS X version which should prove helpful to Mac OS X games. See **http://www.montalcini.com** for details.*

Configure Input Sprocket

If your game and controller are both compatible with the Input Sprocket, then configuration is simple. The controller should say on the box that it's compatible with Input Sprocket or Game Sprockets, and it should include a CD that allows you to install drivers for its particular characteristics. (In other cases, it might not require a special driver and will work with the Input Sprockets that are already installed on your iMac.) You'll install a driver for your particular controller (in some cases), then you'll install a compatible game. Once support for both has been established, you're ready to set things up.

In the game itself, look for an option to change controller preferences. That will cause a special dialog box to appear—the Input Sprocket configuration dialog box (see Figure 16-2). In

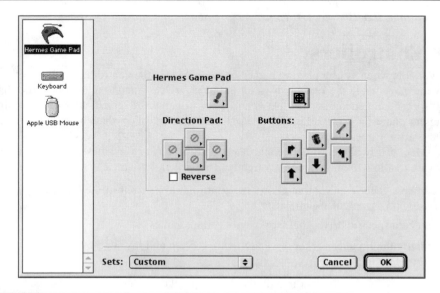

FIGURE 16-2   Configuring a joystick using Input Sprocket

this dialog box, you'll be able to choose what each button on your controller will do. Click a particular button to see a list of different options available for your particular controller. Each game has its own control mappings, so look carefully at each. For instance, in the game "Future Cop" (the Ariston Hermes example shown in Figure 16-2), there are three different weapons at my disposal—each needs to be mapped to a particular button on the gamepad.

Since this dialog box is designed as part of Apple's Input Sprocket software, you'll find it's similar for nearly every device you use and every game you play that supports Input Sprocket.

16

Chapter 17

Tracking Your Schedule and Contacts

How to...

- Schedule appointments on your calendar
- Deal with your To Do's
- Jot down quick reminders
- Track your contacts
- Sync your iMac with a Palm OS handheld computer
- Install Palm applications

The iMac ships with the Palm Desktop, an application from Palm, Inc., that allows a Palm Pilot or Palm OS handheld computer to synchronize data with a Macintosh computer. Of course, the iMac doesn't come with a Palm device (don't I wish), but the Palm Desktop is perfectly functional with or without a Palm handheld computer. On its own, the Palm Desktop is a fairly complete calendar and contact manager, allowing you to track appointments, To Do lists, notes, and information about people you know in your work or personal life.

> NOTE   *Palm devices are popular handheld computers that use the Palm OS. In addition to Palm, Inc., other companies also make handheld computers that run the Palm OS, including IBM's Workpad and the Handspring Visor. The Palm Desktop software works with those handheld computers, too.*

In fact, Palm Desktop is a good program precisely because Apple wrote it—at least, initially. When it was clear that the Palm handheld computer was going to be popular with Mac users, 3Com bought Claris Organizer, a datebook and contact manager program, from Apple. (Claris was a subsidiary company of Apple before it was folded back into Apple in early 1998. The Claris people are the same folks who wrote AppleWorks, which was once called ClarisWorks.) Using Claris Organizer as a basis, the Palm Computing/3Com folks wrote the new Palm Desktop software that not only tracks appointments and contacts, but also syncs up nicely with a Palm handheld computer. Then, even cooler, they released the software for free and allowed Apple to bundle it on the iMac.

> NOTE   *You can still download the software for free from Palm Inc. (**http://www.palm.com/**). You can also get the Palm Desktop software when you purchase a Palm OS handheld computer or a Palm connection kit. At the time of writing, a native Mac OS X version has been announced, but isn't yet available. You can use Palm Desktop from within the Classic environment, however.*

Get Started with Palm Desktop

In most cases, you'll find Palm desktop in the Palm folder inside the Applications (Mac OS 9) folder. Double-click the Palm application to launch it.

In other cases, you may need to install the Palm software—with some iMac versions, the Palm folder holds a Palm Desktop installer. Double-click it to install the program.

Once Palm Desktop is started up, you're presented with a dialog box, where you can enter the name you'd like to associate with your Palm data. Enter your name (first name is usually OK) and click Continue. After you enter a name, you can choose whether or not to set up HotSync. If you click Setup Now, you'll be asked to choose the type of connection for your Palm OS handheld's connection—with the iMac, you're likely to use a USB connection for your Palm OS handheld. (You'll need a special USB connection kit, which is a separate purchase for some Palm devices.) To set up HotSync later (or to not set it up at all if you don't have a Palm OS device), click Setup Later.

The Instant Palm Desktop Menu

With Palm Desktop installed and your iMac restarted, you may see something different about your iMac's menu bar in Mac OS 9. It will likely have a small icon up in the corner of the menu bar, next to the clock. This is the Instant Palm Desktop menu, a special menu that allows you to quickly access the Palm Desktop software and the HotSync capabilities for getting your iMac to talk to a Palm OS device.

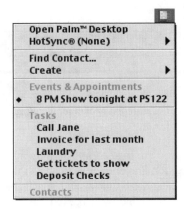

The menu also has a Create menu, which allows you to select individual items you'd like to create within Palm Desktop. And, if you have anything that's currently scheduled or due, you can see those things quickly by looking at the menu instead of opening up or switching to the Palm Desktop software.

If you need to launch Palm Desktop, switch to it if it's already open, or to quickly check your current tasks and appointments, select this menu. It's a lot easier than finding the Palm Desktop icon and launching the program. (Note that in Mac OS X you'll only see the Palm Desktop menu while a Classic application is active.)

If you'd like more information about a particular task or appointment that's listed, select it in the menu. A dialog box will appear for that particular item, with the complete text of the item, the date, times, and whether or not an alarm is set. You can change things in the dialog box or just click OK to dismiss it.

17

 *If you don't see the Instant Palm Desktop menu in Mac OS 9 or Classic, you need to change a setting. Choose Edit | Preferences and click the General button. Turn on the Show Instant Palm Desktop Menu option. The menu will appear after you restart your iMac (or after you restart the Classic environment, if you're working in Mac OS X).*

The Palm Desktop Interface

Once you've gotten the Palm Desktop launched or switched to, you'll see a more complete application ready for just about any data you'd like to organize. The nerve center of the Palm Desktop software is its toolbar, which gives you quick access to just about every major command available in the software.

 You can use the mouse to point at a button in the toolbar if you don't know what it does. Its name will appear just below the button. If you don't see the name, click the disclosure triangle at the far-left end of the toolbar so that it's pointing down. Now you'll be able to see the names of buttons.

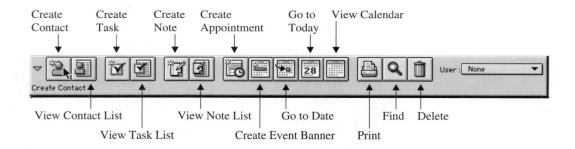

As you can see, the toolbar allows you to accomplish quite a lot without ever touching a menu. Just point your mouse at a button and click it to execute that command.

By default, you'll also see the Calendar window, and you'll likely keep it up most of the time, since it can be tucked behind other windows (like the Task List, Note List, and Contact List), always hanging out there in the background.

To quit the Palm Desktop, choose File | Quit.

Manage Appointments, Events, and Tasks

Since the Calendar is what you'll see first in the Palm Desktop interface, let's go ahead and talk about it first. The Calendar allows you to manage three different things—appointments, event banners, and tasks. You can also manage these things from three different views—Daily, Weekly, and Monthly. Each gives you a different overview of the items you've scheduled. Figure 17-1 shows the Daily calendar; Figure 17-2 show the Weekly calendar; and Figure 17-3 shows the Monthly calendar.

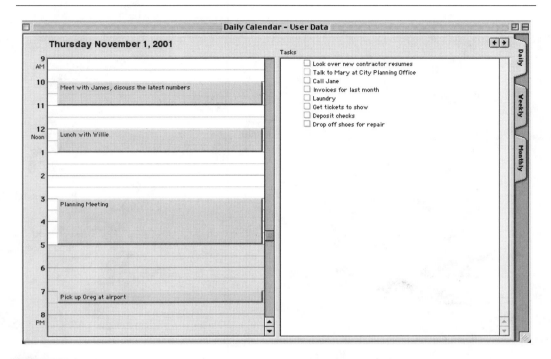

Daily Calendar – User Data

Thursday November 1, 2001

Tasks

☐ Look over new contractor resumes
☐ Talk to Mary at City Planning Office
☐ Call Jane
☐ Invoices for last month
☐ Laundry
☐ Get tickets to show
☐ Deposit checks
☐ Drop off shoes for repair

9 AM

10   Meet with James, discuss the latest numbers

11

12 Noon   Lunch with Willie

1

2

3   Planning Meeting

4

5

6

7   Pick up Greg at airport

8 PM

Daily   Weekly   Monthly

FIGURE 17-1   The Daily calendar gives you a look at the day's appointments and tasks.

To change the view, click the tab on the far right side of the Calendar window. This immediately switches you between different views. If you're currently viewing a Weekly or Monthly view, you can switch to a Daily view by double-clicking a date (the actual number) in the calendar.

As you can see, the different views are useful for different reasons. Daily lets you jump into today (or some day in the future) and get an exact idea of all the appointments you have and the tasks that need to happen. The Weekly view gives you a sense of what's going on over a five-day period, especially when it comes to appointments. The Monthly view is simply useful for knowing roughly what's going on at some point in the month and just generally what a busy person you are.

TIP   *The toolbar has buttons for Go To Date and Go To Today, if you'd like to quickly get to a particular date on the calendar.*

17

The Calendar views can be handy not just for getting a sense of what you need to do, but also for creating events and moving things around. For instance, most items on your calendar will respond to drag-and-drop—just point at an item and hold down the mouse button. The mouse pointer should turn into a fist. Now, drag the item to the time or date where you'd prefer to see it and release the mouse button. It's moved.

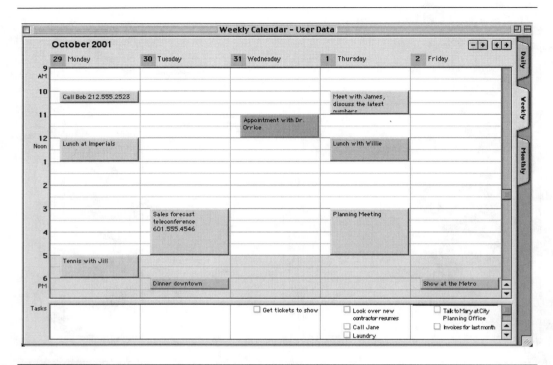

FIGURE 17-2 The Weekly calendar is good for getting a handle on your immediate tasks.

If you'd like to see just the appointments or just the tasks in a particular view, select View | Calendar, then choose either Show Appointments or Show Tasks. The Show command that you select will have its check mark (in the menu) removed and those items will no longer be shown. To see them again, return to the command and select it to replace its check mark. The items reappear in the calendar.

Before you can move events around, though, you'll probably need to create some.

Create an Appointment

To create an appointment, you can do a number of different things, depending on where you are in the Calendar view (or even if you're not looking at the calendar):

■ From anywhere in the Mac OS, pull down the Instant Palm Desktop menu and choose Appointment from the Create menu.

■ From within the Palm Desktop software, click the Create Appointment button in the toolbar.

■ On a Monthly view, double-click the box that represents the day on which you'd like to set the appointment. In the dialog box, select Appointment and click OK.

■ On a Weekly or Daily view, point at the start time within the day's schedule area and hold down the mouse button while dragging to create the new appointment. If you aim well, you can create the appointment for the correct start and end time. You can then begin typing the text for your appointment. When you're done, click elsewhere on the calendar.

In all but the last case, you'll see the Appointment dialog box, where you can enter the text for your appointment, set the date and time, set an alarm, and choose categories for the appointment.

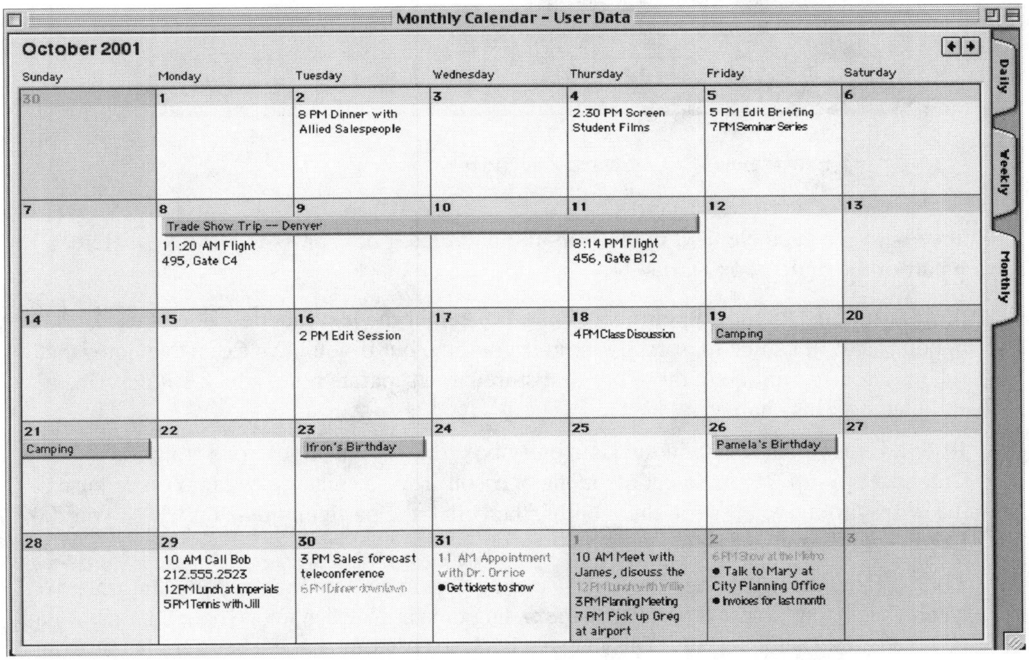

FIGURE 17-3   The Monthly calendar shows you an entire month at a glance.

17

In Weekly or Daily view you can double-click any appointment to see its dialog box, which you'll need to do if you want to set an alarm or the categories for the appointment.

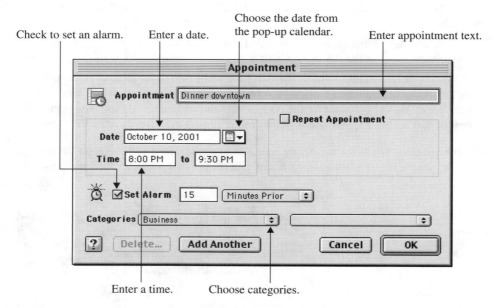

To move between each element in the Appointment dialog box, press the TAB key. Here's how each part of the dialog box works:

■ **Appointment**   In the Appointment entry box, enter the text that described the appointment. It can be reasonably long, if you like, but if you have extensive notes that relate to the appointment, those are best stored as a separate note, which I'll describe a little later in this chapter.

■ **Date**   Either enter a date in the Date entry box, or you can choose one from the Calendar pop-up menu. Select the menu and you'll see a small calendar. You can use the arrows to move between the months, then click the particular date on which you'd like to set this appointment.

■ **Time**   Enter the beginning time and the ending time in the entry boxes. Note that when you enter a beginning time and press TAB, the ending time is switched to one hour after the beginning time automatically. This may not be what you want, but it's helpful when it's right.

■ **Set Alarm**   Check this box if you want to be reminded (by a tone and an alert box) of this appointment. Once checked, you can enter a number and then choose from the pop-up menu whether the number represents the number of minutes or hours before the appointment that the alarm should appear.

■ **Categories**   You can choose a category for this appointment from the pop-up menu. If you like, in fact, you can choose two categories.

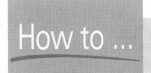 **Set a Repeating Appointment**

If you have an appointment that needs to repeat on a regular basis, you can set that in the Appointment dialog box. (If you're not currently viewing the particular appointment's dialog box, double-click the appointment in the calendar.) To set a repeating appointment, place a check mark next to Repeat Appointment in the Appointment dialog box. (So far, it ain't brain surgery.)

Next, you'll see a pop-up menu appear. Select from that pop-up menu how often you'd like the appointment to repeat. If you don't see the right timeframe in the menu, you can select More Choices to set the frequency yourself. In the More Choices dialog box, use the radio buttons, pop-up windows, and check boxes to determine exactly how often this appointment should occur. When you're done, click OK.

Back in the Appointment dialog box, you'll see an entry box labeled Until. Enter the date when this repeating appointment should stop repeating or choose it from the Calendar pop-up menu. Now, your repeating appointment is scheduled and added to your calendar.

When you're done creating the appointment, you can click the OK button to dismiss the dialog box or click the Add Another button to add another appointment without getting rid of the dialog box. This clears it out and let's you create a new appointment without going to the hassle of invoking another command.

Create a Banner Event

Do you have an event that isn't quite an appointment and doesn't exactly fit the bill of a task? Then it's probably a banner event. Banner events can span one day, many days, or many weeks, if desired, and they aren't tied to a particular time. As a result, you can set an alarm for a banner event, and they don't show up in lists like tasks do.

I use banner events in two ways. The more obvious way is for vacations, trade shows, or anything that will take me a couple of days, or for events that take one day but are special. With a banner event, you'll see immediately when you have a trip scheduled or a birthday or anniversary coming up, especially in Weekly and Monthly views.

The other way I use them is to track project deadlines. Since I'm a writer (by trade if not by calling), a lot of what I deal with are chapters. I'll create banner events for each chapter and place them on the dates when they're due or when I plan to get them done. Then, when I need to reschedule (as my editors well know, this happens more often than not), I can simply drag the banner event to a new day. If things are getting tight, I can drag two or more banners to a particular day and virtually see the work starting to pile up.

In any case, creating a banner event is easy. Here are the different ways to do it:

■ From the Instant Palm Desktop menu, choose Create | Banner Event.

■ With the Palm Desktop software active, click the Create Banner Event button in the toolbar.

17

■ From the Palm Desktop software, choose Create | Banner Event.

■ From a Monthly view, double-click a day's box and choose Event Banner from the dialog box, then click OK.

■ In a Weekly or Daily view, double-click just above the appointment area, just below the date and day of the week.

After choosing one of these fabulous options, you'll see the Event Banner dialog box. Don't worry—this one is easy.

Enter the text for the banner.   Choose a   Click if this event repeats every year.
                                     start date.

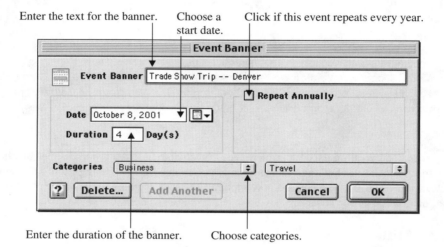

Enter the duration of the banner.   Choose categories.

In the Event Banner entry box, type the text for your banner. Then, enter a start date in the Date entry box (or choose it from the Calendar pop-up menu) for the banner. Next, enter the duration of the banner if you want it to last more than one day. Choose categories for the event banner from the Categories menus, if desired.

 *If this is an event that repeats annually, click the Repeat Annually check box. Once selected, you can choose to be reminded of the event a number of days before it happens—perfect for birthdays and anniversaries.*

When you're done, click the OK button to dismiss the dialog box, or click Add Another if you'd like to create another Event Banner. When you're done, you'll see your event banner back in the Calendar window. The banner will span the relevant dates in the Monthly view, or you'll see it at the top of the window in the Weekly view or the Daily view.

Add Your Tasks

Aside from appointments and banner events, you can use the Palm Desktop to manage your tasks, or To Do's. By default, your tasks appear in the calendar on the day for which the tasks are scheduled. Plus, tasks will be held over and shown on subsequent days if you haven't checked off the task once it's completed. If you often use Daily or Weekly views in the calendar, then you'll be able to conveniently view both your appointments and tasks from those views.

You can also manage your tasks in a special list. The list makes it easy to see all pending tasks, including those scheduled for the future. And it's a simple matter to add and delete tasks from the Task List. I'll cover both ways in the following sections.

Create a Task

First, you need to create a task. You can do that in a number of ways:

- From the Instant Palm Desktop menu, choose Create | Task.

- With the Palm Desktop software active, select the Create Task button in the toolbar.

- From the Palm Desktop software, choose Create | Task.

- From a Monthly view, double-click a day's box and choose Task from the dialog box, then click OK.

- In a Weekly or Daily view, double-click in the Tasks area of the windows. (In the Weekly view, this is at the bottom of the window. In the Daily view, tasks are on the right-hand side.)

Once you've chosen to create a task, you'll see the Task dialog box. Here you'll enter the information for this particular task.

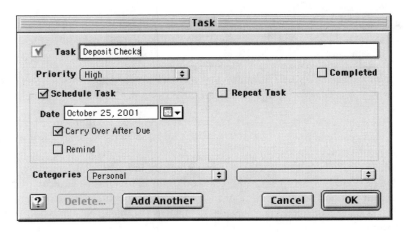

Here are the different items you can enter or set for your task:

- **Task** Enter the text that describes the task.
- **Priority** Choose a priority level. In the various task areas and the Task List, you can sort by priority so that the most important tasks appear at the top of the list.
- **Schedule Task** If selected, the task will have a due date. If you check the box to deselect it, then the task will simply appear in your Task List on the current day.
- **Date** Enter the due date or choose it from the pop-up calendar.
- **Carry Over After Due** If you'd like this task to continue to appear in your task areas or the Task List after its due date, select this box. Now it won't ever leave until you purposefully mark the task as done.
- **Remind** If selected, this option will allow you to enter the number of days before the due date that the software will remind you of the task (via an alert box).
- **Categories** If you'd like to associate particular categories with this task, select the categories from the pop-up menus.

When you're done entering the information for your task, you can click the OK button to store the task, or click the Add Another button if you'd like to continue adding tasks without dismissing the Task dialog box.

Manage Tasks in the Calendar

Once you've entered some tasks, you'll see them in your Calendar window. They're easier to see in the Weekly and Daily views, since those calendars have special areas for tasks. In the Monthly view, tasks appear in the same listing as appointments, below the appointments in a date box. (They have a bullet point before the task description instead of a time.)

In the Weekly and Monthly views, you can select a task and drag it to another day. This changes the start date of the task, not the due date. If you drag a task past its original due date, the due date will disappear.

NOTE   *Tasks without due dates will have the date the task was created in parenthesis after the task description. Tasks with due dates will have "due:" plus a date in those parenthesis.*

In the Daily view, you can't drag a task to a different day, because there aren't other days to choose from. Instead, you can drag a task to a different location in the task area if you'd like to see your tasks in a different order.

To edit a task, double-click it in any view. This brings up the Task dialog box.

In the Daily and Weekly views, you can do one other thing to a task—you can mark it as complete. When you've completed a particular task, click the small check box that precedes it in the task area. You'll see a check mark, marking that task as complete. Now it won't show up in the task area in future days' listings. (To do this in the Monthly view, double-click the task and place a check in the Completed box.)

 *Don't forget that your current tasks also show up in the Instant Palm Desktop menu, so you don't even have to open the Palm Desktop software in order to see what you need to accomplish for the day.*

Manage Tasks in the Task List

Want to see all your tasks in one place? Just click the View Task List button in the Palm Desktop toolbar or choose View | Task List from the menu. Now you'll see the Task List (see Figure 17-4).

The Task List can make it easier to view and manage your tasks all at once. It allows you to view quite a bit of information about the tasks, including the description, priority, date, and any categories.

Here are some management tasks you can accomplish in the Task List:

- To check off a completed task, click the check box at the far left of the item's row. If you check an item you haven't completed, you can click the check box again to remove your check mark.

- To edit a task, double-click it in the Task List. You'll see the Task dialog box, where you can change the description, priority, schedule, or categories for the task.

- From the View menu in the top-left corner of the Task List, you can choose to view all tasks, this week's uncompleted tasks, or today's uncompleted tasks. You can also create your own views by selecting View | Memorize View. You'll then see a dialog box that lets you give the view a name and decide what, exactly, is memorized. Once you've created a memorized view, you can select it at any time from the View menu. (You'll want to change things around elsewhere in the Task List, as described in the next bullet points.)

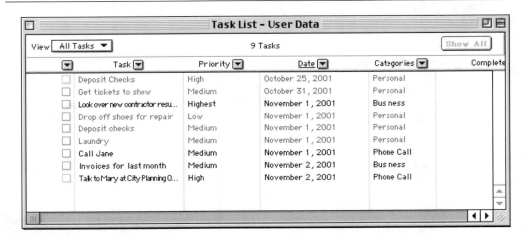

FIGURE 17-4   The Task List lets you manage tasks without flipping through the calendar.

17

■ You can sort the list by any of the columns listed. For instance, if you want to sort by date, click the heading Date in the Task List. Your list is sorted by date.

TIP *Want to move the columns around? Click and drag the column's name to a new location in the Task List and it'll appear when you release the mouse button.*

■ You can also use filters to help you see exactly what you need to see in the Task List. To do this, select the small triangle next to one of the column headings. In the pop-up menu, you can choose one of the filters. For instance, if you choose the Priority column's pop-up menu, you can see only tasks with the Highest priority by selecting that filter. With the Date column's pop-up menu, you can view tasks dated for the next week or for today and tomorrow, for instance. To return to the unfiltered view, choose the pop-up menu again and select No Filter.

SHORTCUT *If you've filtered like mad and you want to quickly get back to the entire list of tasks, choose the Show All button up in the top-right corner of the Task List. This will immediately do away with all filters and show you the complete list.*

■ You can create your own filters if you don't see one that meets your needs. From a column heading's pop-up menu, choose Custom Filter. You'll then see a dialog box that allows you to create a filter that will work for that column head—each dialog box is different since each column offers a different type of information.

TIP *The checked column has its own filter menu, too. You can choose that pop-up menu and select Unchecked if you'd like to see only the tasks that haven't yet been checked as completed.*

To close the Task List, just click its Close box. You can get back to it at any time through its toolbar button or the View | Task List command.

Manage Your Contacts

Aside from serving duty as your taskmaster and date book, the Palm Desktop can also replace that dog-eared address book you have floating around your desk ... somewhere. You can create and manage individual contact records for everyone you know, then view them all at once and edit at will. If you've got a Palm OS handheld computer, you can then synchronize your Contact List with the handheld so you can carry your address book with you.

Plus, contacts can be attached to calendar items in the Palm Desktop software. If you've got an appointment with John Doe or Jill Buck, you can attach that contact to the appointment and access that person's information quickly from within the calendar.

Create a New Contact

Before you can manage your contacts, you'll need to create some. These can be colleagues, family members, or friends.

TIP *If you need to create colleagues or friends, you might consider getting a job; starting a business; or joining a sports team, hobby group, or a fraternity or sorority. Creating family members is something I'll leave up to you.*

Once you have these sorts of people at your disposal, you can create a contact record within the Palm Desktop software to track them. There are, of course, a number of ways to create a contact record:

■ From the Instant Palm Desktop menu, choose Create | Contact.

■ From within the Palm Desktop software, click the New Contact button in the toolbar.

■ In the Palm Desktop software, choose Create | Contact.

Now you're ready to enter information about your contact in the Contact dialog box.

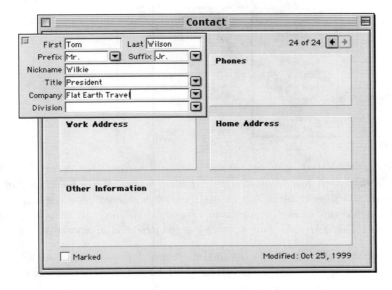

To enter information, just begin typing. The first entry box by default is the First name—type this person's first name, then press the TAB key. Keep entering information in each entry box. If you get to an entry box that you don't have information for or you otherwise want to skip, just press the TAB key again.

SHORTCUT *Each item has a small triangle pop-up menu next to it. After you've entered a few contacts, you'll notice that these arrows will include the entries you've made previously. And, you'll notice a little "auto-fill" going on: As you type the first few letters of items in many fields, they will be automatically filled in with previous entries. If those entries aren't correct, just keep typing. If the auto-fill entry is correct, just press TAB to move to the next field. This is a great way to quickly enter data that you've typed before.*

17

The Contact dialog box is divided into various sections, each of which includes different entry elements that help you enter information about this person. When you reach the end of one section (like the Name section), pressing the TAB key takes you to the first entry box in the next section. If you'd like to go directly to another section, select it with the mouse pointer and click once.

You'll also find that some of the entry options include pop-up menus. For instance, in the Phones section you can choose the type of phone number you're entering from the pop-up menu next to each entry. Options include Fax, Home, Main, Mobile, Work, and others.

		Ext.	
Work ▼	(212) 555-3452	300	☐
Home ▼	(212) 555-7869		☐
None			
Business	(212) 555-3450		☐
● Cellular ▶	917-232-2332		☐
Fax			
Home	ss		
Main			
Pager			
School			
Toll Free			
Work			
Other...			
Edit Menu...			

TIP   *You can create your own entries for these menus. Choose Other to enter a one-time name for this menu, like "Upstate" or "Vacation home." When you choose the Other command, you'll see a dialog box that lets you enter this one-time name. If you'd like to permanently add an item to the menu, choose Edit Menu from the pop-up menu. Now you'll see the Edit Menu dialog box that lets you delete, edit, or add items to the menu.*

Now, just move through each section and add information that you have about this person. You'll find that in some of the boxes you can choose the type of information you're entering from a pop-up menu—for instance, you can choose the type of address you want to enter from a pop-up menu in one of the address sections. You don't have to enter a Work Address and Home Address (the defaults). You can choose School or Business or you can customize the menu to reflect a different type of address (like billing, shipping, vacation, or whatever you'd like to enter).

In the Other Information section, you'll see a number of Custom entry boxes. To change the name of a Custom entry box, double-click the existing name. In the dialog box, you can customize a number of features, including the name, whether or not items in the entry box are capitalized automatically, whether or not the entries typed are saved to the triangle pull-down menu, and whether or not the entry will include a button icon that runs an AppleScript when clicked. You'll notice, in the Script File menu, there are a few AppleScripts that have already been set up for you.

Know something about AppleScript? If you do, you can create more scripts to associate with buttons in the Contact dialog box. Place those scripts in the Scripts folder inside the Palm folder on your hard disk and the scripts will appear in the Script File menu.

Done with all that data entry? Click the Contact dialog box's Close box and the entry is saved.

View the Contact List

Once you've gotten a few contacts entered, you're ready to manage them from the Contact List. To open the Contact List, click the View Contact List button in the toolbar or choose View | Contact List from the menu. You'll see the Contact List in all its shimmering glory, as shown in Figure 17-5.

	Full Name ▼	Company ▼	Phone 1 ▼	Phone 2 ▼	Categories ▼
	Kim Chen	The Candlelight Restaurant	W:(408)555-0900	H:(503)555-4655	Customers
	Mr. Dennis Copley Ph.D.	International Bakery	W:(913)555-3234	H:(913)555-8752	Employees
	Samuel Corning	International Bakery	W:(803)555-7911	H:(513)555-1987	Employees
	Vern Critser	International Bakery	W:(603)555-3322	H:(205)555-2388	Employees
	Pamela Dreyfus	International Bakery	W:(712)555-5245	H:(715)555-9987	Employees
	Nancy Eison	International Bakery	W:(616)555-3698	H:(719)555-4477	Employees
	Denise Garcia	Bakery Supplies, Inc.	W:(814)555-7777	H:(408)555-5684	Suppliers
	Doris Gerhard	International Bakery	W:(407)555-8297	H:(408)555-6241	Employees
	Faye Johnson	International Bakery	W:(518)555-2211	H:(315)555-0011	Employees
	Irfon Kohn	The Spice Exchange	W:(606)555-5468	H:(712)555-5245	Suppliers
	Heidi Lee	Finest Flours, Inc.	W:(208)555-8135	H:(616)555-3698	Suppliers
	Mary Jo Licklighter	Delightful Diner	W:(505)555-8822	H:(814)555-7777	Customers
	Jeremy Lin		W:(503)555-4655	H:(408)555-0900	Customers
	Sonia Long	Best Bakery Equipment, Inc.	W:(601)555-6899	H:(913)555-3234	Suppliers
	Bob Nguyen	Bakery Middlemen, Inc.	W:(401)555-3258	H:(803)555-7911	Customers
	Jennifer Norris		W:(717)555-4688	H:(603)555-3322	Customers
	Matt Peterson	General Repair Service, Inc.	W:(513)555-1987	H:(712)555-5245	Suppliers
	Lei Richley	Wholeworld Wholesalers, Inc.	W:(205)555-2388	H:(616)555-3698	Customers
	Rajesh Shah	International Bakery	W:(715)555-9987	H:(503)555-4655	Employees
	John Shaw	Popular Promotions, Ltd	W:(719)555-4477	H:(601)555-6899	Suppliers
	Janet Swanson	Deli Delights	W:(408)555-5685		Customers
	Meni Waters	ABC Legal Services	W:(408)555-6241	H:(717)555-4688	Suppliers
	Bob Wilford	Ace Accounting Service, Inc.	W:(315)555-0011	H:(513)555-1987	Suppliers
	Mr. Tom Wilson Jr.	Flat Earth Travel	W:(212)555-345...	H:(212)555-7869	None

View [All Contacts ▼]   24 of 24 Contacts   [Show All]

Contact List - Todd

FIGURE 17-5   The Contact List shows you contacts and selected information about them.

17

Once you've got the Contact List open, there are plenty of management tasks you can perform:

- To edit a contact, double-click it in the Contact List. You'll see the Contact dialog box, where you can change the information for this contact.

- If you have a contact who has information that's similar to another contact you'd like to create, select that contact and choose Edit | Duplicate Contact. Now you can change what's different about your new contact, but leave the other information intact.

- You can sort the list by any of the columns listed. For instance, if you want to sort by company, click the heading Company in the Contact List. Your list is sorted by company.

TIP   *Want to move the columns around? Click and drag the column name to a new location in the Contact List and it'll appear when you release the mouse button.*

- You can also use filters to help you see exactly what you need to see in the Contact List. To do this, select the small triangle next to one of the column headings. In the pop-up menu, you can choose one of the filters. For instance, if you choose the Categories column's pop-up menu, you can see only contacts within your Personal category by selecting that filter. With the Company column's pop-up menu, you can view people who work for a particular company by selecting the company name. To return to the unfiltered view, choose the pop-up menu again and select No Filter.

SHORTCUT   *If you've been filtering a bit and you want to quickly get back to the entire list of contacts, click the Show All button in the top-right corner of the Contact List. This will immediately do away with all filters and show you the complete list.*

- You can create your own filters if you don't see one that meets your needs. From a column heading's pop-up menu, choose Custom Filter. You'll then see a dialog box that allows you to create a filter that will work for that column head—each dialog box is different since each column offers a different type of information.

- From the View menu, you can choose All Contacts if you've been filtering and sorting. If you've created a series of filters and sorts that really tickle your fancy, you can store that view of the Contact List by selecting View | Memorize View. You'll then see a dialog box that lets you give the view a name and decide what, exactly, is memorized. Once you've created a memorized view, you can select it at any time from the View menu.

TIP   *You can view different columns of information, if you'd like to. To select the columns to view, choose View | Columns. In the Columns dialog box, click an item to place or remove the check mark that denotes whether or not the item will appear in the Contact List. You can then drag items to new locations to change the order in which the columns will appear. A small number next to the check mark indicates its order (from left to right) in the Contact List.*

Attach Contacts to Items

One of the really powerful features in Palm Desktop is the ability to attach a contact to appointments, events, or tasks on your calendar. This makes it easy to associate data between the different parts of your calendar in many different ways. For instance, you can associate a contact with a particular task that involves that person, like a task you create that reminds you to call Nancy. If you attach Nancy's contact info to the task, you won't have to go digging for her number.

Attach From the Contact List

One way to attach a contact to a particular item is from within the Contact List. With the Contact List open, select the Attach menu next to that contact's name (it's the file folder icon with a paperclip on it). In the menu, choose the item you'd like to attach this contact to from the Attach To menu. If you choose Existing Item from the Attach To menu, a small window opens up at the bottom of the screen.

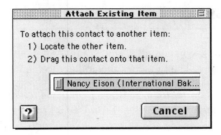

You'll notice that this window holds a little draggable version of the contact you've chosen. Now, switch to the Calendar or Task List and find the item to which you'd like to attach this contact. Once you've found it, drag the contact from its Attach Existing Item window to the event. When you drop the contact on the event, they become attached.

Attached icon

Now, when you encounter that event, you can select the attached icon to bring up a menu that allows you to view the attached contact, detach the contact, or attach it to another item.

 *If you have both the Contact List and the Task List or Calendar open, you can drag a contact straight from the Contact List to the item to which you'd like to attach the contact. This attaches the contact instantly.*

17

Auto-Attach

If you don't feel like opening the Contact List, you can attach contacts from within the Calendar or while you're creating an item. If you create an item that has part of a contact's (or more than one contacts') name in the entry, you'll see the Auto-Attachments dialog box after you've created the item. For instance, creating an appointment called "Lunch with Bob" will bring up the Auto-Attachments dialog box, complete with listings of contacts that may fit the description.

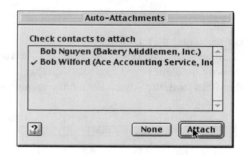

If one of the contacts matches, you can click that contact to place a check mark, then click the Attach button in the dialog box. That attaches the contact to the item you've created.

 *If you want to attach a contact to an existing item that includes part of the contact's name, click the item, then choose Create | Attach To | Instant Attach. That will cause Palm Desktop to analyze the event and see if any contacts might match.*

Create and Manage Notes

If you synchronize the Palm Desktop software with your Palm OS handheld computer, you'll probably see the immediate value of creating notes in the Palm Desktop program. After all, it can be nice to have extensive notes and reminders on your handheld computer, but it can cramp your style to have to write all of those notes on the handheld's little screen. Well, what if you could type them up (or copy and paste them from your iMac's applications) first, then get them on the handheld computer with a quick menu command?

Even if you don't have a handheld, the Notes feature in Palm Desktop is worth using. It's a great place to put thoughts, ideas, lists, or anything else you'd like to keep track of. Plus, you can attach notes to events, appointments, and tasks in your calendar, making it easy to add extra text to a calendar event. If you've got directions to a meeting, for instance, you can store them in a note, then attach them to an appointment (or to a task or contact). That way the note is safely stored away, and it can be attached to a future item if necessary.

Create the Note

If you've been reading along in this chapter so far, you know there are multiple ways to create items with Palm Desktop. Creating a note is no exception. Here's how:

■ From the Instant Palm Desktop menu, choose Create | Note.

■ From within the Palm Desktop software, click the New Note button in the toolbar.

■ In the Palm Desktop software, choose Create | Note.

All of these result in a new Note window appearing in Palm Desktop, as shown in Figure 17-6.

To create your note, just enter a title in the Title entry box, then press TAB to move on to the Date. Today's date and time are entered automatically, but you can edit them if desired. (Usually, the date is used to reflect when the note was created.) Next, you can select a category or categories for the note. Then, you're ready to edit. Type your note in the text area of the note.

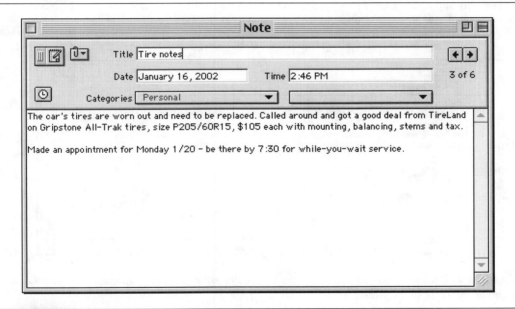

FIGURE 17-6   The Note window allows you to title, categorize, and edit your note.

17

 *Want to insert the current date and time without typing them? Click the small clock icon on the left side of the window, just above the text area. That automatically inserts the current date and time at the insertion point. You can do this at different times if you like to keep a running journal or to add to an existing note.*

Notes are plain text—you can't format with fonts, boldface, italics, and other styles. One of the reasons for this is simple—most Palm OS handheld computers can't handle too much styled text, so anything you do in the Note window wouldn't translate well anyway.

Once you're done creating the note, you can click the Close box in the Note window. Your note is done.

 The Note window is also used for reading notes that you've written previously. In the top-right corner, you'll find two arrow keys that can be used to move back and forth between the notes that you've saved. This makes it easier to read notes quickly.

View the Note List

Like contacts and tasks, you can view all of your notes using the Note List. To open the Note List, click the View Note List button in the toolbar or choose View | Note List.

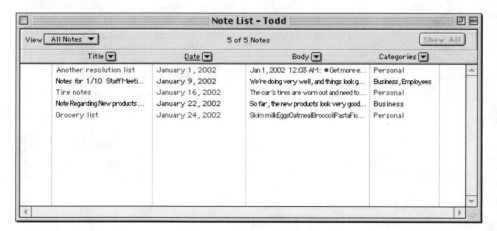

And, as with the Contact List and the Task List, there are a number of management tasks that you can accomplish in the Note List:

- To edit a note, double-click it in the Note List. You'll see the Note window, where you can re-title, edit, or add to your note.

- You can sort the Note List by any of the columns listed. For instance, if you want to sort by title, click the heading Title in the Note List. Your list is sorted alphabetically by title.

Want to move the columns around? Click and drag the column name to a new location in the Note List and it'll appear when you release the mouse button.

■ You can use filters to help you see exactly what you need to see in the Note List. To do this, select the small triangle next to one of the column headings. In the pop-up menu, you can choose one of the filters. For instance, if you choose the Categories column's pop-up menu, you can see only notes in your Personal category by selecting that filter. To return to the unfiltered view, choose the pop-up menu again and select No Filter.

If you've been filtering a bit and you want to quickly get back to the entire list of notes, click the Show All button in the top-right corner of the Note List. This will immediately do away with all filters and show you the complete list.

■ You can create your own filters if you don't see one that meets your needs. From a column heading's pop-up menu, choose Custom Filter. You'll then see a dialog box that allows you to create a filter that will work for that column head—each dialog box is different since each column offers a different type of information.

■ From the View menu, you can choose All Notes if you've been filtering and sorting. If you've created a series of filters and sorts that really tickle your fancy, you can store that view of the Note List by selecting View | Memorize View. You'll then see a dialog box that lets you give the view a name and decide what, exactly, is memorized. Once you've created a memorized view, you can select it at any time from the View menu.

Attach Notes

Like contacts (and most other events, for that matter) you can attach notes to other events in Palm Desktop. This is great for situations where you'd like to store extensive notes about something—say, a log of phone conversations or written directions to a meeting site—and then associate them with a contact, appointment, or other event. Plus, you can associate one note to any number of events, making it easy to cross-reference an important document while you're viewing an event or contact.

Attaching a note works much the same as attaching any other event. There are two basic ways to accomplish it:

■ From the Note window, open the Attach menu (the small menu that looks like a folder and paperclip.) Select Attach To, then choose the type of item. If you choose Existing Item, an icon for the note appears in a floating window. Locate the existing item and drag the note icon from the floating window to that item.

■ From the Note List, drag a note to an item in the Calendar, Contact List, or Task List.

17

Synchronizing with a Palm Device

Although Palm Desktop is a powerful organizer program in its own right, ultimately its goal is to synchronize calendar and note-taking data with a Palm OS handheld computer. If you have one of those, and you have a USB-based PalmConnect kit (which allows a Palm cradle to connect to an iMac via USB), then you can synchronize your calendar, contacts, and notes with the handheld computer easily.

NOTE   *You don't have to have a PalmConnect USB connection kit, although that's certainly the easiest way. Some USB adapter manufacturers make USB-to-serial connection kits that allow you to connect a serial PalmConnect cable to a USB port on your iMac. See Chapter 26 for details on adapters.*

Set Up HotSync

Once you have your Palm's cradle connected to your iMac, you'll want to make sure you've got HotSync configured correctly. From within Palm Desktop, choose HotSync | Setup. Now, in the HotSync Software Setup window, check to make sure that HotSync is enabled. You may also wish to make sure that the Enable HotSync Software At System Startup option is checked so that you can sync data by pushing the cradle's HotSync button instead of using a menu command.

Click the Serial Port Settings tab to set up the connection for your Palm's cradle. With these settings, you can choose whether you'll be synchronizing over a local connection (most likely the USB cable), a modem connection (if your Palm OS handheld has a modem), or both if you'd like the option of switching between the two. Then, set up the speed and port for each relevant setup. (For the local setup, you'll likely choose As Fast As Possible and PalmConnect USB from the pop-up menus.)

Set Conduit Settings

Your next step is to determine what, exactly, you'd like to have synchronized when you perform a HotSync between the Palm OS handheld and your iMac. To do that, choose HotSync | Conduit Settings.

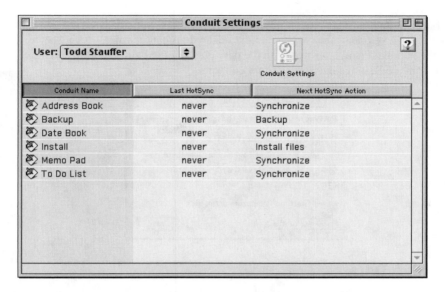

The Conduit Settings window shows you the currently installed applications that include a conduit. For the Palm software, a *conduit* is a mechanism by which a Mac OS application and a Palm OS application can share data. For instance, all of the standard applications on a Palm OS computer (To Do, Memo Pad, Address Book, and Date Book) have conduits that allow them to share data with their counterparts in the Palm Desktop software. Likewise, if you install other applications that can share data via a conduit, that conduit will appear in the Conduit Settings window.

To alter a particular conduit, double-click it in the window. Now you'll see a Settings dialog box that gives you the options for that particular conduit. (While the bundled conduits are similar, you'll find that third-party conduits vary more significantly.) Change whatever settings you think are necessary, or leave things as they are, and click the OK button when you're done.

Note that for the bundled applications, the conduit settings allow you to change the way a HotSync works. By default, a HotSync causes all data to be synchronized between the two devices—that is, any event or item that appears on one computer but not the other will now

17

appear on both computers. That's useful, but it may not be how you always want things handled. If you'd prefer to have one of the two computers be the dominant partner—for instance, so that all data on the handheld is overwritten with the data that's in the Palm Desktop software, you can choose that from the Settings menu for certain conduits.

Synchronize Data

Once you've got your settings in place, synchronizing between the Palm OS handheld and the Palm Desktop software is simple. Simply place the handheld in its cradle and press the HotSync button. You'll see the HotSync alert box appear and a status bar will indicate that your Palm OS handheld is being located, then that data will be synchronized.

> **NOTE** *If you're working with Palm Desktop in the Classic environment of Mac OS X, it should still synchronize properly, but you'll need to have the Classic environment loaded before pressing the HotSync button. Your best bet is to have Palm Desktop front and center, then synchronize.*

If you don't see the HotSync alert dialog, check the connection between the Palm's cradle and your iMac. You should also ensure that HotSync is enabled on the HotSync Enabled dialog box and that your local connection settings are correct on the Serial Port Settings tab.

Install Palm Applications

You can also use the Palm Desktop software to install applications on your Palm OS handheld. To do that, choose HotSync | Install Applications from the menu. In the Install Handheld Files dialog box, drag Palm OS applications to the Applications list. (Palm applications have the three-letter extension ".prc" as part of their filenames.) Figure 17-7 shows files being dragged to the Install Handheld Files window.

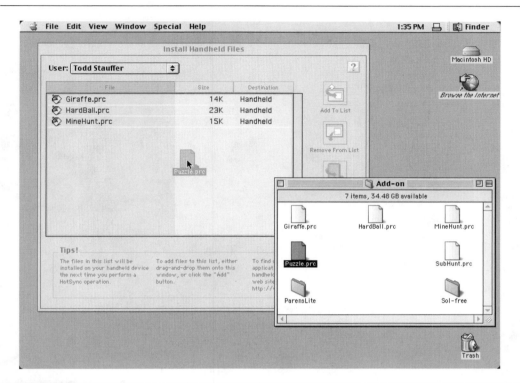

FIGURE 17-7   Installing files on your Palm OS handheld

Now, the next time you perform a HotSync, these files will be installed on the Palm OS device. To perform the HotSync immediately, place the Palm OS handheld in its cradle and press the HotSync button.

17

Part III

Get Online

Chapter 18

Get Serious About E-mail

How to...

- Set up your e-mail account(s)
- Use Mac.com mail
- Organize your e-mail
- Get attachments, add signatures, and build rules

You may have bought your iMac for the express purpose of getting e-mail—a lot of people do. Even if it wasn't your primary goal, you probably think e-mail is a big part of the computing experience. Electronic mail (e-mail) gives you the opportunity to communicate inexpensively and rather quickly in a written format. What were once letters between family, friends, and business associates have become electronic messages. What used to take days now arrives in seconds.

In this chapter I'll focus on two different e-mail applications—Apple Mail, Mac OS X's full-featured e-mail program, and Microsoft Outlook Express, both of which are included with your iMac. If you're using Mac OS 9, then Outlook Express is your main option, although you can also use Netscape Communicator's Messenger e-mail component (which isn't covered in this chapter). In Mac OS X, you can use either Mail or Outlook Express, although you should be warned that Outlook Express runs as a Classic application.

Is Your Account Set Up?

The first thing you'll need before you can send and receive e-mail is an e-mail account. Most likely you already have one—an e-mail account is created for you when you sign up for Internet access. And the best part is, with most ISPs, you'll have an e-mail account that corresponds to your Internet account name. If you were given the user name *myusername* when you created the Internet account, for instance, then your e-mail address is probably *myusername@myisp.net*.

If you've walked through the Setup Assistant (Mac OS X) or the Internet Setup Assistant (Mac OS 9) discussed in Chapter 1, then you may already have your account set up—in that case, you can just fire up your e-mail application and begin sending and receiving. Likewise, if you signed up for iTools using the Mac OS X Setup Assistant, then you're automatically already set up to send and receive Mac.com mail. If not, then you may need to dig deeper into your e-mail settings, as discussed in this section.

Configure the Internet Pane or Control Panel

Using the Internet pane (Mac OS X) or Internet control panel (Mac OS 9), it's possible to quickly and easily customize your e-mail account setup, regardless of the e-mail application you're using (see Figure 18-1). You've likely already used the Setup Assistant, so the basics are already entered regarding your e-mail account. If you dig into the Internet pane, though, you can change some options, too. In Mac OS X, launch the System Preferences application, then select the Internet icon. In Mac OS 9, choose Apple menu | Control Panels | Internet. In both cases, once the Internet window appears you can click the E-mail tab.

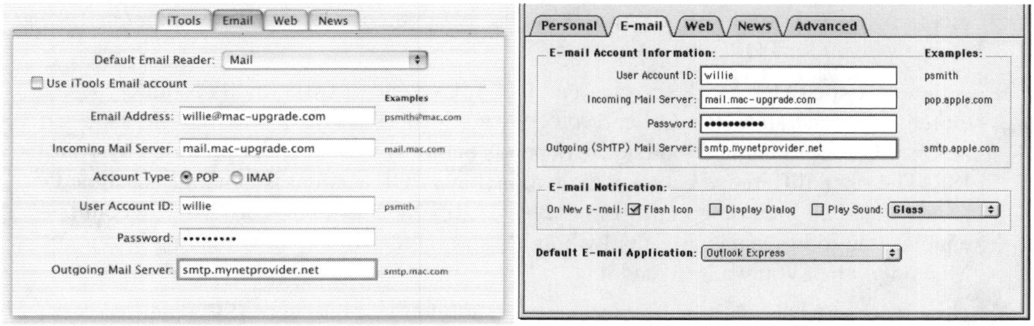

FIGURE 18-1   On the left, the Internet pane in Mac OS X; on the right, the Internet control panel in Mac OS 9.

With the E-mail tab displayed, you're ready to enter the information your e-mail program will need to access the ISP's server computer and get your e-mail. Many of these entries may have already been completed for you by the Setup Assistant. You can change them if desired or necessary—sometimes you'll get a new password or an e-mail server address from your system administrator.

In Mac OS X, the first item you may notice is a special option—Use iTools E-mail Account. If you click the check box next to this option to turn it on, the Internet pane will automatically use the iTools member name and password you entered on the iTools tab to extrapolate the rest of the information it needs to set up your Mac.com account. Once you've turned this option on, you don't have any other decisions to make—you can close the System Preferences application and move right to launching Mail and working with your Mac.com account.

If you need to set up a different account, or make changes to an existing account, you'll enter and edit those items on the E-mail tab. (Note that E-mail Address is on the Personal tab of the Internet control panel in Mac OS 9.)

■ **Default Mail Reader (or Default E-mail Application)**   Select the application you want to use as your default for reading and replying to e-mail messages. If that application doesn't appear in the pop-up menu, choose Select from the menu and use the Open dialog box to locate that application.

■ **E-mail Address**   This entry can be confusing. It's here that you should type your *reply-to* address—the e-mail address that others use to send you e-mail. This may be different from your user name and the actual account that you log into to receive e-mail. For instance, my reply address might be *willie@mac-upgrade.com,* but my user account with my ISP could be *todds56* or something similar. This isn't always the case, but it's fairly common. (Note that this entry box appears on the Personal tab of the Internet control panel in Mac OS 9.)

18

- **Incoming Mail Server**   This is the address of the mail server computer where your incoming e-mail should be retrieved. Usually, it's in the form of *mail.myisp.net* or *pop.myisp.net* for POP e-mail accounts.

- **Account Type (Mac OS X only)**   You likely have one of two e-mail account types, either a POP account (Post Office Protocol) or an IMAP account (Internet Message Access Protocol). Which you choose depends on the type of account provided by your ISP. The main difference between the two is that a POP account is generally designed to download all incoming mail from the server to your Mac, while an IMAP account enables you to browse your e-mail while it's still on the server, downloading it to your Mac only when you want to read it.

- **User Account ID**   This is the user name used to log you into your ISP's mail server. In many cases it's the same as the first part of your e-mail address, but not always.

- **Password**   This is the password that, along with the User Account ID, enables you to log into your ISP's mail server and retrieve your e-mail.

- **Outgoing Mail Server**   This is the mail server computer used for outgoing messages, usually in the form of *smtp.myisp.net*. (SMTP stands for Simple Mail Transport Protocol.) This address is often different from your incoming mail server.

TIP

In most cases, you should use the outgoing mail server provided by the ISP that you actually sign into for Internet access, not necessarily the ISP that hosts your e-mail account. For instance, if you sign onto the Internet using a cable modem, but you access an e-mail account provided by a different ISP, then you should use the cable modem ISP's outgoing mail server to send your e-mail. Otherwise, you may get "forwarding" error messages from the outgoing mail server because you aren't recognized as a valid user.

With all of these items configured, you should be ready to launch your e-mail application and start receiving, reading, and replying to e-mail messages. Close System Preferences or the Internet control panel, then launch Mail or Outlook Express to begin working with e-mail.

Use More Than One Account

Do you have more than one e-mail account? You'll be happy to know that both Mail and Outlook Express can handle messages from more than one e-mail account, allowing you to download from all your accounts at once, manage your messages from one Inbox, and, as you'll see, send your e-mail from the account of your choice.

NOTE

You can use this system for the different people's e-mail accounts in your household or organization, but a better approach is to create multiple users, as discussed in Chapter 27. In that way, each individual can have his or her own e-mail preferences and archives—in fact, you can use different e-mail programs altogether, if desired!

Create a New Account in Mail

Creating a new account differs slightly depending on which e-mail application you're using. Here's how to add an account to Mac OS X's Mail:

1. Choose Mail | Preferences.

2. In the Mail Preferences window, click the Accounts icon, if it isn't already selected.

3. To create a new account, click Create Account.

4. In the dialog sheet that appears, enter information regarding your account—this is pretty much the same information discussed previously in the section "Configure the Internet Pane or Control Panel." The only differences that may cause confusion are the Host Name entry, which corresponds to the Incoming Mail Server discussed earlier, and the SMTP Host, which corresponds to the Outgoing Mail Server.

5. If you'd like to set advanced options for this account, click the Account Options tab at the top of the dialog sheet. You'll see a number of interesting options, including the option to "Delete Messages on Server After Downloading" (you'll generally want to turn this option on if this iMac is your primary e-mail computer) and an option to "Show This Account Separately in the Mailboxes Drawer" if you'd like to see a separate Inbox for this account in the Mailboxes drawer. When you're done setting preferences, click OK.

The account is created. Now, whenever you create a new message you have the choice of using the new account to send the message (via the Account menu in the Composition window) instead of your original one. When you select Get Mail, both (or all) of your e-mail accounts will be accessed and the new e-mail will show up in the Inbox, unless you opt to change these options on the Account Options tab discussed in step 5.

You can also check this account individually. Choose Mailbox | Get New Mail in Account | *Account Name* to check messages for a particular account.

Create a New Account in Outlook Express

Outlook Express 5 also supports multiple accounts, and they're easy to add, thanks to a special Setup Assistant. Here's how:

1. Choose Tools | Accounts.

2. Choose Mail from the New button menu.

3. Now the Account Setup Assistant takes over from here. You can use the assistant to set up an existing or new e-mail account. You can also create a free Hotmail account (a special Web-based, Microsoft-hosted account that you can access via Outlook Express) from within the assistant.

4. If you want the newly created account to be your default account (the one that you've automatically set up to send e-mail from, unless you change it), then choose Make Default. When you're done entering information, click OK.

18

The account is created. Now, when you select Send and Receive, both (or all) of your e-mail accounts will be accessed and the new e-mail will show up in the Inbox. (Notice that each message has a column entry that tells you what account it was sent to.) To send a message from this account, simply choose it in the From menu of a composition (or reply) window.

You can check this account individually by choosing the account name from the Send and Receive button menu or by selecting Tools | Send and Receive, then the name of the account that you want to check.

TIP   *Want this account to not get checked when you check others? Open the Accounts window (Tools | Accounts) and double-click the account name. Now, you can use the Include This Account in My "Send and Receive All" Schedule option to determine whether or not it is checked when you check others.*

Use Your Mac.com E-mail Address

Once you have an iTools account (see Chapter 6), you automatically have a Mac.com e-mail address in the form of *membername*@mac.com. This account is designed to be used in conjunction with your e-mail application, whether that's Mac OS X's Mail application, Microsoft Outlook Express, or another program. You can set up your Mac.com account in two different ways.

Set Up Mac.com Mail Automatically in Mac OS X

The easiest way to set up your Mac.com e-mail account is via the Internet pane in the System Preferences application. The only caveat to this approach is that, at the time of writing, it works best with the built-in Mail application in Mac OS X. (This may change in later versions of third-party e-mail applications that take advantage of this feature in Mac OS X.)

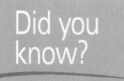

Mac.com in OS X Mail

If you have a Mac.com account in addition to a standard POP account, you'll notice that the Mac.com account, by default, appears with its own Inbox and mailboxes in Mac OS X's Mail application. That's because the Mac.com account is an IMAP account—one that enables you to view your messages "live" on the server before downloading them. When you select a message to read it, it's then downloaded. Because of this difference in operating, Mac.com mail doesn't show up in your standard Inbox. That also means it's important to regularly move items from your Inbox to other folders (or *mailboxes,* as they're called in the Mail application) so that they're downloaded from Apple's servers. Otherwise, you may eventually run up against the storage limits (20MB) set by Apple for your iTools account.

First, you need to have signed up for iTools and entered your member name and password on the iTools tab in the Internet pane. Then, select the E-mail tab in the Internet pane. Click the check box next to the Use iTools E-mail Account option. You'll see your e-mail information automatically filled in on the E-mail tab.

 Setting up your Mac.com account in this way makes your Mac.com your default e-mail account. If you'd prefer some other account to be your default, use the manual approach to setting up Mac.com mail, described in the next section.

Now, all you have to do is launch the Mail application. You'll note that your Mac.com e-mail account is automatically added to your list of Mailboxes. (In fact, it may be your only account if you've not previously added any accounts within Mail.)

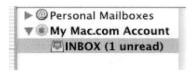

You can then immediately begin sending and receiving e-mail via the Mac.com account, as discussed in Chapter 6. (In fact, you'll probably already have one e-mail message you can read—an automatic welcome message from Apple.)

Set Up Mac.com E-mail Manually

The other method you can use for setting up Mac.com e-mail is the manual approach. You'll use this procedure to add the Mac.com e-mail account to any third party e-mail application, or to add it as a secondary (that is, not the default) account in the Mail application. You do this by launching your e-mail application and creating a new account. (See the earlier section "Use More Than One E-mail Account" for details.)

Next, you'll need to enter the account information for your Mac.com account. Again, different e-mail applications will ask for this information in slightly different ways, but it should be fairly easy to figure out:

- **Account Name** The account name for your Mac.com account is the member name you've been assigned, as in "willieh345" or "sjobs."
- **Mail Password** Your e-mail password is the same as your iTools account password.

18

- **POP Mail Server** This may also be listed as "incoming mail server." Enter **mail.mac.com**.

- **SMTP Mail Server** This may also be called the "outgoing mail server." For this entry, you can simply enter **smtp.mac.com**. (If you have trouble with outgoing mail, change this to your ISP's SMTP server address, such as **smtp.earthlink.net** if you sign onto the Internet via Earthlink.)

- **Reply-to Address** This will sometimes also be listed as simply "E-mail Address." In most cases, you should simply make this *membername*@mac.com. You can, however, often enter a different e-mail address for this option if you'd prefer that your recipients use a different address when they click the Reply command.

- **Full Name** This may be given different names in different programs, but it's simply asking for the name you want your recipients to see next to your e-mail address in their e-mail applications. Enter your full name or, if you'd prefer "Arcon the Death Warrior" or "Kitty Lover;" you can generally enter such names here with no harm done (except to your recipient's sensibilities).

Once you've set up the account, you can begin using it for e-mail, just as you would any e-mail account.

Mac.com E-mail Options

Apple offers a few other options that are accessible from the Web for your Mac.com e-mail account. Visit **http://itools.mac.com/** and click the Mac.com E-mail option. Then, sign into your iTools account (if asked). Once you're on the Mac.com E-mail page, you'll see (at least) three options:

- **Forward Your Mail** You can select this option if you'd prefer that any messages sent to your Mac.com address are forwarded to another e-mail account. This means you won't be able to use the Mac.com address for your replies (you'll use the account to which the messages were forwarded). Forwarding has the advantage of allowing you to check your Mac.com e-mail from anywhere that you can check your other e-mail account. (For instance, if you forward to a Yahoo!, Excite, or Hotmail account, you can check those accounts from any Web browser.)

- **Auto Reply** Select this option if you'd like iTools to reply to all received messages with an automatic message you select. Enter an Auto Reply message that says "I'm out of the office for two weeks…" or "I'm on a meditation retreat in Nova Scotia…" and turn on the Auto Reply option. You'll still receive the e-mail messages whenever you check them in your e-mail program, and you'll still be able to reply to messages you've received, but, in the meantime, your senders won't be left wondering what happened to you and why you don't love them anymore. (Don't forget to turn *off* Auto Reply once you're back and functioning again in your day-to-day life.)

■ **Spread the Word**   iTools gives you another chance here to send an iCard to anyone who needs to know your new Mac.com address. Just follow the onscreen instructions and you can quickly let an entire list of folks know how to keep in touch with you via your Mac.com e-mail address.

Organize Your E-mail

You saw the basics of reading, responding to, and creating e-mail messages in Chapter 6. Once you've received more than a few messages in your e-mail application, you'll probably want to start organizing them. Mail makes that easy enough to do, via the Mailboxes drawer and the multiple personal folders (which Mail calls *mailboxes*) that you can create for storing messages. Outlook Express, likewise, enables you to create and use folders in the Folder List for storing your read messages.

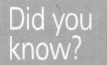
Did you know?

Customize the Toolbar in Mac OS X Mail

Delete, Reply, Reply All, and Compose are handy commands to have on the Mail toolbar, but they're not the only commands possible. What's more, you can decide exactly what commands appear on the toolbar and in what order. And, if you've read Chapter 4, you'll recognize the system that's used to customize Mail's toolbar—it's the same approach you can use to customize a Mac OS X Finder window's toolbar.

Select View | Customize Toolbar and you'll see a large dialog sheet appear, featuring many different icons and controls that you can add to the toolbar. Now, just drag items up from the dialog sheet to Mail's toolbar—you can even drag existing icons around on the toolbar itself to change the icons' positions. Also, at the bottom of the dialog sheet, you can select from the Show menu what you'd like to see in the toolbar: Icon & Text, Icon Only, or Text Only. To return to the default toolbar, simply click the default set near the bottom of the dialog sheet. When you're finished customizing, click the Done button.

Want even more power? You can choose View | Customize Toolbar when you're viewing an open Composition window—either during a reply or while creating a new e-mail message. There, you can use the same process to customize the toolbar for editing and sending your messages.

Create and Delete Mailboxes in Mail

To create a new mailbox in Mail, first select the group where you'd like the new mailbox to appear. Most likely, you'll select Personal Mailboxes, although you may wish to select a particular e-mail account if you have more than one that appears in the Mailboxes drawer (such as a Mac.com account).

Creating a new mailbox is simple—just choose Mailbox | New Mailbox. In the dialog box that appears, enter a name for the new mailbox and press RETURN or click OK. The mailbox appears in the Mailboxes drawer, complete with a small folder icon (suggesting that this is a personal mailbox that you've created to organize messages).

To move messages to the new mailbox folder, select them in the message list, then drag-and-drop items from the message list to that mailbox. You can also CONTROL-click on a particular message, choose Transfer from the contextual menu, then select the target mailbox folder.

> **TIP**   *If you'd like to create nested mailbox folders (that is, subfolders inside the main mailbox folders), you do that by typing the name in the form* mailbox/subfolder, *such as* **Family/Grandma**. *Note that you can only create a nested folder if the main mailbox folder doesn't yet exist. If you've already created a standalone mailbox folder called Clients, then you can't create subfolders for that folder. But if you begin by creating Clients/East, then you can later add Clients/West and so on.*

To delete a mailbox, select it in the Mailboxes drawer, then choose Mailbox | Delete Mailbox. Note that when you delete a mailbox, any messages in that mailbox are deleted immediately—they are *not* moved to the Deleted Messages mailbox folder.

Create and Delete Folders in Outlook Express

Outlook Express, like Mail, has a special Folders List that's available in the main mail viewer screen. (Select View | Folder List to hide or show the list.) Within that list, you can create new

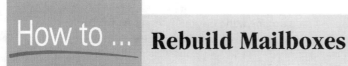

Rebuild Mailboxes

After working with mailbox folders for a while in Mail, you'll find that it's a good idea to *rebuild* those folders—a process that cleans up the database entries and recovers the storage space that had been used for deleted files. This is especially true if it seems to take a long time to view a particular mailbox or if you believe odd things are happening—messages don't seem to appear correctly or deleted messages still remain in the mailbox folder.

To rebuild a mailbox, select either Personal Mailboxes (to rebuild all mailboxes under the Personal Mailboxes) or an individual mailbox folder, then choose Mailbox | Rebuild Mailbox. You'll see the progress of the rebuild indicated on the status line.

In Outlook Express, you don't individually rebuild mailboxes—instead, you can rebuild the entire OE database by holding down the OPTION key while launching Outlook Express. You'll see a dialog box asking if you want to compact the message base. Click Yes if you want to perform a reasonably quick compacting operation. Click No, however, and you'll see another option—a complex rebuild. Choose this if you want the best results and/or you're having trouble with Outlook Express and you want to attempt to recover problematic messages. (It's also a good idea to have a backup of the Outlook Express database files first—they're found in a folder called Microsoft User Data, often found in your main Documents folder.)

folders by selecting File | New | Folder. An untitled folder appears in the Folder List—begin typing immediately to give it a name.

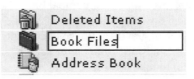

Press RETURN and the folder jumps to its position, alphabetically, in the list of folders. To create a subfolder, select a folder in the list and choose File | New | Subfolder. The subfolder appears under the selected folder.

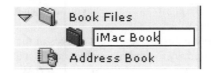

18

You can also drag one folder to another. Once dropped, the originally dragged folder becomes a subfolder of the target folder. The parent folder will now have a disclosure triangle, indicating that it has subfolder(s) within it.

To move items to a folder, simply select them in the main message list and drag them to the folder. Note that you can select multiple messages by holding down SHIFT (for contiguous messages) or ⌘ while clicking messages with the mouse. You can also highlight messages and select Message | Move To and a folder from the list that appears in that menu. And you can drag items directly to subfolders as well. If the subfolder isn't revealed, drag the messages to the disclosure triangle next to the parent folder in the Folder List and hover there for a second—the triangle should pop "open" revealing its subfolders.

To delete a folder, highlight it in the list and click the Delete button in the toolbar or press the DELETE key on your keyboard. If the folder is empty, it's deleted immediately. If the folder has messages in it, you'll see an alert box asking if you're sure that you want to delete the folder. Click Delete if you're sure you want to delete the folder and messages.

Attachments, Signatures, and Rules

Beyond the basics of managing your e-mail, you may want to customize the experience further. In this section, we'll talk about sending and receiving computer files as attachments to e-mail messages. You'll also see how to add custom signatures to your messages and how to automate certain e-mail tasks with the built-in rules features of Mail and Outlook Express.

Send and Receive Attachments

Most any Mac e-mail application can help you send an attached file—a document, application, or compressed archive of different sorts of files—to recipients through Internet e-mail. In fact, you can even send attachments to recipients using Intel-compatible PCs. The only major limitation is that it can take a while to upload and download attachments. While most e-mail messages are about 5–10 kilobytes in size, the typical graphical image document—a photo, for instance—begins at 50,000 kilobytes and spirals upward from there. Sending and receiving such documents over a modem connection can seem to take forever.

There are two rules about sending attachments to someone. First, etiquette dictates that the person should be expecting the attachment. It's important to remember that a lot of people pay for their time online and their e-mail service—a very large download could cost them time or money. Also, some clever computer viruses are sent as e-mail attachments and can even appear to have come from a trusted friend. So, if your recipient knows ahead of time that you intend to send an attachment, she is less likely to simply toss your message as a safeguard against infection from a virus.

Second, you should make sure that the attachment arrives in the correct format for your recipient to use. Ideally, you should try to store documents in formats that will be easily translated on the other computer—if you're sending a Microsoft Word document to the other user and she also has Microsoft Word, the conversion should work. If you don't have the same word processing program, it might be best to send the document in RTF (Rich Text Format) instead, which can be handled by most word processing programs, including AppleWorks and Mac OS X's TextEdit.

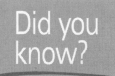

Encoding and Compressing

By definition, Internet e-mail programs are designed to send text, not computer files like documents, programs, or system code. There is a way to get around this limitation, though, and it's exactly what Outlook Express and Mail do to send an attached file—it's called *encoding*. Through the process of encoding, a file made up of binary data (ones and zeros) is literally translated into a transmittable format following a particular encoding method. Once the file arrives on the other side of the Internet transmission, it's decoded back to its original form.

In the meantime, even after you've sent or received the file, it's useless until it's decoded.

The Mail application uses a specific type of encoding, called *Base64/MIME,* which is the most popular encoding/decoding format for most types of computers, including Macs and Microsoft Windows PCs. (Outlook Express uses *AppleDouble* by default, which is a special variation on Base64 that's compatible with all types of computers.) If your recipients ask you what format you're using, however, you may need to tell them—not all e-mail programs handle these attachments automatically.

It's also recommended that you compress files—particularly large documents or groups of documents—before sending them. If you're sending to Mac users, you can use the StuffIt format; for Windows PC users, you might want to use PKZip. In either case, see Chapter 20 for more details on compressing files and creating file archives.

Add the Attachment

In Mail, you add an attachment to an outgoing message by dragging it from the Finder into the Composition window, clicking the Attach button in the toolbar or by selecting Message | Attach File. (In either of the latter two cases, you'll see an Open dialog box where you should locate the file to attach.) Once the file is attached, you'll see the file's icon appear in the message window. Now, send your e-mail as usual and the attachment goes right along for the ride. If you decide you don't want to send a document that you've already attached, select Message | Remove Attachments or highlight the attachment's icon in the compose window and press DELETE.

In Outlook Express, you can add attachments by dragging them from the Finder to an open message window. You can also select Message | Add Attachments. In the message window, you'll find an Attachments section—click the disclosure triangle to see what items are currently attached. You can click Add to add more attachments (using an Open dialog box) or you can select an attachment and click Remove.

▽ Attachments: Annual Budget 2.cwk		
📄 Annual Budget 2.cwk	47 K	⊕ Add
		🔍 Find
		✖ Remove
Encode for any computer (AppleDouble); no compression		

Get an Attachment

If you receive an e-mail message that includes an attachment, you'll see the attached file's icon appear in the message area (in Mail) or in the Attachments area (in Outlook Express) when you read the message. To work with the attachment, you can drag it from the message window to your desktop or to an open Finder window. In Mail, you can also single-click the name of the attachment (you'll notice that it looks like a hyperlink), which will load the file in its associated application, if possible. (In Outlook Express, you can double-click an attachment's icon to launch it.) If an application can't be found, you'll see a dialog box asking if you'd like to save the attachment. Click Save and you'll be presented with a Save dialog box.

 Opening attachments to e-mail messages is one known way to contract a computer virus. You should only open or use attachments from known senders and only when the attachment is expected from that user. It's possible for some viruses to send virus-infected attachments automatically from a user's e-mail program, making it look like the user sent the message to you. If you're not expecting an attachment, don't open it until you've talked to the sender and confirmed that he or she meant to send you the attachment.

Create and Add Your Signature

A signature, in e-mail parlance, is a block of text that you add to the end of your e-mail messages to help identify you. For professional purposes, people often put their corporate title, address, and phone numbers; for personal signatures, you might put your name, Web site URL, and a favorite quote. In either case, signatures are generally composed ahead of time so they can be easily reused. In general, you should use about three to five lines of information, but make sure it's not too personal (home phone numbers and so on) for the Internet.

To create a signature in Mail, open Mail Preferences (Mail | Preferences) and click the Signatures icon. Now, click the Create Signature button to open a new signature dialog sheet. In the Description box, enter a description for the signature, then in the main entry area, enter your signature.

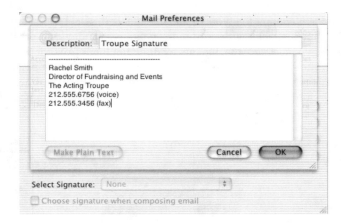

Click OK when you're done editing. Back in the Mail Preferences window, you can opt to create additional signatures if you'd like to be able to rotate between them—just click Create Signature again. If you do create multiple signatures, you can use the Select Signature menu to determine which signature is used by default in your messages; or, if you'd prefer to choose the signature in the Composition window, turn on the Choose Signature When Composing E-mail option. (Click the Mail Preferences' Close button to close the window.) With this option selected, you'll find a Signature menu in the Composition window, where you can choose which signature to use for that particular message.

In Outlook Express, the process is similar. Choose Tools | Signatures to see a list of existing signatures. To create a new one, click New. Now, in the Signature window, give the signature a name in the Name entry box, then type the signature in the window. When you're done, close the window. Whenever you're composing a message, you can select the signature you want to use from the Signature menu in the button bar.

Automate Using Rules

Need to automate your e-mail? Both Mail and Outlook Express enable you to create *rules,* or filters, that look at incoming mail and compare the messages against criteria that you specify. If an e-mail message matches a criterion, then a certain action is taken—the message is deleted, moved to a particular mailbox folder, or automatically forwarded, for instance.

To create a rule in Mail, choose Mail | Preferences. In the Mail Preferences window, select the Rules icon. Now you'll see a list of the current rules. By default, Apple has some rules here to change the color of messages sent to you by Apple. (Nice of them, eh?) You can open one of these rules (select it and click Edit) to see the basic structure of a rule.

You'll also notice in the rules list that you can turn a rule on or off by clicking its check box in the Active (Mail) or Enabled (Outlook Express) column. You can also drag rules around to change their order—each incoming message is applied against the rules in order, starting with the first rule on the list.

To create a new rule in Mail, click the Create Rule button. You'll see a dialog sheet appear, where you can begin building your rule (see the image on the left in Figure 18-2).

In Outlook Express, you create rules by first choosing Tools | Rules, then selecting the tab that's appropriate for the type of message retrieval you'd like to automate. (For typical incoming messages, you'll likely choose Mail (POP).) Then, to create the rule, click New. Give the rule a name in the Define Mail Rule window (see the image on the right in Figure 18-2).

18

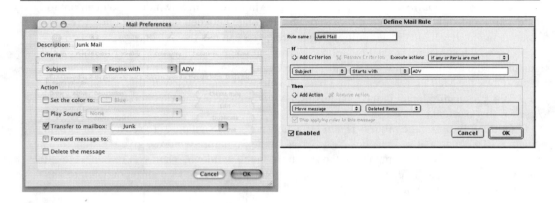

FIGURE 18-2   On the left, a rule in Mail; on the right, a rule in Outlook Express.

Building rules can be a thinking game—in a sense, it approaches the logic you need to create an AppleScript or a similar computer program. It's a basic "IF…THEN" statement—in order to use mail rules, you'll have to think that way.

Once you get your mind set to the problem, you'll find solutions. For instance, consider the idea of automatically moving messages to a particular folder. In this case, let's focus on advertising mail. Junk mail messages, when properly formatted, ideally have the letters "ADV" in the subject of the message. So, you can begin creating the rule using the Criteria menus (in Mail) or the pop-up menus in the IF section (in Outlook Express) and entry box:

```
Subject Begins With ADV
```

Now, if the criterion is met, actions can be put into play. To enable an action in Mail, click its check box, then complete the options. (You can activate any or all of the actions, if desired.) For instance, to move the message to a new folder, you'd turn on the Transfer to Mailbox option and select the destination mailbox folder from the menu.

In Outlook Express, you enable actions in the Then section of the Define Mail Rule window. Select an action from the pop-up menu, then complete the action's other options. To add an additional action, click the Add Action button.

When you're done creating the rule in either program, click the OK button. Now, whenever new messages are received (or, in some cases with Outlook Express, when they're sent out), they'll be compared against the active rules and, if criteria are met, the actions will be activated.

TIP   *If you'd like to run a rule against e-mail messages that have already been received, select those messages in the viewer window (hold down the SHIFT key while clicking to select multiple messages) then, in Mail, choose Message | Apply Rules to Selection. In Outlook Express, choose Message | Apply Rule and choose the rule from the menu.*

Chapter 19

Cool Browser Tricks

How to...

- Choose the default browser
- Surf HTML frames
- Choose a home page
- Enter data at secure sites
- Track an online auction
- Use Java, instant messaging, and plug-ins

In Chapter 6, you saw the basics of getting up and running on the Internet and using a Web browser. Indeed, using Internet Explorer, which is included with both Mac OS 9 and Mac OS X, is fairly easy, particularly for plain old surfin'. But Internet Explorer—and the greater Web itself—offers some interesting prospects for going deeper with the technology. In this chapter, you'll see some of the interesting things you can do with a Web browser, including some advanced browsing topics, customizing your Web home page and using some special features of Internet Explorer.

Advanced Browsing

Chapter 6 showed you how to browse the Web—for the most part, you just click hyperlinks or images, and, in turn, your Web browser locates and loads a new Web page. You can then use the bookmarks or Favorites feature of the Web browser to store and manage the sites you visit often. But as you're browsing, you'll encounter some other behavior as well, which we'll cover in this section.

Use a Different Browser

Mac OS X ships with a native version of Microsoft Internet Explorer, although most iMacs also include classic versions of Internet Explorer and Netscape Communicator on the hard disk. Check out the Internet folder on your hard disk, which may be inside the "Applications (Mac OS 9)" folder. If you're in Mac OS X, you can run these classic browsers, if desired, although I wouldn't recommend doing so with a modem-based Internet connection. (They tend to work fine with higher-speed DSL and cable connections.) If you're using Mac OS 9, these two will be your main choices.

If you like, you can set which browser is your default browser in either OS version. In Mac OS X, launch the System Preferences application (you can choose it from the Apple menu) and click the Internet icon. That launches the Internet pane. Click the Web tab, then locate the Default Web Browser menu. Pull down that menu to select a different default browser—you can choose Select from the menu to use an Open dialog box to locate the browser you want to use.

In Mac OS 9, you choose the default browser in a similar way—launch the Internet control panel (Apple menu | Control Panels | Internet) and click the Web tab. Choose the browser you'd like to set as the default from the Default Web Browser menu.

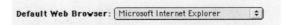

What's this good for? In Mac OS 9, the default browser is launched when you double-click the Browse the Internet alias on the desktop or when you choose Browse the Internet from the Apple menu. In both operating systems, the default browser is often used when hyperlinks are clicked in *other* applications, such as e-mail programs or word processors. When such a link is clicked, the default browser will be launched in order to view the Web page that results.

Click a Multimedia Link

Most of the time when you click a hyperlink in your Web browser, you'll load a new Web page. But a hyperlink can be used to load other things, such as images or multimedia, or you might even click a link that enables you to download a file. Other than loading a new Web page, four different things can happen when you click a link:

- ■ *A helper program is invoked.* Your Web browser recognizes many types of files and passes them on to the appropriate application. For instance, if you click a link to a Microsoft Word document, the document might be downloaded and handed over to Microsoft Word to display, assuming you have Word installed. Similarly, clicking a hyperlink that leads to a mailto: URL activates your e-mail application.

- ■ *A plug-in is activated.* The most common plug-in is QuickTime, which enables you to watch movies from within your Web browser's window. Or, you can choose plug-ins for Macromedia Flash documents, virtual reality documents, audio and video formats, Java applets, and more. The plug-in takes over a portion of the browser window and displays its data as part of the Web page.

NOTE   *Plug-ins are discussed in more depth later in this chapter.*

- ■ *A file is downloaded.* If a link points to a file that the browser can't display, the file is then downloaded to your iMac's hard disk, often directly to your desktop. You can view it with another application, decompress it with StuffIt Expander if necessary (which is often done automatically), or perform a similar task. (In some cases, an FTP link shows you a listing of files you can then click to download.) In Internet Explorer, downloaded files appear in the Download Manager (Window | Download Manager).

File	Status	Time	Transferred
✓ gliderosx.hqx	Complete	< 1 minute	2.0 MB
✓ OmniWeb-4.0.1.dm...	Complete	< 1 minute	3.3 MB
fm55_trialosx.sit		< 1 minute	5.6 MB of 8.4 MB, 223 KB/sec

Download Manager

19

In the Download Manager, you can see the progress of an item as it downloads. You can also double-click an item to view more information about it, including Cancel and Reload buttons that you can use to stop and restart a download.

■ *The item isn't recognized.* Sometimes, you click a hyperlink to a particular file and the Web browser won't recognize it. In this case, you'll usually see a dialog box, where you can choose to download the file, ignore it, or search for the correct application in which to view it, as instructed by a dialog box that appears when errors are encountered.

Work with Frames

With some Web sites, you encounter an *HTML frames* interface, which is a special sort of page that actually breaks a single Web browser window into different window panes (hence *frames*) used to display different pages. In most cases, the idea is to click a link in one of the frames, and then have the page change in another frame. Frames enable you to view many pages' worth of information without refreshing the entire window every time (see Figure 19-1).

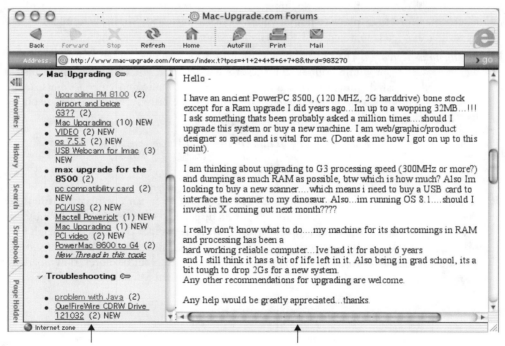

Click items in this frame …   … and the page in this frame changes.

FIGURE 19-1   The Forums section of my Web site uses an HTML frames interface.

If necessary, you can choose commands to let you go back, forward, and so on within that particular frame. Click and hold the mouse button within a frame to see a pop-up contextual menu. (You can also hold down the CONTROL key and click within the frame.) You can then choose Back, Forward (if applicable), and other commands that affect only that frame.

Choose a Home Page

If you plan to spend a lot of time online, you want to get organized. The best starting place I know for getting organized is a good home page. In any browser, you can choose a particular home page where you want to start your Internet adventure every time you sign on. (In fact, the home page is usually loaded every time you open a new browser window.) You can link to your company page, a page you particularly enjoy reading, a professional *portal* page (a home page with news, sports, and other topical headlines) from one of the big Internet companies, or even a page you create yourself.

Change Your Home Page

If you use IE for your Web surfing, your home page is already set for you—it's the Apple Excite home page. If you don't need or want to change from these defaults, skip down to the section "Edit the Home Page." You can change the home page if you find one you like more or if you want to experiment.

Popular sites that enable you to customize your own home page include the following:

Apple Excite (offers Apple news)	**http://apple.excite.com/**
Earthlink Personal Start Page	**http://start.earthlink.net/**
Go Network	**http://mypage.go.com/**
Microsoft Network	**http://www.msn.com/**
My Excite	**http://my.excite.com/**
My NBCi	**http://my.nbci.com/**
My Netscape	**http://my.netscape.com/**
My Yahoo	**http://my.yahoo.com/**

You needn't go with one of the big names. Equally useful may be a smaller site you enjoy visiting—one associated with a hobby or interest of yours. Of course, the site should also be the sort of page that changes often—making a home page out of a page that's never updated is a little dull, unless it's filled with interesting hyperlinks.

Making any page into your home page is simple:

1. Open your potential home page in your browser.
2. Highlight the URL and choose Edit | Copy or press ⌘-C.

19

3. In Mac OS X, open the System Preferences application (Apple menu | System Preferences) and click the Internet icon. In Mac OS 9, open the Internet control panel (Apple menu | Control Panels | Internet).

4. Select the Web tab in the Internet pane or control panel.

5. In the Home Page entry box, highlight the contents of the box and delete the address currently there.

6. Select Edit | Paste or press ⌘-V to paste your home page URL into the Home Page entry box.

7. Quit the System Preferences application (or close the Internet control panel) and your settings are saved.

TIP

Note the other interesting options on the Web tab of the Internet pane or control panel, including settings to select a default Search page, choose your default Web browser, and change the location where files you download from the Web are saved.

Now, the Home button in your Web browser should lead you to the new home page whenever you click it. Similarly, you'll see the home page every time you open a new browser window while you're connected to the Internet.

NOTE

Browsers can also have their own internal settings for home pages. If you notice your home page isn't changing, it's possible the setting in the browser's Preferences dialog box is overriding the Internet pane or Internet control panel's settings. Check the application's Preferences command to see if you should set the home page within the application.

Edit the Home Page

If you're using one of the major services for your home page, you can probably edit it, if desired. Look for a link that says "Personalize This Page" or something similar. Click that link and you'll likely find tools that enable you to change what you view on the home page and the order in which you view it.

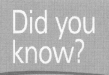

The Cookie Issue

For most custom home pages to work—along with many other customization features and, sometimes, even e-commerce features, such as online shopping carts—you need to have the cookies feature enabled in your browser. *Cookies* are small bits of data a Web server can store on your hard disk, making it possible for the site to identify and remember you. Some users don't like to enable cookies because they allow Web servers to track their browsing, store personal information, and so forth. Although cookies are generally harmless, you can enable and disable them in IE Preferences. Choose Explorer | Preferences (or Edit | Preferences in Mac OS 9), and then click the Cookies item on the left side of the Preferences dialog box. Locate the When Receiving Cookies menu and choose how you want to be notified of a site's attempt to place a cookie with your browser.

In most cases, you place a check mark next to items you want on the page. Then, you enter a number next to each item to choose how you want it prioritized—whether you want the item to appear at the top or the bottom of the page, for instance. You should be able to choose from a variety of topics—finances, news, entertainment, and so on.

You'll also probably be asked for some demographic information, as well as for your ZIP code and perhaps your birthday (especially for horoscopes). If you're worried about the information getting out, look for a link to the company's privacy statement. Also, look for an option you can check telling them they can't sell or use your information for advertising and junk mail purposes.

Fill in a Form and Buy Things Online

Web browsers are capable of displaying Web pages that include HTML form elements. Interface items you might find in a dialog box within the Mac OS can be added to a Web page, so you can send information back to the Web server computer. These elements include familiar items like entry boxes, menus, check boxes, radio buttons, and regular buttons. All these form elements are used much as they are within the Mac OS.

The difference is, you're usually filling in personal information, which you plan to send to the Web server computer, so it can be processed in some way. Perhaps you're buying computer software or subscribing to an online newsletter—or maybe you're setting up a home page, as discussed earlier in this chapter.

Fill in the Form

Filling in a form is usually pretty easy—you just enter the information necessary by typing in entry boxes and choosing items in lists or menus (see Figure 19-2).

19

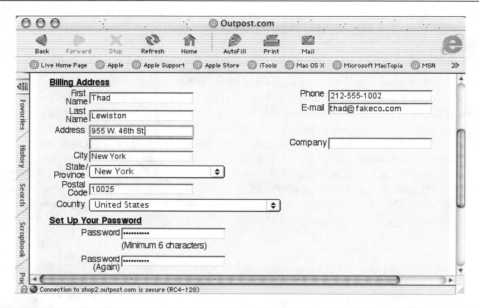

Web pages can enable you to fill in information and send it across the Internet.

Other elements should also be familiar. Press TAB to move among most of the parts of the form (you'll probably have to use the mouse to choose items from pull-down menus).

Once you fill in the form, you need to look for a way to submit that form. Your data needs to be sent to the Web server computer, but it can't go until you say it can. In most cases, you can see a Send or Submit button that you click with the mouse. You might also see a Clear button, which clears the form of everything you just entered. Don't click that button unless you're sure you want to clear the form.

Click Submit (or Send, or Search, and so on) and your data is sent over the Internet to the Web server computer where it's processed. In most cases, clicking the Submit button also loads a new page into your Web browser that either includes results from your data or a page telling you your submission has been received.

Did I say your data is sent over the Internet? But what if it's private data like credit card numbers, salary figures, or e-mail addresses? Are you sure you want them floating around?

Check for a Secure Connection

In most cases, when a Web site wants you to send financial or private information, it does so over what's called a *secure* server. What this means is simple—the Web site and your browser establish a connection over which data is encrypted. Your data is coded like a military transmission. The code can only be broken once your data gets to the server computer.

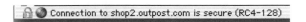

In IE, you see the locked padlock icon and a message at the bottom of the screen attesting to the page's security. (Note that RC4-128 is the more powerful, North America-only encryption scheme. If you see RC4-56 or something similar, that's OK encryption, but not the strongest. Most likely, though, neither type would be easily defeated.)

 Encryption *simply means it's more difficult for someone to intercept your personal information while it's en route. You should still consider the reputation and reliability of any Web sites to which you're sending your personal information, and you should look into your credit card company or financial institution's policies regarding online use and protection before paying for things online.*

Track an Online Auction

Speaking of buying things, IE includes a special feature called the Auction Manager, which you can use to track an auction item on a site such as eBay (**www.ebay.com**) or Amazon.com auctions (**www.amazon.com/auctions**). When you're viewing an auction item, tracking the auction is easy. Choose Tools | Track Auction. In the dialog box that appears, enter your user ID for the auction service (you'll need to have registered with eBay or Amazon or whatever Web site you're using) and click Track.

The auction will be checked every 15 minutes and you'll be alerted when bidding changes. (You can click the Customize button in the Track Auction dialog box if you'd like to alter when and how IE alerts you to changes.) You can also open the Auction Manager (Tools | Auction Manager) to see all of your auctions that are currently being tracked.

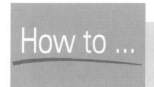 **Use AutoFill in Internet Explorer**

In IE, you might see the Forms AutoFill dialog box that asks if you want to use the form to set up AutoFill. *AutoFill* is a feature that enables you to enter common form data (your name, address, phone number, and so on) once in IE, and then you can click the AutoFill button on the toolbar whenever you encounter a new form. Click Yes in the dialog box to view and edit your AutoFill profile. Or, at any time, you can click the AutoFill button to enter your AutoFill profile manually.

In the Preferences dialog box, you see entries for items about yourself that online forms typically request. Edit those and then click OK in the Preferences dialog box. Now, whenever you visit a site requesting your information, just click the AutoFill button in the toolbar and IE fills in as much information as it can.

Internet Plug-Ins, Java, and Instant Messaging

You've already seen that your Web browser is capable of displaying and arranging images and text in the browser window. But Web browsers are also capable of giving over part of the browser window to other mini-applications that enable you to interact with an online program of some sort. These fall under the heading of *embedded* content, which just means they're small programs that enable you to perform a simple task. Some of them rely on plug-ins, special add-ons that different companies make for browsers. Other embedded programs rely on Java, which works with your browser to enable small applications, such as calculators, interactive content, and even full-fledged programs like the instant message applications discussed later in this section.

Embedded Plug-in Files

Using plug-in technology, the Web browser can actually give control of part of the browser window to another little program, which can be responsible for dealing with user input and displaying things on the screen. In most cases, these plug-ins add more multimedia, perhaps offering animated graphics, a unique interface to the Web site, and so on. One popular plug-in technology is Macromedia's Flash (**http://www.macromedia.com/software/flash/**) plug-in, which enables you to view animated graphics within the browser window (see Figure 19-3). Flash plug-ins are already included and installed on your iMac, whether you're running Mac OS X or Mac OS 9. You will occasionally want to visit the Web site and update the plug-in, however.

Other plug-ins let you view a variety of embedded multimedia documents, like the Real Network's RealPlayer (**http://www.realnetworks.com/**). With RealPlayer, which is currently only available for Mac OS 9, you can view streaming audio and video (audio and video played as they arrive across the Internet in a data stream, so you don't have to wait a long time for the data to download). Other popular plug-ins offer 3-D vistas, Virtual Reality Modeling Language

| FIGURE 19-3 | Plug-in technology adds interactivity (and visual effects) to Web pages. |

(VRML) controllers, and so on. A great place to find many of the plug-ins available today for Web browsers is at Netscape's Browser Plug-in Web pages (**http://home.netscape.com/plugins/index.html**).

> **NOTE** *Of course, one of the most important plug-ins is the QuickTime plug-in, which is installed automatically. (See Chapter 14 for more on using the QuickTime plug-in.)*

Add Plug-ins

You install plug-ins differently depending on which Mac OS you're using. (Indeed, the plug-ins need to be specifically compatible with the Mac OS version you're using.) In Mac OS X, plug-ins need to be placed in one of two folders—either the Internet Plug-ins folder located in your personal Library folder (inside your home folder), or in the Internet Plug-ins folder in the main Library folder on your startup disk. To install the plug-in in the main Library folder, you need to be logged into an administrator's account (see Chapter 27), but doing so makes the plug-in available to all users on your multi-user iMac (assuming you have multiple users, also discussed in Chapter 27).

Mac OS 9 also has an Internet Plug-ins folder, found inside the System Folder, which can be used—in theory—as a central repository. In practice, however, most Classic Web browsers rely on their own Plug-in folders, which you'll generally find inside the application's (such as Netscape Communicator's or Internet Explorer's) own folder inside the Applications (Mac OS 9) folder.

If the plug-in has an installation program, just let it do its thing. But, if you simply downloaded the plug-in to your desktop, you need to drag it to the appropriate Internet Plug-ins folder. Once the plug-in is installed there, you can restart your Web browser, which then automatically searches for and detects new plug-ins. The plug-in's functionality is noted and the next time you encounter an embedded multimedia document, the correct plug-in is loaded and the multimedia content is displayed in the browser window.

Work with Java

With most applications, you have to specifically buy a Mac OS application or a Microsoft Windows application. And, as you know, one type of application won't easily run on another type of computer. Java changes that by allowing a Java program to run using a *virtual machine*—an emulator of sorts—which runs on top of the actual operating system. That means that Java applications don't have to be written for a specific operating system—instead, they're written to run in the virtual machine. The Java virtual machine, in turn, is written specifically for the particular OS—Mac OS 9 has the Macintosh Runtime for Java (MRJ) and Mac OS X has its own virtual machine, both of which make it possible to run Java applications on your iMac.

NOTE   *You should update Java regularly to get the latest versions—use Software Update (Chapter 29) in both Mac OS 9 and Mac OS X to search for and install recent updates.*

In most cases, Java works seamlessly on your iMac—there's nothing in particular you need to do. In fact, if you download and install a Java application on your iMac, it should work just like any other iMac program.

Often, though, Java applets are loaded over the Internet and displayed in your Web browser. To use Java applets, if it requires any user interaction, simply point and click the mouse like you would with any Mac application.

Instant Messaging and Java

One popular use of Java deserves its own mention here—instant messaging (IM). IM is a popular application that enables you to type messages back and forth with friends and colleagues in real-time, over the Internet. It's sort of like a chat room on AOL or elsewhere, but conducted privately between individuals.

IM *clients* are often actual, standalone applications from America Online, Yahoo!, and others that offer instant messaging services. These clients are written specifically for various operating systems and made available for download. At the time of writing, however, Mac OS X clients were still on their way—only Mac OS 9 clients can be downloaded and used immediately. Enter Java. Because many IM clients come in a Java version, you can still chat away (assuming you've registered and have an account) using a Java client (see Figure 19-4).

These Java-based clients are not only useful for services that don't yet have a Mac OS X version. You can also use them when you don't have the time or inclination to download the standalone client—particularly if you're using someone else's Mac or you're accessing instant messaging in a library, café, or some similar locale.

Troubleshoot Java Applets

If you're encountering trouble with Java and your browser, the problem is most likely an issue with settings. In Mac OS 9, you can change the virtual machine and alter some other options in Internet Explorer. (As of this writing, Netscape 6.1 (and lower) uses its own Java virtual machine, which can't be changed.) In IE, here's how to choose the Java virtual machine:

1. Choose Edit | Preferences in IE.

2. Click the Java button.

3. At the top of the preferences window, make sure Enable Java is checked.

4. In the Java Virtual Machine menu, choose MRJ. (Or choose Microsoft Virtual Machine, if desired.)

5. Click OK.

If you've changed the Java machine you're using, you'll need to restart Internet Explorer. If you continue to have trouble, you may need to increase the amount of memory that's allocated to Internet Explorer (or run IE with fewer applications in the background). See Chapter 29 for more on Classic and Mac OS 9 memory issues.

In Mac OS X, the Java virtual machine is built-in, so you won't be likely to change it. However, current versions of Internet Explorer ship with Java turned off, so if you're having Java trouble, you may want to select Explorer | Preferences, click Java, and make sure the Enable Java option is on. You should also stay on top of updates to Mac OS X via the Software Update pane of System Preferences—the Java virtual machine is a work-in-progress in Mac OS X, and it's getting steadily better with each update to the operating system.

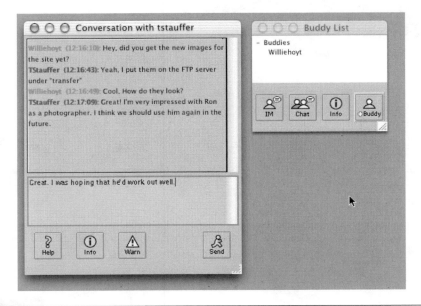

FIGURE 19-4   This AOL Instant Messenger client is actually running in a Web browser window and using Java.

19

Chapter 20

Master Files Online

How to...

- Use your iDisk
- Get an online "floppy disk"
- Use the File Transfer Protocol to upload and download files
- Compress and decompress files
- Use disk images
- Find and use shareware and freeware applications

Your iMac, more than many computers, is designed to live on the Internet. It's built to transfer files online, back up files online, and get most of its updates, new installations, and new third-party applications, such as an FTP program, so you can access the wealth of files that are available on the Internet for downloading.

In this chapter, you'll see how to use your iDisk—if you've signed up for Apple's iTools service—to store and retrieve files over the Internet. You'll also learn how to upload to and download from the Internet using an FTP application. And you'll see how to work with some of the unique archiving file formats you often use for transferring files and learn some ways to get new applications and application updates into your iMac over the Internet.

Work with Your iDisk

It's just my opinion, but I think iDisk is the coolest iTool that Apple offers. For one, iDisk is an interesting solution to the conundrum of the floppy-less iMac—using iDisk, you can actually store files online, using Apple's servers, enabling you to access those files from another Mac, when necessary. iDisk also enables others to download those files (if you choose to make them public) for easy file exchange, as discussed in Chapter 21. And iDisk works with both Mac OS 9 and Mac OS X.

iDisk is essentially a bit of server disk space (by default, 20MB) that you can access over the Internet. When you sign into your iDisk, a small disk icon appears on your desktop. You can drag files and folders to the iDisk, thus copying them over the Internet and storing them on the remote server. In fact, iDisk is great for backing up your most important files so that they're saved in two places—on your iMac and remotely on Apple's servers. That way, if some catastrophe strikes your iMac you can still get to those important documents.

TIP   *Want more than 20MB of storage space? Apple has an option (at the time of writing) that let's you pay monthly for additional storage, up to 400MB worth. Check the iDisk page online at **http://itools.mac.com** for details.*

Access Your iDisk

If you have an iTools account (discussed in Chapter 6), you already have an iDisk available. All you have to do is access it, and Mac OS X gives you two easy ways to do that. In both Mac OS 9 and Mac OS X, the most basic way to access your iDisk is to connect to the Internet and sign onto **http://itools.mac.com/** with your Web browser, click the iDisk tool, then enter your user name and password. On the iDisk page, click the Open Your iDisk button. Your iDisk will open on your desktop, revealing its contents (see Figure 20-1).

You've got a few other options for quickly launching your iDisk (assuming you're connected to the Internet), including:

■ In Mac OS X, choose Go | iDisk from the Finder menu. After a brief delay (it can seem more than "brief" if you have a modem connection to the Internet), your iDisk is mounted on the desktop.

SHORTCUT *If you want to access your iDisk even faster, you can use the View | Customize Toolbar command in the Mac OS X Finder to add an iDisk icon to your Finder window toolbar. Then you simply click the icon to sign into your iDisk. (In Mac OS X 10.1, if you have that version, you'll notice that the iDisk icon is there by default.)*

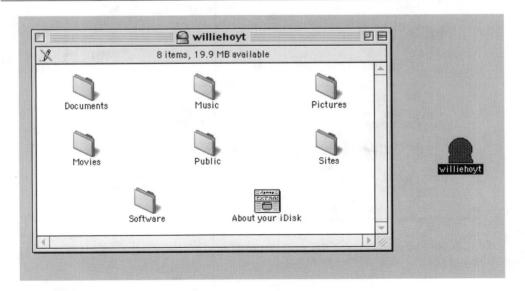

FIGURE 20-1   Your iDisk appears on the desktop much like any other network or removable disk.

■ You can also sign into your iDisk using the Connect to Server window in Mac OS X, which is useful if you're accessing your iDisk from another Mac or if you want to access a different iDisk (from the Internet pane default) on your iMac's desktop. Choose Go | Connect to Server. In the Connect to Server window, enter **afp://idisk.mac.com** in the Address entry box and click Connect.

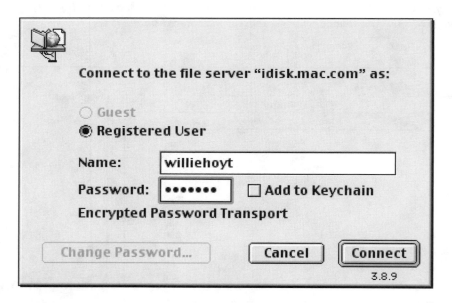

■ In Mac OS 9, open the Network Browser (from the Apple menu), then choose Connect to iDisk from the Shortcuts button (the disk and globe icon). You'll be immediately connected to the iTools server, assuming your Internet connection is active. Then, you'll see the Connect to Server dialog box. Enter your iTools member name and password, then click Connect.

That's it. Assuming your member name and password are valid, your iDisk will appear on the desktop and you're ready to work with it.

> TIP
>
> *In both Mac OS 9 and Mac OS X, a special iDisk favorite appears in the Open and Save dialog boxes. Select it and, if you're connected to the Internet or if your Internet connection is automatic, you'll be able to open or save directly to your iDisk. Also, once your iDisk is open, you can create an alias to it, which you can then double-click at a later date to sign back in.*

Explore Your iDisk

Once you have the iDisk on your desktop, you can start taking a look around. You'll notice right away that the iDisk is pre-organized for you—you'll find a Documents folder (where you'll store a lot of your files) as well as folders for specific uses: Music, Pictures, Movies, Public, Sites, and Software.

> NOTE
>
> *If things don't match the description here, it's possible that Apple has changed the iDisk somewhat, which is done periodically. See the main iTools Web site (and/or the iDisk section of the iTools site) for details.*

So what are each of these folders for? Here's a rundown:

- **Documents**   This folder is for storing anything you'd like to save or back up online. Others can't access this folder—it's your private spot for storing and backing up documents. You can create subfolders and organize your files in whatever way that you'd like.

- **Music**   Place files here for use with iTunes or if you'd like to add music to a Web site you create with the HomePage tool.

- **Pictures**   Copy image files to this folder (in JPEG or GIF format) to use with the HomePage tool or with iCard, both discussed in Chapter 21. Note that you can store your pictures in titled subfolders within this folder (Vacation, New Car, Baby's Steps)—tools such as iCard and HomePage can still access them within the subfolders.

- **Movies**   If you create a Movie with iMovie (or any other QuickTime movie) that you'd like to use on your HomePage Web site, you can copy that movie to this folder.

- **Public**   Copy files to this folder that you'd like to share with others on the Internet. (You'll also need to create a File Sharing Web page, which is discussed in Chapter 21.)

- **Sites**   This is the folder where your Web pages are stored if you use the HomePage tool. You can also upload your own HTML files to this folder, if you know something about HTML. Place a file called index.html in the root of the Sites folder, and it will be accessible at the URL **http://homepage.mac.com/***membername***/index.html** where *membername* is your iTools member name. All other files and folders will be similarly accessible using that base URL.

- **Software**   The Software folder is a special case. Here, Apple has made available a number of shareware, freeware, and demo applications that you can copy *from* the Software folder *to* your iMac. You can then run the installers and work with the software. Note that you can't copy files *to* the Software folder, only from it. It's simply a convenient way for you to gain access to shareware and similar applications and it doesn't count against your 20MB file limit.

For the most part, you can work with your iDisk just as you would any removable disk (such as a Zip disk) or any network volume. A few caveats exist, however. First, you can't add folders or files to the first level of the iDisk—if you want to create subfolders for arranging your personal files, you should do so inside the Documents folder. And remember that you're accessing your iDisk over the Internet, so some operations can feel slow—painfully at times. That's just the nature of the beast. If you can't stand the slow speeds, the best plan is to upgrade your Internet service. (See Chapter 23 for details.)

NOTE *When you delete items from your iDisk, they're deleted immediately; they aren't stored in your Trash. Also, you can't delete items from the Software folder or its subfolders and you can't delete any of the first-level folders just discussed.*

Close Your iDisk

When you're done working with your iDisk, you can eject it from the desktop by dragging its icon to the Trash. Alternatively, you can highlight the iDisk icon and press ⌘-E or you can hold down the CONTROL key, click the iDisk icon, and choose Eject from the contextual menu.

If you leave your iDisk on your desktop while you're working in other applications, periodically you'll get warnings that the iDisk will be automatically ejected if you don't work with it. (This isn't necessarily true in Mac OS X 10.1 and higher, which uses slightly different technology for the connection.) If you see such messages, you can simply wait for your iDisk to automatically log out or, if you want to keep the iDisk open, simply double-click a folder so that some activity is registered by Apple's server. If you don't plan to use the iDisk again in the near future, eject it.

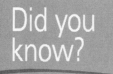

The Virtual Floppy Disk

If there's any downside to iDisk, it's that it's only accessible to Mac OS 9 and Mac OS X-based computers. What if you want to store files online that you can access from any computer, including Unix or Windows? In that case, check into one of a number of Web sites that offer a service called the *virtual disk*. In essence, a virtual disk is a few megabytes of storage space available via Web browsers, allowing you to transfer a file up to the Web site using a Web browser on one computer, then get it again using a Web browser on any other computer, even if it isn't a Mac. These services are usually provided free of charge because they sell advertising. Check out iMacFloppy.com and FreeDrive.com, among others.

Use File Transfer Protocol

File Transfer Protocol, or FTP, is a client-server system for transferring files via the Internet. Like a Web browser, an FTP application is designed to access special FTP server computers on the Internet. But instead of viewing pages and images, the FTP application's sole purpose is to upload and download files.

If you're using FTP to access online FTP resources (such as an FTP server at your organization or a public FTP server for shareware downloads), then all you really need to worry about is getting an FTP application. If you want to use FTP for storing your personal files, you'll need both an application and a virtual "place" where you can send your files. In this second case, you need to get some FTP storage space, most likely through your Internet service provider (ISP).

The FTP Application and Server Space

So which FTP application should you use? It's up to you, although any of them need to be downloaded from the Internet before you can use them. My personal favorite is an FTP application called Transmit, shown in Figure 20-2. First, I like the way Transmit looks and, second, I like the way Transmit makes it easy to see what's on your computer versus what's on the Internet computer. Transmit has both a Classic and a native Mac OS X version available.

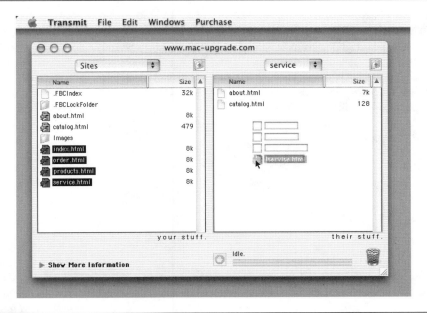

FIGURE 20-2   Transmit makes transferring files via FTP easy—here I'm dragging-and-dropping from my iMac to my Web server.

20

Transmit is written by Panic Software and can be downloaded from **http://www.panic.com**. It costs $24.95 to license the software if you like it. (Transmit is shareware, which is discussed later in this chapter.)

Other popular FTP programs available for Mac OS 9 and Mac OS X include Fetch (**http://fetchsoftworks.com**) and Interarchy (**http://www.interarchy.com/**), both of which are shareware programs with a long history on the Mac platform. They work a little differently from Transmit, but the concepts are the same.

Once you have the FTP application, you may also want some FTP storage space, most likely through your ISP. You may also want to have two different folders in that space—public and private—with different privilege settings (ask your ISP how to set these). The public folder on the server will be accessible to other Internet users—perfect if you need Bob in San Francisco to be able to log in and download a long report. The private folder is accessible only to you. The private folder can be used for backing up your important documents and application in a secure, online location, so your files are accessible if you ever have trouble with your iMac.

If your ISP offers storage space for a Web site that you can access via FTP, you may also be able to use that space for personal file storage. In that case, you should ask your ISP to help you create a private folder on the FTP site, so others can't access your files via the Web (unless that's what you want them to do, of course). Otherwise, you might ask the ISP if you can rent private FTP storage space—it's often available for a small fee.

The FTP Address

FTP servers have an address, just as Web servers do. The difference is, some FTP servers require you to log in as a registered user of that server, and then you get access to certain or all files on that server. You can use the FTP program to upload and download files stored in your Internet space. So, the burning question you need to ask your ISP is, "What is the address I use to access my Internet space?" In most cases, this is an address like ftp.mac-upgrade.com or www.companyname.net, depending on the type of server computer. (Most dedicated FTP servers start with "ftp" in their name, but if you're uploading directly to a Web server computer it may have "www" as part of its name.)

NOTE   *Some FTP servers, called* anonymous *servers, allow you to log in and download files without having a specific account on the system. Anonymous FTP access is discussed later in this chapter. For servers where you'll upload files, you generally need to be a registered user.*

To access a non-anonymous FTP server, you'll need an account on the remote computer and you'll need to know your user name and password. (If you're trying to access space made available by your ISP, then your user name and password are most likely the same as your user name and password for the dial-up connection, but they may be different. Ask your ISP.)

Upload Files Using FTP

Once you have your FTP program installed and you've made sure your Internet connection is active, you're ready to transfer files to the distant site. Uploading is done in two steps: first you prepare the file(s) for uploading, and then you send them.

In most cases, files must have a proper filename extension to work correctly when uploaded and downloaded from FTP servers. For instance, if you upload a TIFF image from your Mac called Image01 to your FTP server, and then subsequently download it, your Mac won't immediately know this is a TIFF image. If you include the filename extension .tif or .tiff, as in Image01.tif, however, then your Mac (or any other computer) should be able to work with the file properly. The same goes for AppleWorks (.cwk) or Microsoft Word (.doc) documents. And, you should always add filename extensions if you're making the files available to Microsoft Windows or Unix users.

> **TIP** *For best results, you might also want to compress the file(s) into an archive, as discussed in the section "Compress and Decompress Files."*

Now you're ready to upload. In FTP parlance, uploading a file uses the Put command and downloading a file requires the Get command. If you're using Transmit, you won't see these commands by default, but Interarchy and Fetch both use them.

1. Start up the FTP application and enter an FTP server computer address. (In some programs, you may need to choose File | Connect or a similar command first.) You should also enter user name and password information, if relevant. Click the button that enables you to log on.

2. Once you successfully log on, you see a file list. On the remote server, you should create a folder you can use for uploading and downloading files. (In Transmit, use File | New Folder; you then select Their Stuff in the New Folder dialog box.) I like to call my folder Transfer because that's what I tend to use it for.

> **NOTE** *If the FTP space offered by your ISP is for a Web site, then you may be shown, by default, a folder available to everyone on the Web. If you're not uploading Web documents that you want publicly available, you'll need to create a private folder for your files. Consult your ISP.*

3. Double-click the new folder.

4. Now, if you're using Transmit, you can select the files you want to upload in the My Stuff file list, and then drag-and-drop the files to the Their Stuff file list. If you're using Fetch or Interarchy, you can drag files from the Finder to the open window in that application. (You can also use the Put command in Fetch or Interarchy.)

 *Some FTP applications may reveal hidden folders or files (such as .FBCIndex in Mac OS X) on your iMac's hard disk. Don't delete or move these files, because they're used by the Mac OS at the system level for important tasks. (They should not be copied to remote servers, either.)*

That's it—you should see the files available now in the remote folder.

Download Files

To retrieve or download a file, the process is reversed—you can drag-and-drop a file from the server folder to your desktop or a folder in the Finder. Or, you can select the remote file and drag it to the My Stuff window (in Transmit), click the Get button (in Fetch), or choose the File | FTP Download command (in Interarchy). The file is downloaded and saved on your hard disk.

Compress and Decompress Files

Because large files take a long time to transmit over the Internet, sometimes it's preferable to compress them. Using sophisticated algorithms, the compression software can reduce redundant information in a document or program and make the file more compact. The catch is the file is completely useless until it's expanded, using the reverse of the compression scheme.

The other thing you can often do with most compression schemes is create a compressed archive of more than one file, so a number of files, or an entire folder, can be stored and sent within a single archive file, almost as if it were a shipping envelope. Once the file arrives at its destination, the decompression program is used to separate the files and bring them back to full size.

To do all this, you need to pick a compression scheme. Three major schemes are used for compressing files on the Internet, which are

- **StuffIt**   This format (with the filename extension .sit) is used almost exclusively by Macs, although a Windows version of StuffIt Expander is available. Windows users who have Expander for Windows can expand stuffed archives created on a Mac.

- **Zip**   This format is used almost exclusively in the Windows world. Utilities are available on the Mac to create PKZip (or just .zip or ZIP) files, and StuffIt Expander can expand .zip files.

- **Gzip and Unix Compress**   These formats are generally used by Unix machines (the files have .gz and .Z extensions). Because Mac OS X is based on Unix, you occasionally encounter these types of compressed files, although most day-to-day compression in Mac OS X uses the StuffIt format. StuffIt Expander can decompress these formats.

StuffIt and DropStuff

For decompressing files you download, StuffIt Expander works with any files created on a Mac, even older formats like Compact Pro. It can also decompress most common Windows ZIP and Unix archives. DropStuff is a shareware program, also available from Aladdin Systems, that's used for compressing StuffIt archives. Because DropStuff is shareware, you should pay for it (about $25) if you find it's useful.

*Your iMac includes StuffIt Expander by default, but newer versions might be available. Check **http://www.aladdinsys.com** to find a new version of StuffIt Expander or to download DropStuff—remember to get the native Mac OS X versions if you're using Mac OS X.*

The procedure for *decompressing* most archives is simply to drag-and-drop the archive onto the StuffIt Expander icon. When you drop an archive on StuffIt Expander, it expands the archive, if possible. And StuffIt knows quite a bit about expanding archives.

You can usually decompress .sit files easily by double-clicking them. Also, many Web browser and e-mail applications, including those bundled with your iMac, automatically decompress .sit files by sending them to StuffIt Expander when you download them.

How about *compressing* files? If you're sending a file to a Macintosh, compress it as a StuffIt file. To do this, simply drag-and-drop the file, folder, or group of files (and folders) to the DropStuff icon. When you release the mouse button, DropStuff goes into action, stuffing the files into an archive.

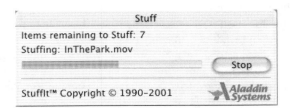

If you're only stuffing one document, then the archive file is named for that document with a .sit filename extension. If you're stuffing more than one document, you get a file named archive.sit. You can rename the file, just as you can rename any other file. One suggestion, however: Keep the .sit part in the name so that your receiving party (assuming you're sending this to someone else) knows to drag it to StuffIt Expander.

If you encounter a file with the extension .sea, it's a self-extracting archive. This doesn't require StuffIt Expander to decompress—just double-click it and it decompresses itself (a tiny version of Expander is built in).

20

Compress Using PC/Unix Formats

If you're sending a file to a user of a Microsoft Windows machine, you'll probably want to use the PKZip format instead of the StuffIt format. And, if you're sending to a Unix machine, third-party utilities are available. Here are the main ones:

Utility	Description	URL
StuffIt Deluxe	The deluxe version of DropStuff. Creates and decompresses StuffIt, ZIP, and Unix-style archives	**http://www.aladdinsys.com/**
ZipIt	Creates and decompresses Windows ZIP archives	**http://www.awa.com/softlock/zipit/**
DropZip	Creates Windows ZIP archives	**http://www.aladdinsys.com/**
Pack Up and Go	Creates Unix-style archives and compressed files	**http://www.stone.com/PackUpAndGo/ PackUpAndGo.html**
OpenUp	Decompresses a variety of formats, including Unix-style archives	**http://www.stepwise.com/Software/ OpenUp/**

Work with Disk Images

When the iMac was first released so many years ago, the lack of a floppy drive was much maligned. While most of that has died down now (particularly with the latest models sporting writeable CD drives), the legacy of the floppy disk lives on in something called disk images. A *disk image* is a special sort of document—when you double-click it, it gets "mounted" on the desktop, almost as if the file itself was a removable disk, like a CD or a floppy.

Once the disk image is mounted, it acts like any other disk. You can drag files to its icon, in some cases, to copy files onto the disk image. Similarly, you can double-click the disk image to open its window and copy files from (and sometimes to) that window. But the disk image isn't a disk at all—it's a special kind of file, which you can copy to other disks, copy over a network connection, or even send over the Internet.

There are two different kinds of disk images—self-mounting images (.smi) and regular disk images (.img or .dmg). A *self-mounting image* can be used on any Macintosh because it mounts itself. This is how most electronic software updates are distributed by Apple these days, which makes it easy to download the images and double-click to mount them. Then you can install from them as if they were actual disks.

To use regular image files, you need the Disk Copy software, which comes preinstalled with both Mac OS 9 and Mac OS X. Then, you need to find a disk image file. Once you have one, double-click it to mount the disk image on the desktop. In this example, for instance, the disk image files are on top and the mounted disk images below them:

Once the disk icon appears on the desktop, you can work with it, just as if it were another removable disk. Double-click it to open a Finder window and reveal its contents. Then, double-click installer applications to launch them or drag-and-drop files from the disk image's window to another Finder window or to the desktop. When you've finished with the disk image, drag its disk icon to the Trash and it'll be *unmounted* or removed from the desktop. (Dragging the disk image file itself to the Trash places it in the Trash for deletion.)

Find and Use Shareware and Freeware Programs

One of the main reasons to learn the nuances of uploading and downloading programs is so you can start to work with shareware and freeware programs. These are computer programs available on the Internet (or online services) for downloading and using immediately on your iMac.

If the software is shareware, you'll find yourself with a grace period during which you can use the program—often 30 days. If you go past the time limit, a number of things might happen. You might be unable to save documents anymore. You might not have access to all the features. Or, you might be able to use the program as before, but you'll see *nag* screens—screens that pop up reminding you to pay for the program—more frequently.

NOTE   *Demo versions of commercial software often work like shareware, at least in some respects. Usually, you have a demonstration period where you can use all or most of the program's features. After the demo period expires, you generally have to pay for the software to continue using all its features.*

With freeware, the program is simply free, although other licensing restrictions might exist. (It might be free in certain settings, like education and nonprofit, but not free for corporate use, for instance.) As you can tell, much of shareware is sold on the honor system. This keeps overhead low for smaller publishers, plus it allows for more targeted applications—which may have a smaller audience than big-time software—to be distributed and sold, hopefully, at a small profit for the author.

Don't for a moment think shareware and freeware aren't good programs because they aren't sold at electronics stores. (By way of comparison, shrink-wrapped, packaged programs are called *commercial* software.) A lot of great shareware and freeware is available for downloading—programs that do amazing things and have wonderful interfaces. In fact, you already learned about Transmit, Fetch, and Aladdin's StuffIt products, all of which are distributed as shareware. (And StuffIt Expander is freeware!)

20

If you're using Mac OS X, remember to try and get the Mac OS X native version of any freeware, shareware, or demo application you download. Earlier versions might not function correctly or they might require the Classic environment to be launched.

Find Good Shareware

Fortunately, you're not on your own when it comes to finding decent shareware. You can use your browser for shareware in a number of ways, including great services that help you search for exactly what you want. You can usually search by keywords or you can look at the most popular downloads, most recent additions, and so on. And, as mentioned, Apple makes a great deal of shareware available as a simple drag-and-drop download via the Software folder on your iDisk.

*These days, some of the Macintosh magazines—MacAddict (**http://www. macaddict.com**), Mac Home (**http://www.machome.com/**), Inside Mac Games (**http://www.imgmagazine.com/**)—and many of the large Macintosh user groups, like Arizona Mac Users Group (AMUG, **http://www.amug.org/**), offer CD subscriptions. Subscribe and you'll regularly receive a CD-ROM in the mail, enabling you to sample the latest shareware and freeware, as sampled by the editors of that magazine or CD service.*

You can begin by heading out to a Web download site using your browser. There, you can search using keywords to locate shareware and freeware that can solve the problem or fill the gap you want filled. Many of the sites even feature weekly updates, stories that suggest new programs, and ways to determine what would be best for you.

Here are a few of my favorite places to find shareware on the Web:

Resource	Description	URL
CNet's Download.com	Repository of all sorts of downloadables, including shareware, demos, patches, and updates	**http://www.download.com**
CNet's Shareware.com	Great search engine for shareware and freeware	**http://www.shareware.com**
ZD's MacDownload.com	Mac focus with ratings from the Ziff-Davis Mac magazine staffs (*Macworld, MacWeek*)	**http://www.macdownload.com**
Version Tracker	Tracks new programs and new versions, both commercial and shareware, available on the Internet	**http://www.versiontracker.com**
SoftWatcher	Tracks new programs and updates; offers a Mac-specific section	**http://www.softwatcher.com/mac/**

Each of these sites has its strengths, including cataloging, reviewing, and rating popularity. In most cases, you search or browse for a particular title, then you follow the links to download the file. The file shows up in your default folder for downloads (which is set using the Internet control panel) or on the desktop.

Often, these sites point you to the original Web site offered by the program's author or to some FTP repository of Mac software. But, what if you could access such an FTP site directly?

Anonymous FTP Sites

One of the main repositories of Mac software is the *Info-Mac archive,* which is maintained by the Info-Mac organization. This is distributed to many, many different mirror sites, however, so you won't ever access the Info-Mac servers themselves; instead, you access a site that serves as a mirror image of the original archive at Info-Mac.

You can log in to a number of such FTP mirror sites anonymously. Two FTP mirror sites are Apple's (**ftp://mirror.apple.com/mirrors/Info-Mac.Archive/**) and America Online's (**ftp://mirrors.aol.com/pub/info-mac/**).

Once downloaded, you're ready to decompress, install, and use the shareware, freeware, or demo on your iMac. You've already seen how to do all this stuff earlier in this chapter. Now you're ready to make it happen!

Downloading files can increase your chance of catching computer viruses because infected files are usually transmitted via the Internet. Many public archives check their files with virus checkers, but not always. If you prefer to be on the safe side, read about virus checking in Chapter 29.

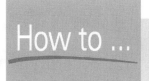 **Log in to Anonymous FTP**

In many cases, public servers are available for accessing downloadable software. With FTP, you get less information and a less-friendly interface than with a Web site. You probably need to know the exact name of the file you want to download. Armed with that knowledge, however, you can easily log in to an FTP site and access these files using your FTP program. You can also often use a Web browser to access an FTP site—remember to enter the URL to the site as **ftp://ftp.***mysite.***com/** instead of **http://ftp.***mysite.***com/** in the browser's entry box. This tells the browser you want to initiate an FTP session.

The trick is to log in anonymously—enter **anonymous** as your user name in your FTP program when accessing one of the public servers. (You skip this step if you're using a Web browser.) You can probably get by without a password, but etiquette suggests you enter your e-mail address as your password—this way, the public server administrators can reach you if a problem or concern occurs. It's very, very unlikely that anyone would ever contact you using the e-mail address, but adding it can't hurt. (Some sites, like those from Apple and Microsoft, don't require you to enter a user name or password.)

20

Chapter 21 Build Web Pages

How to...

- Build your own Web page
- Create Movie and Photo Album pages
- Share files on the Web
- How to send a personal iCard

Ready to put your own pages on the Web? It's not uncommon. Even though the Web has been around for a while now (it's creeping up on ten years old!), you may not yet have encountered a good reason to build your own Web site. Now that you're working with an iMac, though, you may suddenly find yourself ready to take on the Web and create your own pages.

iTools includes a Web browser-based interface for creating your own Web pages, called, cleverly enough, HomePage. HomePage is easy to use, even if you have no Web development experience and, what's more, the space is free as part of your iTools account. And ... in the best infomercial tradition ... *that's not all!* Possibly the coolest part of HomePage is that you can use it to display not only pictures, but also QuickTime movies that you copy to your iDisk—presumably movies that you create yourself in iMovie.

In this chapter, you'll see how to create different types of Web pages with HomePage. You'll also see how to create a Web page that enables you to share files with others and you'll see information on uploading your own Web pages (created in another Web editing program, for instance) so that they can be viewed via your iTools account.

Build Your Own Web Page

To begin your Web page, you'll need to sign into iTools and launch the HomePage tool. You'll then select a template for your page and begin editing the text that will appear on that page. Next, you'll edit links, add images, and make some other basic choices. Finally, you'll preview the page and publish it on the Web.

Here's how to begin:

1. Connect to the Internet (if necessary), launch your Web browser, and enter the URL **http://itools.mac.com**.

2. Click the HomePage button (or image) to launch the HomePage tool. If you haven't recently signed into iTools, you'll see a screen asking for your member name and password. Type them and click the Enter button.

Now you'll see the main HomePage screen. If you haven't created any pages thus far, you won't see anything in the Edit a Page section of the HomePage tool. Scroll down to the Create a Page section, and you can begin to see how HomePage works.

HomePage enables you to create Web pages based on templates that Apple has created for you. The templates are arranged by topic, with the topics appearing as buttons down the left-hand side. HomePage offers a number of different types of templates that can change anytime Apple gets the urge (so they may be different from what's pictured here). Categories include Personal (newsletters, mostly), Invites, Baby (different types of pages for featuring a newborn), Resume, and Education for teachers and students. Other categories—Photo Album, iMovie, and File Sharing—are different types of pages we'll discuss more later in the chapter.

Select one of the topic buttons, such as Resumes, and the page will reload, showing you the different template choices you have, as in Modern Resume, Classic Resume I, and so on for the Resume topic. When you see a template that you like, click it.

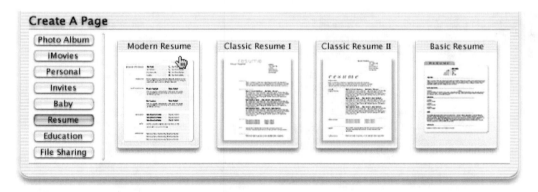

Edit the Text

After you've selected a template, you'll see a screen that enables you to edit the page. In the top-right corner on this screen, you'll see the Change Theme, which enables you to change to a different template at any time. If you click this button, you'll see the same template options you saw previously (such as Modern Resume, Classic Resume, and so forth). The only difference is that when you use the Change Theme command, any changes on your page will be saved and will appear in the new template, which is handy if you change your mind about the design of your page, but you still want to publish this text and information.

You'll also see the Edit Text button, which you should click so that you can edit the text that appears on the page.

After you've clicked Edit Text, you'll see entry boxes that enable you to edit the contents of the page. Make the changes that you'd like to make by clicking in each entry box and editing the text (see Figure 21-1). When you're done with your alterations, scroll back to the top of the page and click the Apply Text button.

Note that you can add hypertext links while editing some portions of your page by enclosing them between the standard HTML anchor tags, such as **<a href="http:// www.apple.com/">Click to visit Apple's site</a>**. Likewise, you can use a mailto URL if you'd like the clicked link to lead to an e-mail address, such as **<a href="mailto:steve@mac.com">Click to send me your reply.</a>**. In some cases, you can use other HTML tags, such as **boldface** or **<i>italics</i>**

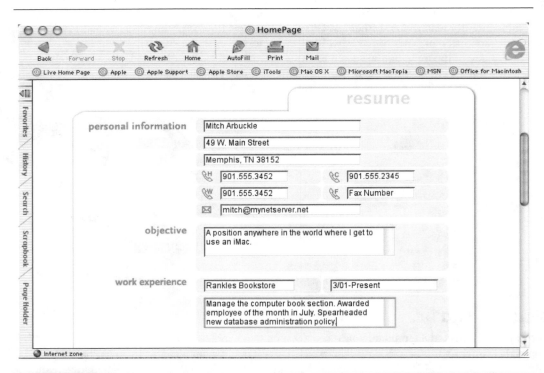

FIGURE 21-1 Click Edit Text and you can begin to change the text for your Web page.

to alter your text. (HTML tags usually work in larger text areas that support a lot of text—short lines for addresses and names may not properly recognize the HTML tags, instead leaving them as part of the text. Just re-edit that line to remove the unrecognized tags.)

Alter the Layout, Links, and Images

After you've clicked the Apply Text button, you'll be back to the main editing screen, where you may be able to make additional decisions about your page. For instance, on some templates you can click an Add/Remove button (with a plus sign and a minus sign) to add or remove a particular line from the site. Click the plus-sign button to add a new line or element with those same features, or click the minus-sign button to remove an item if you don't need it for your page.

education   **University of Memphis**   - +

Coursework (Junior Year), Computer Science

Memphis CC   - +

Associates Degree, Computer Studies

Institution   +

Degree, Subject

You may also see Edit Link buttons at various points on your page, where you can click to edit the URL to a particular item on the page that HomePage believes should have a hyperlink associated with it. (On a resume, for instance, it will assume you want a link to the company names listed in your work history.) Click the Edit Link button and a small entry box appears—enter the URL for the associated item, then click Apply. Now, once published, the underlined text will be a hyperlink to the URL you entered.

Some special links are specifically designed for e-mail addresses, such as those used for the RSVP section of party invitation pages. In those cases, simply enter the e-mail address you want to use—don't use http:// or mailto: as part of the entry.

Some templates offer yet another option for adding individual images to the page you're creating—particularly invitations, newsletters, and some of the templates under Education. The Choose button enables you to choose a single graphic image that you've previously uploaded to the Pictures folder on your iDisk. Click Choose, then use the Choose an Image screen to locate the image you want to use (to open folders, click the folder name and click the Open Folder button). When you select an image, you can click Preview to see the image in the preview area, or click Apply to add the image to the Web page.

Choose an image from the Pictures folder on your iDisk.

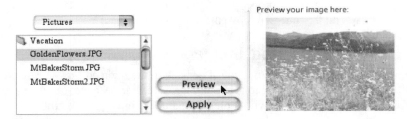

You'll notice other controls on the page, including a button that enables you to switch to your Movies folder (so you can add a QuickTime movie instead of an image) and an Update button that will refresh the list if you've added images to your iDisk that don't appear on this page.

 *The Image Library button leads to a number of clipart and free images that Apple makes available for you to add to your pages, if desired.*

Once you click Apply or Back to Template (if you opt not to add an image), you'll be returned to your page's main editing screen.

Preview and Publish

When you're done with all of your changes, you can click the Preview button in the top-right corner of the HomePage interface, which will cause the page to appear much as it will to your site's visitors. If you don't yet like the way things look, you can click the Edit button to return to the main edit screen.

  Otherwise, you're ready to publish your page—just click the Publish button. You'll see a confirmation page that congratulates you for finishing the page and shows you the URL by which that page can be accessed. To test, open another Web browser window and enter the URL given—you'll see the page just as your visitors will in the future!

 Are you in a spot where you've created a page you don't want to keep? Just click the HomePage button at the top of the screen or close the browser window. When you return to the main HomePage screen, you'll be able to start over again or start on a different page.

From the confirmation screen, click the Back to Home button to return to the main HomePage screen, where you'll see the page you've just created (along with any others you've created in the past) in the Edit a Page section. If you'd like to change the page, you can select it and click Edit Page. To delete a page, select it and click Delete Page. To set the page as your Start Page (meaning users will see it when they access your base URL at **http://homepage.mac.com/ membername/**), select the page in the list, then click Set Start Page.

Incidentally, HomePage automatically creates small text links at the top of each page once you have more than one page created. These links make it possible for your visitors to move back and forth between each of the pages you've created. That's one reason it's important to give each page you create a unique name. You do that while editing the text of the page by changing the name that appears in the This Page Is Currently Called entry box. If you give each page a meaningful name, the links that appear at the top of your pages will make sense to your visitors.

My Resume | Housewarming Invite | Family Newsletter

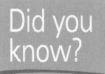

Publish Your Own Pages

The Web pages you create in HomePage are the same type of HTML documents you could create on your own using an HTML or Web page editing application such as Adobe's GoLive or Macromedia Dreamweaver. (Even Netscape Communicator—which is included on your iMac and runs as a Classic or Mac OS 9 application—includes a special Composer tool that you can use to create Web pages.)

So, it would follow that you can post pages you create without HomePage and still display them using your iTools server space, right? That's true. All you have to do is copy the HTML documents (and any associated files, such as image files) to the Sites folder on your iDisk, and they become immediately available on the Internet at the URL **http://homepage.mac.com/*membername/pagename*.html**, such as http://homepage.mac.com/steve/mypage.html. Remember to name one of your pages **index.html** if you'd like it to load automatically as the index page for the site.

Publish Movies and Images

Aside from the pages discussed thus far, HomePage offers a few other special types of templates that require a little preparation. One of those is an iMovie page, which can be used to display an iMovie (or, actually, any QuickTime movie) that you've uploaded to your iDisk and placed in the Movies folder.

> **NOTE** *Although the HomePage screens often say you can display "iMovies" on a Web page, you're actually displaying a QuickTime movie, not an iMovie project file. Using iMovie, you should export using the "Web Movie, Small" option as discussed in Chapter 15 in the section "Export to QuickTime." QuickTime movies should be 240 × 180 pixels, although HomePage can stretch the templates to fit larger movies. (Movies can be saved as "hinted" if desired, using QuickTime's Expert options.) Remember, too, your 20MB limit in iTools, as QuickTime movies can take up a lot of space.*

If you've selected a template designed for a QuickTime movie, you'll see a Choose button when editing the page. Click it and the contents of the Movies folder on your iDisk will be displayed. Select a movie file, then click either Preview (to see the movie playback onscreen) or click Apply to add the movie to your page. Now, use Edit Text to change the text on the page, and, once you've clicked Apply Text, you can then click the Publish button to add the page to your site.

If you're working with a page designed to display a photo album, you'll need to do a little prep work. Photo album pages work by either displaying the entire contents of your iDisk's Pictures folder, or displaying the contents of a subfolder that you create within the Photos folder. So, your first order of business should be to open your iDisk and copy a series of images to your Pictures folder—or, better yet, create a subfolder within the Pictures folder and copy images into that folder. The images should be in GIF or JPEG format.

> **TIP** *Images for the Web should be relatively small in both dimensions and file size. If you have an image-editing program (GraphicConverter, $35 shareware from **http://www.lemkesoft.com**, is a great option), edit your images down in size (if you used a digital camera, somewhere between 320 × 240 or 640 × 480 is a good size for the Web) and set the resolution to 72 dots per inch. That way, the images will be relatively small in file size so they take up less space on your iDisk and less time to download to your visitor's browser.*

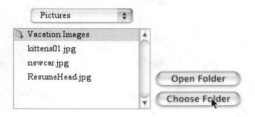

Now, once you have the subfolder set up, select a Photo Album template from the main HomePage screen. On the Choose a Folder of Images screen, you can either click Choose Folder immediately to select your main Pictures folder on your iDisk, or you can highlight the name of a folder and click Choose Folder. By default, every image in that folder will be included on the photo album page(s) that you create.

Once you've selected the folder, you'll see all the images in that folder appear as thumbnails (smaller versions of the images) on a photo album page. If there's a particular image you don't want to show in the album, click the Hide button beneath it. Once clicked, the Hide button changes to a Show button, which you can click again to cause the image to appear on the page.

Don't like the order of the images? You can drag one image to the location of another to place it there. Click and hold the mouse button on the first image you want to move, then drag it to another image. When the second image becomes highlighted, release the mouse button and all of the images will scoot over one spot so that the dropped image will appear in the new location.

Once you've gotten all the images in the right order, click the Edit Text button to edit the text on the photo album page, including the text beneath each image if you'd like to give them a cutline that's more descriptive than the simple filename. When you're done editing, click Apply Text. Finally, click Publish to add the photo album page to your growing Web site. Now, when visitors access this page, they can click the thumbnail images to see them full-size in their Web browsers.

Share Files in Your Public Folder

As mentioned in Chapter 20, the Public folder is a special folder on your iDisk where you can place files that you'd like other people to be able to access and, ideally, download to their own computers. To do that, access your iDisk and copy the files you want to share into your Public folder, or create a subfolder within the Public folder and copy files there.

TIP   *Remember that it's a good idea to store these files in compressed form, using a utility like Aladdin's DropStuff (**www.aladdinsys.com**). See the discussion in Chapter 20.*

Next, sign into the iTools server using your Web browser and choose the HomePage tool. One of the template types available should be called File Sharing. Select this topic, then click the template you think looks good.

Now, click the Edit Text button and edit the text that described this page—tell visitors what they can expect about the files and why you're making them available. You'll notice that the page already lists the contents of your Public folder. You can also place files in a subfolder of the Public folder, if desired, and users will be able to access the subfolder as well.

Business Files ⬍			
File Name	**Size**	👁 **Preview**	⬇ **Download**
Articles.sit	38 K		⬇
Business Plan.rtf.sit	3 K		⬇
house_photos.sit	242 K		⬇

When you're done editing the text on your File Sharing page, click Apply Text; then you can click the Preview button to take a final look at it. If everything looks good, click the Publish button to add it to your site. Now, users can access this page in order to click and download the files in your Public folder using their Web browsers.

 **Send a Personal iCard**

iTools features another little application that's similar to HomePage, but is designed to send an e-mail "postcard" to others. iCards are great for sending a quick birthday greeting, a party invitation, or just a cute digital greeting card for no particular reason. In fact, iCard doesn't require an iTools account—because the whole thing is Web-based, anyone with a Web browser can send an iCard.

iTools members do have one other advantage though—you can build your own iCard using images in your Pictures folder. Here's how:

1. Access the iCards application by clicking it from the iTools site or going directly to **http://icards.mac.com**. Locate the Create Your Own button and click it.

2. If you're already signed into your iTools account, you'll immediately see the Pictures folder on your iDisk. (If not, you'll need to enter your member name and password.)

3. Select an image and click Preview. If you like the image, click Select This Image.

Now, finish the card using the onscreen instructions. You'll type some text, select a font and decide whether you should allow the iCards application to trim your image so that it fits properly on the card. On the screen that follows, you'll enter information about yourself and your recipient(s), then click Send Your Card to send the personalized photo and message on its way!

Chapter 22

Get on America Online

How to...

- Sign onto AOL
- Customize your screen name, including Parental Controls for kids' accounts
- Get e-mail and send some of your own
- Visit the different channels on the service
- Check out the chat rooms
- Post in message areas
- Send instant messages
- Get on the Internet with AOL's tools

There's often confusion over what, exactly, America Online is. AOL is an online service that uses its own special application software for accessing the information, e-mail, chat groups, and message areas that are run by AOL staff. Ultimately, your iMac uses the AOL application to dial into server computers in AOL's headquarters in Virginia, which send requested information (news, stocks, e-mail) back to your iMac.

AOL is not the Internet, although you can use AOL as your Internet service provider and you can access Internet services through AOL. AOL has a built-in version of Internet Explorer, for instance, and its e-mail tools can be used to send and receive e-mail on the Internet. Instead, the AOL service is its own distinct place, complete with news, sports, magazines, interest groups, chats, and more. With more than 20 million users, it's a very popular place to be.

AOL is easy to use, it's accessible from most anyplace in the United States (and most places around the world), and it offers a lot of unique content. If you don't want to mess with other ISPs, then sign onto AOL and enjoy yourself.

NOTE   *America Online is available for both Mac OS 9 and Mac OS X. I'll cover both versions in this chapter. Note that the Mac OS X version of AOL is still in development at the time of writing, so if you don't seem to have it, try downloading it from AOL at **http://www.aol.com/** or via the AOL service (keyword: upgrade) using the Mac OS 9 version.*

Sign Up and Dial In

For the America Online service, you'll need an account name and password—if you don't have those things, you can sign up directly via the service. If you already have an AOL account, then you can skip a few steps. For any connection, though, you'll need to start up AOL by double-clicking its icon, which is located in the main Applications folder (in Mac OS X), or in the AOL subfolder of the Internet folder, inside the Mac OS 9 (Applications) folder if you're running AOL from Mac OS 9 or in the Classic environment.

> TIP
>
> *Before starting this process, check the sound volume on your iMac (particularly in Mac OS 9) and turn it down a bit. When AOL goes to dial the modem the first time, it can be very loud and obnoxious and you can't change the volume until it's done dialing.*

Dial In the First Time

The AOL software is designed to connect in one of two ways. Either you sign on using your iMac's modem—directly calling an AOL access number—or you can sign on over an existing Internet connection, as if AOL was just another Web browser or e-mail program. This second option is good for a few reasons. First, it's useful if you happen to have a high-speed cable modem or DSL connection—AOL is much faster over these connections. Second, AOL offers lower rates for its "Bring Your Own Access" plans, so even if you use a modem, it's cheaper to dial in to your regular ISP (such as Earthlink) then connect to AOL over the Internet. Of course, if you don't have another ISP, then direct-dialing into AOL is your solution.

> NOTE
>
> *AOL can't dial out directly using the modem when it's run from the Classic environment within Mac OS X, although it can connect over a TCP/IP connection.*

Here's how to set up the connection once you've launched AOL for the first time:

1. You'll see the AOL Setup Assistant screen. Choose Begin Automatic Setup and click the right-facing arrow. AOL will try to find your iMac's modem, which it should do with no problem. Wait until this process is complete.

2. Next you'll see the Confirm Your Connection screen, where you're asked to confirm that you want to use the iMac's internal modem. If you want to do this, just click the right-facing arrow. If you'd prefer to sign on to AOL using your ISP then turn on the "Internet Service Provider or Local Area Network (TCP/IP)" option.

> NOTE
>
> *If you've chosen the TCP/IP option, AOL will attempt to log in over your existing connection (you may need to use Remote Access in Mac OS 9 or Internet Connect in Mac OS X to establish the connection first). If AOL succeeds in connecting, move ahead a bit in this chapter to "Create an Account."*

3. If you're using a direct-dialed modem connection, now you'll need to make some dialing choices. If you have a pulse-dial phone (unlikely, except in very rural areas) turn off the Use Touch-Tone Service option. If you have special dialing needs, select the appropriate check boxes and make whatever changes are necessary for your particular phone system. (A comma, entered in any situation where numbers will be dialed, tells the AOL software to pause for a few seconds at that comma.) Click the right-facing arrow.

> TIP
>
> *Turning off call waiting via your phone service's special code is usually a good idea, as the tones that the call waiting service uses can interrupt your modem while it's connected to AOL.*

4. Now, choose the country you're dialing from and, if appropriate, the area code where you are currently located. Click the right-facing arrow.

5. AOL is about to dial its special toll-free number. Make sure the phone line is connected to your iMac's modem port and that no one is on another extension, then click the right-facing arrow.

6. The dialing takes place. Hopefully, everything is successful and you'll move on to the Search for AOL Access Numbers screen.

7. Now choose a local phone number for AOL to access (assuming one is listed). Highlight that number on the left and click the Add button. Your iMac is most compatible with V.90/Flex connections, but it should work fine with any of the other V.90 connections, as well as 33.6, 14.4, and so on. The smaller the number, the slower the connection, with V.90 being the fastest. Each time you click Add, you'll see a screen that asks you to set up the number exactly as it should be dialed.

Your modem will dial this access number *exactly* as shown:

1010111,212-417-7640

1010111,212-417-7640

This number is in New York, NY, United States, area code 212.

8. Edit the number to the exact series of digits that should be dialed (my example shows a fictitious "10-10" long distance dialing code), then click OK in the dialog box. You're back to adding numbers—you can add more than one if more than one local number is available and you'd like AOL to be able to try a series of numbers. After you've selected all the phone numbers you want to use, click the right-facing arrow.

9. Now AOL dials in to the first local access number you've selected. It will attempt to connect to the service (you'll hear the modem screeching). If successful, you'll see the Create an Account screen. At this point, things diverge slightly, depending on whether you're creating a new AOL account or signing on with an existing account.

Create an Account

If you plan to create a new account, follow these instructions. If you already have an account, head to this chapter's next section, called "Use Your Existing Account."

Here's how to create a new account:

1. Select You Want to Create a New Account in the Create Your America Online dialog box. Click Next.

2. Now, enter a bunch of information about yourself, pressing TAB to move to each entry box. Click Next when you're done.

3. Now, read all about the exciting new membership that awaits you, then click Next.

4. Choose the credit card you want to use for your billing, or explore other options by clicking the Other Billing Options button. If you click that button, other credit cards and a checking account option are shown. Select one and click Next.

5. You'll then pass through various screens that ask you to enter credit card information, verify it, and so on.

6. After entering your credit card or banking information, you'll read and accept the member agreement. To read it, click the Read Now radio button, then click Next. If you've read it and you agree, click the I Do button and click Next.

7. Once all that is out of the way, you can choose your screen name. Enter the name you'd like to use for your main AOL account. Enter something that sounds good and click Next.

8. AOL may report that it's able to set up your screen name, but probably not. (With over 20 million users—and potentially 140 million screen names—many common names are already taken.) Instead, AOL will offer a contraction of what you entered, probably with some randomly generated numbers. If you like that screen name, click Next. Otherwise, choose the radio button next to I'd Like This Screen Name Instead. When you select the button, another text box appears and you can enter a different name. Click Next when you've typed it. You may have to go through this a few times, but, eventually, you'll either break down and accept that awful name, or you'll hit on something that works.

9. Next, you confirm your screen name and click Next.

10. Now you'll enter a password. Your password should be at least six characters long and can include both letters and numbers. The best passwords have nothing to do with your life—but those can be tough to remember. So, a combination of remembrances—something like your childhood house number plus that funny name your college roommate used to have for his one green sock—can mix into something no hacker could ever guess. After you've entered the password twice (to verify that you're trying the same thing both times), click Next.

11. Now you may be asked dumb demographic question(s). Click to answer them.

That's it. You're online. You'll be "welcomed" and told that "you've got mail." Don't get too excited, though—the e-mail is just a canned message from Steve Case, president of AOL. If you like, you can click the Tell Me About AOL option in the dialog box and take a tour of AOL. (Notice you can click Don't Show Me This Again if you don't want and don't need a tour of AOL, thanks very much!)

OK, now skip the next section in this chapter (lucky you!) and jump ahead to see how you'll generally go about signing on and off AOL.

Use Your Existing Account

If you already have an AOL account and you just want to set up your iMac to use that account, you can do that, too. Here's how:

1. On the Create Your America Online page, choose You Already Have An AOL Account You'd Like To Use.

2. Two entry boxes appear where you can enter your name and password. Do so, then click Next.

Easy enough, right? As long as you've entered a valid user name and password, you're set. AOL will finish signing on and your member name will become the default for the AOL software. Now you can learn about signing on and off in the next section.

Sign On and Off

Generally, you'll start your AOL session at the Welcome screen, where you'll see your screen name (and any others you've created) along with space for your password. Here's how to sign on:

1. If you're using a modem-based connection, make sure your modem and phone line aren't currently in use. (You can't sign on while someone is talking on the phone or while your iMac is busy accepting a fax.)

2. Choose a screen name you'd like to use to sign on from the Select Screen Name menu.

3. Enter the password for the chosen screen name.

4. Choose the location you're dialing from, if appropriate, in the Select Location box. (If you're going to connect over TCP/IP, you'll generally choose TCP/IP from the Select Location box.)

5. Click Sign On.

Now the modem will dial (if your connection uses the modem) and the familiar connection screen appears. Watch the messages to see how things are going. Once you've gotten through the log-on process, you'll see the regular screen and you'll be welcomed, then told "you've got mail" if, in fact, you have some.

Once you're signed on, there are really three ways to sign off. First, you can sign off and allow someone else to access AOL or otherwise leave AOL active so it can be used again. (It won't be using the modem; it'll simply be open and waiting at the Welcome screen.) To do this, choose Sign Off | Sign Off. You can also choose Sign Off | Change Screen Name if you'd like to change to a new user without being forced to redial the modem or otherwise reconnect.

You can also quit AOL, which will sign off and quit the program all in one swift motion. Just choose File | Quit.

Create a New Screen Name

One of the first things you might want to do is add a second screen name to your account. In fact, you can give each member of your family a unique screen name up to AOL's limit of seven total screen names. Each screen name gets its own individual e-mail, its own storage folders, and even its own 2MB of storage space for Web pages. You can also change the Parental Controls for a particular screen name, limiting what can be done on AOL while that screen name is signed on. And the best part is, only the original screen name is the administrative account, so as long as you keep that screen name's password to yourself, you have total control over the other screen names.

To create, add, or delete screen names, sign on to the service under your original screen name (that's the administrative account) and wait until you've been fully connected. Once you've seen the main screens, you can select My AOL | Screen Names. (Pop-up menus appear when you select many of the buttons in AOL.) On the AOL Screen Names screen, click the Create a Screen Name option. Now you'll see the Create a Screen Name assistant, which walks you through the steps for creating a screen name. The assistant is fairly self-explanatory—you'll pick a name, enter a password for that screen name, and choose a Parental Controls category, as described in the next section. When you're done, you've got another account ready for a family member or anyone else with whom you'd like to share your AOL account.

Parental Controls

AOL really gives you a lot of control over how your account and screen names can be set up. Parental Controls allow you to choose what parts of the service a particular screen name can use, which allows you to decide, for instance, that a particular screen name can't accept e-mail with attachments or can't chat in chat rooms.

Beyond that, you can move on to the Custom Controls, which allow you to fine-tune the Parental Controls to the levels that you feel are appropriate for a given screen name. So if you don't like the AOL defaults, you can change them.

As mentioned previously, you can choose the Parental Controls for a particular user as you're creating his or her screen name. Later, though, you can go back and set or change Parental Controls at any time:

1. Choose My AOL | Parental Controls.

2. Now, on the screen that appears, choose the Set Parental Controls button.

3. In the Parental Control window, you'll see a menu at the top of the screen that allows you to choose one of the screen names associated with your account. Choose one from the menu, then, at the very bottom of the screen, click the category that's most appropriate for this screen name: General Access, Mature Teen, Young Teen, and Kids Only.

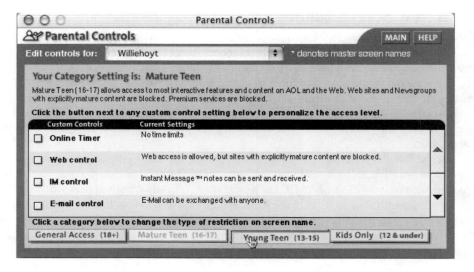

4. Now, if you'd like to dig deeper, you can personalize the settings by clicking the button next to one of the Custom Controls you'd like to change (Online Timer, Web Control, IM Control, E-mail Control, and so on).

5. Once you've chosen a Custom Control, you'll see a dialog box or an assistant that gives you various options to set regarding that particular control. (For instance, the Online Timer lets you specify when and for how long a particular screen name can sign onto

AOL—you could limit access to 30 minutes per weekday night, for instance.) When you're done setting the Custom Control, you're returned to the main Parental Controls screen where you can do more management.

Once you've made all the Parental Controls decisions for that particular screen name, you can select another from the pull-down menu, or close the Parent Controls window. The settings and restrictions will be in place the next time that screen name is accessed.

Delete a Screen Name

To delete a screen name, you need to be signed on with the original account name (or a Master Screen Name). Here's how you do it:

1. Select My AOL | Screen Names.

2. In the dialog box that appears, click Delete a Screen Name.

3. Click Continue in the Are You Sure dialog box.

4. Now, choose the screen name to delete from the menu, then click Delete. The screen name is deleted.

Restore a Screen Name

Just because it's deleted doesn't mean a screen name is gone forever—at least, not if it's been less than six months since you deleted it. To recover a screen name:

1. Select My AOL | Screen Names.

2. In the dialog box that appears, click Restore a Screen Name.

3. Now you'll see a dialog box that includes recoverable screen names. Select one, then click Recover.

Click OK in the dialog box that confirms recovery, and you're ready to roll with the screen name, now back from the dead!

Get Your E-mail

If you're like most AOL users, you're itching for that e-mail. Well, reading your e-mail is easy, assuming you have some. You'll usually know—if the volume control is allowing any sound to get through your iMac's speakers, you'll hear "you've got mail" when you sign onto the service if you've been sent some. To read that mail, just click the You Have Mail icon that appears in the corner of the Welcome screen.

You'll see the Mailbox with a list of messages you've received.

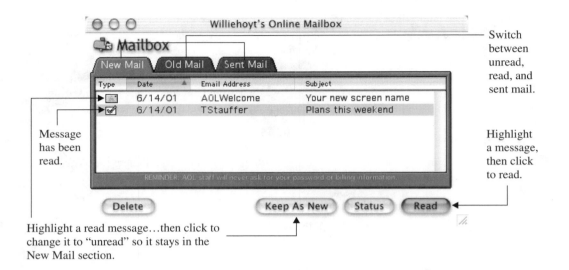

Switch between unread, read, and sent mail.

Message has been read.

Highlight a message, then click to read.

Highlight a read message...then click to change it to "unread" so it stays in the New Mail section.

If a particular message looks interesting, double-click it (or select it and click Read) to open it up in its own window (see Figure 22-1). This window allows you to read the message using the scroll bars down the right side of the message window. But it also allows you to do a lot more than that. You can reply, forward the message, delete it, or just move on to another message.

Here's what each of the controls does:

- **Arrows** If you choose the right arrow, you can move to the next message without returning to the Mailbox. The left arrow gives you the previous message in the list.

- **# of # Box** This is actually a button, which shows the current message you're reading of a certain total number of messages. Clicking the button returns you immediately to the Mailbox.

- **Delete** Clicking the Delete button causes the message to immediately leave the Mailbox. A deleted message is not kept in the Old Mail folder (part of the Mailbox); messages that are read but not deleted are left in the Old Mail folder for a few days or weeks (depending on your volume of mail) before they're deleted.

- **Remember Address** This adds the sender's e-mail address to the Address Book, which can be accessed from the Mail Center button menu in the AOL toolbar.

- **Reply** Highlight the text you'd like to *quote*—text that you'd like to appear in your message reply that reminds the recipient what he or she originally said in the e-mail to you. Then, click the Reply button to create a new message that includes the sender's e-mail address as the recipient of the reply. Now type your message and click the Send Now or Send Later button to send the reply.

■ **Forward** Click Forward, then enter an e-mail address in the Address section of the new message. Click Send Now or Send Later once you have the forward message addressed properly. (You can also type a few lines, if you like.)

■ **Download Later** If you have an attachment with this message, you can choose to add it to your Download Manager—a part of AOL where different download files can be specified. Then, at a given time, you can choose to download them all at once, instead of waiting for each to download. This allows you to get up and move around, since the Download Manager can even sign off automatically. (Read about it later in the Did You Know? sidebar called "Use the Download Manager.")

■ **Download Now** Clicking this button downloads any attached files to your iMac immediately. You'll get a Save dialog box so you can choose where you'd like the attached file saved.

And, as always, you can simply close the message you're reading by clicking its Close box. A check now appears next to its name in the Mailbox. The next time you open the Mailbox, the read message will have been moved to the Old Mail tab.

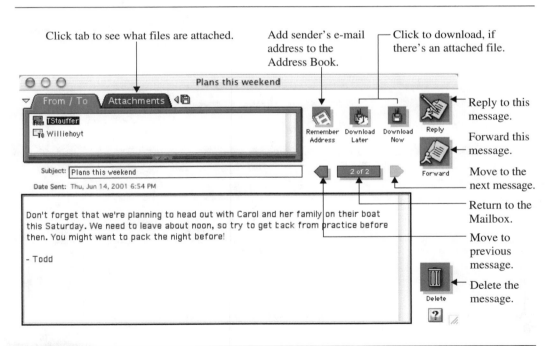

FIGURE 22-1 The Read E-mail window gives you a number of choices for dealing with your incoming messages.

 *Just FYI—AOL staff members will never ask you for your account password, nor will they direct you to a Web site that asks you to enter such information. Any e-mail you get that suggests that you need to enter your password (usually in exchange for something free) is a hoax. That's just evil users trying to get your password so they can create some mischief. Little devils.*

Create a New Message

If you'd like to create a new message from scratch, the beginning part is simple—just click the Write button in the AOL toolbar. That causes a new message window to appear (see Figure 22-2).

By the way—you don't have to be connected to start a message. You can write messages without being signed on to AOL, then choose Send Later (after writing the message) to send it once you've signed on. You'll see how to do that at the end of this section.

Once you've got the new message window open, you're ready to address the message. To do that, either type an e-mail address that you happen to know for your recipient, or click the Address Book button, then choose a name from the Address Book window. Note, in the Send To area, that the To: icon is actually a menu, where you can choose to send the message as a CC (carbon copy) or BCC (blind carbon copy).

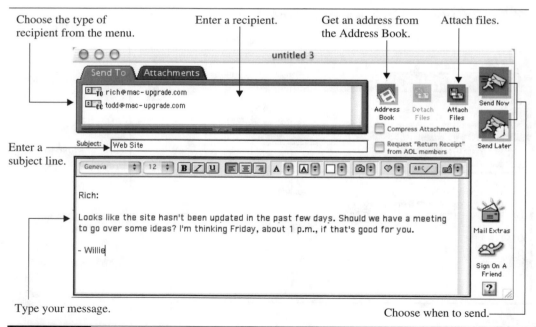

FIGURE 22-2   The new message window offers many options for formatting your e-mail.

TIP *For AOL addresses, you can simply type a screen name. For Internet addresses, type the entire address.*

If you've added a recipient but decided not to send the message to that person, select the name in the Send To window and press the DELETE key.

If you want to attach a file to this message, click the Attach Files button. An Open dialog box appears, where you can find an attachment. Select it, then click the Attach button. If you choose to compress the attachment, click the Compress Attachments check box. (The attachments are compressed with the StuffIt format, which is not recommended for sending to Microsoft Windows or Unix users.) The file(s) are now attached—you can see them by clicking the Attachments tab. You can then remove a file, if necessary, by highlighting the filename and clicking the Detach Files button.

Now you can click in the body of the message and type your message. Remember that you only need to press RETURN at the end of a paragraph, just as when you're typing in a word processor. At this point you might want to make formatting decisions about your e-mail—again the tools for changing fonts, font size, and attributes such as bold, italic, or underlining are like those you'll find in a typical word processor, as shown in the next image. Along with those controls, AOL also offers some other formatting tools for your messages, which allow you to do more e-mail-specific things.

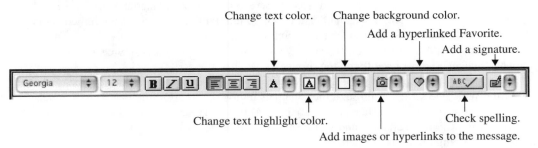

Change text color.　　Change background color.
　　　　　　　　　　　　　　　　　Add a hyperlinked Favorite.
　　　　　　　　　　　　　　　　　　　　Add a signature.

Change text highlight color.　　　　　Check spelling.
　　　　　Add images or hyperlinks to the message.

AOL offers many options that you can learn more about from the Mail Extras button down in the bottom-right corner of the message. Most of them allow you to add Web page-like tools—such as hyperlinks and graphics—to your e-mail documents.

When you've completed the message, you might want to click the Check Spelling button, then you can click Send Now to send the message immediately. If you're not currently connected to AOL, you can click Send Later and it'll be sent when you sign on.

Send Waiting Mail

If you've elected to Send Later, you can send your mail all at once. You do that by opening the Mail Waiting to Be Sent window from the Mail Center button menu. You'll see the window, which allows you to click Send All or select individual messages and click Send to send them over the Internet.

This is great if you want to compose your messages offline, then sign onto AOL and send them quickly. It keeps you from tying up the phone lines, spending money on long distance, or eating into your connect time if you have a limited-time plan for your AOL access.

 *You can also use Auto AOL to log into and out of AOL to send and receive e-mail, even when you're not at your Mac. Choose Mail Center | Set Up Automatic AOL to configure AOL for automatic connections.*

Move Around the Service

There's a lot to do on AOL besides get your e-mail. In fact, figuring out where to go can be tough, so there are different ways to search and be guided around AOL to get a full sense of how it works.

In most cases, moving around AOL is simple. You click buttons to move to another section—sometimes there will be hyperlinks, too, which take you to a new topic. If you want to get rid of a window, click its Close box or button.

Welcome

Aside from access to your Mailbox, the Welcome screen usually offers the latest and most exciting news on the service. You can click any link to jump into a news or entertainment story. You can also click the AOL logo to find a special section, What's New on AOL. Once you become a seasoned AOL surfer you'll probably spend some time with this service, since it tells you what's changed most recently on the service.

The place to start is probably the Channels, which you can access by clicking on the far-left side of the Welcome screen or through the Channels button on the AOL toolbar. The Channels allow you to quickly explore different topic areas on AOL like Travel, Finance, Education, Sports, and Kids Only. Choose a channel and you'll see its main page. From there click the latest links to see what's going on in that particular topic area.

People Connection

I'll discuss this section in more depth in the section "Chat, Message Boards, and Instant Messages." The People Connection is an area where you'll learn about AOL chatting, find out what's available online that day (what celebrities and notable folks are chatting today), and discover how to go about all this chat business. Plus, there's plenty of advice on meeting people and getting to know one another better, virtually. You can get to the People Connection by choosing People | People Connection.

Find by Keyword

Keywords are quite a commodity on AOL—if you happen to know the keyword for a particular area, you can get there immediately by typing the keyword into the entry bar at the top of the screen and clicking Go or pressing ENTER. Keywords often make sense. The keyword **writer** opens the Writers Club, the keyword **dog** opens the Pets Interest page, the keyword **finance** takes you to the Personal Finance area, and the keyword **Mac Community** takes you to the Mac Center Community page.

Keywords and searches can work on the World Wide Web, too—enter the keyword **Time**, for instance, and AOL takes you to *Time Magazine*'s Web site. You can figure out an AOL area's keyword pretty easily once you've visited it. Just check the lower-right corner, where you'll see the keyword.

Download Files

Great shareware and freeware libraries exist on the service, and AOL staff generally performs a thorough check for computer viruses. Plus, you can use the Download Manager to manage all your downloads at once. What could be better?

The main repository of downloadable files on the service is available through the Mac Computing's Download area, which you can get to by entering keyword: **Download Software**. You'll see a list of shareware titles you can browse through. Or, click Software Search to narrow things down a bit.

AOL Has Favorites

If you find a place you like on AOL or while browsing the Web from within AOL, you can turn it into a Favorite. That way, it's easily accessible from within the Favorites button menu. To create a Favorite, all you need to do is locate the small heart in the top-right corner of the window—it should show up in any window that can be designated a Favorite. Click that heart. Now you'll see a dialog box that allows you to choose what to do with this particular page. In this case, you want to add it to the Favorites menu.

To use a Favorite, click the Favorites button in the toolbar, then select the Favorite from the menu that appears.

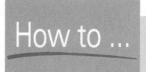

Use the Download Manager

The Download Manager stores a reference to any file that you choose to download later—whether that's a shareware item or an e-mail attachment. In either case, the files appear in the Download Manager. You can access the manager by choosing My Files | Download Manager.

When the Download Manager appears, you'll be able to see downloads that have been completed and those that are waiting to be downloaded. If you'd like to download a waiting file, make sure the To Be Downloaded icon is selected (and highlighted), then click the Download button. You can also select individual items in the To Be Downloaded folder and click Download.

If you'd like to change the location where the downloaded files will be saved (by default they're saved in a subfolder of the AOL folder called Online Downloads in Mac OS 9, or on your desktop in Mac OS X), you can click the Save To button. This allows you to select a folder.

Once the download starts you'll see the File Transfer dialog box. You can choose to have AOL sign off after all files have been transferred by checking the Automatically Sign Off When Completed check box.

Chat, Message Boards, and Instant Messages

Another major reason to fire up America Online and spend some time connected is to get to know people through special interest groups, informal chats, or online forums. First, of course, you've got to find that stuff.

Chat: The People Connection

Using the People Connection, you can find chats on all sorts of topics, ranging from romance to fan chats to particular, and serious, topics regarding current events, the news, or regional discussions. Here's how:

1. Open the People Connection by selecting People | People Connection.

2. In the People Connection window, click Find a Chat.

3. Now, highlight a category, then click View Chats. You'll see the Chat Groups list change on the right side of the window.

4. When you see a chat that interests you, highlight it and click the Go Chat button. Now you'll enter the chat room.

You'll also find chat rooms elsewhere on the AOL service, including in special interest and hobbyist areas. Instead of searching for those, you'll generally just click an icon to enter the chat room.

NOTE *Sometimes a chat room is full. If that's the case, AOL will ask you if you'd like to be automatically routed to a similar chat topic.*

Once you're in a chat room, you'll find a standard AOL interface for the chat (see Figure 22-3). You'll see the people who are chatting on the right side of the window, while the actual chat lines scroll down the left side. (These are lines that have been typed by other folks who are participating in the chat.)

Chatting is actually pretty easy. You just type a line of text in the entry box, then click the Send button or press RETURN. Once you click Send, your message (sometimes after a brief delay) will appear in the Chat window.

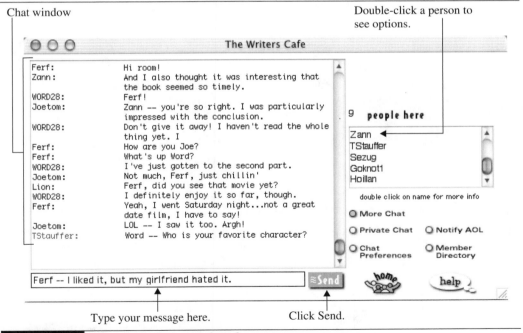

FIGURE 22-3   The AOL chat room interface

The real options come when you're dealing with individual users. In the list of people, you can double-click a particular member name to bring up a dialog box about that person. Here's what you can do:

■ Turn on the Ignore option if this person is annoying, obnoxious, or bothersome. You now will no longer see that person's comments in the Chat window.

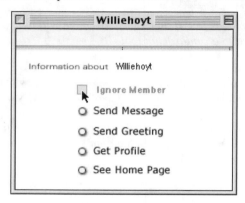

NOTE *You can also use Ignore Member in a more positive way—if you're chatting in a large room with many people in it, you might choose to ignore members that aren't currently participating in your conversation. That will make the discussion easier to follow.*

■ Click Message to send an Instant Message to this user. Instant Messages are special one-on-one chats between AOL users (or Internet users with the special AOL Instant Message software installed).

■ Click Get Info to see if this person has a Member Profile on file.

TIP *You can create your own Member Profile by choosing My AOL | My Member Profile.*

Read and Write in Message Boards

You'll find message boards more often in the special interest areas on AOL. While you're wandering around AOL, anything that says "read what others have to say" or "exchange messages with like-minded folks" is probably a message board. Message boards are areas that work almost exactly like Usenet newsgroups—you read the messages, post your replies, mark things as read, and so forth.

Click such an entry and you'll see the message board interface. Double-click a topic to see its listing window, then double-click a subject to read the posts. Posts are simply a series of replies to a particular topic of discussion. Once you get down to the post level, you're seeing each individual message.

To read the next post in this same subject, click the Next Post button; to read the next subject, click the Next Subject button. To reply to the subject (that is, to add your own post to the ongoing discussion), click Reply. You'll see the Reply window, which offers some features of its own (see Figure 22-4).

Notice that your reply can be sent two different ways—you can post it to the message board or you can send it as an e-mail directly to the person who is shown in the message when you click Reply. You can also do both, or you can enter a different screen name if you'd like to send this message to someone else (perhaps to alert them to an interesting topic).

It's important to note that if you decide to post the message, it doesn't actually have to be a reply to the original poster. You don't even have to quote their message—you can simply go off on some other topic and post the message at the end of the particular subject. Or, you can highlight text, click Quote, then reply specifically to a particular person's comments. It's up to you.

When you're done entering your post, click Send.

NOTE
Your post is available for all to see, including AOL. Make sure your post doesn't violate AOL's terms of service and that you're really saying what you want to say to people—not just something angry in the heat of the moment. You should also double-check the entries to make sure you're doing what you want with the reply. If you're trying to send an e-mail, for instance, you'll want to make sure that you've checked only the Send Via E-mail option.

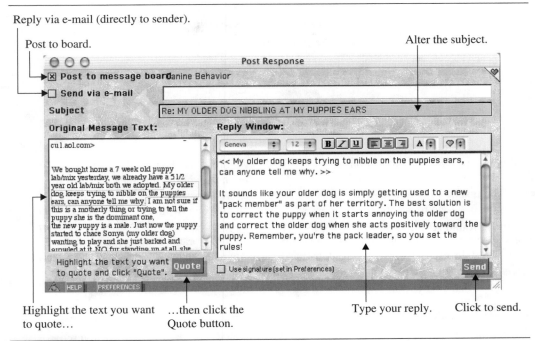

Reply via e-mail (directly to sender).

Post to board.

Alter the subject.

Highlight the text you want to quote...

...then click the Quote button.

Type your reply.

Click to send.

FIGURE 22-4   The Post Response message window

Send Instant Messages

One of the hottest technologies that AOL offers is instant messaging, which gives you the ability to chat one-on-one with others by typing in a chat window. To initiate an instant message session, choose People | Instant Message from the America Online toolbar. In the Instant Message dialog box that appears, enter the Member Name of the person you want to contact, then enter a message and click Send. If the member isn't online, you'll see an alert box telling you so. (You can also enter a Member Name and click Available to see if the user is available.) If the member is online, then you'll see an Instant Message window appear, with the conversation at the top and your entry area at the bottom, where you type and click Send to send your messages.

TIP *As you type, pressing RETURN simply adds a line return. However, you can hold down ⌘ and press RETURN to send the message without needing to click the Send button.*

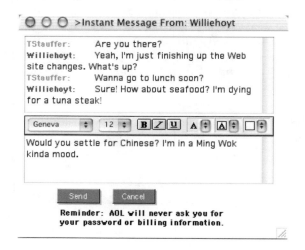

When you're done with the conversation, you can simply close the window. (You can also close the window when you get an IM request for another user whom you don't want to chat with.) The Instant Message feature can be used with any AOL user whose Parental Controls settings enable them to accept instant messages. You can also chat with users who have signed up to use AOL Instant Messenger via a regular Internet connect—no AOL account is required. Instead, users can use a standalone AOL IM application, or they can use a Java applet from within a Web browser (as discussed in Chapter 19). As long as they're signed on via the Internet, you can chat with them just as if they were on AOL.

Get on the Internet

You may already have noticed that AOL is tightly integrated with the Internet. As you move from topic area to topic area, you'll find that Internet links are mixed in with the regular links—after all, AOL 5 has an integrated Web browser that is actually a version of Internet

Explorer. The browser tool is certainly capable, and assuming you have a reasonably fast connection, it's pretty painless to surf the Internet from within America Online.

But you can also, as mentioned, use AOL as your Internet service provider and run other Internet applications, using AOL as your connection to the Internet. All you have to do, in most cases, is fire up the Internet application and start working. AOL takes care of the rest. We'll see more on how that works in the section "AOL Link and Internet Applications."

AOL's Web Browser

You've already seen that you can load AOL's internal Web browser tool simply by clicking on a Web link of some sort. You can also choose a Favorite that happens to point to a Web site. If you do, then the browser tool opens and you'll view that site.

If you'd like to enter a URL directly, you can do that, too. In the entry box in the toolbar, enter the URL directly. Press RETURN and AOL will attempt to load that page. You'll notice in this illustration that the AOL toolbar actually turns into a sort of browser toolbar, complete with Back, Forward, Refresh, and Home buttons as well as the location entry box.

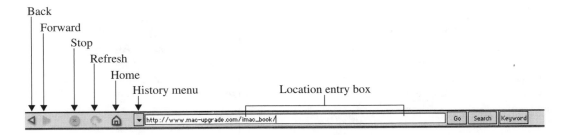

Back
Forward
Stop
Refresh
Home
History menu
Location entry box

http://www.mac-upgrade.com/imac_book/   Go   Search Keyword

You can access the History menu (the arrow just to the left of the location box) to revisit pages you've loaded recently. You can also click the Search button on the toolbar to open up the AOL Search page on the Web and begin searching the Internet.

TIP

Want to set your own home page? Choose My AOL | Preferences. In the Preferences dialog box, click WWW. Now you can enter a new home page, and many other preferences regarding Web browsing. Click OK when you're done.

Other Internet Tools

AOL offers support for FTP as well. (FTP, short for File Transfer Protocol, is a common way to transfer files to and from other computers over the Internet.) You can use keyword: **FTP** to get to the special FTP tools, or enter an FTP URL in the location box and use the browser tools to download files.

And AOL has tools built in for accessing Usenet newsgroups. You can get there by entering the keyword: **Newsgroups**. The controls are similar to AOL's message board interface discussed in this chapter.

NOTE *FTP is discussed in Chapter 20.*

AOL Link and Internet Applications

AOL uses special technology to allow America Online to serve as an ISP connection for some of your other Internet software. If you're connected through a dial-in connection to AOL, you can actually use any TCP/IP application—such as a Web browser or FTP client such as Transmit or Fetch. That way, you can use faster or more full-featured Internet programs than those provided by AOL's client software.

NOTE *Occasionally in Mac OS 9, you'll notice AOL asking you to switch to AOL Link as you're starting up. AOL does this if the TCP/IP control panel is set to use some other connection (like Ethernet or Remote Access) and you're trying to use AOL to dial your modem, instead of using AOL over an existing Internet connection. If that's the case, AOL will switch to AOL Link in the TCP/IP control panel to run its Web tool and other Internet programs. In Mac OS X, all of this happens behind the scenes.*

So, with AOL up and running over a modem connection, just double-click Internet Explorer or launch your FTP tool to get started. Note that e-mail programs will work, too, but only for accessing e-mail from ISP-based (such as Earthlink) or Mac.com accounts, not AOL accounts. (And you may have trouble sending e-mail via your e-mail application if your ISP's SMTP e-mail server doesn't allow remote access.) You can, however, access your AOL e-mail from any browser (when you're away from your iMac) by visiting **http://www.aol.com/** on the Web and signing in.

Did you know? **AOL's Web Storage Space**

Every AOL screen name gets access to 2MB of storage space that can be used for Web pages. The pages can be accessed by anyone with a Web browser and an Internet connection by entering the URL **http://homepage.aol.com/*username/*** where the *username* is one of your screen names. Upload pages through the My FTP Space interface, which works almost exactly like the FTP controls discussed in the previous section, "Other Internet Tools." In order to upload your Web files, you'll access keyword: **My FTP Space**, then upload your documents to the My FTP Space directory. Those files will then be available to anyone who has Web access.

Chapter 23

Get Faster Internet Access

How to...

- ■ Configure a modem connection
- ■ Configure a cable-modem connection
- ■ Configure a DSL connection
- ■ Use the Location Manager

The iMac is usually simple to get up and running with an Internet service provider (ISP)—that's part of the reason I've left all the gritty details to this chapter, instead of explaining all the Internet-related settings and control panels earlier in the book. After all, there are the Setup Assistant (Mac OS X) and Mac Setup Assistant (Mac OS 9), which help you get online when you first open the box. Plus, we discussed the Internet Connect (Mac OS X) and Remote Access (Mac OS 9) windows in Chapter 6, so you may already know everything you need to know to make your Internet connection work. If that's the case, then there isn't much reason to read this chapter.

But if you need to add a new connection or you're interested in exploring new, faster Internet connection technologies, read on.

Configure a Modem Connection

If you plan to use your iMac's modem to connect to an ISP, called a *dial-up connection*, then you'll find that setup is fairly simple in both Mac OS X and Mac OS 9. What you'll need is a valid account with your ISP, a phone number for local access (if possible), and you may need to know the Domain Name Server (DNS) addresses that your ISP uses. (DNS computers are used by your Mac to look up URLs so that the computer can figure out what numeric address a text address such as "www.apple.com" actually refers to.)

Dial Up in Mac OS X

Once you have those three things, you're ready to set up the connection. Here's how to do it in Mac OS X:

1. Launch System Preferences (Apple menu | System Preferences) and click the Network icon.

2. In the Network pane, select Internal Modem from the Configure menu.

3. On the TCP/IP tab, you'll see another Configure menu. Select Using PPP from that menu. In the text entry box under Domain Name Servers, enter the IP addresses your ISP supplied, if necessary.

4. Click the PPP tab. Enter the name of your service provider, the telephone number, and alternate telephone (if you have one). You can enter a full telephone number, including area code, if it's required. Also you can use commas to pause the dialing between different numbers—for instance, **9,16015553452** might be used to first dial a 9 for an outside line, then pause, then dial a long-distance access number. (Of course, most U.S. entries will be standard seven-digit phone numbers for local calls.)

5. With the phone number entered, move on to the account name and password. If you want the password to be remembered and entered automatically when you sign on, click the Save Password option.

Account Name: rich1181

Password: ••••••••

☑ Save password
Checking this box allows all users of this computer to access this Internet account without entering a password.

PPP Options...

TIP *Click the PPP Options button and you'll see a dialog sheet with additional options for the PPP connection. Most of them you'll only need to mess with if your ISP tells you to. The one at the top, "Connect Automatically When Starting TCP/IP Applications," is most interesting. Turn it on if you'd like to have your modem automatically dial out whenever you launch an Internet application or check e-mail. Click OK in the dialog sheet to dismiss it.*

6. Click the Modem tab. From the Modem menu, select Apple Internal 56K Modem (v.90). If you have trouble connecting to the ISP, you can also try Apple Internal 56K Modem (v.34) which is slower, but sometimes more reliable. Then, make other choices about Sound (Do you want to hear the modem?) and Dialing (Do you have a tone or pulse phone line?).

NOTE *A stutter dial tone (the tone that phone companies use for voicemail alert) can confuse a modem into believing it's not hearing a dial tone. If you have phone-company voicemail or a similar feature and you can't seem to get your modem to dial out successfully, try turning off the Wait for Dial Tone Before Dialing option.*

7. Now, click Save in the Network pane and you're configured for a dial-up connection. The next step is to use the Internet Connect application to make the actual connection, as discussed in Chapter 6.

Dial Up in Mac OS 9

For a dial-up connection in Mac OS 9, the settings are the same, but the places where you'll enter those settings are different. And there's another caveat to Internet connections in Mac OS 9—if you use TCP/IP for sharing files (as discussed in Chapter 28) then you can't use TCP/IP for a modem connection. (Instead, your solution would be to get Internet access over the network itself, as discussed in Chapter 28.) If you use AppleTalk for networking or if you don't have a local network, then you're free to use TCP/IP for a modem connection.

Here's how to set up a dial-up connection in Mac OS 9:

1. Open the TCP/IP control panel (Apple menu | Control Panels | TCP/IP).

2. If you're creating your first Internet configuration, skip to step 3. If this is an additional
Internet configuration, choose File | Configurations. In the Configurations window,
select a configuration and click Duplicate. Give the duplicate a new name and click OK.
Now, select that duplicate and click Make Active.

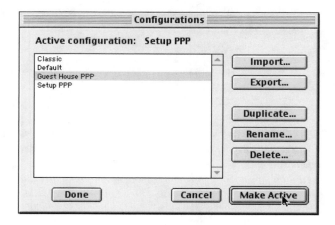

3. In the TCP/IP window, choose PPP from the Connect Via menu at the top.

4. In the Configure menu, choose Using PPP Server. In the Name Server Address entry box,
enter the IP address for your DNS computers, if your ISP supplied you with any. Close
the TCP/IP window.

5. Open Remote Access (Apple menu | Control Panels | Remote Access). If you'd like to create
a new configuration, select File | Configurations and follow the instructions in step 2.
(Multiple configurations are particularly useful if you tend to dial out from different locations
that require different phone numbers.)

6. In the Remote Access window, enter the user name assigned by your ISP in the Name
entry box and enter your password in the Password entry box. (Turn on "Save Password"
if you want Remote Access to be able to connect automatically.) Enter a phone number
in the Number entry box.

7. To connect, simply click the Connect button. If your phone line is plugged into the iMac correctly, you should hear the modem dial out and, if all goes well, you'll see connection information from Remote Access, as discussed in Chapter 6.

TIP

Remote Access has an Options button. Click it and you'll see the Options dialog box. On the Protocol tab, if PPP is selected in the Use Protocol menu, you'll see the Connect Automatically When Starting TCP/IP Application option. Turn it on if you'd like Remote Access to dial out automatically whenever a TCP/IP application attempts to access an Internet resource.

Configure a Cable (or Direct Ethernet) Connection

One high-speed option is a cable modem, which gives you high-speed service over the same coaxial cable as your cable television service. Cable modems are available in many large and medium-sized cities—in fact, cable modems are outpacing DSL and other high-speed solutions for consumers. In most of the deals I've seen, cable access is only $40–$50 a month, and most cable company technicians are reasonably comfortable around iMacs these days, thanks to the little guy's popularity.

NOTE *Because a cable modem (or any Ethernet-based Internet solution) needs to plug into your iMac's Ethernet cable, you won't be able to use Ethernet for a local network. If that's a problem, though, there's a solution—an Internet router. See Chapter 28 for details.*

The majority of cable modem connections are "always-on" connections that work directly with the TCP/IP protocols built-into your iMac—you don't need additional software. (These steps also work for other types of Ethernet connections that don't require additional software, such as corporate T-1 and other hard-wired Internet connections.) Once you've gotten the cable modem hooked up and an Ethernet cable between the cable modem and your iMac, you'll either configure your iMac with manual settings (from the ISP) or you'll select DHCP (Dynamic Host Configuration Protocol) to have your iMac configured automatically. Here's how to set up access in Mac OS X:

1. Launch System Preferences and choose the Network pane.

2. Select Built-in Ethernet from the Configure menu in the Network pane, then make sure the TCP/IP tab is selected.

3. In the second Configure menu, choose either Using DHCP or Manually, depending on your ISP's (in most cases, the cable company's) instructions.

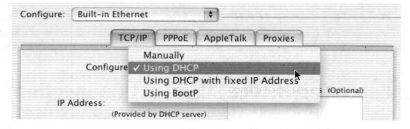

NOTE *If you choose Using DHCP, you may need to enter a code in the DHCP Client ID entry box that appears. Some ISPs require an ID number to help uniquely identify your iMac on the network.*

4. If you chose Manually, enter an IP address, subnet mask, and router address, as specified by your ISP. With either Manually or Using DHCP, you should enter DNS addresses in the Domain Name Server entry box, if your ISP requires them.

5. Click Save or Apply Now at the bottom of the Network pane and close System Preferences. You should now be able to access the Internet.

In Mac OS 9, you'll use the TCP/IP control panel to choose the same settings:

1. Open the TCP/IP control panel (Apple menu | Control Panels | TCP/IP).

2. If this is your only TCP/IP configuration, you can skip to step 3. Otherwise, you can create a new configuration (so you can switch between these settings and some other TCP/IP settings) by choosing File | Configurations. In the Configurations window, select a configuration and click Duplicate. Give the duplicate a new name and click OK. Now, select that duplicate and click Make Active.

3. In the TCP/IP window, choose Ethernet from the Connect Via menu at the top.

4. In the Configure menu, choose Manually or Using DHCP Server, according to your ISP's instructions. If you chose Manually, enter an IP address, subnet mask, and router address, according to your ISP's instructions. For either manual or DHCP connections, enter the IP address for your DNS computers in the Name Server Address box, if your ISP supplied you with such an address. Close the TCP/IP window and you should be able to access the Internet.

NOTE   *Again, the TCP/IP control panel has a special DHCP Client ID box that you may need to use if your ISP requires that you have a special ID code for access.*

To test your Internet connection in either OS, you should launch a Web browser and check to see if you're able to access Web sites. You can also launch your e-mail application and try to check for e-mail. If all goes well, then you're connected. If you have trouble, check your settings again (particularly your DNS addresses), make sure the Ethernet cable is properly connected to the cable modem (or similar device) and that the cable modem is working properly.

Did you know?

Cable Speed and Security

The way a cable-based Internet connection works is a little weird. Because cable television is installed for individual neighborhoods at once, cable modems operate on that same neighborhood *loop*. That means that the Internet *bandwidth* (which loosely translates as downloading speed) is shared between households in a given neighborhood. The more people in your area that access a cable modem at once, the slower your connection will seem. That fact leads to the cardinal rule of cable modems—never brag about them at neighborhood barbecues.

The other issue is security. Because of this local networking loop, everyone in your neighborhood is actually on something similar to a local area network. That means that with some cable services others may be able to see and access your iMac if you have File Sharing or Web Sharing enabled. While that generally isn't a problem (particularly if you disallow Guest access and have good passwords for all your remote users), it's still something to think about if you use a cable modem. If you don't have any reason to share files, turn off File Sharing and Web Sharing (as well as FTP and Remote Access in Mac OS X's File Sharing pane) just to be safe. (See Chapter 28 for more details on File Sharing.)

Configure a DSL (or PPP-over-Ethernet) Connection

Digital Subscriber Line (DSL) connections use your home or business phone line to provide high-speed access to a special DSL modem, which you then connect to your iMac via Ethernet. You can even continue to use the phone line for voice conversations. DSL is generally offered by the phone company in small-to-large cities, although you'll find some other ISPs that offer DSL, including national companies such as Earthlink. (The ISP still has to work with your phone company, which ultimately provides portions of the service.) The location where you plan to have DSL service needs to be reasonably close to the phone company's local buildings (usually within 15,000 feet), which means that it's a less likely option for rural areas.

If DSL is available in your area, you should find that the phone company is familiar with Macs and capable of installing the service. While some DSL connections are as easily configured as cable modems, in general DSL service can be a bit more complex. That's because DSL tends to use a protocol called *PPP-over-Ethernet* (PPPoE) in order to complete the connection. PPP-over-Ethernet is similar to a modem connection in that the DSL modem "dials out" to the ISP's server, but PPPoE connections are generally negotiated within a few seconds, instead of the minute or so it can take your iMac's built-in modem to connect.

NOTE *If your DSL service doesn't use PPPoE, follow the service's instructions for setup, which may be similar to configuring a cable modem, as described earlier.*

The other difference is that the ability to deal with a PPPoE connection is built into Mac OS X, but it generally requires a third-party *dialer* application in Mac OS 9. Let's look at how to set it up in each.

NOTE *Some ISPs require your iMac's Ethernet ID number (the MAC number) to configure the service. You can find this in one of three ways. The easiest way is to look on the bottom of your iMac, where the Ethernet ID is printed. In Mac OS 9, you can also open the TCP/IP control panel and click the Info button; in Mac OS X, the ID number is shown on the TCP/IP tab when you've selected Built-in Ethernet from the main Configure menu of the Network pane.*

PPPoE in Mac OS X

In Mac OS X, you configure a PPPoE connection by opening the Network pane of System Preferences and selecting the PPPoE tab. On the PPPoE tab, click the check box next to Connect Using PPPoE.

This automatically changes your TCP/IP settings (on the TCP/IP tab) to Using PPP, and it enables you to enter more information about your PPPoE account. Now, enter an Account Name and Password. (Service Provider and PPPoE Service Name are optional.) You can have your password saved (using the Save Password check box) if you don't want to be forced to enter your password each time you connect.

Click the PPPoE Options button if you'd like to change some of the advanced options. You may, in particular, wish to check the Connect Automatically When Starting TCP/IP Applications option if you'd like the connection to come up automatically whenever you work with an Internet application. When you're done making changes, click Save or Apply Now in the Network pane.

NOTE *If your ISP requires that you manually enter DNS addresses, click the TCP/IP tab and do so before moving on.*

The next step is the cool part—you use Internet Connect to initiate the PPPoE connection. Launch the Internet Connect application (in the Utilities folder inside your Applications folder) and choose Built-in Ethernet from the Configuration menu. Now, click Connect. If everything is properly configured in the Network pane and you've successfully connected your DSL modem to your iMac via Ethernet, you should see the connection completed in Internet Connect. To disconnect, click the Disconnect button.

TIP *You can drag Internet Connect to the Dock for quick access; also, in version 10.1, Internet Connect offers an option to turn on an indicator in the menu bar.*

PPPoE in Mac OS 9

Setting up the first part of a PPPoE connection in Mac OS 9 is fairly simple—you'll open the TCP/IP control panel and select PPP from the Configure menu. (If this isn't an option, that's probably because you need to install software that came with your DSL modem.) The next step, connecting to the ISP, will likely require a third-party application. If your DSL service supports Mac OS 9, you'll receive the dialer application from your DSL provider. Install it and launch it to configure with your user name and password. Once it's configured, you're ready to dial out— click the Connect (or similar) button. If all is correctly configured, you should be up and running. Figure 23-1 shows one popular PPPoE dialer, MacPOET.

Change Locations (or Configurations) Quickly

Both Mac OS 9 and Mac OS X feature another trick that you might find handy for customizing network connections—the Location Manager. The Location Manager allows you to create different saved *location sets,* which you can then switch back and forth between easily. For instance, if you often move your iMac between your beach house, your pied-à-terre, and your regular residence, you could create a location set for each of those, with different ISP phone numbers, TCP/IP settings, and so on.

FIGURE 23-1   MacPOET (shown in a Bell Atlantic branded version) is used by many ISPs for PPPoE connections in Mac OS 9.

Then, you can quickly switch between the settings by choosing a location. Note that this is also useful if you don't move your iMac, but, for instance, you have two different dial-up ISP accounts you'd like to be able to switch between easily.

To create a new set in Mac OS X, choose New Location from the Location menu in the Network pane of System Preferences. A dialog sheet will appear, where you can name the set. Give it a meaningful name ("Beach House" or "Modem at Home") and click OK. Now, you'll have a blank slate of TCP/IP, PPP, PPPoE, and Modem settings that you can assign for this set. Once you have more than one set created, you can switch between different sets by selecting them in the Locations menu of the Network pane, or you can choose the location from the Locations menu in the Apple menu. Once you've switched, you can immediately begin using the new settings.

In Mac OS 9, you create new locations by first creating different configurations in the TCP/IP and Remote Access control panels, as detailed earlier in the chapter. For instance, you might create a TCP/IP configuration called "Beach House" and a Remote Access configuration called "Beach House." Now, set both of those control panels to the "Beach House" configuration so you can set the Location Manager.

Next, open the Location Manager control panel (Apple menu | Control Panels | Location Manager). To create a new location, choose File | New Location, give the location a name (for instance, "Beach House"), and click Save. Now, place a check mark next to the items that you want to track with this particular location, including AppleTalk & TCP/IP and Remote Access. (As you can see, you can track more than Internet information, if desired.)

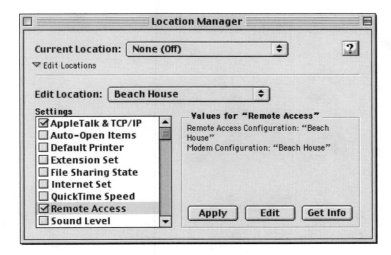

Close or quit the Location Manager and you'll be asked to save changes. Click Save. Now, whenever you switch back to this newly created set by opening the Location Manager and selecting it, the stored configurations (in our example, the "Beach House" configurations) will be automatically applied to the TCP/IP, Remote Access, and any other control panels you've chosen to track. The settings are changed automatically, and you should be able to use them immediately.

TIP   *In Mac OS 9, if you have the Control Strip enabled (via the Control Strip control panel), you'll find a Location Manager control strip module that you can use to quickly change locations.*

Part IV

Customize Your iMac

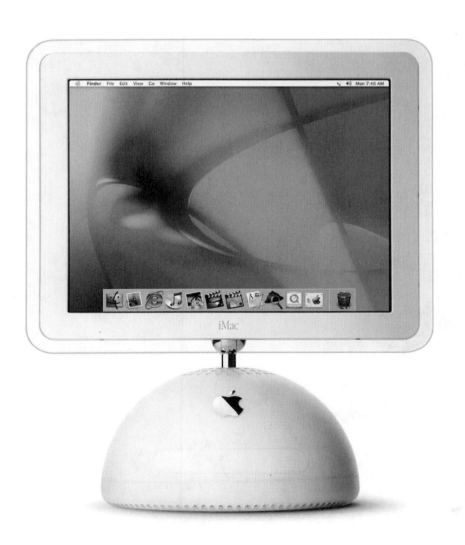

Chapter 24

Change iMac's Appearance and Attitude

How to...

- Change the resolution and color depth of your iMac's screen
- Change the dimensions of your iMac's display
- Calibrate the screen's colors
- Set basic preferences for how your iMac looks and acts
- Set the time and date
- Save energy and automate startup, shutdown, and sleep
- Customize how your iMac uses memory
- Set up your keychain

In this chapter I discuss the atmospheric, behavioral settings for your iMac—what it looks like and how it operates. You can change these settings using control panels or Preference panes. Other settings are discussed in other chapters—those that govern networking, the Internet, and your modem, for instance. In this chapter, we'll focus on the control panels built into the Mac OS that handle appearance, the monitor, sound, memory, and other basic settings.

Make Adjustments in Mac OS 9 and Mac OS X

You'll make most of these adjustments in one of two places, depending on the operating system version you're using. In Mac OS 9, you'll access different control panels, found in the Control Panels menu in the Apple menu. Select a control panel and it appears onscreen, enabling you to make settings choices and changes.

In Mac OS X, settings have been brought together in a single application, called System Preferences. Select Apple | System Preferences or click the System Preferences tile in the Dock to launch the application. Then, click one of the preference icons to load the *preference pane* that corresponds to that item. When your changes are made in the pane, you can click the Show All icon to see all available icons, or click one of the icons at the top of the System Preferences window to switch to a different pane.

> TIP   *You can drag icons from the main portion of the System Preferences window up to the toolbar to add them for quick access.*

Note that, in some cases, these settings may require an Administrator's password before you can set them. If you're logged into an Admin account (such as the account you first created on the Mac OS X system), then you won't have any trouble changing settings in System Preferences. If not, however, you may need to click the small Padlock icon that appears in the System Preferences window, and then enter the name and password of an administrative user, particularly for some system-level preferences such as Date and Time or Energy Saver. If you don't know that name and password, you'll have to ask for it before you can make some of the changes discussed in this section. (See Chapter 27 for more on the different types of user accounts.)

Adjust Your iMac's Monitor

Instead of using knobs and buttons on the outside of the monitor, you can control quite a bit about your iMac's display from within the Monitors control panel in Mac OS 9.

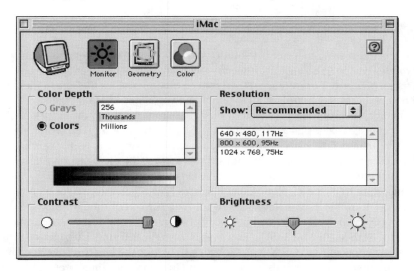

NOTE   *If your iMac has an earlier version of the Mac OS, you'll find these same controls in the Monitors and Sound control panel.*

There are three different parts of the Monitors control panel that concern your monitor—the Monitor, Geometry, and Color settings. Each will affect how your iMac's screen looks, and each has its own area of responsibility.

In Mac OS X, you'll use the Displays pane of System Preferences to change monitor settings; with the Displays pane, you'll find tabs for Display, Geometry, and Color, each similar to their counterparts in Mac OS 9.

Adjust the Monitor and Display Settings

Click the Monitor button in Mac OS 9 or the Display tab in Mac OS X and the controls change to show you the monitor settings.

Color Depth

Your iMac can display a range of colors from 256 to thousands to millions. This represents the color *palette* available to your iMac—the number of distinct colors that could potentially be shown on the screen. The more colors that appear on screen, the more photo-realistic the images on your screen. A JPEG photo file displayed at 256 colors will offer less detail than one rendered at millions of colors.

In most cases, Thousands or Millions of colors is appropriate. You can change the color depth, though, if you find that you have images that don't look right—they seem less than sharp in places, have too much gray or black in the image, appear too light or dark, or simply seem jagged. To change the color depth, simply click one of the options in Mac OS 9, or select a different number of colors from the Colors menu in Mac OS X.

Resolution

The iMac supports three different screen resolutions: 640 × 480; 800 × 600; and 1,024 × 768. So what does *resolution* mean? Technically, it means the number of pixels that appear on the screen, expressed in terms of a grid. For instance, 800 × 600 resolution divides the screen into 800 pixel columns and 600 pixel rows. Multiply it all together and you'd get 480,000 pixels on the screen.

The significance of resolution is two-fold. First, the more pixels on the screen, the more information you can see—at 1,024 × 768, you can see a lot more of a given word processing page, for instance, than at 640 × 480. Second, the more pixels on the screen, the smaller the pixel. In order to see more of the page on your iMac's screen, the elements on the screen will have to get smaller, since the size of your monitor stays the same.

It's most important to pick a resolution that balances how much information you want on the screen with how comfortable you are looking at it for long periods of time. In Mac OS 9, you'll likely pick 800 × 600, which offers a good balance between the use of screen space and the size of elements on the screen. In Mac OS X, however, I'd suggest trying 1,024 × 768; the larger icons and visual elements in Mac OS X make it better suited for the larger resolution. Ultimately, however, it's your choice—if the words on screen seem too small or things seem a little fuzzy, you might want to run Mac OS X at 800 × 600.

NOTE *On most any iMac current at the time of writing, the Refresh Rate setting in Mac OS X is only mildly interesting; the iMac has three refresh rates, and each is available at a particular resolution. The higher the Refresh Rate, the better the image quality, with less shimmering. Also, Mac OS X version 10.1 includes an option, Show Displays in Menu Bar, that enables you to add a quick-access menu for switching resolutions to the Mac OS X menu bar.*

Contrast and Brightness

These options are relatively self-explanatory. You can use the sliders to change the brightness and contrast shown on your screen. There are two considerations. First, you should never set any computer monitor to its highest brightness setting, since that can wear out the monitor more quickly, causing it to dim prematurely. If you feel you need to brighten this screen, make sure you've tried different contrast settings before setting brightness all the way up.

Second, changing brightness and contrast may affect how the screen looks compared to printed documents, especially color documents. You'll calibrate the monitor to correct for lighting conditions and to create optimum color output later in this section. You might want to calibrate (described later) before going nuts with the brightness and contrast.

Change the Geometry

The iMac's software settings include the ability to fine-tune the screen characteristics so that you get a perfectly square image with all the right proportions—assuming that's your desire. For most people, Murphy's Law of Vertical Hold takes effect—the more you mess with any of these controls, whatever your intent, ability, or skill level, the worse the picture looks. Maybe you'll have better luck.

You get to these controls by clicking the Geometry button in the Monitors control panel, or the Geometry tab in the Displays pane. (Note: The iMAC G4 doesn't require geometry settings.)

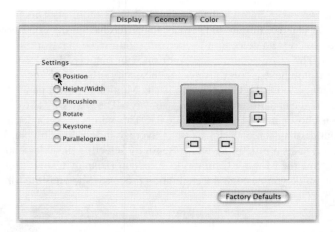

Now, you can go about changing many, many different settings regarding the size and dimensions of your monitor's picture. Here's what each does:

- **Position**   With this setting, you can change the vertical and horizontal placement of the screen image so that it's centered as much as possible.

- **Height/Width**   This setting allows you to change the size of the screen's image. You may notice that your screen, by default, doesn't fill the available space. That may be a good thing, since the very edges of a monitor tend to distort the picture somewhat. But you might also be able to tweak out a slightly larger picture using these controls.

- **Pincushion**   If your screen appears to bow in or out at the middle or edges (giving it a pear or an hourglass shape) then you can use Pincushion controls to take it back to a rectangular shape.

- **Rotate**   The screen may appear slightly higher in one top corner than the other. If that's the case, you can rotate the image to bring it level again.

- **Keystone**   If the top or bottom of the screen is bowed in or out, you can change that with the Keystone setting.

- **Parallelogram**   If the screen rectangle slants in one direction or the other, you can shift it back with this control.

To change a setting, just click the radio button next to the setting you want to alter and the controls on the right side of the window will change to reflect that. Click the little control buttons that appear around the image of an iMac screen to make your changes. You should see the screen react immediately.

If you mess it up beyond recognition, click the Factory Settings or Factory Defaults button. This will reset the picture to the way it was calibrated back at the Apple assembly line.

Calibrate the Display

Apple has created a technology, called ColorSync, which makes it possible for you to fine-tune the color, brightness, and other characteristics of your iMac's monitor. This is useful for two reasons—first, it allows you to calibrate the display for different lighting conditions. Secondly, ColorSync allows you to create a color profile for your monitor, so that printing to a color printer looks as true as it can. The more accurate the color on your display, the closer it will be to the final, printed product if you have a color printer that also supports ColorSync.

To begin calibrating, choose the Color button in the Monitors control panel or the Color tab in the Displays pane. You can calibrate in one of two ways. The easy way is to simply make sure that the *iMac* profile is chosen in the Display Profile list. This will give you a decent approximation that should cause your display screen to look fine in average indoor lighting conditions.

The second method takes a little more work. Begin by selecting the iMac entry, then click the Calibrate button. Now the Monitor Calibration Assistant (Display Calibration Assistant in Mac OS X) appears to guide you through the calibration process. (Shown is the Mac OS 9 version.)

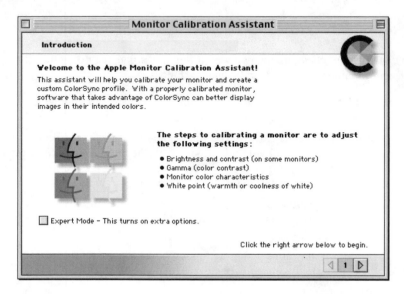

You may have trouble with the Assistant if you have red-green or similar color vision impairments.

Walk through the steps of the Assistant, following its instructions. When you're done with the Assistant, you'll have a newly calibrated display, and perhaps even a more richly colored screen. In the last step of the Assistant you'll give it a unique name—that name is added to the ColorSync Profile list. For instance, you might name the color settings Bright Day and Night. Now, whenever you want to change calibrations, you can quickly select different profiles from the ColorSync Profile list.

Alter Sound and Alert Settings

In the Sound control panel (in Mac OS 9) or the Sound settings pane (in Mac OS X) you can make some sound adjustments. You're able to adjust the volume, change the input device for recording, and enable 3-D sound. You can also change your system alert and, if desired, record some alerts of your own.

Change Sound Settings in Mac OS 9

If you have Mac OS 9, you'll use the Sound control panel to make your sound settings. At the top, you'll see tabs for the different types of settings. Click one of those and the control panel changes to show your choices.

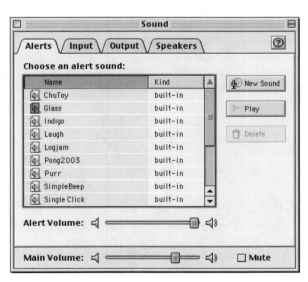

The Sound control panel lets you choose the input device and output device for sound on your iMac, plus it lets you manage the speakers, volume, and other basics. Most of the time you won't need to play with these too much. By default, the settings will allow you to record from the iMac's microphone, play audio CDs, and so on. If you need to get serious about recording or outputting audio to different equipment, that's when you'll dive into the Sound control panel. Here's what you can do in each section of the control panel.

Alerts

Select the sound you'd like to use as an alert sound whenever the iMac encounters a problem or otherwise needs your attention. You can also set the Alert Volume and, if desired, click the New Sound button to record a new alert sound (for instance, your own speaking voice).

Input

Click the Input tab and you'll be able to choose a device for sound input in the top of the control panel. In most cases you'll be choosing between the Built-in option and the Internal CD or DVD player. Once you've chosen, you'll have options in the Settings for the selected device. For instance, in some cases you can place a check mark next to Play Sound Through Output Device if you'd like to hear the sound from this input source on the output device. (For instance, sound from an internal CD to your speakers should play through—that makes sense. If you're using the microphone to record your voice, however, you may not want it to play through, since that could cause feedback.)

Output

In the output section you'll choose the device that the iMac should use for sound sent out of applications. If you don't have any external speakers or receivers attached to your iMac, you'll see Built-in as the only option. You can set the volume for output sound using the slider in this window. If you have other output devices attached, you'll select them here.

Speakers

In the Speaker Setup section you can test the arrangement and volume of your speakers. Click the Start Test button and you'll hear a static tone that helps you set the balance of your speakers using the small volume sliders under each speaker. When you're done, click the Stop Test button.

Change Sound Settings in Mac OS X

In Mac OS X, sound settings are currently much more basic. Select the Sound pane in System Preferences and you'll see, at the top of the pane, sliders for system volume and balance between left and right speakers. You'll also see a Mute check box, which you can select to turn the volume off immediately.

At the bottom of the pane, you'll find a slider for alert volume, enabling you to select an individual volume setting for the alert sounds that are played when Mac OS X needs to get your attention. Below that, you can select your alert sound in the scrolling list. In Mac OS X version 10.1, the option Show Volume in Menu Bar, which is on by default, enables you to select the volume by clicking the speaker icon that appears on the menu bar.

Set Date and Time

One of the basic settings for your iMac is the time and date. You probably set these when you first plugged in, turned on your iMac, and ran the Setup Assistant. But you may have some reason to revisit them, including a move to another time zone or perhaps recognition that something is set incorrectly. To change the time and date, head to the Apple menu, then choose Control Panels | Date & Time in Mac OS 9.

The Date and Time pane in Mac OS X is similar, although it offers its controls on four tabs across the top of the pane. Here's a look at the different things you can set regarding the date and time:

■   *Edit date and time.* In the Current Date (Today's Date) section, click in the Date entry box and either type or use the arrows to change the date. You can do the same thing for setting Time in the Current Time section.

NOTE   *If you can't edit the Date and Time in Mac OS X, it's because you're set to use a Time Server on the Network Time tab. Turn that option off to change date and time manually.*

■ *Format date and time.* In Mac OS 9, you can click the Formats button to change the date and time formats. Each section provides several options for the time or date display.

NOTE   *In Mac OS X, these settings are found on the Date and Time tabs of the International pane.*

■ *Set the time zone.* In Mac OS 9, click the Set Time Zone button to choose your locale. You can also click the check boxes if you want to automatically track daylight savings or to let the iMac know that daylight savings is currently in effect. In Mac OS X, click the Time Zone tab, then select your approximate time zone on the map, followed by a more exact time zone in the pop-up menu.

■ *Use a time server.* In Mac OS 9, the Time Server option can synchronize your iMac's clock to an Internet Time Server clock. (Internet Server Time is based on official atomic clocks, making them very accurate.) There's also a Server Options button that checks the clock against the server closest to you. In Mac OS X, click the Network Time tab, then click Start to turn on synchronization and Stop to turn it off. If your Mac is on a larger Mac OS X network, you may need to select From NetInfo to access a network time server setting.

NOTE   *In Mac OS X version 10.1, you simply turn on the Use a Network Time Server option, and then select the server from the NTP Server menu.*

■ *Turn menu bar clock on or off.* Want a clock on your iMac's menu bar in Mac OS 9? Click the On radio button. You can set other options (fonts and colors) by clicking the Clock Options button. In Mac OS X, click the Menu Bar Clock tab, then turn on the Show the Clock in the Menu Bar option.

Set General Controls

Once, General Controls was the main control panel for specifying the look of a Mac. These days, it's relegated to a smaller, but still important, role in Mac OS 9, where it gives you basic controls over how the Finder and menus work. In Mac OS X, it's even more limited, focusing only on colors and how scroll bars work.

Set General Controls in Mac OS 9

To access the General Controls control panel, select Apple | Control Panels | General Controls.

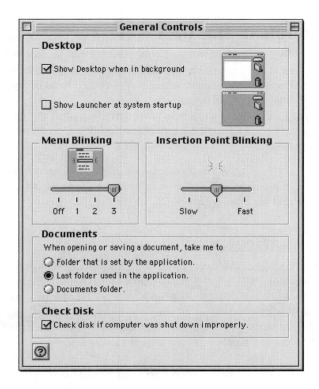

24

Here's what everything does:

■ **Desktop/Launcher**   These controls determine whether or not the desktop or the Launcher appears in the background when you're using other applications. (The Launcher is a special window that quickly launches applications. Drop aliases in the Launcher subfolder of the System Folder to access them through the Launcher.)

■ **Blinking**   Change the speed and number of times the insertion point and menus blink.

■ **Documents**   Choose what folder the Open and Save dialog boxes will display by default. This is especially useful if you find yourself frustrated when opening and saving documents—set the default to the Documents folder and you always know how Open and Save dialog boxes will behave by default.

■ **Check Disk**   If your iMac is shut down incorrectly (due to a freeze up, crash, or power failure), you'll get a warning and Disk First Aid will check your iMac's hard drive. If you don't want this option, remove the check from the check box.

Set General Controls in Mac OS X

Open the General pane of System Preferences and you'll see options to choose the Appearance and Highlight color for your iMac's interface. The Appearance setting can be important; graphic artists tend to opt for the Graphite appearance, which is less colorful and distracts less from the colors used in photos and other graphical documents.

The only other option governs how scroll bars react when you click on them. Choose either Jump to Next Page to quickly page through documents or Scroll to Here to move directly to the selected spot in the document.

 *Mac OS X version 10.1 adds a few more options, including control over the appearance of scroll arrows, the number of recent items that appear in the Apple menu's Recent menus, and how text smoothing works.*

Save Energy Automatically

The Energy Saver control panel allows you to do some interesting things—you can actually schedule your iMac to sleep or, in Mac OS 9, to shut down and start up automatically. You can also cause it to dim the monitor and even go to sleep after a period of inactivity. When your iMac sleeps, the processor, hard disk, and monitor all consume much less energy, but the power stays on and applications and documents stay open. Tap a key on the keyboard and the iMac will spring back to life. In Mac OS 9, choose Apple | Control Panels | Energy Saver.

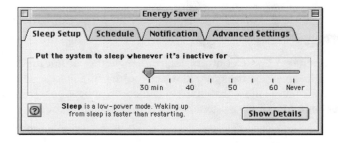

In Mac OS X, choose the Energy Saver pane in System Preferences, where you'll find controls similar to the Sleep Setup controls discussed next. (Mac OS X doesn't support scheduling sleep and/or shutdown.)

Set the Sleep Timer

To set how quickly your system goes to sleep during periods of inactivity, choose the Sleep Setup tab in Mac OS 9, or simply locate the slider labeled Put System to Sleep Whenever It's Inactive For in Mac OS X. Then, move the slider to the amount of time you want the iMac to wait before it puts itself to sleep.

If you'd like to turn off the display and hard disk sleep options or change the default settings, click the Show Details button in Mac OS 9. You'll see separate sliders for the display and hard disk (they're shown by default in Mac OS X). If you want to set separate sleep times for the display or hard disk, click the check box next to each entry, then move its slider bar.

> NOTE *Your iMac's display consumes the most power, so you may want it to sleep reasonably quickly compared to the hard disk and the rest of the iMac's components.*

Schedule Sleep (or Shutdown) in Mac OS 9

You can schedule your iMac to automatically sleep, start up, and shut down, if you'd like. To do that, click the Schedule tab in Mac OS 9. Now, place a check mark next to the option you'd like to automate, then from the menu choose the days of the week that this should take place. Finally, choose a time when the startup or shutdown should take place.

> NOTE *To schedule startup and shutdown in Mac OS 9, you'll need to turn on the "Scheduled Shut Down instead of Scheduled Sleep" option. Otherwise, the available options let you automate putting the iMac to sleep and waking it up at certain times.*

That's it—close the Energy Saver control panel and the system is armed.

Adjust Memory Settings in Mac OS 9

The Memory control panel offers an opportunity to manage the RAM in your iMac and, perhaps, get a little more performance out of your system. (This isn't necessary in Mac OS X, which features advanced memory-management built in.) Some of the settings are automatic, but you can make changes. Choose Apple | Control Panels | Memory.

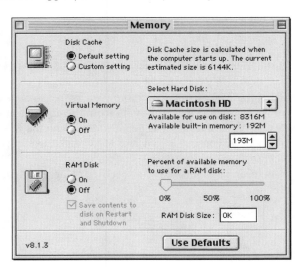

Here's what each setting does:

- **Disk Cache** This setting determines how much system RAM is set aside for a disk cache. A *disk cache* is a special portion of memory where "look-ahead" data is stored to be accessed more quickly than if the Mac OS was forced to load the data straight from the disk. Usually, this is set automatically, but if you'd like to enter your own number, click Custom Setting and enter an amount, in kilobytes, for the cache.

- **Virtual Memory** Virtual memory allows your iMac to use part of the hard disk to store items that should be in memory, but can temporarily be placed on the hard disk. This makes it possible to run more programs at once. Click the On and Off radio buttons to turn Virtual Memory on and off. (You should always have Virtual Memory turned on unless you have an application or utility that specifically suggests you turn it off.) Choose an amount in the entry box or use the arrows. How much? Add between 1 and 10MB to the current built-in memory.

NOTE *I only recommend turning off virtual memory if you have 192MB of RAM or more, and even then it's a trade-off. Turning off virtual memory generally makes applications perform a bit quicker, but it makes them launch a bit slower.*

- **RAM Disk** A RAM disk allows you to create a sort of "virtual" disk that's actually stored in RAM. The advantage of this is that RAM is much faster than a hard disk, so placing data or applications on the RAM disk can make your iMac run a little faster. The disadvantage is that a RAM disk is just as volatile as regular RAM. Don't store important data on a RAM disk since one system freeze or power surge could wipe away all the data. To create a RAM disk, click the On button and choose a size. To get rid of the RAM disk, go to the Finder and delete everything from the RAM disk, then click Off in the Memory control panel.

NOTE *File Sharing needs to be turned off in order to get rid of a RAM disk.*

The more RAM you have, the more you can devote to a RAM disk. If you have 32MB-64MB of RAM, then you really can't spare any for a RAM disk—your iMac is using all of that RAM just to function. With 96MB or 128MB of RAM (or more) you're free to have a RAM disk, if you find one useful. Remember, a RAM disk subtracts from the amount of RAM used for running applications. Check Save on Shutdown to make sure data on the RAM disk is saved when you shut down your iMac. The contents saved on a RAM disk can survive a restart, but not a shutdown, unless you choose to save the data.

Don't like the Memory control panel settings you specified? Click the Use Defaults button to return to the original settings.

24

> TIP
>
> *What do you put on a RAM disk? Here are a few good options: Place your Web browser's cache storage here by using the Preferences control panel in your Web browser to change the location of stored cache files. Also, store QuickTime movies here so they'll run smoother and be easier to edit. Otherwise, it's best to store non-documents such as applications and games—you'll speed things up and save energy.*

Change the Appearance in Mac OS 9

Another major control panel in Mac OS 9 is the Appearance control panel. This allows you to choose how the Mac's interface looks—the colors, the textures, the behaviors—as well as how the arrows work on the scrollbars and what sort of sounds are made as you're working. To manage all that, it has to have a lot of tabs. Choose Apple | Control Panels | Appearance.

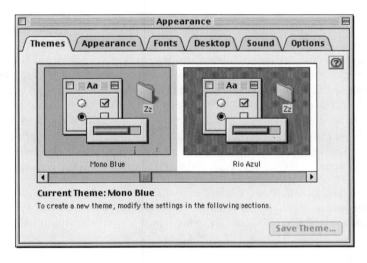

> NOTE
>
> *Mac OS X doesn't offer this level of control over the appearance, although you can choose a desktop picture by selecting Finder | Preferences. In Mac OS X version 10.1, that option is available via the Desktop pane in System Preferences.*

Here's what happens on each tab:

- **Themes**   Themes are, overall, cohesive collections of all the other settings tabs—appearance, color of the desktop, sounds, and so on. Each theme offers a different overall experience. To use a theme, select it from the scrolling list. Close the Appearance control panel and work with that theme, or you can alter it. If you alter it (by visiting the other tabs), return to the Themes tab to name and save your altered creation using the Save Theme button.

■ **Appearance**   Your iMac ships with a default appearance, but theme files (offered by third-party companies) can be stored in the System Folder within the Appearance subfolder. This changes the whole look of the windows, icons, and everything. You can also change the highlight color (the color used when you select text or an icon) and the variation color (used for the highlight bar in menus and for the scroll boxes in windows).

■ **Fonts**   With the Fonts tab, change the font face used for different parts of the Mac OS. Feel free to experiment. You can also experiment with font *smoothing*—this technology causes fonts larger than a certain point size (which you can change with the arrows and Size entry box) to be smoothed or *anti-aliased* onscreen. This makes some fonts look better onscreen, although the overall look varies depending on the fonts used. Text smaller than 14 point can sometimes be too blurry to read when smoothed, so it's probably best to leave this option on for 14 point or higher text.

■ **Desktop**   This tab allows you to place a pattern or picture on the desktop to give your iMac some personality. To place a pattern, use the Patterns list. To place a picture, click the Place Picture button and find the picture in the Open dialog box (the Desktop Pictures folder in the Appearance folder inside your System Folder has some sample desktop images), then click Choose. Back in the Appearance control panel, position the image using the Position menu. You can choose Tile on Screen (several copies pasted together to fill the screen), Center on Screen, Scale to Fit (filling the screen while maintaining the correct ratio), or Fill the Screen (regardless of dimensions). You can also leave it at the default, Position Automatically, especially if the image is already the same resolution as your desktop. When you've made your choices, click Set Desktop. To remove the picture, click Remove Picture and click Set Desktop again.

> TIP   *It's a good idea to match your desktop image's resolution to your screen's resolution—if you're running at 800 × 600, then the desktop picture can also be 800 × 600. Also, you can use any PICT, JPG, or GIF image, and it can be stored anywhere on your hard disk.*

■ **Sound**   Choose a soundtrack for your theme. The soundtrack offers preset sounds for many different things you can do in the Mac OS, including selecting from menus, moving icons, scrolling windows, and so on. Choose a soundtrack from the menu, then, by checking or unchecking the different sound effects, choose the sounds you'd like to hear.

■ **Options**   This last tab offers you two check boxes. First, should your scroll arrows appear at just one end of the scrollbar? And, two, should you be able to double-click a title bar in order to invoke the Windowshade command? Make your choices.

If you've changed the settings extensively, don't forget to return to the Themes tab and give your new theme a name. Otherwise, you're done—click the Close box to exit the Appearance control panel. Your new appearance is now in effect.

Create and Access a Keychain

In Mac OS 9 and Mac OS X, you can use your personal *keychain* to store user names and passwords for servers, encrypted files, and, in some cases, Internet sites. Many items that you access on your iMac using a password can be stored on your keychain, just like you can store the keys for your car, house, office, and safety deposit box on a real keychain.

With your Mac OS keychain, you only need to remember one password. The keychain stores the passwords for many other resources, all of which are locked behind a single password that you memorize. Now, instead of looking up passwords on that hidden sheet of paper taped to the bottom of a desk drawer, you can unlock your Mac OS keychain and access passwords automatically.

How does it work? In certain applications, you'll find an Add to Keychain option, which allows you to add a user name and password to the keychain automatically. Now, the next time you try to access that user name and password, the application will attempt to retrieve it from your keychain. If your keychain is unlocked, then that password-protected connection (or item) will be opened automatically—you won't have to enter a password! If your keychain is locked, though, you'll have to enter your keychain password before the application can continue. So, as long as you're diligent about locking your keychain, others won't be able to access it and get into your password-protected items.

NOTE   *In most cases, applications need to support the keychain in order for it to work. (For instance, applications like Apple's Mail and OmniWeb use your keychain to store mail server passwords and password-protected Web sites.) Network Browser (Mac OS 9) and Connect to Server (Mac OS X) support the keychain, so you can automatically store your network logins using keychain technology. Likewise, the Apple File Security application in Mac OS 9 supports the keychain, so you can encrypt files on your iMac for safe storage and store the password in your keychain.*

In Mac OS X, you can also specifically create your own keychain items, thus extending its usefulness to things like storing personal passwords, ATM PIN numbers, and other items you need to remember on a regular basis, but would like protected in your keychain.

Create Your Keychain

In Mac OS X, your keychain is created automatically, and it's assigned the password you used when you first created your user account. In Mac OS 9, you'll need to create your keychain, first. If you've already created a keychain (or if one has been created for you, which may have happened if you're using the Multiple Users feature), then you'll probably see a dialog box asking you for your keychain password when you open the Keychain Access control panel.

If you haven't created a keychain before, you can create one. Here's how:

1. Open the Keychain Access control panel.

2. If you haven't created a keychain, you'll see a dialog box asking if you'd like to create one. Click the Create button.

3. In the Create Keychain dialog box, enter a name for the keychain (for instance, your name) and a password. (You can press TAB to move between entry boxes.) You'll enter the password twice—once in the Password box and once in the Confirm box—to ensure that you type it the same way each time. Click Create.

The password you use should be at least six characters long and ideally include a mix of letters and numbers. If you create a password that the Keychain Access control panel determines isn't very secure, you may be asked to reconsider your password. (Click No and change your password.) Also, don't forget your password! There's no way to get into your keychain if you do.

View Your Keychain

You access your keychain or keychains by opening the Keychain Access control panel in Mac OS 9, or the Keychain Access application in Mac OS X (it's found in the Utilities folder inside the Applications folder). When you launch either of these, you'll see the Unlock Keychain dialog box if your keychain is locked. Choose your keychain from the Unlock Keychain pop-up menu, then enter your password for the keychain. Click the Unlock button and your keychain will be unlocked.

Once your keychain is unlocked (or if your keychain was already unlocked) Keychain Access opens the keychain's window. Now you can see the items that are stored on your keychain. (Shown is the Mac OS 9 version.)

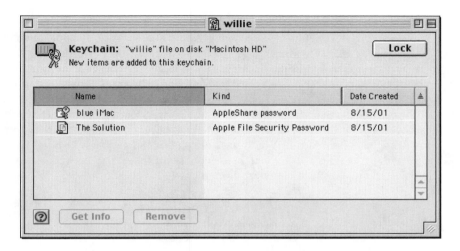

To learn more about an item, select it in the window and click the Get Info button. If you want to remove an item, select it and click Remove. If you'd like to lock your keychain, just click the Lock button. This immediately locks the keychain. The next time an application attempts to access it, the keychain will ask you for your password to ensure that you want the application to have access to your keychain.

In Mac OS X, you can add keychain items yourself—it's a convenient way to store passwords that you use for Web sites or applications that don't automatically add items to keychains. For instance, if you have a user name and password for accessing your credit card statement online, you can add those to the keychain. If your keychain is unlocked, you'll be able to access the password; if it's locked, then no one can see what your password is.

To add an item, you'll use an additional button, not pictured before—click Add. In the New Password Item window, enter a name for this item, an account name (if appropriate), and the password you're storing. Click Add and it's added to your keychain—in the future, if you need to remember this password, simply select this item in the keychain window and click Get Info.

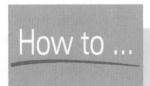 **Use the Keychain (and Encrypt Files)**

In Mac OS 9, you don't really add items to your keychain using the Keychain Access control panel, although in some cases you can drag items (like Internet location files) to Keychain Access. In the meantime, you'll generally add keychain items using applications. One that supports the keychain is the Network Browser, discussed in Chapter 28.

Another application that supports the keychain is Apple File Security, an application in Mac OS 9 that *encrypts* files in the Finder. (Apple File Security isn't yet available in Mac OS X.) Encryption is a process that turns the document into a jumble of nonsense, as far as any snooping eyes are concerned. Like an encrypted transmission between nations at war, it'll take a passphrase to get into this file. Without it, you won't be able to open this file.

Drag-and-drop a document or program onto the Apple File Security icon, located in the Applications folder on your iMac. (You can also CONTROL-click an item in the Finder and select Encrypt from the pop-up menu.) You'll see a dialog box asking you for a *passphrase,* which is the same thing as a password. Enter a password twice (press TAB between entries) and make sure the Add to Keychain option is selected.

When you click the Encrypt button, the file is encrypted. At the same time, the password for this item is stored on the keychain. Now, if you double-click the encrypted item in the Finder, you'll be asked for your keychain password if it's locked. Then, once unlocked, the password for this encrypted file is accessed automatically and the file is decrypted!

Set Keychain Options

You can also set some important preferences for your keychain using the Keychain Access control panel. Select Edit | *Name* Settings (where *Name* is the name you've given to your keychain). You may be asked to enter your keychain password. Now, in the Change Settings dialog box, you can change the password for your keychain. You can also turn on some options:

- ■ **Allow Access Without Warning** If this is turned on, applications will be able to immediately access your keychain if it's unlocked. If the option is turned off, you'll often see a dialog box that confirms that you want a particular application to have access to your keychain.

■ **Lock After Minutes of Inactivity**   Turn on this option and enter a number of minutes of system idle time the control panel should wait before automatically locking your keychain. I'd recommend turning on this option, especially in an office or organizational environment. If you forget to lock your password and you leave your workstation, then the keychain will be locked automatically after the idle time has passed.

■ **Lock When the System Sleeps**   Select this option if you'd like your keychain to lock itself whenever the system sleeps. That way you can simply put your iMac to sleep for increased security when you need to step away from it for a few minutes.

Click the Save button to save your changes in the Change Settings dialog box.

Chapter 25

Print Your Documents and Send Faxes

How to...

- ■ Choose your printer
- ■ Set up your Printer and iMac
- ■ Print documents and manage print jobs
- ■ Understand and add fonts to your iMac
- ■ Send and receive faxes from your iMac

You probably want to print stuff. Whether you already have an iMac-compatible printer, you're wondering if you can make your current printer iMac-compatible, or you're still in the shopping phase, let's take a look at your needs and figure out how to get you up and printing. It's actually pretty easy with an iMac, especially if you're able to buy a USB printer.

To begin, let's talk about the different types of printers you can get and what the advantages are of each. Then, we'll take a look at how you set up a printer and print to it. Later we'll discuss fonts, as well as how to send and receive faxes.

Choose a Printer

There are two major types of printers that are used in the home, home office, or most businesses and organizations: laser and inkjet.

Inkjet printers tend to be less expensive, they can generally print in color, and, depending on the model, they can offer good-to-exceptional print quality. Inkjets can be slightly easier to set up than laser printers, but they rely strongly on their own software drivers, whereas most laser printers use a driver written by Apple that integrates well with the Mac OS. At this time, many inkjets don't have full-featured Mac OS X drivers, so you'll want to shop carefully if you're printing from Mac OS X.

Laser printers are often faster and quieter than inkjets. Most inexpensive lasers don't print in color and laser printers tend to be more expensive at the outset. Many laser printers will connect to an iMac using the Ethernet port, making it easy to share the printer with a number of different iMacs or other computers. Laser printers tend to have more professional-level options—paper trays and envelope feeders, for instance. And laser printers that use the PostScript printer language are preferred for professional-level printing.

If you're trying to decide between the two, probably the most important considerations are your volume of printing, the need for color, and the desired quality of black-and-white printing. If you expect to print hundreds or thousands of pages a month—or if you'll be in situations where you need to quickly print 20- to 100-page documents and send them somewhere—then you'll likely want a laser printer. You'll also want a laser printer for a lower cost-per-page over the long term. And you'll want a laser if you print many important documents that are mostly text and require no color.

Inkjet technology has improved remarkably and you can get a good color printer for less than $150. Inkjet printers are great if you run a small business and plan to print brochures, signs, menus, thank you notes, invitations, overhead slides, and so forth. While not always workhorses for hundreds of pages per month, an inkjet printer provides flexible printing with a variety of options. Look for an inkjet that accepts a number of different types of paper and transparencies, especially if you plan to make full use of color on business cards, overhead slides, and photos.

If you want to share one printer between two or more computers, a laser or high-end inkjet printer with an Ethernet connection is best, as it allows the printer to be an independent entity on your network. (It also tends to make the printer much more expensive.) Most USB printers, however, can be shared between Macs using Apple's USB Printer Sharing technology, the only downside being that the Mac connected to the printer must be left on.

25

Connect the Printer to Your iMac

Printers also offer a variety of ways that they can be connected to your iMac. There are two ways to directly connect to an iMac—by USB and by a network (either Ethernet or wireless). In the case of USB, you should be able to connect the printer directly to an available USB port on your iMac using an "A-to-B" USB cable.

Laser printers will often connect via Ethernet, although how you're connecting dictates the type of Ethernet cable you need. If you're only connecting the laser printer to your iMac, you'll need an Ethernet *crossover* cable, which is designed to allow two Ethernet devices to talk to one another. Connect the cable to your iMac's Ethernet port and to the Ethernet port on the printer.

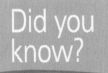

All-in-One Printers

Once virtually non-existent in the Mac market, all-in-one or multifunction printers (that include scanning, copying, and often fax capabilities) now abound from manufacturers such as Canon, Epson, HP, and Lexmark. Usually for less than a scanner and a printer separately, you can get a single box that performs all those tasks for your home or small office.

So should you? Keeping in mind the adage "jack of all trades, master of none," a multifunction printer can be a good investment, with a few caveats. First, these devices are highly dependent on driver software, although they may have drivers for Mac OS 9, it may take a while before drivers specifically written for Mac OS X are available. Second, some multifunction devices offer fewer features for Macs than for PCs, so read the box (and Mac-oriented magazine reviews) carefully. Finally, consider whether you want to pay extra for the ability to copy or fax without having your iMac powered on—devices with standalone features tend to be pricier, but more convenient and better performers, making them a good fit in a busy small office setting.

You'll need an Ethernet hub and a standard Ethernet *patch* cable if you plan to use the laser printer with more than one computer. You can do that easily with all the devices plugged into the hub; all the computers (especially if they're Macs and compatible with the printer) will be able to "see" and connect to the printer once you've set them up properly.

If you have an older printer designed for a Mac, it may not have either USB or Ethernet ports. In that case, you're dealing with either a LocalTalk printer (one that could be networked using LocalTalk cabling) or a direct serial printer designed to connect to the Printer or Modem port on older Macs. For those types of printers, you'll need an adapter that enables you to connect the printer to one of your iMac's ports. Table 25-1 shows a listing of adapter manufacturers.

NOTE   *These adapters will often work with Mac OS 9, because the printer driver software for the older printer can run in Mac OS 9. In Mac OS X, however, most serial printers are completely unsupported because their printer driver software hasn't been updated for Mac OS X. (Many LocalTalk printers are supported, particularly if they are PostScript printers.)*

Printer Languages

Printers can use different languages for describing a page. If your printer uses the PostScript language, then it's generally capable of more graphically complex pages. Professional publishers tend to use PostScript-language printers for their high-end printing needs. A PostScript-language printer includes a special processor, its own RAM, and some PostScript Type 1 fonts built into the printer itself. In this case, a program that wants to print to the printer simply sends a series of PostScript commands to tell the printer how the document should be printed. Then, the printer does all the work using its own processor to create the printed page.

Many inkjet printers use a different language, the Printer Control Language (PCL), a standard originated by Hewlett-Packard Corporation. In this case, the printer requires a special driver so that your iMac can speak the PCL language, create the page, and send it to the printer in the proper format. Your iMac does all of the processing, which is why inkjet printing can be slower than laser printing; it's also why most inkjet printers are cheaper, since they don't have their own processor, RAM, and so on—they rely on the iMac for all that.

Manufacturer	Adapter(s)	Web Site
Belkin	USB-to-serial	**http://www.belkin.com**
Keyspan	USB-to-serial	**http://www.keyspan.com**
New Motion	USB-to-serial	**http://www.newmotiontech.com**
Proxim	USB-to-LocalTalk USB-to-serial	**http://www.proxim.com**

TABLE 25-1   Printer Adapter Manufacturers and Their Web Sites

This situation is also why inkjet printers (and many USB-based laser printers) need to have special driver software written for them, while PostScript-language printers, even if they aren't specifically designed to be Mac-compatible, often work just fine using the built-in LaserWriter driver discussed later in this chapter.

> NOTE   *Earlier non-PostScript printers were made specifically for Macs using the QuickDraw printer language. For instance, HP's DeskWriter series in the mid-1990s, although nearly identical to the DeskJet series, used QuickDraw instead of PCL for the Mac version. These days that's much less common, especially for USB-based printers.*

Set Up Your Printer and iMac

You've seen a number of different ways to attach an iMac and a printer, including special adapters and cables. In most of those cases, you'll either connect the printer directly to a USB port on your iMac or you'll connect the printer via Ethernet.

The next step is to tell your Mac about the printer and assign it a printer driver. If you have a USB or serial-adapted printer, you'll use an individual printer driver from the manufacturer. (If your printer came with a CD-ROM, run that CD's installation program first to install the software driver.) If you have a laser printer that's connected via Ethernet, you'll likely use the LaserWriter driver that's built into both Mac OS 9 and Mac OS X.

In Mac OS 9, you'll use the Chooser, accessed from the Apple menu, to set up the printer; in Mac OS X, you'll launch the Print Center, which is located in the Utilities folder inside the main Application folder.

How to ...   Use a PC Printer

Need to print to a PC printer that has a parallel port? With a product called PowerPrint USB from Strydent Software (**http://www.strydent.com/**), it's possible to connect a parallel-port PC printer—either an inkjet or a non-PostScript laser printer—to your iMac, using the USB-to-PC parallel port adapter and special driver software for Mac OS 9.

PowerPrint works with Canon, Epson, Lexmark, and NEC printers as well as HP's LaserJet and DeskJet series. During the installation process choose the type of printer drivers you want to install, or a generic set of drivers, if appropriate.

After the installation is complete, simply access the printer's driver in the Chooser as discussed later in this chapter. The printer is treated the same as if it were a regular Mac-compatible printer.

Choose a USB Printer

In Mac OS 9, with the Chooser open and your printer driver installed, you'll set up the printer by selecting its driver on the left-hand side of the window. The driver will have the printer's name (or the printer's class, if the same driver is used for different printers), such as DeskJet 880, USB LaserJet, Epson 740, or something similar.

Hopefully, your iMac will find the connection to the printer and display it on the right side of the Chooser, where you'll see a small icon and the printer's name. (It's also possible you'll see a Printer Port symbol if you're using an adapter.)

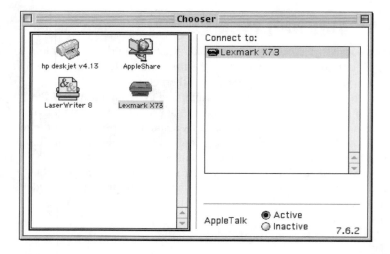

When you've selected the connection, click the Setup button (if one appears) to set basic printer preferences. Otherwise, just click the Close box and your printer is set. In most cases, a new printer icon will appear on the desktop.

NOTE *If your particular printer's driver doesn't appear in the Chooser, then you may not have installed it. Printer drivers are installed right in the Extensions folder in your System Folder, just in case you want to look for them. Your printer may also require some other support files in the Extensions or Control Panels folder.*

In Mac OS X, you'll need to add the printer in the Print Center. If the Add Printer dialog sheet doesn't appear automatically, select Printer | Add Printer. Use the pop-up menu to select USB. Now, you should see a listing of any USB printers that are attached to your iMac.

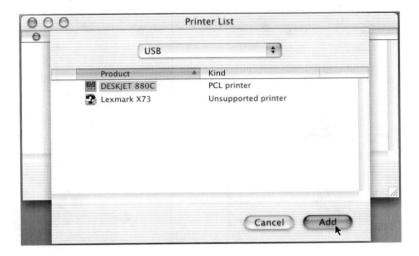

If a driver isn't installed for the printer, you'll see "Unsupported Printer" in the Kind column. You'll need to locate or download a Mac OS X native driver and install it. If the printer is recognized, simply select it in the sheet and click Add. Now you can close the Printer List or quit the Print Center.

> NOTE   *Mac OS X has basic drivers for Canon, HP, and Epson inkjets built in. For more features and better printing, check the manufacturer for an updated, full-function driver for your printer.*

Choose an Ethernet Printer

If your printer is connected via Ethernet, either using a crossover cable or plugged directly into an Ethernet hub, setting up the printer is usually very simple.

In Mac OS 9, open the Chooser and select the LaserWriter 8 printer driver (or the driver you specially installed for your laser printer). Now, on the right side of the Chooser window, select the printer you want to use. In cases where your iMac resides on a large network, you may see more than one choice.

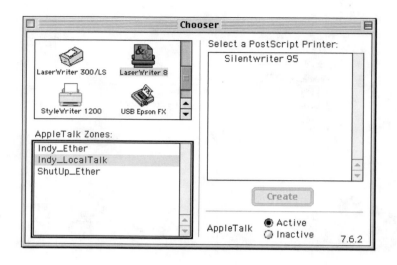

Not all networks will have the AppleTalk zones pictured here. If yours doesn't, you'll simply see all available PostScript printers when you click the LaserWriter 8 driver. If your network does have zones, you may need to select the appropriate zone for the printer you want to print to. Ask your system administrator for details.

Select the PostScript printer and click the Create button. This allows you to create (or use) a PostScript Printer Description (PPD) file that can be used to control this printer.

If you believe you have a PPD installed for this printer (PPD files are stored in the Extensions folder inside the System Folder), then you can choose Select PPD and search for it. If not, then you're best off choosing Auto Setup where the LaserWriter driver will help you decide what the printer is capable of. You can get information about the printer by clicking the Get Info button. If you have your printer manual around and you want to set some options for your particular printer, click the Configure button. Otherwise, click OK.

Now, close the Chooser. When you do, your desktop printer icon for this printer will appear.

If you don't see your printer when you select the LaserWriter 8 driver in the Chooser, you may need to turn on AppleTalk in the Chooser or in the AppleTalk control panel. If the printer is a TCP/IP-based printer, you'll need to use the Desktop Printer Utility (located in the LaserWriter Software folder, inside the Apple Extras folder inside the Applications [Mac OS 9] folder) to configure it.

In Mac OS X, you connect to the Ethernet printer in the Print Center. Once it is launched, select Printer | Add Printer. In the dialog sheet, choose AppleTalk from the pop-up menu if you're attempting to connect to an AppleTalk printer, or select LPR Printers using IP if you have an IP-only Ethernet printer.

If you choose AppleTalk, your next step will be to select the printer and click Add. (Again, if your AppleTalk network has zones, you'll select the appropriate zone where the printer is located in the Local AppleTalk Zone pop-up menu.)

NOTE   *If you don't see your printer, you may need to launch the Network pane of System Preferences, select the AppleTalk tab, and turn on AppleTalk for your iMac's built-in Ethernet port.*

If you choose to configure an LPR Printer, you'll need to know the IP address for the printer. (If you're not sure about this number, ask your system administrator or whoever set up the printer.) Enter it in the Line Printer's Address entry box, then choose a PPD for the printer from the Printer Model pop-up menu. Click Add to add the printer.

Print Stuff and Manage Print Jobs

Once you have your printer set up, you're ready to print. Before you send the page to the printer, though, you may want to check the options in Page Setup, so that you know everything is set up correctly.

Then, after you've invoked the Print command and sent the print job to the printer, it's passed to either the print spooler or the desktop printer. In the case of a spooler in Mac OS 9, you'll simply see its entry in the Application menu—you can switch to it if desired to see your progress. (In Mac OS X, this is handled by the Print Center application.) If your print driver uses a desktop printer in Mac OS 9, you can manage the print job from there.

Page Setup

When you've created a document and you're ready to print it, begin by choosing File | Page Setup. That brings up the Page Setup dialog box, shown in Figure 25-1.

Actually, you don't need to visit this dialog box every time you plan to print—only when you need to change a major option for your printer or when you've recently changed printers (while the application was open) and you need the application to recognize the new printer. But it's also where you set some important options, which can vary somewhat between print drivers and between Mac OS 9 and Mac OS X:

- **Page (or Paper) Size**   Choose what size paper the application should plan on printing to. (The default is 8.5 × 11-inch paper.)

- **Scaling or Scale**   Enter a percentage if you'd like the document to be printed at anything other than 100 percent.

■ **Orientation**   Choose whether the document should be printed in Portrait mode (regular orientation on the page) or in Landscape mode (lengthwise, as with ledger sheets).

■ **Settings Menu or Options**   If the Page Setup window has a Settings menu, an untitled pop-up menu, or an Options button, select it to see the options that it may provide that are unique to your particular printer model.

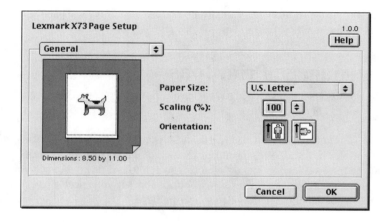

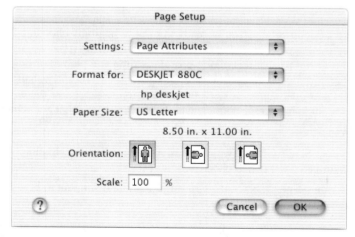

FIGURE 25-1   On the top, Page Setup in Mac OS 9; on the bottom, Page Setup in Mac OS X

When you've finished making changes, click OK in the Page Setup dialog box.

Select Print

When you've made your Page Setup choices, you're ready to print. In general, Mac OS 9 and Mac OS X offer similar Print dialog boxes, as you can see from Figure 25-2. In some cases, you'll find an oddball Print dialog box in Mac OS 9, particularly with a USB printer that has a third-party printer driver. In Mac OS X, the Print dialog boxes tend to be pretty uniform.

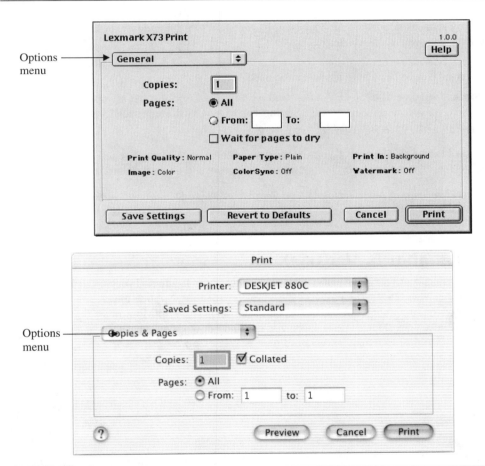

FIGURE 25-2   On the top, the Print dialog box in Mac OS 9; on the bottom, Mac OS X's standard Print dialog box

Note that most Print dialog boxes have an untitled options menu (it defaults to General or Copies & Pages in many cases) that enables you to choose different settings options. Here's a look at some of those options:

- **Printer** At the top of many dialog boxes, you'll find a Printer menu where you can select the printer you'd like to use for this document.

- **General or Copies and Pages** Here you can enter the number of copies you want to print and choose the range of pages that you want printed. (Remember that the number is inclusive, so printing from pages 2 to 4 will include both page 2 and page 4.)

- **Print or Quality Modes** Many inkjet printers will enable you to choose different quality settings depending on how quickly you want to print and how laser-like in quality you want the final output.

- **Color** Choose whether or not you want a color document printed in color and whether you want a color matching system to be used.

- **Application-Specific** You'll often find a category of options that are specific to the application you're printing from, enabling you to make different decisions based on that application's document types and capabilities.

When you're done making all of your printing selections, click Print. The job is sent to the printer and you've nothing left to do but monitor its progress and await the output.

NOTE *Most Print dialog boxes have a Saved Settings or Make Default option that enables you to store the changes you've just made for future use. If you find yourself making the same changes all the time, save those changes for quicker access.*

The PrintMonitor in Mac OS 9

Once the print job is sent, you'll probably hear the printer come to life and prepare to feed paper and print. In Mac OS 9, you may also see a new entry in the Applications menu called the PrintMonitor (or something similar, like Epson Monitor). The PrintMonitor works in the background to allow your iMac to print while you continue to work on other things. You can also use the PrintMonitor to manage your print jobs.

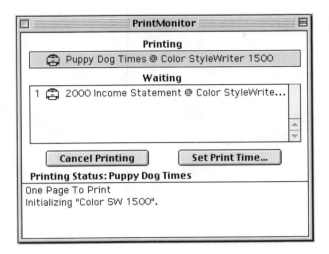

Using the PrintMonitor, you can view the print jobs that have been sent to the printer; if you've sent more than one document to the printer, each appears in the PrintMonitor queue, with the current job at the top. Select a print job and click Cancel Printing to clear the job from the print queue, or click Set Print Time to schedule the print job to print sometime in the future.

While the PrintMonitor is open you can also select File | Stop Printing to suspend printing for the moment. If you'd like to continue printing, select File | Resume Printing.

The Desktop Printer

Many Mac-compatible inkjet printers and Ethernet laser printers will create a desktop printer icon that you can use to manage your print jobs in Mac OS 9. It works a lot like the PrintMonitor, but is a little friendlier and a little more powerful.

Once you've sent a print job to the printer, you should see your desktop printer icon change to reflect the fact that it has a document that's ready to be printed.

If you need to, you can manage that print job by double-clicking the desktop icon to open the print queue window, where you can see the scheduled print jobs.

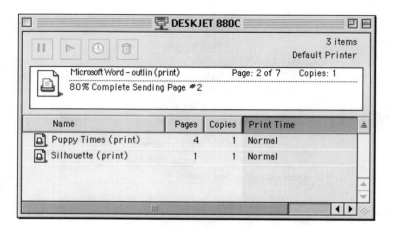

Select a print job in this window, then use the controls at the top of the window to control it—you can pause a job, start it again, give it higher priority, schedule the print job, or delete it.

> **TIP** *Dragging a print job from the queue list to the current print job window will change its priority to Urgent, moving it to the top of the queue.*

You'll also notice that while the desktop printer queue is open, there's another command menu in the Finder's menu bar—the Printing menu. Pull it down and select Stop Print Queue to halt all printing; choose Start Print Queue to continue printing. Click the Close box to close the queue window and the printer will continue printing in the background.

> **SHORTCUT** *If you have more than one desktop printer, then you don't have to return to the Chooser to switch between them. A small printer icon appears on the menu bar, very near the Application menu in the top-right corner. Click that icon and you'll get a menu where you can change the active printer.*

Print Center

In Mac OS X, you can monitor current print jobs using the Print Center application. Once launched, you can double-click an active printer to see its queue window. In that window, you'll see the status of current jobs, as well as the current job that's printing, shown at the top of the window.

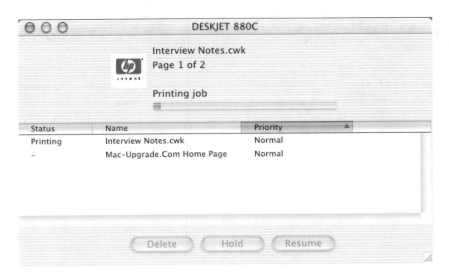

To hold a job, select it and click Hold; other jobs will continue printing. To release that particular document, select it again and click Resume. To delete a job (so that document won't print), select it and click Delete. To stop the entire queue, choose Queue | Stop Queue from the menu; to start it again, select Queue | Start Queue.

Understand and Add Fonts to Your iMac

A *font* is a collection of letters, numbers, and punctuation marks with a particular typeface, weight (bold or not bold), and size in plain or italic. However, the word "font" is also frequently used to mean a typeface with a particular design, such as Courier or Arial. I'll use the term "font" loosely.

When you select a font the application passes that information to the Mac OS, which helps the application render that font. Fonts in Mac OS 9 are stored in a subfolder of your System Folder called the Fonts folder; Mac OS X has a few different folders where fonts can be stored.

The font files serve two purposes. First, font files tell your printer how printed text should appear. Second, they tell your iMac how to display text on the screen.

Add Fonts in Mac OS 9 and Classic

You can buy both TrueType and PostScript Type 1 fonts from computer stores or online computer sales outlets—any such fonts should work fine with your iMac. To add a font for your iMac's applications, just drag-and-drop the font file onto the System Folder icon.

A dialog box will appear telling you that this file will automatically be added to the Fonts folder. Click OK.

> **NOTE** *If you're using PostScript Type 1 fonts with Mac OS 9, you should have Adobe Type Manager (ATM) installed and working on your iMac. ATM is a control panel that's installed along with Adobe Acrobat Reader, so by default, your iMac should have it active. If you have Mac OS 9 installed on your iMac, you'll need ATM Lite or higher; older versions are incompatible. Mac OS X has its own rendering engine and doesn't require ATM.*

Fonts in Mac OS 9 can either be stored loose in the Fonts folder, or they can be saved in a special kind of folder called a *suitcase*. Because there's a limit of 128 items in the Fonts folder, a suitcase can be used to get around that minimum by, for instance, grouping all the Times New Roman fonts (TrueType and bitmap versions) in the same suitcase.

Arial Black

You can also use suitcases for organization—drag as many fonts as you want to into a suitcase and name it "Special Design Fonts" or something similar. Now, drag this suitcase into the Fonts folder before you launch QuarkXPress, GraphicConverter, or another application that you use with these fonts. At other times when you're working in regular applications, you can store the font suitcase in a different folder on your iMac, so that those fonts aren't used. The fewer fonts you have active, the faster your applications will run. If you open the Fonts folder, you'll see that many of the fonts are already stored in suitcases.

Double-click a suitcase and you can drag-and-drop fonts in and out of the suitcase. The best way to create your own suitcase is to create a duplicate of an existing suitcase and rename it. (You'll also want to delete the fonts in your duplicate suitcase by dragging them to the Trash.)

> **SHORTCUT** *If you'll deal with fonts a lot, you might clean out a duplicate suitcase and save it as your "master" suitcase. You can duplicate your master suitcase whenever you need a new suitcase. This way, you won't have to clean out the fonts every time.*

The renamed suitcase can now store font files. Just drag all fonts for that suitcase—both bitmap and TrueType fonts, if you've got them—onto the suitcase icon.

Note that you need to manage fonts in the System Folder's Fonts folder for both Mac OS 9 and the Classic environment within Mac OS X; however, the Finder in Mac OS X won't let you open font suitcases, so you'll need to boot into Mac OS 9 to manage fonts for Classic applications.

Add Fonts in Mac OS X

In Mac OS X, fonts can be stored in a number of different places. If you'd like to add fonts that everyone can use, copy the font files to the Fonts folder inside the main Library folder on your hard disk. If you'd like to install fonts for your own personal use, install them in the Fonts folder that's inside the Library folder inside your home folder. Ideally, Mac OS X applications are updated instantly with font changes, but in practice many applications need to be restarted.

25

Fonts in the Classic System Folder are also recognized and made available in native Mac OS X applications. So if you intend to use fonts (aside from bitmapped fonts, which aren't recognized in Mac OS X) in both environments, you can install them in the Mac OS 9 Fonts folder.

Mac OS X also supports a different type of font, called an OpenType font. This is actually a hybrid of PostScript and TrueType technologies, and it's likely the font of the future. To install an OpenType font, simply drag it to one of the Mac OS X Fonts folders (in the main Library folder or in your personal Library folder) and it's ready to be used.

Delete Fonts

To delete a font, just open the Fonts folder and drag the font (or suitcase) to the Trash.

It's a good idea to think carefully before deleting a font file, because you can't always anticipate when an application or document might need that particular font. If you want to simply deactivate a font, drag it to a folder outside of the System Folder or the Library folder where it's been stored. (Create a "Disabled Fonts" folder on your hard disk, for instance.) Now that font won't appear in the Font menu of any of your applications. If you get error messages requiring the use of a disabled font, you can still drag the font back into the Fonts folder if it's needed.

Remember, too, that many of the files in the Classic Fonts folder are actually suitcases that have more than one font inside of them (usually, but not always, in the same typeface family). If you don't want to delete the entire suitcase, you can double-click the suitcase to open it, then drag the font files to the Trash individually.

Fax with Your iMac

Your iMac comes bundled with a program called FaxSTF that makes it possible—perhaps even easy—to send and receive faxes in Mac OS 9. All you have to do is plug your modem into the telephone line and make some basic preference settings. The rest of it should be set up and ready to use.

At the time of writing, FaxSTF for Mac OS X isn't yet bundled with iMacs, although that may be the plan for the future.

Send a Fax

Obviously, your iMac, right out of the box, doesn't offer the full functionality of a fax machine, since it doesn't have a mechanism for feeding pages to fax into your iMac so you can send them along. If you have a scanner (see Chapter 26), you can replace your fax machine. Without one, you're relegated to sending documents that you create—in AppleWorks, Microsoft Word, QuarkXPress, Adobe PhotoDeluxe, or other programs—to distant fax machines. In that sense, faxing is just a substitute for printing.

In fact, that's how it works on your iMac. While you're viewing a document you want to fax, hold down ⌘-OPTION while selecting the File menu. If your fax software is working, you won't find a Print command on the menu. Instead, you'll see a Fax command. Select it and you'll see the FaxPrint dialog box.

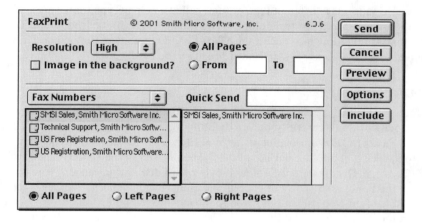

In the dialog box, choose the resolution of the fax, which pages to send, and so on. (A low-resolution fax will send a bit quicker but look worse at the other end.) Then, select your recipient from the list of names and drag it to the Destinations window pane. If your recipient isn't listed, add him or her through the FaxSTF Browser (discussed in the next section). You can add a fax number by selecting Temporary Address or New Entry from the Fax Numbers pull-down menu. Then, fill out the dialog box and click ENTER.

With your addressee chosen, click Send. (You can click Preview, first, if you'd like to see what your fax will look like.) After you click Send, your modem will dial the number for the distant fax machine and transmit the fax. You'll see the Fax Status window, apprising you of the success or failure of the connection.

Receive a Fax

FaxSTF, unfortunately, doesn't have an option that allows you to manually accept a fax. In order to have your iMac receive a fax, you'll need to configure the FaxSTF Browser application to listen for the phone ringing. Here's how:

1. First, launch the FaxSTF Browser, which is located in the FaxSTF folder inside the Applications (Mac OS 9) folder.

2. With the browser open, select Edit | Preferences.

3. Select the Fax Modem icon on the left side of the dialog box or select Fax Modem from the Panel menu, depending on your FaxSTF version.

4. Locate and open the Answer On menu and choose the number of rings the fax software should wait before it picks up the phone line.

5. Click OK.

Now the iMac will answer after the designated number of rings and attempt to receive a fax, if one is incoming. When the iMac detects a call on the line, you'll see the Fax Status window appear to tell you if a fax has connected and is being transmitted. The Fax Status window includes a Stop button, which will allow you to stop an attempted connection, just in case you decide it's a person on the line that you need to speak with.

Received faxes appear in the FaxSTF Browser window. First, launch the FaxSTF Browser, which is located in the FaxSTF folder inside the Applications (Mac OS 9) folder. On the left side of the window, select the Fax In folder and a list of received faxes will appear on the right side of the window.

To view a fax, double-click it. It'll appear in its own window. From there, you can print the fax using the File | Print command. You can also use the Action menu to alter the fax somewhat, making it look better, print faster, or align correctly.

25

Did you know?

Receive Faxes Online

A number of different fax services such as j2 Communications (**www.j2.com**) and eFax (**www.efax.com**) enable you to receive faxes as e-mail attachments. When you sign up, the service assigns you a phone number, which you can give out to friends and colleagues or clients. (Often you'll pay a premium to get a phone number in your area code or a toll-free number.) When someone sends a fax to that number, the fax is turned into an image file and sent to you via e-mail. You can then double-click the image and, in some cases, view it in an application such as GraphicConverter (**www.lemkesoft.com**). In the case of eFax, there's a special Macintosh application that runs in Mac OS 9 or the Classic environment, enabling you to view or print the fax.

Chapter 26

Upgrade Your iMac

How to…

- ▪ Install applications
- ▪ Run DOS and Windows programs
- ▪ Add USB and FireWire peripherals to your iMac
- ▪ Add a removable drive
- ▪ Add a CD-R or CD-RW drive
- ▪ Add speakers or a USB microphone
- ▪ Upgrade the RAM in your slot-loading iMac
- ▪ Install the AirPort card in your slot-loading iMac

When the iMac was introduced back in 1998, one of the revolutionary gambles Apple took was abandoning older *port* technologies in favor of two simple Universal Serial Bus (USB) ports. USB ports were faster than those they replaced, and less troublesome, but the market for USB devices (printers, keyboards, CD burners, and so on) was small. Fortunately, it worked out tremendously, as the iMac's success drove the market for USB devices, and hundreds of peripherals are available for the iMac.

In addition to USB, nearly all slot-loading iMac models also offer another option for upgrading—*FireWire*. FireWire ports offer very high-speed data transfer with similar convenience to USB, making FireWire perfect for certain demanding devices, such as digital camcorders, high-speed external disks, and removable storage drives.

If you absolutely must connect older peripherals that don't support USB or FireWire, that's possible, too. You simply need the right adapter for the job. We'll take a look at all those options in this chapter, as well as the steps for installing applications and driver software.

> **NOTE** *This chapter doesn't cover printers, although many of them use a USB port on your iMac. See Chapter 25 for information on installing and configuring a printer.*

Install Your Own Applications

While the iMac comes pre-installed with a host of applications—as evidenced by the middle section of this book—you'll eventually come across a reason to install some of your own. Generally, installation is simple—you launch an installer application, choose a disk and/or a folder for the application, then let the installer do its work.

Depending on the operating system you're using, however, there is an important caveat or two. In Mac OS 9, Apple has added more structure to the folders than in previous versions. So, it's recommended that you install applications in the Applications (Mac OS 9) folder that appears on the hard disk. This is also true if you're installing a Carbon application—one that can run in either Mac OS 9 or Mac OS X. Note that this isn't a hard-and-fast rule—you can install applications anywhere on a Mac OS 9 system and they'll work fine. But for the sake of uniformity and for the best results in Mac OS X, using the Applications (Mac OS 9) folder is a good idea.

Installing in Mac OS X can be more demanding due to its multiuser nature. If you're the original user of your iMac and/or you have administrator privileges, you can use an installer application to install native Mac OS X programs in the main Applications folder (or in a subfolder such as the Utilities folder). Once installed here, the applications are made available to all users on your iMac, regardless of their privilege level. If you're installing an application that you don't want or need to share with other users on the iMac, you can install that application in your personal home folder, or in a subfolder within your home folder. (You can create a subfolder called My Applications, for instance.)

> NOTE   *Mac OS X's reliance on privileges means that only administrator-level users can install software in the main folders, such as Applications and Library. The first user created on your iMac is an administrative user, so if you remember the password you used in the Setup Assistant, you can install applications that require a password. See Chapter 27 for more details on creating and using administrator accounts.*

With some installers, you won't have much choice—the standard Package Installer built into Mac OS X generally requires an administrator's password and will automatically install in the main Applications folder. With other applications, you simply drag-and-drop the application to a folder for which you have write privileges. The third case is the typical third-party installer, which will enable you to pick your target folder, often by choosing a Select Folder option in the installer.

Now you'll see a standard Open dialog box, where you can choose the folder where you'd like the application installed.

> NOTE   *Many downloadable applications come as disk images, which you first double-click to mount on the desktop, as if they were removable disks. Then you double-click the mounted "disk" and launch the installer, or drag-and-drop the application onto your own hard disk. Disk images are discussed in Chapter 20.*

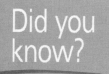

Run DOS and Windows Applications

Have a need to run an application that hasn't been written for Mac OS 9 or Mac OS X? If it's compatible with Microsoft DOS or Windows versions (or, for that matter, Linux) you may be able to run it using a product called VirtualPC, from Connectix (**www.connectix.com**). Virtual PC runs as an application on iMacs (in either Mac OS 9 or Mac OS X), but it emulates a Windows-compatible PC. Then, depending on the version you buy, you can use Virtual PC to run Windows 98, ME, 2000, and later. You can also opt to install different versions of Linux on VirtualPC or a straight PC-DOS configuration, if desired. For more information, visit Connectix's site, as well as MacWindows.com, an excellent site for information about integrating Mac and Windows applications and computers, hosted by one of this book's technical editors, John Rizzo.

Upgrade with USB and FireWire

All iMacs include USB ports for upgrading. USB is a technology designed to allow other technologies that have traditionally been connected to Macs via "serial" ports to connect to a faster, more modern equivalent. The connector, the speeds, and the methods of connection have all been updated.

iMac DV and later slot-loading iMac models also include FireWire ports, another technology that enables you to easily and quickly hook up peripherals. FireWire is much faster than USB, meaning it's better suited for devices that transfer a lot of data to and from your iMac. Those devices include hard disks, removable drives, scanners, and similar devices.

Why USB?

USB offers three major improvements over the serial ports that have been used in both Windows-based PCs and older Macintosh computers for nearly two decades:

- **Speed**   Each USB bus on an iMac can transfer data up to 12 megabits per second, or over 12,000 kilobits per second. USB is fast enough for external removable disks and other devices that require reasonably high-speed connections.

NOTE *On slot-loading iMac and iMac G4 models, there are two USB buses so that the ports' capabilities are better distributed. On earlier iMacs, that 12 megabits per second is shared by their two USB ports, which means a device on one port can slow down a device on the other port if they're both in use at the same time.*

■ **Ease of Use**   Aside from being *hot-swappable* (meaning you can plug and unplug devices without damaging them or your iMac), USB ports can also provide power to some peripherals, which means fewer of them require their own power cords and adapters.

■ **Device Support**   USB can support up to 127 devices per bus, as long as those devices don't mind sharing the connection. That means you'll easily be able to hook up a scanner, joystick, printer, Zip drive, digital camera, mouse, keyboard, and most anything else without much trouble.

> NOTE   *On slot-loading iMacs and iMac G4 models, each USB bus can support 127 devices, and there are two buses. So, just in case you need to hook up 254 devices, you're set.*

With these improvements you can see why USB is a boon for the iMac—not only is it quick and extensible, but it's also simple to use.

26

Why FireWire?

If you have a slot-loading iMac, you have FireWire ports available for connecting devices to your iMac. FireWire is very fast compared to most other external port technologies. FireWire can transfer data at up to 400 megabits per second, which is quite a bit more than USB, older serial ports, or even external SCSI ports. That makes FireWire ideal not only for connecting external DV camcorders, but also for high-speed devices like external hard disks and removable disk drives.

FireWire is just as easy to hook up as USB, with up to 63 devices supported between the two ports. FireWire, like USB, can supply power to external devices, when necessary, meaning even some hard drives don't require a wall plug. And, unlike USB, FireWire devices don't require a hub—you can actually *daisy-chain* them together by plugging one device into the iMac, the next device into the first device, and so on. USB, by contrast, requires a hub.

> NOTE   *While FireWire hubs are available, hubs aren't necessary for FireWire devices; they're simply convenient. A FireWire hub allows you to connect and disconnect FireWire devices without affecting other devices. If you have devices arranged in a daisy chain, disconnecting one of them may interrupt others on the chain until you get the whole thing plugged back in again.*

The real advantage, though, is choice. With a FireWire-supporting iMac model, you can choose to buy higher-speed peripheral devices that use FireWire for best performance. Then, you'll also have USB ports available for Zip drives, input devices, and other lower-performance external devices. You've got the best of both worlds!

USB Ports and Hubs

Your iMac has two USB ports. One of those ports probably has your iMac's keyboard plugged into it, with a mouse plugged into the keyboard.

That leaves one port open on the keyboard and one port open on the side of the iMac. After a rough count, that's two ports available for devices. Hardly comes close to 127 (or 254, for slot-loading iMacs), does it?

In order to use more than two devices, you'll need to get a device called a *USB hub*. This device will probably have its own AC adapter so it can provide power to the USB ports. It'll also have four, eight, or more USB ports that you can use for additional devices (see Figure 26-1).

Hubs are reasonably inexpensive, but you won't even need one until you have more than two additional devices for your iMac—one can plug into the keyboard, which is a passive hub in its own right (it doesn't supply power), and the other can plug directly into the iMac. If all you have is a printer and a joystick, for instance, you might plug the joystick into your keyboard and the printer into your iMac's side. Once you get more than two devices, though, it's hub time.

A number of vendors sell hubs. Here's a partial list of the vendors and their Web sites:

Asante	**http://www.asante.com/**
Belkin Components	**http://www.belkin.com/**
CompuCable	**http://www.compucable.com/**
MacAlly	**http://www.macally.com/**
Xircom	**http://www.xircom.com/**

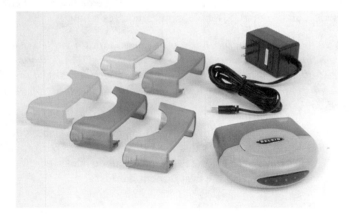

FIGURE 26-1   With USB, hubs are necessary to connect more than one device to a single USB port. (Photo courtesy Belkin Components.)

Install a USB or FireWire Device

Some USB and FireWire devices require drivers that are placed in the Extensions folder, in Mac OS 9, and used whenever the device is connected and recognized by the Mac OS. For Mac OS X, USB devices will sometimes require a special driver, called a *kernel driver,* that needs to be installed using the manufacturer's installation application. Keyboards and mice don't necessarily require drivers (plug them in and they should work), although they will require special drivers in some cases—for example, to program more than one mouse button or to remap the Windows keys (the Microsoft Windows-specific keys on some keyboards) to the Mac's special ⌘ command keys. All of these require special driver software.

The normal game plan with external devices is to install the driver software, then connect your device to the iMac. If all goes well, your device will be recognized and the driver will be properly loaded and used with the device. (This can sometimes appear to freeze the iMac while the driver gets situated. You should always wait a few seconds after you've plugged in a device before you panic.) In other cases, you may need to restart your iMac in order for the device to be recognized. If the device is a game controller that uses Game Sprockets drivers in Mac OS 9, you won't be able to use the device until you're playing a game that supports Game Sprockets. (See Chapter 16.)

In order to use many USB and FireWire products reliably, your iMac needs the latest software, Mac OS, and iMac firmware updates. (This is especially true in two cases—older iMacs and any iMac running Mac OS X, which is still improving USB and FireWire support.) See Chapter 29 for more on updating your iMac.

Add a Mouse, Keyboard, or Controller

All controllers and input devices use USB for their connection, since FireWire is overkill for a mouse, keyboard, or controller. Mice and keyboards are generally the easiest devices to add—in many cases, they don't even require special drivers. Apple's USB software has built into it some generic drivers that can recognize nearly any USB mouse or keyboard that's been plugged into an available USB port and use it easily.

In other cases, though, you will need a driver. This will usually come in the form of an extension or control panel, which you drag to the System Folder (in Mac OS 9) or install using the device's installer application (in Mac OS X). After you've restarted your iMac, you'll have access to the device. If the driver is a control panel, you can open that control panel to set preferences for the device.

Keyboards usually require even less customization, unless the keyboard has special features like a built-in pointing device. Some keyboards originally designed for Microsoft Windows require a special driver that allows their special command keys and other keys to be used as Mac OS equivalents. Although the keyboards are basically the same, the Mac OS recognizes the ⌘ and POWER keys, as well as the VOLUME and EJECT keys, making it a good idea to get Mac-compatible keyboards whenever possible. A number of companies offer unique pointing devices and keyboards for the iMac. Here are a few of those companies and what they offer:

Belkin	**http://www.belkin.com/**	Mouse, keyboard
CompuCable	**http://www.compucable.com/**	Mouse
Contour Design	**http://www.contourdesign.com/**	Mouse
Kensington	**http://www.kensington.com/**	Mouse, trackball
MacAlly	**http://www.macally.com/**	Mouse, keyboard, trackball, joystick
Microsoft	**http://www.microsoft.com/**	Mouse
Wacom	**http://www.wacom.com/**	Pen tablet

What's a pen tablet? It's a flat surface that allows you to use a pen for moving the mouse cursor—great for drawing, touch-ups, or just for a familiar interface for moving the mouse pointer.

Add an External Drive

A removable drive can be an important addition, since the iMac lacks a floppy drive and many users aren't connected to local area networks. Online file transfer is certainly one option, especially if you have a higher-speed connection. (Online storage is discussed in Chapter 20.) But if you'd like to be able to back up your important files to physical disks, then a removable drive or an external hard drive is a good idea.

External drives come in both USB and FireWire varieties. In most cases, FireWire is preferable if you have an iMac that supports it, since FireWire is much faster for copying data to and from the drive.

There are two basic approaches to removable media—removable disks and writeable CD technology. Removable disks include Iomega's Zip drive, Imation's SuperDisk, and the Castlewood Orb drive. All of these are designed to use compact floppy-like disks that can store between 100MB and 2.2GB, depending on the drive used. Here's a look at each:

■ **Iomega Zip (http://www.iomega.com/)**   The Zip drive is a popular choice for removable storage, offering 100-250MB of storage space. (For 250MB, you'll need the special Zip250 drive.) It's reasonably quick and Zip disks are very popular with Mac and PC users alike. If you plan to share media among different computers, this may be the best solution.

- ■ **Imation SuperDisk (http://www.superdisk.com/)**   The SuperDisk offers the unique ability to read traditional 1.4MB floppy disks as well as the special 120MB LS120 disks. The SuperDisk is a touch slow compared to other removables, but very flexible. This is a good solution if you need to read floppy disks but also want extra capacity.

- ■ **Castlewood Orb (http://www.castlewood.com/)**   The Castlewood Orb drive offers 2.2GB of storage on reasonably inexpensive media, making it easy to back up nearly your entire iBook to a single disk. If you plan to rotate your media, a single Orb disk should suffice for each backup session, even if you have a lot of files.

You'll also find some external drives on the market that don't quite fit the "removable" mold but are popular ways to extend your iMac nonetheless. A few companies make floppy drives for iMacs, allowing you to use a typical 1.4MB floppy diskette. Other companies make actual external hard disks in gigabyte capacities.

If your iMac doesn't support FireWire, then you may opt for a USB-based hard disk. Be warned that USB is a little slow for use with a hard disk; the external disk will never be as fast as your iMac's internal disk. That doesn't mean it won't be useful, though, since having such a large capacity for backup—along with the option of unplugging the drive and using it with another computer—is a convenient touch. Here are some manufacturers of floppy and hard disks for iMacs:

Imation	**http://www.imation.com/**	Floppy drive, LS120 (120MB floppy)
MacAlly	**http://www.macally.com/**	Floppy drive, hard disk
LaCie	**http://www.lacie.com/**	Hard disk
SmartDisk	**http://www.smartdisk.com/**	Floppy drive, hard disks
Teac	**http://www.teac.com/**	Floppy drive

If you have a slot-loading iMac model that does support FireWire, you'll find external FireWire hard disks that are fully as fast and useful as your iMac's internal disk. In fact, FireWire hard disks are a great addition to your iMac, since you can easily back up to the disk, transport the disk, and move the disk between iMacs and other Macs that support FireWire. VST Technologies, LaCie, MacTell (**http://www.mactell.com/**), Maxtor (**http://www.maxtor.com/**), QPS (**http://www.qps-inc.com/**), and other manufacturers make FireWire hard disks as well as other FireWire-based external removable drives.

Install an External Drive

External removable drives often require special software for installation on an iMac, since each may have its own unique USB or FireWire driver. Hard disk drives often don't require additional drivers, as the Mac OS has drivers built in to support hard disks.

26

Once the driver is installed, hooking up the drive should be simple. Just plug the USB or FireWire cable into the drive, then into either the port on your iMac's keyboard (for USB), the port on the side of the iMac, or an available port on your USB hub. (FireWire devices can usually be plugged into an available port on the side of your iMac or the back of another FireWire device.) Right after you plug in the drive you'll either have success or you'll see a message that suggests you haven't correctly installed the drive's software. Success is generally indicated by the appearance of the disk on the desktop or in the Finder.

CAUTION *If you're connecting multiple FireWire devices in a daisy chain, make sure that none of the connections loop back on any of the already connected devices. Device 1 should be connected to the iMac's FireWire port, device 2 to device 1, device 3 to device 2, and so on.*

You'll want to be careful with your removable drives, because some of them don't react well in certain configurations. In some situations, you also need to consider *where* you put your removable drive on the USB bus. Some removable drives work better with older iMacs if they have access to their own port. With slot-loading iMacs, each USB port is its own 12Mbps bus. In this case, you'll probably get better performance if you place the removable drive on a different port from your other demanding peripherals, like scanners or printers. While you're not likely to encounter errors, placing your demanding peripherals on separate ports may help you get the best performance.

NOTE *Earlier versions of Mac OS X have trouble with many external USB devices, and using them may cause kernel panics, or system crashes that result in text on the screen. If this happens, remove the device and restart your iMac, then check the device manufacturer's Web site or customer service for details or improved drivers.*

If you can't dedicate a whole USB port to the removable drive, it's best to connect and use your drive while other peripherals on the same connection are inactive. That is, you'll see worse performance if a scanner, removable drive, and keyboard or mouse are all being used on the same bus at the same time. It's not a huge problem, although there's a chance it could result in data loss.

NOTE *Another consideration—Iomega's documentation for the Zip drive suggests you not plug in or unplug other devices on the USB while the drive is in active use. This also translates to other types of removable drives, since it could be a problem to have the iMac looking for a USB driver while it's supposed to be paying attention to the drive. This shouldn't be a problem on newer slot-loading iMacs, especially if you're plugging in and unplugging devices that are connected to the other USB port or to a FireWire port.*

With older iMacs, it isn't possible to boot from USB-based disks and drives, even if the disk has a compatible Mac OS System Folder on it. With slot-loading iMacs, it is possible to boot from external USB peripherals, thanks to the dual-channel nature of the USB implementation; likewise, you can often boot from FireWire devices. (At the time of writing, you can't boot Mac OS X from any external disks other than an Apple CD.) If you'd like to boot from a removable drive, insert a disk that includes a valid Mac OS 9 System Folder, then open the Startup Disk control panel. Select the removable drive and close the control panel. Now, when you restart, your iMac will start up from the removable drive.

With any iMac, you can still boot from a CD in the internal CD-ROM or DVD-ROM drive. Place a CD with a valid System Folder (or a Mac OS X startup disc) in the drive and restart your iMac. Immediately after you hear the startup tone, hold down the C key until the Welcome to Macintosh message appears.

Back Up to a Removable Drive

The Iomega Zip drive comes with special software to help you manage backing up to the drive—other removable drives may include similar software. Whether or not you use the included software or a backup application like Retrospect Express (**www.dantz.com**) or shareware solutions, you can use the removable drive to automatically back up your important files to the removable disk.

You've already seen (in Chapter 20) that online backup can be automated in this way, and with great success. When you're dealing with disks, though, there are some things to consider:

- **Rotate Media**   If you can, rotate backups between three or more different disks. If you need to back up often, you can back up Mondays, Wednesdays, and Fridays. Then, the next week, you can use your software to do an incremental backup, which simply adds files that have changed since the last backup. If you don't want to back up that often, back up once a week and rotate new media in each week for three or four weeks, then start over.

- **Archive**   This is important: Every so often (say, once a week in a business situation, once a month at home) archive one of your removable disks—that is, drop it out of the rotation and store it somewhere safe. This does two things. It gives you a reasonably up-to-date emergency copy of your data. It also gives you a copy of your data that's fixed in time. If your iMac subsequently gets infected with a virus, or if you accidentally delete or change a file, you still have the older copy to return to.

NOTE   *If you're serious about archiving disks, you should consider a CD-R, CD-RW, or DVD-R drive (discussed in the next section). CDs are much better for long-term storage than many removable disks. CDs are also cheaper than most removable disks, making it less expensive to back up to CDs over the long haul. Plus, the latest iMacs have CD-RW drives built in, as discussed later in this chapter and in Chapter 3.*

- **Test**   Especially in a business situation (or even with your thesis, business plan, novel, or personal investment portfolio), test the backup media occasionally to make sure they're working OK.

Once you get into the swing of things, you should find it's easy to automate the backup process. In many cases, it's just a question of telling the backup software when to schedule the backup, then leaving the right disk in the drive when it's time for the backup.

Install CD-RW and DVD-R Drives

You might also want to consider a CD-R (CD-Recordable), CD-RW (CD-Rewriteable), or DVD-R drive for your iMac. These drives work a lot like other removable drives, although they tend to be a little slower for saving data, as the data must be *burned* to the disc. The discs, on the other hand, can often be cheaper.

A CD-RW drive can write once to a CD-R disc, which can then be read by nearly any CD-ROM drive. This is a convenient way to transfer files or send files great distances, since CD-R discs are cheap, they can hold up to 650MB of data, and they're pretty resilient. CD-R discs are also a great media for archiving important documents from your hard disk since the CD-R discs store well, don't take up a lot of space, and can be popped into any Mac if there's trouble with your iMac.

CD-RW disks are slightly more expensive, but allow you to erase information on the disc and write to it again. In this way a CD-RW is very much like a Zip or similar removable drive. CD-RW drives tend to be capable of writing to CD-R media, too, so you can have the best of both worlds.

DVD-R and DVD-RAM (rewriteable) drives can write data to recordable DVD discs, which can store quite a bit more information than CDs—between 2.6GB and 4.7GB (for write-once DVD-R media) to 4.7GB to 9.4GB for DVD-RAM discs.

Companies making CD-RW and DVD-R/DVD-RAM drives for the iMac (via USB and/or FireWire) include:

EZQuest	**http://www.ezq.com/**
Fantom Drives	**http://www.fantomdrives.com/**
Formac Electronic	**http://www.formac.com/**
LaCie	**http://www.lacie.com/**
QPS, Inc.	**http://www.qps-inc.com/**
SmartDisk	**http://www.smartdisk.com/**
Sony	**http://www.sony.com/**

Some CD-RW drives are compatible with Apple's Disc Burner software, which enables you to burn data CDs from the Finder, as well as audio CDs using Apple's iTunes software. In order to fully gauge compatibility, it's good to know the manufacturer of the CD-RW mechanism inside your drive—often that's a large, recognizable company such as Sony, Panasonic, Pioneer, or Yamaha. Check your drive's documentation and consult **http://www.apple.com/itunes/** to see which devices are supported directly by Apple. If your external CD-RW drive works with Disc Burner, then you can use the commands discussed in Chapters 3 and 14 to create data and audio CDs.

In other cases, or when you want more features than Disc Burner offers, you'll need to turn to a third-party solution. The most popular option is Roxio Toast (**www.roxio.com**), a program that allows you to burn an entire CD or DVD at once. You can also write to a disc in *sessions,* meaning you can write to the disc at different times, storing data sequentially on the disc. Toast also lets you create audio CDs, video CDs (that can be played back in some commercial DVD players), and CDs designed to use the file format that Windows computers generally read. Toast should be available for Mac OS X by the time you read this.

Scanners and Digital Cameras

Scanners and digital cameras are also being designed to support USB and FireWire these days, offering an easy way to get digital images into your iMac for use in newsletters, reports, and Web sites. Scanners allow you to place an image or document flat on the glass bed of the scanner's top—like a copy machine—and digitize the image or document so that it can be used on your iMac's screen. In fact, some scanners include special Optical Character Recognition (OCR) software that allows a scanned document to be turned into a regular word processing document, enabling you to edit and store the document in an application like AppleWorks.

Add a Scanner

Scanners for the iMac tend to be inexpensive and they include decent bells and whistles. If you're comparison shopping, look for high-end color support (32-bit color or better), high *true* resolution (600 × 600 or better), and extras like Photoshop plug-ins and OCR software. Here are some scanner manufacturers with iMac-compatible products:

AGFA	**http://www.agfa.com/**
Canon	**http://www.canonusa.com/**
Hewlett-Packard	**http://www.hp.com/**
Microtek	**http://www.microtek.com/**
Umax	**http://www.umax.com/**

Generally, you'll simply install the scanner's software, plug in the scanner, and start scanning, at least in Mac OS 9. In Mac OS X, you may need to look for updated drivers and/or scanning software from the manufacturer in order to work with the scanner, although some scanners work well in the Classic environment.

Add a Digital Camera

There are two different types of iMac-compatible digital cameras. One is a *still-image camera,* designed to be carried around and used just like a typical 35mm camera. The difference with a digital camera is that, instead of taking pictures on film, it takes pictures that are stored in a computer-compatible format, often JPEG. These images can be downloaded from the camera and used immediately in a photo-editing program, in a desktop layout, or for Web pages.

The other type of digital camera is a *digital motion camera*. These all come in two varieties—DV camcorders and low-end video capture cameras. Nearly all DV camcorders support FireWire, making it simple to transfer digital movies from the camcorder to your iMac DV model. If you plan to make home movies, corporate videos, or other high-quality video, a DV camcorder that supports FireWire is the best choice.

> **NOTE** *Attaching a FireWire-based DV camcorder to your FireWire-equipped iMac is covered in Chapter 15.*

If you have an older iMac or you don't want to invest in a DV camcorder, you can get small cameras that are attached via USB and create video of you and your immediate surroundings. These cameras offer lower resolution and picture quality than your typical video camcorder, but they're useful for Internet conferencing and similar applications. These cameras have their own software and drivers that must be installed in Mac OS 9; Mac OS X support for most of these, at the time of writing, is still in the works.

In the case of a digital still camera, you get the images into your iMac in one of two ways. The first way is via a USB connection and software that enables you to acquire the images the same way you acquire a scanned image—either in photo-editing software such as PhotoShop, or via the scanner's own software application. (In Mac OS X, you can use the Image Capture application, included in the Applications folder, to capture images from USB-based still cameras.)

The other method is to remove the SmartDisk or CompactFlash card from the camera and plug it into a card reader. This causes the card to appear on the desktop as if it were a removable disk, enabling you to copy the images directly from the card. Card readers are made by a number of companies, including VST Technologies (**www.vsttech.com**), SanDisk (**www.sandisk.com**) and many others.

> **TIP** *These days you can also purchase* video capture *devices that enable you to hook up a VHS camcorder and digitize video via the USB port. You'll generally do this if you want to create QuickTime movies from videos you've filmed using a traditional camcorder.*

Here's a list of current digital camera manufacturers. Note that many digital still-image cameras support USB as an interface. If you buy one of these cameras, make sure it includes Macintosh driver software. Here's some of what's available at the time of this writing:

Belkin Components	**http://www.belkin.com/**	Video capture device
Epson	**http://www.epson.com/**	Still cameras
Formac Electronic	**http://www.formac.com/**	Video capture device
Logitech	**http://www.logitech.com/**	Video cameras
Kensington	**http://www.kensington.com/**	Video cameras
Kodak	**http://www.kodak.com/**	Still cameras
Ricoh	**http://www.ricoh.com/**	Still cameras
XLR8	**http://www.xlr8.com/**	Video capture device

Digital cameras, like removable drives, can be demanding on the USB bus, so it's recommended that you use digital video cameras and similar devices on a different USB port from removable disks and/or while the removable disk isn't operating. You'll get better performance that way.

Add Older Mac Devices Using Adapters

Because USB and FireWire are newer technologies, not all devices designed to work with Macs in the past will work with an iMac. In a sense, that's a good thing, since it means only the latest technology works with an iMac and that technology is more likely to be fast enough and advanced enough to integrate well with the iMac. At the same time, though, it means you can't hook up older peripherals that you may already own.

Fortunately, there are a number of companies making adapters for the USB ports on the iMac (and the FireWire port on recent iMac models) to allow you to connect other sorts of devices that don't natively support USB or FireWire. We already saw some adapters for hooking up printers in Chapter 25. Here's a list of some adapter manufacturers and the types of adapter products they offer:

Belkin	http://www.belkin.com/	USB-to-serial USB-to-parallel USB-to-SCSI
CompuCable	http://www.compucable.com/	USB-to-serial USB-to-parallel USB-to-ADB
Griffin Technology	http://www.griffintechnology.com/	USB-to-ADB USB-to-serial
Keyspan	http://www.keyspan.com/	USB-to-serial
MidiMan	http://www.midiman.net/	USB-to-MIDI
Opcode	http://www.opcode.com/	USB-to-MIDI
Orange Micro	http://www.orangemicro.com/	FireWire-to-SCSI
Second Wave	http://www.2ndwave.com/	USB-to-SCSI FireWire-to-SCSI

What are all these technologies? Here's a quick look:

- **Serial**   Pre-iMac Macs use serial ports for many connections, including external modems, some digital cameras, PDA synchronize cables, and non-PostScript printers. (Note that serial-to-USB adapters can be designed to work with PC serial ports, which are different from Mac serial ports. In most cases, if you're trying to connect an older Mac peripheral, you'll want a DIN-8 Mac serial adapter.)

- **ADB**   Apple Desktop Bus is used to connect keyboard, mice, and other pointing devices for pre-iMac Mac computers.

■ **SCSI** Used by Macs and PCs to connect external drives and scanners to the computer, SCSI is a faster technology than USB, so a USB-to-SCSI connector isn't recommended for daily use (although a FireWire-to-SCSI adapter should work well). USB-to-SCSI is a great way to hook up an existing scanner or hard disk occasionally, if only to get a few files or images transferred to your iMac.

■ **Parallel** Parallel adapters are used on Intel-compatible PCs to connect to many printers (and some other devices). These adapters can be used to connect PC printers to your iMac, as long as you have a driver that allows your iMac to print to that printer.

■ **MIDI** The Musical Instrument Digital Interface allows you to connect MIDI keyboard synthesizers and other devices to your iMac to edit music and play back songs.

Add Microphones and Speakers

All tray-loading and some slot-loading iMacs can support an external microphone through the sound-out ports on the side of the iMac; likewise, all iMacs can support external speakers. The only caveats are this: For speakers, choose powered, computer-shielded speakers, preferably those designed to be used with the iMac. This is important because speakers not designed specifically for a computer can affect the monitor picture and other aspects of the computing experience.

> NOTE *Your iMac actually has a microphone built in—it's that small hole at the top (or in the lower-left corner, on the iMac G4) of your display. If your Mac has a microphone port as well, you can use that for a higher-quality microphone or for another audio-in device, such as an audio component from which you'd like to record.*

The output for speakers is actually a line-level output, which means you can plug your iMac directly into a stereo amplifier, if you like and if you have the right audio cable adapter, and listen to iMac sounds through your stereo system. To connect, you'll need an adapter from the iMac's 1/8" RCA stereo mini-plug connector to the inputs on your stereo system.

The microphone port is also a line-level device, meaning you'll need either a special Apple PlainTalk microphone (available in Mac-friendly computer stores) or a signal from a powered microphone or from a line-level device, like an external receiver or even an audio device like a CD player. Typical karaoke-style microphones won't work. If you want to use an inexpensive microphone, Griffin Technology (**http://www.griffintechnology.com/**) offers a special adapter for connecting such microphones to your iMac.

> NOTE *Newer iMacs no longer include a sound-in port for microphones, although they still include the built-in mic; if you need something higher-quality, the solution is a USB microphone, such as the models made by Macsense (**www.macsense.com**) and others.*

Install RAM or the AirPort Card

The slot-loading iMac and iMac G4 models make it easy to install RAM and the AirPort card, Apple's special wireless networking card. You'll need to get inside your iMac to make these upgrades, but it's not tough to do.

 *Whenever you're inside your iMac, you need to avoid static electricity discharge, which can damage components. You can get a grounding strap, which attaches to your wrist and discharges static, from most computer and electronics stores.*

Unfortunately, you can't get into the original iMac to install RAM as easily as you can the later models. Because installing RAM in the original iMac requires removing screws and connectors and carefully sliding the iMac's main circuit board and CD-ROM drive out of the iMac, I'm not covering it in this book. If you feel adept at such upgrades, you'll find instructions in Apple's Knowledge Base at http://docs.info.apple.com/article.html?artnum=43012 on the Web. I have, however, noted which RAM you'll want to use to upgrade your iMac, in the next section.

Determine RAM Type and Install RAM

The type of RAM your iMac requires depends on the model. All iMacs have two memory slots, one of which is filled with the base memory that shipped with the iMac. It's possible to remove the base memory and install a larger memory module, if necessary, to bring the iMac to the maximum allowable amount of RAM.

If you have an iMac 233, iMac 266, or iMac 333, your iMac uses 3.3 volt SO-DIMM SDRAM. Specifications are: unbuffered, 64-bit wide, 144-pin. Speeds should be 100 MHz and 10 ns or faster (which would mean a number lower than 10).

Officially (according to Apple), the revision A iMac 233 supports 64MB modules in each slot; the iMac 266 and iMac 333 support up to 128MB modules in each slot. However, it is possible to get larger memory modules and install them successfully. Note, however, that if you plan to install memory in the "lower" slot on these iMacs (which is where the base memory is installed), you'll need a specially designed smaller module to fit that slot (consult Apple dealers for details).

The slot-loading iMacs support standard PC-100 DIMMs that are 3.3-volt, 64-bit wide, 168-pin modules. There should be a maximum of 16 memory devices (chips) on the DIMM and it needs to be unbuffered with a maximum height of 2.0 inches. Most Mac vendors will pre-certify RAM for compliance with these specifications, but you should look carefully if you're buying standard PC-100 DIMMs from a different source, like a PC-centric vendor.

NOTE *According to Apple, slot-loading models made in 2001 can support PC-133 DIMMs as well.*

On slot-loading iMacs, you'll find two DIMM slots accessible from the bottom of the computer. (All models already have one of the slots filled.) You can release the upgrade panel simply by turning its screw with a coin. You then have access to the DIMM slots, as shown in Figure 26-2.

NOTE *The handbook that comes with your iMac includes step-by-step instructions and drawings to help you install RAM. Make sure you place the iMac face-down on a soft surface (like a lint-free towel) and touch the metal cage that surrounds the slot in order to discharge static electricity. Also, make sure you press the DIMM all the way in so that the small plastic guards snap up snug to the DIMM. Don't force it—the DIMM is only designed to go in one way (look to make sure the notches in the DIMM match up with the DIMM slot).*

The maximum DIMM size for each slot is 512MB. With the two slots full, the maximum RAM is 1GB of RAM, and note that you'll need to remove any RAM already installed before adding both DIMMs.

On the iMac G4, the user-installable RAM slot supports a PC133 144-pin SO-DIMM up to 512MB. The second slot is not user-serviceable, according to Apple; you'll need to have an authorized dealer change RAM in that slot. RAM is installed in the base of the iMac's unit and can be accessed by removing the metal access plate that's held in place by four screws. For detailed instructions, see your iMac's User's Guide or http://docs.info.apple.com/article.html?artnum=26239.

Install and Configure an AirPort Card

Slot-loading iMacs and iMac G4 models also support an AirPort card for wireless networking. If your iMac didn't come with the card pre-installed, you can buy an AirPort card separately and install the card yourself. You'll need to install both the card and its software.

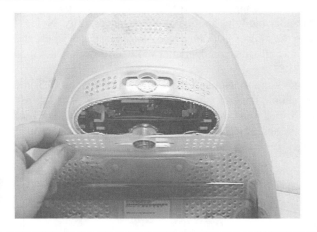

FIGURE 26-2 The slot-loading iMac's upgrade panel opened

Install the Card

You install the AirPort card in the slot-loading iMac using the same opening that you use to access the memory DIMMs. Here's how to install the card in the slot-loading iMac:

> **TIP**
>
> *The iMac G4's instructions are a bit different; view them in your iMac User's Guide or at http://docs.info.apple.com/article.html?artnum=26237 on the Web.*

1. Shut down the iMac and unplug all cables except the power cable. (This electrically grounds the iMac.) Place the iMac screen-down on a soft surface or cloth.
2. Using a coin, open the access door.
3. Touch the metal shield inside the port door (just behind the plastic). This will discharge static electricity.
4. Detach the antenna from the plastic guard on the side. Pull the plastic antenna cap away from the guard, then pull the antenna out of the plastic cap.
5. Attach the antenna to your AirPort card and insert the card into the slot until it's locked in. (Don't press too hard, but you should feel when it locks into place.)
6. Close the access door, plug everything back in, and fire up your iMac.

Configure the Software

Once you've installed your AirPort card, you'll need to install the AirPort software. Here's how:

1. Insert the AirPort CD in your iMac's CD or DVD drive.

> **NOTE**
>
> *In some cases, you'll probably want to download the latest version of the AirPort software from http://asu.info.apple.com or http://www.apple.com/airport/ on the Web. If you've been using the Software Update feature, you may have the latest version on your iMac already, particularly if you're using Mac OS X.*

2. Double-click the Installer icon.
3. In the installer, choose a disk for installation, read the Read Me file, and agree to the license agreement (click Continue between each screen).
4. On the Install/Remove Software screen, click Start. This installs the software. Once installed, your iMac will need to be restarted. (Click the Restart button.)
5. When you restart the iMac, you'll see the AirPort Setup Assistant appear. (If you've configured AirPort in Mac OS X, note that version 10.1 is the first to include the AirPort Setup Assistant, which is in the Utilities folder inside the main Applications folder.) The AirPort Setup Assistant helps you set up your iMac to access an existing wireless network or set up an AirPort Base Station. Walk through the Assistant, clicking the right arrow to move to the next screen.

Once the software is installed in Mac OS 9, you can use the AirPort control strip or the AirPort application (in the Apple menu) to turn the AirPort card on and off or to change your network connection (for instance, to connect computer-to-computer instead of using a Base Station). In Mac OS X, you'll use Internet Connect and the AirPort dockling (or the AirPort menu bar icon) to control the connection. See Chapter 28 for details on networking with AirPort.

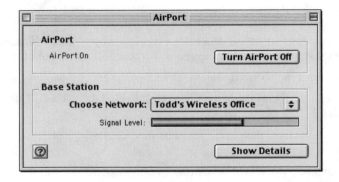

Chapter 27

Create and Manage Multiple Users

How to...

- ■ Work with the Multiple Users feature
- ■ Turn on and create users in Mac OS X
- ■ Log into Mac OS X
- ■ Turn on Multiple Users in Mac OS 9
- ■ Log in and out of Mac OS 9

While it may not appear so at first blush, Mac OS X is designed to be used by multiple users, where each user logs into the account using a unique user name and password. If your iMac came pre-installed with Mac OS X or if you've recently installed Mac OS X, you may still only have one user account—in fact, you may not even log into your Mac currently. If that system works for you, then there's no reason to change it. But you can.

Mac OS 9 works the same way initially—it starts up and works for one user. But enabling multiple user accounts in either operating system can be useful in many different settings. Each person in your household or office can have a distinct user name and password. Then, each user also gets a home folder where personal documents, applications, and preferences can be stored. Almost anything about a user's iMac experience can be customized—the Dock or Launcher, the background and colors, desktop icons, and even the iMac's settings. And with multiple user accounts, that customization won't affect other users.

If this sort of personal approach sounds appealing, you'll want to dig into the world of multiple users. I'll cover Mac OS X's implementation first, then you'll see how to enable multiple users in Mac OS 9 later in the chapter.

Set Up Multiple Users and Mac OS X

In Mac OS X, you can create two types of accounts—an administrator's account and a regular account. A regular account is for day-to-day stuff—getting work done. A regular account can't install applications in the Applications folder, for instance, and a regular account only has access to a limited number of the options and settings available in the System Preferences application. By contrast, an administrator account (one that's in the Admin group) has enough *privileges* to install applications in the Applications folder, make changes in the main Library folder (where fonts, driver software, and other important files are installed), and make system-level decisions in the System Preferences application.

As mentioned, the first user account created in Mac OS X is automatically placed in the Admin group. That means that this account has the capabilities to do all of these tasks, as well as create other user accounts. When you create a new user, you're also creating a new home folder for that user, giving that user a "virtual workspace" of sorts on the iMac. And you're separating that user's files and preferences from any other users, so that each individual who accesses your iMac can have a personal space that's free from meddling by others.

 *It's important to note that being an Admin user does mean you have to be careful. Deleting items in the Application or Library folders can lead to problems for your iMac, as can choosing the wrong settings in the System Preferences application. And if you're digging into other administrative utilities—particularly the Terminal application and the NetInfo Manager application—you could damage some of your iMac's files or misconfigure Mac OS X.*

Create and Manage Users

If you've decided you'd like to have multiple user accounts on your iMac, you're ready to begin creating them. To do so, launch the System Preferences application by either clicking its tile in the Dock or by selecting System Preferences from the Apple menu. Then, in the System Preferences application, click the Users icon to launch the Users pane.

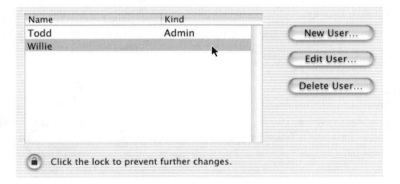

You'll notice immediately that all of the currently created accounts are listed in the User pane. You can also see which of those accounts are Admin accounts. (Regular accounts don't have an entry in the Kind column.) If your account is not an Admin account, then you'll either need to log out and log back in using an Admin account or, alternatively, you can *authenticate* by clicking the small padlock icon at the bottom of the pane and entering the user name and password of a valid Admin account. (Remember that the first account created, during the Setup Assistant steps discussed in Chapter 1, is an Admin account.)

If the padlock icon is already unlocked, you're signed into an Admin account. You're ready to begin creating and managing users. Click the New User button and the User dialog box appears. From there, creating a new user is easy:

1. Enter the user's first and last name in the Name entry box. Press TAB.

2. In the Short Name entry box, you'll see a suggested short name. This is your user name on the system and for accessing this Mac via a network. You can press TAB again to accept it, or edit it before pressing TAB.

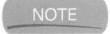

In Mac OS X version 10.1 and higher, you'll be able to select a Login Picture for this user by clicking one of the default options or clicking the Choose button and locating a picture on your disk. Then, to continue with these steps, click the Password tab.

3. Enter a password for the user. It should be eight characters long (it can be shorter, but not much) and not easily guessed. The best passwords are combinations of nonsensical words or names and numbers that aren't part of your daily life. (For instance, don't use your birthdate or anniversary.) Press TAB.

4. Since you can't see what you typed in the Password entry box, you'll type the password again in the Verify box to make sure they match. When you type, use the same capitalization— passwords are case-sensitive in Mac OS X. Press TAB.

5. If desired, you can type a hint in the Password Hint entry box. (Don't let the hint be a giveaway!) Later, when this user attempts to log in, the password hint may appear in the Login window (see the section "Set Login Window Options," later in this chapter).

6. Turn on the Allow User to Administer Machine option (by clicking its check box) if you'd like the user to be placed in the Admin group so that this user can create users and work with files in the system-level folders.

When you're done entering user information, click the Save button. The user is saved, a home folder is created for the user, and a new entry will appear for this user in the User pane.

One other thing may happen: If your iMac is currently set for *automatic login,* which means you don't see the Login window when you first start or restart your iMac, then creating a user will cause the Users pane to prompt you to change this. Now that you have two (or more) users on your iMac, you may want to display the Login window every time the iMac is started or restarted, so that different users can log in. In the dialog sheet that appears, click the Yes button if you'd like to enable the Login window. If you'd prefer that automatic login for your main account continues, click the No button.

Change a User's Privileges and Password

You will probably only need to edit an existing user for one of two reasons: to change that user's Admin status or to change that user's password. But those are important reasons—the Users pane is the only way to change a password for a user account, and it's wise to change passwords occasionally, particularly in an organizational environment.

To edit a user, you'll need to be logged into an Admin account or authenticated (by clicking the locked padlock icon) with an Admin user name and password. Now, select that user in the Users pane and click the Edit User button. In the User window, you can change the user's Full Name, although note that you can't change the short name of the user. (That's because the user's home folder is linked to this short name, and can't easily be changed.) You can then highlight, delete, and re-type in the Password and Verify entry boxes to change the user's password; you should also change the user's Password Hint. (You'll need to first select the Password tab in Mac OS X 10.1 and higher.) Finally, you can change the user's Admin status by turning on or off the Allow User to Administer This Machine check box. When you're done making changes, click the Save button.

> **NOTE**   *As an Admin user, you can't simply open the User dialog box and tell another user what his or her password is, because it shows up as dots. Your only choice, if the user has forgotten his or her password, is to edit the user and change the password to something new.*

If you've changed the password for your or another user's account, you'll see an alert sheet appear in the User dialog box when you click the Save button in the Users dialog. The alert informs you that your keychain password will be changed automatically. That means the new keychain password for your account will be the same as the new password that you're entering here.

> **NOTE**   *If you're changing the password for another user's account, you may see a message that says you can't change that user's keychain password in some earlier versions of Mac OS X. This message is actually an error—the password for the user's keychain is changed. For more on the keychain, see Chapter 24.*

Delete a User

To delete a user, you'll need to be logged into an Admin account or authenticated as an Admin user. Then, select that user in the Users pane and click the Delete User button. An alert sheet immediately appears warning you that the user will be permanently deleted. If that's what you want to do, select an Admin account to which you want the privileges for that user's home folder assigned and click the Delete button.

After clicking Delete, you're returned to the User pane and the deleted user will no longer appear in the listing of users. Behind the scenes, however, that user's home folder is renamed with the word "Deleted" appended to it, and the privileges for accessing the folder are assigned to the Admin account that you selected in the alert sheet.

Log In and Set Login Options

When confronted with the Login window, you'll need to type a valid user name in the Name entry box (or, in Mac OS X 10.1, you may be able to select the user name with the mouse) and the associated password in the Password entry box. Then, press RETURN or click the Log In button. If you don't enter a valid user name or password, the Login window shakes from side to side, almost like a toddler saying "No." Try again. If you're entering a valid user name, but your password is entered incorrectly three times, the password hint for that user name will appear. This will continue (every three failed attempts will result in the password hint being displayed) until you give up.

If you successfully enter a valid user name and password, the Login window disappears and the desktop appears. After a few seconds, the Finder appears and you're ready to begin working with your iMac and your personal home folder.

Log Out of Your iMac

In a multiple-user scenario, it's important that you log out of your account whenever you're done working on the iMac. This enables other users to access their own accounts, while avoiding the possibility that another user will have access to your files and settings. (In fact, this even works if you're the only user, adding additional security.)

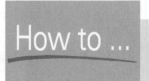 **Re-create a Deleted User**

To re-create a user you've deleted, follow the procedure for creating a new user. You can enter the user's original name, short name, and password, if desired. When you're finished creating the user, click the Save button and that user is created. Now, in the Finder, locate the user's old folder—the one with "Deleted" as part of the name. Open the folder and drag items to the Drop Box folder that's inside the Public folder in the user's new home folder. Items copied to the Drop Box folder automatically become "owned" by that user so that the user, once logged in, will have full Read & Write privileges for moving the files around and storing them in different subfolders inside the new home folder.

To log out, choose the Log Out command from the Apple menu. An alert box will appear, asking you to confirm your decision—click Log Out if that's what you really want to do or click Cancel to stop the log out process.

If you've clicked Log Out, your applications will automatically quit, and you'll be asked to save any unsaved changes in your open documents. Then, eventually, the Finder and desktop will disappear and you'll see the Login window. Now you can log in again, allow another user to log in, or click the Restart or Shut Down buttons to restart or shut down your iMac, respectively.

Set Login Window Options

If you'd like to customize how the Login window looks and works, you can do that by launching the System Preferences application and selecting the Login icon. When the Login pane opens, click the Login Window tab (see Figure 27-1). If you've signed into an Admin account, you should be able to change options in this tab; otherwise, you'll need to click the padlock icon and authenticate.

27

NOTE *In Mac OS X version 10.1, this tab also includes options that enable you to determine whether Name and Password boxes or a list of users appears.*

At the top of the Login Window tab, you can turn on or off the Automatically Log In option if you'd like Mac OS X to bypass the login window and automatically log in a particular user whenever the Mac is started up or restarted. By default the option is turned on if you haven't created additional users. If you've added users, you may have turned off the Automatic Log In option in the Users pane.

FIGURE 27-1 In the Login pane, you can access settings that affect the Login window.

If you want to turn it back on, then click its check box. Now, enter a user name in the Name entry box and that user's password in the Password entry box, then click the Set button. If the user name and password are valid, you'll hear a tone and the Set button will become grayed out. If the user name and password are invalid, you'll see an alert telling you that. To change the user, turn off the Automatically Log In option, then turn it back on again.

 *Turning on the Automatically Log In option means any user who restarts the iMac will have access to the files, folders, and settings of the user you enter here.*

The other options on the Login Window tab enable you to change the way the Login window looks and works. Turning on the Disable Restart and Shut Down Buttons option is generally done as a security measure to keep users who don't have a valid user name from restarting the iMac and starting up from a different hard disk or startup CD that's been inserted in the iMac. (Restarting from a CD is covered in Chapter 29.)

Set Up Multiple Users in Mac OS 9

Unlike Mac OS X, Mac OS 9 isn't designed from the ground up for multiple users. But, it can still handle them, thanks to a special control panel called Multiple Users. When you first set up Multiple Users in Mac OS 9, it creates an account called the *owner account*. There is only one owner account, which is used to create other user accounts that each have a user name and password. Information about those accounts is stored in a folder called Users that only the owner can access. When a user logs in using his or her user name and password, all of that user's preferences are mirrored onto the Preferences folder in the System Folder, so that applications that access the System Folder actually access that user's preferences. That means each user will see a unique workspace, complete with his or her own desktop, applications, and other choices and settings.

Turn On and Create Users

To turn on this system, open the Multiple Users control panel and click the On button next to Multiple User Accounts at the bottom of the window. Now Multiple Users is active. If you do nothing else but close the Multiple Users control panel, you'll find that there's a new Logout command in the Special menu. You'll use this command to leave your owner account and return to the Login screen. The Login screen will now also appear whenever you start up (or restart) the iMac, as long as Multiple Users is active.

 The first time you open the Multiple Users control panel, you may get an error message if you don't have an owner name entered in the File Sharing control panel. Multiple Users uses the owner name to assign an owner account in the Multiple Users control panel.

Now, even with one account, there's a measure of security for your iMac. If you log out of the iMac using the Special | Logout command, only someone who knows your password can log into your iMac. (The password is the same as the owner's password in the File Sharing control panel. You can change that password, as detailed in the section "Change a User's Privileges and Password," earlier in this chapter.) But, of course, the point of Multiple Users is to create additional user accounts, right?

Create User Accounts

Once you've turned on Multiple Users you'll want to create user accounts for everyone to whom you want to give access to your iMac. You do that by clicking the New User button in the Multiple Users control panel. Now you'll see the Edit "New User" window.

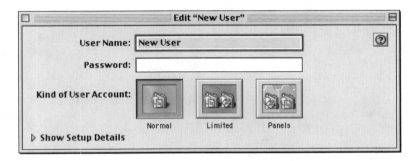

Begin by entering a name for this user in the User Name entry box. Then, press TAB and enter a password for this user in the Password entry box. (Users can change their own passwords as they're logging in, if they like, so you can set up passwords now and they can change them later if they want.) Now, click the button for the type of account you'd like to give this user. There are three choices:

- ■ **Normal**   This type of account gives the user access to all but a handful of control panels that are off-limits to all users but the owner. You can also give these users the ability to manage other Multiple User accounts.

- ■ **Limited**   A limited account uses the regular Finder for the user's interface but allows you (the owner) to choose which applications the user can access. The user can only save documents to his or her own personal folder and can only access system resources (like the control panels, removable media, Apple Menu items, the Chooser, or Network Browser) that you decide they can access.

- ■ **Panels**   This gives you the same control over what the user can access as the Limited account does, but Panels uses a different interface, shown in Figure 27-2. In fact, the Finder doesn't even load for these users—they only use the Panels interface to interact with the iMac.

Once you've chosen the type of account you're going to give the user, you can make some other choices in the Edit "New User" window, if desired. Each set of choices is found on the tabs that are revealed when you click Show Setup Details at the bottom of the window.

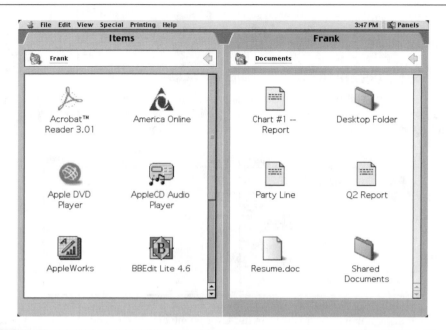

FIGURE 27-2 The Panels interface gives the user a limited but useful way to launch applications and save documents.

User Info

On the User Info tab, you begin by choosing the picture for the user's icon by clicking the small arrows next to the User Picture image. Then, place check marks next to the abilities you'd like this user to have. Here are a few issues:

- Note that if you turn off the Can Log In option, you temporarily disable the account.
- Turn on the Can Manage User Accounts option to allow Normal users to create and edit users.
- You can turn on Access By Others to User's Documents if you want to allow other users to access this user's documents. If you do, you can choose how those users will have access from the pop-up menu: Read Only, Read & Write, or Write Only. In many cases you'll want to leave this turned off, but you may have a case where other users should be able to view this user's documents, such as a young child's.

Applications

For Limited and Panels accounts you can select the Applications tab to decide which applications the user will be able to launch and use. Selecting applications is simple—scroll through the list and place a check mark next to any application that the user should be able to access.

TIP *The full list can be a bit daunting. At the bottom of the window you'll find a Show pop-up window that may make it easier for you to view the applications list by showing all applications but AppleScripts or by showing only selected applications.*

If you don't see an application on the list that you want this user to be able to access, click the Add Other button. You can then use the Open dialog box to find the application you want the user to be able to access. You can also use the Select All or Select None button as a convenient way to select every item on the list or clear the list out, respectively.

Privileges

For Limited and Panels users you can select the Privileges tab to determine what Mac OS components and resources each user will be able to access. Place a check mark next to the items that this user is allowed to access. You should note two special issues—if you opt to enable the user to access CDs and DVDs on the restricted list, you'll create that list later in the section "Set Global Multiple User Options." Second, the Shared Folder option allows this user to access a special folder, the Shared Folder, which is created on your disk when you first enable Multiple Users.

Alternate Password

This tab is only active if you've enabled alternate password usage on the Login tab of the Global Multiple User Options dialog box. It allows you to assign an alternate password—such as a voiceprint password—for this particular user.

Save and Edit Users

Once you've finished setting the user's information, applications, and privileges, you can save that user's settings by clicking the Close box in the Edit window. Now the user will appear in the Multiple Users control panel.

To edit that user account again, double-click the account's icon in the Multiple Users control panel or select it and click Open. If you'd like to create a similar user, you can select that user and click Duplicate. Now you'll be able to rename the user and create a similar account.

Delete a User

You can delete a Multiple User account by selecting the user name in the Multiple Users control panel and clicking the Delete button. You'll see an alert asking if you want to delete the user; click Delete again. Now, you'll be asked if you want to delete the user's folder. If you click Delete, that user's settings and documents are deleted. (It'd be a good idea to have a backup of that user's folder before deleting it.) You can also click Keep, which will leave the user's folder on the iMac. Now, if you ever create another user with this same name, you can use the same folder, settings, and documents, if desired.

Set Global Multiple User Options

The Multiple Users control panel offers some global options that you can set affecting all of your users. These options are accessed by clicking the Options button in the Multiple Users control

27

panel. That brings up the Global Multiple User Options dialog box. In the dialog box you'll see three different tabs where you'll make settings: the Login tab, the CD/DVD-ROM Access tab, and the Other tab. Click a tab to see that tab's options. When you're done setting options, click the Save button in the dialog box to save your settings.

Login Settings

On the Login tab you'll find some general settings that let you determine what users see on the Login screen and how they go about logging in. In the Welcome Message text area you can enter a short message that appears at the top of the Login window.

For better security, turn on the If the User Is Idle For option, then enter a number of idle minutes that Login should wait before taking action. Then, you choose what happens—either the user is logged out of his or her account (Log Out User option) or the screen is locked (Lock The Screen option). In either case, the user will need to re-enter his or her password in order to regain access to the iMac.

The other two settings are special cases. Turn on Allow Alternate Password and select a method from the pop-up menu, if you'd prefer to use either Voice Verification or a third-party method of authentication. (Most of the time you won't, although playing with voiceprint verification can be fun for a while.)

CD/DVD-ROM Access

When you set up Limited and Panels users, one of the options is to restrict those users' access to CD-ROM and DVD-ROM titles. If you do restrict them (as discussed in the section "Create User Accounts"), then you have two options—you can restrict a user from all CD/DVD-ROMs or restrict them to a list of CD/DVD-ROMs. It's on the CD/DVD-ROM Access tab of the Global Multiple User Options window (see Figure 27-3) that you'll build this list of authorized CD/DVD-ROMs.

This can be a bit tedious. What you need to do is insert each CD/DVD-ROM title in your CD or DVD drive so that it's mounted on the desktop. Once inserted, the disc appears in the Inserted pop-up menu (if you have more than one CD/DVD drive you can choose the inserted disc from this menu). Now, to add the CD to the list of authorized titles, click the Add to List button. The title appears in the List for Restricted Users. Now, in the Restrict Content To pane of the window, you can turn on and off individual items on that CD/DVD title so that the user can only access parts of the authorized disc, if desired.

When you're done adding discs, you'll have a list of titles that are the only CD/DVD-ROM titles those users can access. If they insert others, the discs will be ejected and they'll see a message saying they don't have enough access privileges to use the disc.

NOTE   *A restricted user can't play audio CDs, because they can't be added to the list of authorized discs. You can, however, add DVDs. In order to play audio CDs, the user must have unrestricted access to the CD/DVD drive.*

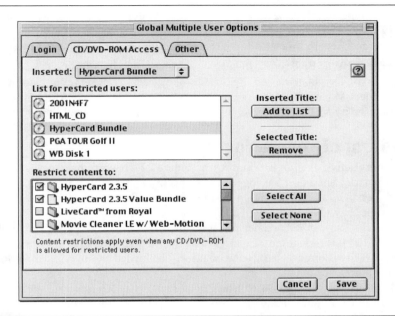

FIGURE 27-3   The CD/DVD-ROM Access tab helps you build a list of discs that your restricted users can access.

Other Options

On the Other tab in the Global Multiple User Options dialog box, you'll find a listing of miscellaneous options you can use to affect the way Multiple Users works. Here's what each does:

- **Allow a Guest User Account**   If you turn this option on, you can create a guest account that allows users who don't have a user name and password to log onto the iMac.

> **CAUTION**   *The Guest User account is given Normal access by default, which is quite a bit of control for a guest. You might want to immediately edit the account so that it has a Limited or Panels interface.*

- **Notify When New Applications Have Been Installed**   If you turn on this option, you (the owner account) will see a dialog box after you or a Normal account user has installed a new application on the iMac.

■ **When Logging In** This option offers two radio button selections: Users Choose Their Names From a List or Users Type Their Names. The first is easier for the users, but the second is more secure, since users are required to remember their login names.

■ **User Account Will Be From** In most cases this should be Multiple User Accounts (Local). If you happen to have a Macintosh Manager account server on your network, you can select Macintosh Manager Account (On Network). (Macintosh Manager is software used by Mac OS X Server and AppleShare IP professional server packages.)

Log In and Out of Your Account

With Multiple Users active, the Login window (see Figure 27-4) appears whenever the iMac is started up, restarted, or after a user has logged out of his or her account. By default, you'll see a list of user account names and icons that go along with them. To log in, you simply double-click a user account name, or click it once and then click the Log In button.

Once you've selected your user name, you'll see the Enter Password dialog box (unless an alternate password has been specified). Enter your password and press RETURN or click the OK button. If the password is correct, your user account will be loaded and the Finder (or Panels interface) will begin to load.

If you'd like to change your password, you can do that as you log into your account. Select your user name from the Login window, then click the Change Password button.

FIGURE 27-4 The Login window is shown before the iMac is completely started up.

> TIP   *If an alternate password is activated, then you'll see the alternate password's dialog box. If this is a Voiceprint Verification password, you'll see the Voiceprint Verification dialog box. As the line scrolls along the dialog box, speak your voiceprint phrase. If your voice matches, then the dialog disappears and the Finder or Panels interface will begin to load. You can click Cancel in the Voiceprint Verification dialog box if you'd prefer to enter your typed password.*

It's important to note that two other things happen at this point. First, any items in your personal Startup Items folder are launched—each user in a Multiple Users setup has his or her own Startup Items folder in the System Folder. That means you can place items in your Startup Items folder if you'd like them launched when you log in.

> TIP   *You can hold down the SHIFT key to bypass your startup items immediately after you've entered your password.*

Second, your keychain is automatically unlocked if you haven't changed your keychain password. (In some cases, your keychain will not be opened automatically if you're the owner, especially if you created and used your keychain before you enabled Multiple Users for the first time.) By default, creating a Multiple Users account also creates a keychain whose password is the same as the Multiple Users account password. If you don't want your keychain opened automatically when you log in, change the keychain password (see Chapter 24 for details).

You'll notice (unless you're the owner, who can store documents anywhere) that you have either a special folder or a special panel that's got your user name on it. This is your personal folder on the system. Store your documents in this folder and others can't access them (unless the owner has allowed access to your files). You can also install applications in this folder, if you have enough privileges. Likewise, Limited and Panels users will have an Items folder (or panel) where aliases to authorized applications are stored.

To log out, choose Special | Logout from the Finder or Panels menu. You'll see an alert box asking if you really want to log out. If you don't, click No. If you do, click Yes or wait 90 seconds and you'll be logged out automatically.

> NOTE   *Before you're completely logged out, any items in your Shutdown Items folder will be executed.*

Chapter 28 Network Your iMac

How to...

- Connect your iMac to a network
- Enter the settings for your network protocols
- Connect to any network server
- Share files on the network
- Set up users, groups, and privileges
- Create your own network

A *local area network (LAN)* is two or more computers connected by special cabling (or, these days, wirelessly) for the purpose of sharing files and resources like printers. With a file-sharing network, you can copy files to and from other computers that are attached to yours either via cabling or a wireless technology.

You begin by attaching Ethernet cable to your iMac(s) or installing AirPort card(s) and, if necessary, an AirPort Base Station. You then configure your iMac so that it recognizes (and is recognized on) the network. Then, in order to share files, you'll connect to a server computer using the Network Browser (Mac OS 9) or the Connect to Server window (Mac OS X).

NOTE   *Only the "slot-loading" iMac models and subsequent models like the iMac G4, support AirPort technology. You'll need to install and configure the card, as discussed in Chapter 26.*

Beyond simply accessing a network server, you can also turn your own iMac into a server computer using File Sharing technology. That way, others on the network can access your iMac to copy files to and from the folders on your hard disk that you give them permission to access.

Set Up the Cards, Cables, and Software

Each iMac or other computer or printer on your network needs to have a way to connect to that network—either via Ethernet cable or an AirPort wireless card. Once you have those cables and cards installed, you'll need to configure them using the Networking pane in System Preferences (Mac OS X) or the AppleTalk and/or TCP/IP control panels in Mac OS 9.

Connect Using Ethernet

Regardless of the size or complexity of your network, your iMac gets connected the same way. If you're using cabling (as opposed to AirPort wireless cards, which are discussed later in the section "Connect Using AirPort"), then you'll connect to other Macs via an Ethernet cable. If you're connecting the iMac to *one* other machine, you can use something called an *Ethernet crossover* cable.

If you're connecting to more than one machine, you'll use a regular Ethernet *patch* cable (called "Category 5") to connect your iMac to an Ethernet hub (or switch), which then allows you to connect to many other machines (see Figure 28-1). A hub is required to connect three or more Macs (or other devices, like network printers and Windows PCs).

FIGURE 28-1   An Ethernet hub allows many computers to connect to one another using Ethernet cables.

You'll notice that the connector on the end of an Ethernet cable looks a lot like a phone cable connector, only it's larger. When you're connecting it to your iMac, make sure you're plugging that cable into the Ethernet port, not the modem port. (The connector won't fit in the modem port, but you could create trouble by trying to squeeze it in.) Once it's connected, you can connect it directly to the Ethernet port of the other Mac (if you're only connecting two computers using a crossover cable) or you can connect it to an open port on the Ethernet hub.

To remove the Ethernet connector, press the small tab on the connector in toward the connector, then pull the cable out. This works just like removing a phone cable connector from a wall jack.

Did you know?

Add Older Macs to the Network

Originally, Macs used a different type of network connection called LocalTalk. Some older Macs—pre-Power Macintosh models, as well as some more recent Performa and PowerBook models—were designed without built-in support for Ethernet at all. (Many, however, can accept upgrade cards for Ethernet capability.) Using the Printer port on these Macs, the LocalTalk cabling could be used to connect a line of Macs to one other. AppleTalk protocols could run over LocalTalk hardware, so it was pretty much as easy as AppleTalk networking today. (TCP/IP protocols, however, cannot run over LocalTalk, so you have to use AppleTalk for such a network.)

But LocalTalk and Ethernet cabling aren't compatible, so you can't simply connect the wiring. Instead, you need to have a *bridge* between the two types of cabling.

One such bridge is the Farallon iPrint (now owned by Proxim, **http://www.proxim.com/**), discussed in Chapter 26 for its ability to hook up LocalTalk printers to the Ethernet port on iMacs. The iPrint handles up to eight LocalTalk devices, so you can use it to hook up a network of LocalTalk machines into your Ethernet hub. Then, all those LocalTalk machines (or just one LocalTalk machine, if that's all you have) are available on the network.

Connect Using AirPort

For an AirPort connection, you'll need an AirPort card properly installed in your iMac, as discussed in Chapter 26. You'll also need an AirPort device to connect *to*—that can be either an AirPort Base Station or another Mac that has an AirPort card installed. The AirPort Base Station is a small, UFO-shaped device that Apple makes available for AirPort networks—it acts as a hub, like an Ethernet hub, allowing AirPort-enabled Macs within a 150-foot radius to communicate with it.

NOTE   *If you're running Mac OS 9, you can actually use an iMac as a base station for other AirPort-enabled Macs and portables, if you'd like to avoid buying additional hardware. If you have an AirPort card installed in your iMac, launch the AirPort Setup Assistant and follow its instructions for setting up your iMac as a software base station. Then, other Macs can share files with your iMac, print to its printer and so on.*

The AirPort Base Station needs to be configured, which you do by running the AirPort Setup Assistant, found in the Utility folder inside the Applications folder in Mac OS X 10.1 (or higher) or in the AirPort folder, located inside the Apple Extras folder inside the Applications (Mac OS 9) folder for Mac OS 9. The Setup Assistant must be run from a Mac that has an AirPort card installed; it will guide you through the process of communicating with the Base Station and configuring the AirPort network.

Once the Base Station is configured, or if you're working with a Base Station that's already configured, you're ready to select a network. If you're using Mac OS 9, launch the Airport utility (it's found in the Apple menu) and make sure AirPort is turned On. If it is, you can now select the wireless network you just created from the Network menu.

TIP   *The AirPort application can also be used to turn the AirPort card on and off.*

In Mac OS X, you'll select your wireless network using Internet Connect. Launch Internet Connect (it's in the Utilities folder inside the Applications folder) and select AirPort from the Configuration menu. Make sure AirPort is turned on. If it is, you can select the newly created network from the Network menu. (The Connect button in Internet Connect is used to tell the Base Station to connect the Internet.)

NOTE   *Mac OS X also has a Signal Strength Dockling that you can use to control your AirPort connection. It has the added advantage of showing you the signal strength for your AirPort connection.*

Once the AirPort card has found the AirPort Base Station, your iMac is "wired" to the base station, so to speak. Now you'll move on to setting up your protocols, turning on File Sharing, and connecting to other Macs on the network.

Choose Your Protocol

Once you have the network set up between your iMac and other Macs (or other computers), you need to choose the protocol you're going to use to pass data between them. There are two major protocols in use today by Macs and iMacs: AppleTalk and TCP/IP. AppleTalk is the traditional favorite of Mac users—it tends to be easier to configure on smaller networks and can allow newer Macs to network with much older (ten years or more) Macs.

TCP/IP, the protocol used over the Internet, is becoming the standard, however. In Mac OS 9, it's possible to set up a small network that includes File Sharing over TCP/IP, which is faster and a little more interoperable with other operating systems. Mac OS X, likewise, is designed for TCP/IP.

Which should you use? It's up to you and circumstances—the wires and airwaves don't really care. If you're connecting to a lab of Macs in an educational or organizational setting, you'll need to be configured to use the protocol that the system administrator has chosen. That may be AppleTalk or TCP/IP. If you're setting up your own LAN, you can choose either, keeping in mind that AppleTalk is best for communicating with older Macs and peripherals, while TCP/IP is faster and may be necessary for tasks like multiplayer gaming.

There's another caveat. While Mac OS X can support more than one TCP/IP connection (for instance, both a modem and an Ethernet connection can have different TCP/IP settings), Mac OS 9 can only support one TCP/IP configuration at a time. So if you decide to use TCP/IP to connect to a network, you may not be able to simultaneously use your iMac's modem for Internet access. If you have a choice, it may be best under those circumstances to connect to your network using AppleTalk so that you can use your modem for TCP/IP access.

Actually, there is another solution. You can use TCP/IP for both Internet and File Sharing access if you have an Internet router or a similar gateway device installed. See the section "How to...Get Internet Access for your LAN," later in this chapter.

Turn On AppleTalk

If you've opted to use AppleTalk as your networking protocol, you'll need to activate it in the AppleTalk control panel (Mac OS 9) or the Network pane (Mac OS X).

Mac OS X version 10.1 is the first version of Mac OS X that can connect to other Macs that are running File Sharing over AppleTalk; if you have an earlier version of Mac OS X, AppleTalk is only used for printing—you'll have to use TCP/IP as your networking protocol, and you'll need to connect to servers that support File Sharing over TCP/IP.

In the AppleTalk control panel, you choose the connection you're going to use for your network. If you choose Ethernet or AirPort, you might also see another menu, the Zones menu. This menu allows you to determine which AppleTalk zone your iMac will appear in. (You'll only see this if you're connected to a large network.)

NOTE — *Zones are designations that network administrators use to artificially separate Macs from one another. For instance, you can separate Accounting computers and Human Resources computers in different zones so that users are less likely to access a hard disk or printer that isn't in their AppleTalk zone. If you're at home setting up your own network, you won't see zones, because they require hardware—either a router or a server computer that acts as a router.*

For AppleTalk networking in Mac OS X version 10.1, you'll activate AppleTalk in the Network pane of System Preferences. Select the port you want to use from the Configure menu (either Ethernet or AirPort), then click the AppleTalk tab. Turn on the Make AppleTalk Active option and, if appropriate, select the AppleTalk Zone where you'd like your iMac to reside. (Again, you'll only see this in larger organizations.) If you need to configure AppleTalk's node and network ID manually, you can do that by choosing Manually from the Configure menu; otherwise, Automatically is standard for most users.

Set Up TCP/IP

In many cases you'll want to use TCP/IP as your networking protocol instead of AppleTalk. TCP/IP configuration is discussed in detail in Chapter 23, and configuring for a local network instead of the Internet isn't really all that different.

You set up TCP/IP in the Network pane of System Preferences (Mac OS X) or the TCP/IP control panel (Mac OS 9). For most local networks, you'll select Ethernet (or AirPort). Next, in the Configure menu, you'll choose either Manually or Using DHCP. Which you choose, again, depends on circumstances and your network administrator. If you have a fixed IP address on your network

How to ...   Connect to a Windows Network

You may find your iMac is better off using a different protocol if you're not connecting primarily to other Macs. For instance, drivers exist that make your iMac capable of speaking to the IPX protocols used by Novell Netware (**http://www.netware.com/**) servers in larger organizations. If your office or organization uses Windows NT Server as a server operating system, you'll likely still sign in using AppleTalk, since Windows NT can allow you to share files and access printers over AppleTalk.

If you're simply trying to connect your iMac to a Windows 95/98 peer-to-peer network, you can use a program called Dave from Thursby Software (**http://www.thursby.com/**). Dave allows your iMac to log into a network of Windows machines running the basic Windows File Sharing protocols. If Macs dominate your network, then Thursby has a similar solution, called TSStalk, which enables the Windows machine to access an AppleTalk network.

In Mac OS X 10.1, support for connecting to some Microsoft Windows-based File Sharing networks is built right in. If you're connected to such a network and it's properly configured, you should be able to connect to a Windows-based server via the Connect to Server window, discussed later in the section "Connect to a Server."

28

(which can be used for both Internet and LAN access, for instance), then you'll enter that IP address, a subnet mask, router address, and name server, if appropriate. In most cases, you'll need to consult your network administrator to learn the correct numbers for this entry.

If you're setting up a LAN for your home or organization, and Internet access isn't a factor, you can opt to use DHCP as the configuration method. This simply means that IP addresses are assigned *dynamically,* or automatically. Usually, you select this option when you have a special DHCP server that's designed to hand out IP addresses. But, in situations where you have a small LAN and you don't have a DHCP server, choosing this setting will cause your Macs to select IP addresses for themselves. File-sharing and Web-sharing servers can then be accessed via the Network Browser (Mac OS 9) or Connect to Server window (Mac OS X).

NOTE   *Mac OS 9 is the first Mac OS version to support File Sharing over TCP/IP. Earlier Mac OS versions can't be used as servers on TCP/IP networks, although they can be used to access TCP/IP-based servers. You do this by clicking the Server IP Address button in the Chooser and entering the IP address for the TCP/IP file server.*

If you have a router or gateway for Internet access (see sidebar), you'll likely need to set up TCP/IP using the Manually setting and enter that router address in the Router entry box. Alternatively, you can set up some routers to act as a DHCP server, in which case you can set up TCP/IP for Using DHCP. Once the router is accessible from your iMac, you should be able to access both local File Sharing and remote Internet data over the same network connection.

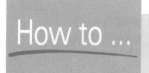

How to ... Get Internet Access for Your LAN

If you'd like to use a broadband modem or similar solution with your network of Macs and iMacs, you can do that by adding an *Internet router* to your network. The router sits between your cable or DSL modem and routes Internet data from that modem to your network, depending on the requests being made by your Macs and iMacs.

Routers are generally hardware devices—popular models in the $250 range for Mac networks include those made by Macsense (**www.macsense.com**) and Proxim (**www.proxim.com**), although it's worth noting that routers are generally cross-platform and can work with any type of computers. Note that routers are also often Ethernet hubs, typically enabling you to connect between four and seven computers and printers.

Note also that some cable and DSL providers prohibit Internet routers on their networks or require you to pay for additional computers that you're connecting—consult them for details. And, if you do opt to provide Internet access to your entire network, you should learn the workings of your router to configure any *firewall* features that are built into the router to block unwanted access. Likewise, you should be vigilant with your File Sharing settings, ensuring that you aren't allowing guest access and that your users don't have easy-to-guess passwords.

Connect to a Server

Once you've got your network set up and AppleTalk or TCP/IP configured for Ethernet or AirPort, you're ready to log into any AppleShare-compatible server computers on the network with your user name and password. In Mac OS 9, you open the Network Browser located in the Apple menu. In Mac OS X, switch to the Finder and select Go | Connect to Server. (See Figure 28-2 for examples of both.)

In either window, the first items you'll see are *network neighborhoods* that represent the different types of servers you'll find on your network. There are a few basic neighborhoods you may encounter. If you're using AppleTalk for your networking, you'll see an AppleTalk neighborhood. (If your LAN has AppleTalk zones active, you'll see the zones inside the neighborhood, which you can then open to reveal the computers associated with each zone.)

You may also see a Local Network neighborhood, which represents TCP/IP-based networks. In addition, if your network has an assigned domain name, you may also see that name in the Network Browser as a neighborhood (like my domain, "mac-upgrade.com").

To open one of the neighborhoods, click it once in the Connect to Server window, or click the disclosure triangle next to it in the Network Browser. Now, you should see the file servers available on that network for logging in. To connect to one of those servers, select it and click the Connect button (in the Connect to Server window) or double-click the server entry (in Network Browser).

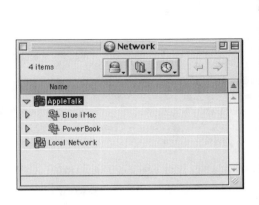

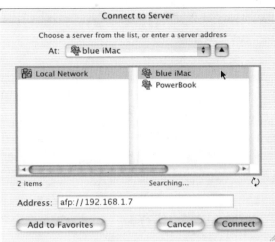

FIGURE 28-2   On the left, the Network browser; on the right, the Connect to Server window

NOTE *In the Network Browser, you can click the Shortcuts button (the pointing hand) and choose Connect to Server, then directly enter an IP address for a TCP/IP-based server. In the Mac OS X Connect to Server window, you can enter an IP address in the Address box (see Figure 28-2).*

Now the Connect to File Server dialog appears. Enter your name and your password, then click Connect to connect to the server. Note that the password is case-sensitive, so don't use uppercase if your original password used lowercase.

TIP *If you want to change your password, click the Change Password button in Mac OS 9 or click the Options button in Mac OS X.*

If you've entered your user name and password correctly, you're shown the different disks or folders available to you from the server computer. Pick a disk and double-click it to mount it on your desktop. That's it: you've logged in and you're able to access files on the network drive as if they were on your own iMac. The disk is mounted on your desktop, just like a removable disk or a floppy disk image (shown is the Mac OS 9 icon for a network volume).

When you're done with a disk, either drag it to the Trash can or select it and choose File | Put Away in Mac OS 9 or File | Eject in Mac OS X. That will unmount the disk. Once you've put away

 **Store Connections on Your Keychain**

As discussed in Chapter 24, you can use your keychain to store often-used login names and passwords in one central place, so that you don't have to remember all your user names and passwords for different servers. Connecting to servers using the Network Browser or the Connect to Server window is one place where this comes in handy.

If you'd like to use the keychain, you should first set it up, as described in Chapter 24. Then, you can add a login to the keychain. Here's how:

1. Locate the computer you want to log into and double-click it as you'd normally do.

2. Now, in the Connect to File Server dialog box, enter your user name and password, then click the check box to turn on the option Add to Keychain. (In Mac OS X's Connect to File Server dialog box, you need to click Options first, then turn on the Add Password to Keychain option and click OK.)

3. Click Connect. Double-click the volume you'd like to access.

4. If your keychain is locked, you'll see a dialog box that asks you to enter your keychain password. If your keychain is unlocked, then your user name and password are added to the keychain automatically.

Now, whenever you log into that server in the future, you won't see the Connect to File Server dialog box. Instead, your keychain will be consulted, and if it's unlocked, the password will be given automatically. If your keychain is locked, you'll be asked to enter your keychain password; then you may see a dialog box asking whether you want to give the Network Browser or Connect to Server window access to the keychain. Once you've set it up, you'll never have to remember your server password again!

all disks and files that you've logged into for a particular server, you'll be logged out of the server computer automatically.

NOTE   *If you're not seeing a server that you're expecting to see, make sure you've properly configured both the server and your iMac to use the same protocols (TCP/IP and/or AppleTalk) and the appropriate hardware (Ethernet or AirPort). Common problems include not turning on the File Sharing over IP option on a Mac OS 9-based server (discussed in the section "Set Up Your Own Network") or forgetting to properly configure AppleTalk or TCP/IP for your local LAN.*

Set Up Your Own Network

Once you have your network connections in place and AppleTalk and/or TCP/IP up and running, you're ready to set up File Sharing and share folders from your iMac on the network. When you set up File Sharing, you're actually turning your iMac into a server computer. Other users attached to your network will be able to sign onto your iMac, access any folders that you make available to them, and copy files to and from your iMac.

CAUTION
Once again, remember that turning on File Sharing poses a security risk, particularly if you turn on File Sharing over TCP/IP (which is the default in Mac OS X) and you have an active Internet connection. If you turn on File Sharing, make sure all of your users have hard-to-guess passwords and that you don't create any users that don't have passwords.

Turn On File Sharing in Mac OS X

File Sharing in Mac OS X is so simple that I'll cover it quickly before we get into Mac OS 9's File Sharing. All you need to do, once your network is configured, is launch the Sharing pane of the System Preferences application. You'll see the File Sharing section at the top of the screen. Click the Start button, and File Sharing will be started. When the message changes to File Sharing On, your iMac is set up as a server.

NOTE
The Sharing pane also has other options, including Allow Remote Login and Allow FTP Access. In general, it's recommended that you leave these options off unless you're an advanced user who intends to use your iMac as an Internet server or in a cross-platform environment. Enabling these services while your iMac is connected to the Internet is an unnecessary security risk.

Unlike Mac OS 9, you don't need to set up users, groups, passwords, and so forth. Instead, File Sharing in Mac OS X uses the same users discussed in Chapter 27. By default, however, regular (non-Admin) users can only see the Public folders of other users. Also, Mac OS X doesn't have an option to turn off Guest access, so realize that anyone who gains access to your iMac's IP address could access Public folders and even upload items to user's Drop Boxes. It's important to remind users not to launch items that appear in their Drop Boxes if they're not sure of the item's origin.

Users with Administrative accounts can see nearly all folders on the hard disk and have access privileges similar to when you're working directly on the iMac. (Actually, an Admin account has slightly more power, so make sure you don't accidentally delete important files when you're logged into a Mac OS X computer via File Sharing.)

NOTE
Any Admin user who accesses your iMac via File Sharing can access other volumes attached or mounted on that iMac, including removable disks and external disks. If you think it's important, you should eject them, disconnect them, or set privileges as discussed in the section "Set Sharing Privileges."

28

Set Up File Sharing in Mac OS 9

In Mac OS 9, you'll use the File Sharing control panel to turn your iMac into a network. The File Sharing control panel requires that you enter an Owner Name, Password, and Computer Name in the top of the control panel. You may already have entries here, particularly if you've completed the Mac OS Setup Assistant that launched after running some versions of the Mac OS 9 installer program.

You can change them, if you like. To start up File Sharing, click the Start button under the File Sharing Off heading. This begins the process of File Sharing. If you have AppleTalk configured and your Ethernet cables properly connected, you're in business—your iMac becomes a server.

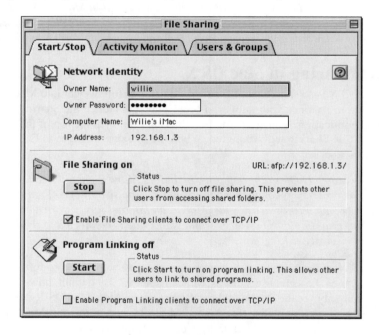

You also have the additional option of turning on File Sharing over TCP/IP. If you'd like to share your files over your TCP/IP network (and you've configured the TCP/IP control panel as discussed earlier in this chapter), you can click the check box next to the Enable File Sharing Clients to Connect over TCP/IP option. This allows anyone who knows your iMac's IP address (which is shown in the control panel, for your convenience) to connect to your iMac and share files.

 *File Sharing over TCP/IP is required if you want Macs running Mac OS X versions prior to 10.1 to access your iMac—those early Mac OS X versions can't connect to a Mac that only has File Sharing over AppleTalk enabled.*

Create Users and Groups

In Mac OS 9, you have the additional step of deciding who can access your computer. By default, *you* can already access your iMac from another computer, using the Owner name and password. (This gives you special access, by the way, allowing you to see every folder and file on the iMac, regardless of what other security measures you've put in place.)

For other users, you need to create user accounts for individuals accessing your iMac over a network. Do that by selecting the Users & Groups tab in the File Sharing control panel.

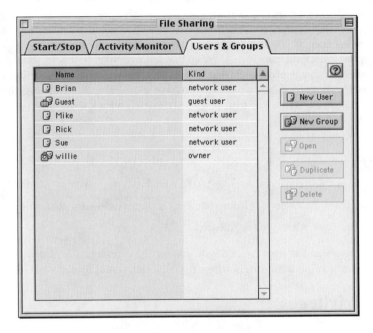

Actually, you don't have to create users if you enable Guest access and you give Everyone privileges to your iMac's files. (See "Set Sharing Privileges," later in this chapter.) It's good to go through the motions of creating users, though, so that you can specify privileges and make sure that no one snoops around your network while you're connected to the Internet or connected via Remote Access. Too much security is better than too little.

If you're using File Sharing over IP, you should be especially vigilant about your Guest access. Since people can potentially access your iMac over the Internet (depending on your configuration), you should only allow users with a user name and password to sign on.

To create a new user in Users & Groups:

1. Click the New User button.

2. You'll see a dialog box that allows you to enter a name and an initial password for this person. If you want the user to be able to change his or her own password, leave the check in the Allow User to Change Password check box.

TIP *Encourage your users to create hard-to-guess passwords that include a mix of numbers and letters that aren't common words or meaningful dates.*

3. Click the Close box to add the person to your list of users.

If you have more than one user (aside from yourself and the Guest account), you may need to create a new group. A group accepts some or all of your users, so you can set sharing privileges for the entire group. For instance, if you want people to have access to a folder you've created on your disk called Accounting Files, you can create a group that has everyone in it who should be able to access that folder, then set things up so only that group can access that folder, as discussed in the section "Set Sharing Privileges." Alternatively, if you have a special folder called Assistant Files that only your assistant, Rick, is allowed to access, you can assign Rick individual privileges for that particular folder.

Here's how to create a group:

1. Click the New Group button.

2. Give the group a name.

3. Drag names from the Users & Groups window to the window for that group.

4. Click the Close box when you're finished.

Now, with your users and groups created, you can set the privileges for those users and groups. Do that by accessing the Sharing settings for each individual folder.

Set Sharing Privileges

Select a folder (or a disk) that you'd like to share with a particular user or group and choose File | Get Info (Mac OS 9) or File | Show Info (Mac OS X). In the Info window, choose Sharing (Mac OS 9) or Privileges (Mac OS X) from the Show menu. Now you're ready to set privileges for this particular folder (see Figure 28-3).

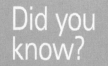

Guest Access

By default, Guest access is turned off in Mac OS 9, which is probably a good thing. If you're unworried about security and want to make it easy for anyone to log into your iMac, however, you can enable Guest access. To do this, double-click the Guest account on the Users & Groups tab, then select Sharing from the Show menu. Turn on the Allow Guests to Connect to This Computer option, then click the Guest window's Close box. Guest access is now enabled—visitors won't need a password to log into your computer if they choose Guest in the Connect to File Server dialog box.

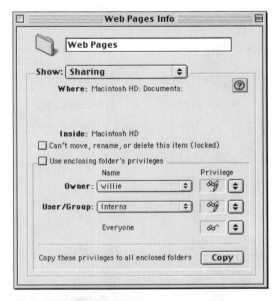

FIGURE 28-3   On the left, Sharing settings in Mac OS 9; on the right, Privileges settings in Mac OS X

Privileges in Mac OS 9

What does it mean to set privileges? In Mac OS 9, you get to decide which user or group can access this particular folder and what he, she, or they can do with it. Here's what the settings do in Mac OS 9:

- **Can't Move, Rename, or Delete This Item (Locked)**   Click this box to deny users permission to alter the folder itself. This locks the folder.

- **Use Enclosing Folder's Privileges**   If clicked, the folder should use the same sharing settings as its parent folder. If the Mac Letter folder is in the Documents folder, then checking the check box means the sharing privileges for Mac Letter will be the same as those for the Documents folder. If you uncheck this box, you can set the privileges separately.

- **Owner**   Choose which user is owner of this folder. That's usually you.

- **User/Group**   Choose which user or group has access to this folder. If you want more than one user to have access, you'll need to place those users in a group. If you want more than one group to have access, you'll need to place users from all those groups in one larger group.

- **Everyone**   If you want to give all users—regardless of their user and group status—certain privileges for the folder, choose from this menu.

 *Consider granting access only to the Owner and a particular user or group, not to Everyone. That will help you manage the security of your files.*

Next to the Owner, User/Group, and Everyone entries, a little icon appears showing the privileges assigned to each.

You can assign to a particular user or group one of four access levels:

- **Read and Write Access** The user or group can both save files and access existing files.
- **Read Access** The user or group can read (open or duplicate) files from a folder but can't save files to that folder.
- **Write Access** The user or group can save files but can't access other files in that folder.
- **None** The user or group has no access to the files in that folder.

Finally, click the Copy button if you'd like these privileges copied to all subfolders.

Privileges in Mac OS X

The Privilege settings are a bit simpler in Mac OS X, because you can't actually select the owner and group as you can in Mac OS 9. The owner is always the person who created the folder and the "group" entry almost always refers to the Admin group. So, if you'd like to set privileges for a folder, first you need to be the owner. If you aren't the owner, you can't change the privilege settings for the selected item. If you are the owner, you'll be able to set the Read and Write access levels for the Admin group (which is also called the "wheel" and "staff" groups in Mac OS X) and for all other users (Everyone).

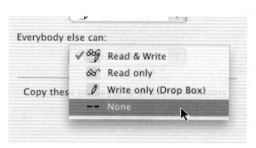

 *Privileges in Mac OS X are used not only for File Sharing, but also for local access for multiple users, as discussed in Chapter 27. The privileges you set for your folder will allow or disallow access to your folders for other users who log directly into your iMac.*

Take the Networking Quiz

Networking can be a bit complex, so, to recap, let's look at a few different scenarios you may encounter and how you'd configure your iMac (and other Macs) under those circumstances. You can then dig back into the chapter to see how to perform each of the tasks. We'll look at networking two Macs, networking two Macs wirelessly, and creating a larger network of more than two Macs.

Connect Your iMac to Another Mac

If you have one Mac that you'd like to connect to your iMac, you can use an Ethernet crossover cable to connect them without an Ethernet hub. Then set up AppleTalk or TCP/IP, turn on File Sharing, and you're ready to sign on.

Here's the procedure:

1. Connect the two computers' Ethernet ports using an Ethernet crossover cable—a special cable that needs to be bought specifically for this purpose. (Ask for an Ethernet crossover cable from the salesperson at a computer shop.)

2. On each computer, do one of two things. Either turn on AppleTalk over Ethernet for both computers, or turn on TCP/IP over Ethernet.

   ■ **AppleTalk**   In Mac OS 9, open the AppleTalk control panel on each Mac, choose Ethernet in the Connect Via menu, then close the control panel. In Mac OS X, open the Network pane on each Mac, select Built-in Ethernet from the Configure menu, select the AppleTalk tab, and click to turn on AppleTalk, then close System Preferences. (Remember that you'll need Mac OS X version 10.1 in order to access another Mac's file-sharing server over AppleTalk.)

   ■ **TCP/IP**   In Mac OS 9, open the TCP/IP control panel and choose Ethernet from the Connect Via menu. In the Configure menu, choose Using DHCP, then close the control panel. In Mac OS X, open the Network pane of System Preferences, choose Built-in Ethernet from the Configure menu, then click the TCP/IP tab and choose Using DHCP from the second Configure menu. Close System Preferences. (For Mac OS 9, this assumes that you don't need Internet access for the duration of the File Sharing session. If you do, and you don't have a DHCP server, you'll likely need an Internet router and manual settings, as detailed earlier in the section "Choose Your Protocol.")

3. On the Mac you designate as the server computer, make sure your Sharing privileges settings are the way you want them for the particular user who's going to sign in. (If it's just you, then you'll want to log into the other computer as Owner in Mac OS 9, or using an Administrator account in Mac OS X.)

4. On that server computer, open the File Sharing control panel or System Preferences pane. Turn on File Sharing.

5. Once File Sharing has started up, use the Network Browser or the Connect to Server window from the other computer to access the server and see if it's available.

6. When you find the server, double-click it to log on. (In Mac OS X, you should click the server's name once, then click Connect.) Enter your name and password and click Connect.

7. Finally, choose the disk you want to mount—double-click it and it'll appear on your desktop.

To log out of the server, choose all the disks you've mounted and drag them to the Trash, or select them and choose File | Put Away or File | Eject from the Finder menu.

28

Connect Two Macs Wirelessly

If you have an AirPort card installed in your iMac, you can use that card to connect directly to another AirPort-enabled Mac without a base station. To do so in Mac OS 9, open the AirPort application on each Mac and select Computer to Computer from the Choose Network pop-up menu. In the dialog box that appears, enter a name for the network. You can also click the More Options button if you'd like to create a password for this network. When you're done, click OK and the network is created—you can close the Airport application.

In Mac OS X, launch Internet Connect, choose AirPort from the Configuration menu, then choose Computer to Computer from the Network menu. In the dialog box that appears, enter a name for the network. Now, you can set each Mac's AppleTalk or TCP/IP settings to AirPort, and share files as discussed in the section "Connect Your iMac to Another Mac."

Network More Than Two Computers

If you plan to network more than two computers via Ethernet, you'll need an Ethernet hub. You're actually creating a local area network, or a LAN, at this point. Connect each Mac's Ethernet port to the Ethernet hub using regular Ethernet patch cable, not a crossover cable. (If you have an AirPort Base Station as part of your network, you'll connect that to the Ethernet hub using a patch cable, too. That way, AirPort-enabled Macs connected to the AirPort hub wirelessly can access the rest of the Ethernet-based computers.)

Once all the machines are connected to the hub, set up AppleTalk or TCP/IP to use Ethernet on each wired machine. Now, decide which Macs are going to be file servers (they don't all have to be) and turn on File Sharing on those machines. Now, set the Sharing privileges for folders or disks on those servers as you see fit.

What you're doing is setting up a peer-to-peer network. One common way to do this is to create a shared folder on each machine so users can log into each other's Macs and swap documents by placing them in each other's shared folders. Here's how:

1. Make every Mac on the network a server by enabling File Sharing on each Mac.

2. Now, on each Mac create a folder that will be its shared folder. For instance, on Willie's Mac, he'd have a folder called Willie's Shared Folder. On your Mac, you'd have a folder called Devoted Reader's Shared Folder. Other people on the network would also have a shared folder. (In Mac OS X, you automatically have a shared folder in your home folder called Public, which others can copy files from and a Drop Box, inside that Public folder, where others can place files.)

3. Next, in Mac OS 9, have everyone set privileges so that others on the system can access their shared folders (probably adding them to a group on each machine and giving that group privileges to see the folder). But only set up Sharing privileges for that one folder so that no one can get into the rest of your files.

4. When you head to the Network Browser or Connect to Server window, you'll see the name of each machine that has File Sharing turned on in either the AppleTalk or Local Network neighborhoods. Log in with your password on that machine (everyone will have to gather around the coffeemaker to make sure you know the user name and password that others have assigned you), and you'll see that person's shared or Public folder. Double-click the folder and it will be mounted on your desktop, ready to use.

TIP   *If you have an Ethernet-based printer, hook that up to your hub as well. That way, all the computers on the network can access the printer. Just plug the printer directly into the hub using a typical Ethernet patch cable. For each Mac to use that printer, select the printer in the Chooser or Print Center. See Chapter 25 for more on setting up Ethernet printers.*

28

Chapter 29

Troubleshoot, Upgrade, and Maintain Your iMac

How to...

- Find technical support resources
- Troubleshoot your iMac's hardware
- Troubleshoot software
- Deal with errors
- Fix freezes and hangs
- Fix extension problems and conflicts
- Reinstall, restore, or update your iMac's software
- Maintain your iMac for long life

It's never good when your iMac starts giving you serious trouble. Hopefully, you won't encounter this much, although the likelihood is that, eventually, you'll have to troubleshoot something. The nature of today's computing is that it isn't all flawless.

Not that it has to be an intolerable experience, either. One of the tricks is adhering to a good maintenance schedule. If you do that, you'll probably have fewer instances of trouble. Better yet, if you do have trouble, a solid backup routine will help you minimize that trouble, allowing you to get back to work as quickly as possible.

So, let's take a look at the three different aspects of keeping your iMac healthy and happy: troubleshooting, updating, and maintenance. Using these three different steps, you can keep your iMac running well, or get it up and running again after you've had some trouble.

Find Tech Support Online

Since this is the Internet-savvy iMac we're talking about, I recommend that you get to know online resources for troubleshooting your iMac right at the outset. Apple's iMac-specific support pages are very useful and offer some great features, including online message areas for iMac users. These sites offer a great way to learn more about your iMac, identify potential problems, and do what is probably the most important step in keeping your iMac tuned—stay up on the latest news and information.

Enter **http://www.apple.com/support/** in a browser, then look around for the link to iMac Support. (There's currently an iMac graphic that you click. Apple likes to change the design of their pages every once in a while, though.) Once you select iMac Support, you'll be taken directly to Apple's special support Web site for the iMac. It's here that you'll find all sorts of information about the iMac, including the latest news, articles on different technologies related to the iMac, and pointers to any software updates that have been released for the iMac.

I won't harp specifically on certain parts of the iMac Support site because the site is likely to change. You'll probably always find a link to the Tech Exchange or a similar message area that allows you to exchange messages with other iMac users and Apple Tech Support specialists.

You'll probably also find links to the latest updates, including updates to the iMac's firmware, to the Mac OS, to the applications that came with your iMac, and to the modem's firmware, among others. (*Firmware* is a type of software/hardware driver combination that can be installed to update your iMac. The firmware updates usually fix bugs or add new features and capabilities to hardware like your iMac's modem or the iMac itself.)

While you're online, you might also want to check out some of the popular Mac-oriented sites, where you'll find news and help on various issues affecting your iMac as well as the entire Macintosh industry. Here's a sampling of them:

Macworld	**http://www.macworld.com/**
MacCentral	**http://www.maccentral.com/**
MacAddict	**http://www.macaddict.com/**
MacFixIt	**http://www.macfixit.com/**
Mac-Upgrade.com (my site)	**http://www.mac-upgrade.com/**

All of these sites can help you find new peripherals, follow the news regarding Apple, discuss Mac and iMac troubleshooting issues, and so on.

Troubleshoot Hardware Problems

There are a couple telltale signs that something has gone wrong with your iMac. Here's what they are, what might cause them, and a few things to try before sending your iMac off to the repair shop.

> TIP   *The Emergency Handbook that comes with many iMac models is also a great source of troubleshooting information. Use it if you don't see the answer in this text. Apple's iMac Support Web pages are equally valuable, especially for getting the most up-to-date information.*

Get Past a Blank Screen or Tones

If you've just tried to turn on your iMac and you've gotten no response, you're seeing a blank screen, and/or you're hearing tones, it's possible there's something wrong with the internals of your iMac, like a RAM module that's not properly installed or something that has come loose. Before you pack it off to the service center though, test a few things:

- Make sure the iMac is plugged in properly and the surge protector (if you're using one) is turned on.

- Check for signs that your surge protector is working correctly and that it hasn't absorbed a power surge, which might cause a fuse to blow on the power strip.

■ Restart the iMac by pressing CONTROL-⌘-POWER (on the keyboard) or by holding down the Power button on the front or back of the iMac for at least ten seconds.

■ Unplug all USB (and FireWire, on later iMac models) peripherals and network connections other than the mouse and keyboard. Try restarting.

■ If that doesn't work, restart the iMac via the Reset button or reset hole, as discussed later in the sidebar "How to…Restart Your iMac."

If none of that works, you may need to take your iMac in for service.

Fix a Blinking Question Mark

If a question mark is blinking in the middle of your screen soon after you start or restart your iMac, it's a sign that the iMac can't find a disk with a working version of the Mac OS on it. Here's what you can do:

■ Wait a minute or so. It may resolve itself. (If this happens, check your Startup Disk control panel or preference pane and make sure it's set to start up from the iMac's internal disk.)

■ Restart with CONTROL-⌘-POWER (or CONTROL-⌘-EJECT) or by pressing the Power button on the iMac for ten seconds.

■ Unplug the iMac, wait a minute, then plug it back in and press the POWER key.

■ If none of the previous steps does away with the blinking question mark, consider performing a step called "zapping the PRAM" to see if that gets your iMac to notice the drive and boot from it. Do that by restarting the iMac. After the startup tone, hold down ⌘-OPTION-P-R until you hear the startup chime two more times. Then, release the keys. That may cause iMac to find the internal hard disk and start up normally. (See the "Did You Know…PRAM" sidebar for more information.)

If these things don't work, start from a recovery CD and run Disk First Aid or a disk doctor application.

Start Up from a Mac OS (or Recovery) CD

Your iMac has the ability to start up from a CD-ROM, which is useful if you need to troubleshoot your main disk, install a new Mac OS version, or start up from a recovery CD such as those included with Norton Utilities or a similar utility program. If you need to start your iMac from a CD-ROM, here's how:

1. Restart. (You can use the Special | Restart or Apple menu | Restart commands or you can reset the iMac as described later in the sidebar "How to…Restart Your iMac.")

2. As the iMac starts, place the CD (the iMac Restore CD, a Mac OS CD, or a recovery CD) in the drive tray or in the CD's slot.

3. Hold down the C key right after the iMac plays its startup tones until you see the Mac OS startup screen and/or hear the CD drive being accessed.

The iMac will start up and the CD will be the main disk that appears in the top-right corner in the Finder. Open that CD, if desired, and launch the disk doctoring utility. (If it's a Mac OS X CD, you can select Disk Utility from the Installer menu.)

Fix a Problematic Peripheral

If a USB device isn't working, check to make sure it's installed correctly. If the non-working device is connected to a USB hub, turn the hub on and off to reset it.

If everything is plugged in correctly, reset the device by turning it on and off. Also, unplug and replug the device's USB connector (which will often reset its USB driver) and follow the manual's instructions for resetting the device.

If you're having trouble with your printer, check to make sure it's selected (highlighted) in the Chooser (Mac OS 9) or Print Center (Mac OS X). Turn it on and off again, or check the printer's manual for a command that allows you to restart the printer.

If none of these work, unplug the device and restart your iMac. Now, with the Mac OS loaded, plug the device back into the USB port. Hopefully, it will be detected and begin working again.

With FireWire devices, you can plug and unplug them if they're not recognized, but be sure you don't plug and unplug devices while they're in use. Also, if a FireWire device requires power from the FireWire bus, plug it directly into the iMac's FireWire port or into a powered hub.

29

PRAM

Parameter RAM (PRAM) is a small portion of RAM that the iMac uses for special settings in control panels, as well as some other internal settings. This RAM always has a little power trickling to it, thanks to a battery inside your iMac. PRAM can also become corrupted, which requires a reset. A reset is usually a last line of defense—but you can try zapping PRAM using the earlier method.

Once you've reset PRAM, it's important to dig into your control panels (in Mac OS 9) or the System Preferences application (in Mac OS X) and make some changes. Your AppleTalk settings, some network settings, the date and time, your iMac's screen resolution, and other settings are stored in PRAM. After PRAM resets, those items need to be manually updated again.

Also, note that the battery that powers PRAM eventually runs out, usually after three to five years. When that happens, the most obvious clue might be that your iMac's clock seems to reset itself to January 1, 1904. If you haven't recently reset PRAM, that's a sure sign it's time to replace the battery, which any Apple Authorized service center can do for you.

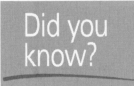

Heat Buildup

One thing that's important to watch out for with any computer is a rising internal temperature, which can lead to erratic performance, crashes, and even component damage. This is particularly true of slot-loading iMacs, which are designed to work without a fan—heat leaves through the air holes in the top of the iMac.

So, it's important to make sure your iMac is in a well-ventilated area, that it's operated at room temperature, and that you don't cover those air holes with paper, books, cloth, cats, or other obstructions.

TIP *Keep up with Mac OS and QuickTime updates from Apple and you'll likely have better luck with peripherals.*

Eject or Rename a Removable Disk

If you're having trouble renaming or ejecting a removable disk, it may not be a problem with the media. Sometimes you'll encounter this trouble when File Sharing is turned on. (It happens more in Mac OS 9, although you can't rename disks in Mac OS X with File Sharing on, either.) The solution is to open the File Sharing control panel or the Sharing pane in System Preferences and turn off File Sharing. Now, rename or eject the volume, and turn File Sharing back on, if desired.

The other side of this problem is a CD that doesn't appear to be recognized and/or won't eject when you select the Eject commands in the Finder or on your keyboard. If File Sharing is turned off, you may be having trouble with the CD being properly recognized. (I've noticed this particularly with CD-RW discs that haven't been completely or properly erased by the Disc Burner software.) If you've encountered such a disc on a slot-loading iMac, your best plan may be to physically eject the disc by inserting a straightened paperclip into the small hole at the far right of the slot. That should activate the mechanism, popping the disc out. Now, the next step is to restart your iMac, particularly in Mac OS 9, just in case it still believes a disc is in the drive.

Troubleshoot Software Problems

There are three basic causes of software problems. Let's define those quickly, then we'll take a look at the symptoms your iMac may be experiencing. Here are the problems that software can encounter on your iMac:

- **Bugs** Bugs are the result of mistakes or oversights by programmers who created applications or the Mac OS. Usually, the only fix is to stop using the program and/or update it.

■ **Conflicts**   Conflicts occur when two pieces of software—two applications, an application and a Mac OS system component, or two system components—don't get along. Conflicts cause crashes and freezes and are usually solved by finding the culprits and updating or disabling them. Extension conflicts (the type between Mac OS extensions that load as the iMac starts up in Mac OS 9 or Classic) are discussed later in "Troubleshoot Extensions and Drivers."

TIP   *Read the Read Me file that accompanies any application causing you trouble. The Read Me file might tell you that the software is known to conflict with other software on your iMac.*

■ **Corruption**   Corruption occurs when data is overwritten with either bad or nonsensical information. This can cause all sorts of trouble, but typically causes crashes and freezes. This is solved by deleting the corrupt data file or finding it and fixing it with a disk doctor program.

Understand Software Symptoms

These are the common symptoms and the First Aid you should perform for the problem:

■ **Error**   This is an error message in the form of an alert dialog box that includes an OK button. It tells you the last command you attempted could not be executed because something went wrong.
First Aid: Click OK and save your work. If the error sounds data-threatening—you're out of memory or disk space, a disk couldn't be found, or there's an error number—it's a good idea to quit the program and restart your iMac in Mac OS 9. In Mac OS X, you can continue computing, but keep an eye on that application in the future.

■ **Crash**   In this case, you get an error message and the application shuts down. Sometimes the application itself tells you about the problem, sometimes the Finder tells you there was an "Unexpected Quit."
First Aid: Save data in other open applications and, if you're working in Mac OS 9, restart your iMac. In Mac OS X, you can continue computing after an application crash, but keep an eye on that application in the future.

■ **Freeze**   Sometimes you'll get an error message, but typically the mouse pointer won't move, the clock isn't ticking, and nothing seems to be happening.
First Aid: Wait. See if anything happens. Check the mouse and keyboard connectors— you may have worked the external keyboard loose. Check for any activity (CD spinning, clicking sounds from the hard disk). Move to the section "Fix Freezes or Hangs."

■ **Hang**   Similar to a freeze, but the mouse pointer still moves and you might see the clock change or the application menu blink (if it was blinking before). In other words, there's activity.
First Aid: Wait. Note if any activity in the frontmost application occurs. If your data is important (and not recently saved) you should wait at least ten minutes before forcing the application to quit, as described in "Fix Freezes and Hangs."

Once you've gotten past the immediate First Aid, you can move on to diagnose the cause of the problem and attempt a long-term solution.

Respond to Error Messages

These are the best sorts of errors to encounter, since they give you some indication of what's going on. If the error didn't crash the application, you'll likely already have some idea what's wrong. A printing error means you should check out your printer or the Chooser; an error loading a Web site or getting your e-mail might have something to do with your Internet connection.

Most of the time, the error message is your guide. Read it, then consult the rest of this section or check out the part of this book where that application or issue is discussed—something may be wrong with your iMac's settings or hardware configuration.

Some of the errors aren't as specific—let's take a quick look at those.

Out-of-Memory Error

Many times, an error message will tell you that you don't have enough memory or "not enough memory to complete task." This can happen for a variety of reasons in Mac OS 9. (In Mac OS X, you will most likely encounter severe slow-downs in the Mac OS before you would encounter an error message.)

If the error occurs in the Finder, quit some of the open applications that you have running. If the problem continues, quit all applications and attempt to restart your iMac. If that doesn't work (or if it freezes your iMac), see the section "Fix Freezes and Hangs."

If the out-of-memory error occurs in the application you're using, do the following in Mac OS 9:

1. Save your data.

2. Switch to the Finder and choose About This Computer from the Apple menu.

3. Look to see how much of the application's memory allocation is being used (does it fill the entire allotted space?) and how much is left in the "Largest Unused Block." If the memory's allocation is filled or nearly filled, you'll want to assign the application more RAM through its Get Info dialog box.

4. If the Largest Unused Block is less than 2MB or so, you might need to quit some of your other applications. You should also check the Memory control panel and make sure Virtual Memory is turned on. (See Chapter 24 for more on the Memory control panel.)

If the problem is with the application's memory allocation, make these changes:

1. Shut down the application.

2. Find the application's original icon. Select the icon and choose File | Get Info.

3. In the Info window, select Memory from the pull-down menu.

4. You'll see entries for the Minimum Size and Preferred Size of the application. This is the amount of memory, in kilobytes, that the Mac OS allocates for the program. You might add about 512KB to the minimum and about 2000KB (or more) to the preferred.

5. Click the Info window's Close box to close the window and register the change.

Now you should quit all applications, restart, and see if the error recurs. (You don't have to restart, but it's best to do so since restarting clears out memory and starts over fresh.)

If you get memory errors even though you've increased the allocation and you've shut down some applications, it's possible that memory has become *fragmented*. This is a temporary condition in Mac OS 9 where memory is filled with unattached bits of data that haven't been properly disposed of after you've opened and closed many applications and/or documents. (It's sort of like application litter.) If memory gets too cluttered by fragmentation, you need to restart the iMac to get it working properly again.

> **TIP** *If out-of-memory errors happen often, consider upgrading the RAM in your iMac. Many iMacs shipped with 32MB or 64MB of RAM, which is a little skimpy, especially if you're running Mac OS 9 and trying to work with graphics applications and games. Consult Chapter 26 for more on upgrading RAM.*

Disk Is Full Error

If your hard disk gets full or close to full, you'll start to see all sorts of errors, including "Disk is Full." Most applications, Internet programs, and games write temporary files, preference files, and other sorts of data to your hard disk, even when you're not actively saving a document. If your hard disk gets full, it will cause applications and the Mac OS to have trouble it doesn't expect to encounter.

If it happens to you, the best plan is to delete any old documents (or any that you have backed up already) and uninstall any applications or games that you don't immediately need.

(You'll find that most application installers also have a Remove or Uninstall choice in their Custom Install menu.)

You should also consider getting rid of image files and QuickTime movies—these are culprits that can take up a lot of disk space, as can games and educational software.

Insufficient Privileges Errors

Privileges problems generally crop up when you're trying to copy items in the Finder in Mac OS X. The basic issue is this—in Mac OS X, thanks to its Unix-like infrastructure, each file has certain privileges assigned to it when it's created or copied. Each file has an owner, a group associated with it, and privileges assigned to "everyone."

If you don't have the proper privileges for a file, then you often can't move or delete it. In some cases, you may not even be able to access a file so that you could load the file in an application and view it. Likewise, privileges can be assigned to folders, where you may not be able to read (view) the file, write (move, delete or save) to the file, or both.

You have a couple of solutions to privilege problems. If you are using a regular Mac OS X account and you have access to an administrator's account, you can log in as an administrator and work with many files, particularly those in the main Applications and Library folders on your iMac. If you don't have access to an administrator's account, or if that still doesn't work, you may need to ask the owner of the file to move or delete the files. (For instance, if you create a folder inside the Shared folder, that folder is owned by you, meaning no other user, not even an administrator, can move or delete it.)

There's a third solution for changing ownership of files. Copy a file to a user's Drop Box, located inside her Public folder and that file becomes owned by that user. This is a great way to make sure that a person you are working with on your iMac has full control over the file, including the ability to delete it if necessary.

NOTE   *Sometimes a removable disk or an external drive may be inaccessible because of privilege problems on that disk. If that's the case, you can do the following. Select the disk, then choose File | Show Info in the Finder. Select Privileges from the pop-up menu in the Info window. At the bottom of the window, turn on the Ignore Privileges on This Volume check box. Now you should be able to access the disk. (If security is a concern, copy the files to another location, then turn the Ignore option back off when you're done.)*

Deal with Crashes

There are a couple different kinds of crashes you'll encounter. Often they'll include an error message or an alert, but sometimes they just happen. Here's a look at what could occur:

- **Error Message or Code**   When an error message appears within the application itself, it means the application *noticed* the error. This can lead you to the source of the problem. It may be a bug in the document or corruption of the document.

- **Unexpected Quitting**   The program disappears, followed by a message in the Finder. This sort of crash often happens because there's a bug in the program or the program encountered a corrupt data file.

■ **No Message**   In this case, the program just quits or disappears. In Mac OS 9, you might notice more error messages in the Finder regarding memory. This could be corruption, but it's likely a bug or a conflict.

Test for Crashing

So what can you do about a crash? The most important thing is to get data saved in your applications and restart your iMac in Mac OS 9. (In Mac OS X, it's generally OK to continue computing after a native application crashes; if a Classic application crashes, you should restart the Classic environment.) After that, your priority is isolating the crash—figuring out when the crash occurs and any factors that contribute to it. Here are some questions to consider when it comes to crashes:

■ *Has your iMac been on for quite a while without restarting or have you been running many different programs?* If so, it might just be that your iMac needed to be restarted, particularly in Mac OS 9. (Mac OS X is designed to run continuously for months.)

■ *Have you added anything recently?* If you've recently installed a new application or utility program, it's possible it installed a new extension that's causing trouble. You can always try disabling any new extensions (see the section "Troubleshoot Extensions and Drivers," later in this chapter, for information on how to do this).

> NOTE   *In Mac OS X, you don't work with extensions in the same way as in Mac OS 9; however, new driver software, particularly* kernel extensions *for peripheral devices, can sometimes cause conflicts. If you suspect such a driver, see the section "Troubleshoot Extensions and Drivers."*

■ *Is the crashing consistent?* If your iMac crashes every time you do something in particular— load a QuickTime movie, check your e-mail, load a particular game—then you may be closer to a solution.

If you can reproduce the error fairly consistently, then there are a few things you can try to test for the error and isolate it further. Here's what to try:

■ *Test different documents.* It's possible that a particular document is corrupt, especially if the crash occurs as you're opening a document, as you're saving a document, as you're printing, or when you move to a particular page in a document. Find a similar document or two and test the application with those to see if the same crash occurs. If it doesn't, you can try running a disk doctor utility (or a special file-fixer utility) or just avoid using that document.

■ *Remove the Preferences file.* Most applications have a preferences file that's stored in the Preferences subfolder of the System Folder in Mac OS 9, or the Preferences folder inside the Library folder that's in your home folder in Mac OS X. Quit the application, move the preferences file to the desktop or another folder, and restart the application. Some of its default behavior may change and the crashing may also stop. If it does, throw away the preferences file and reset your preferences within the application.

29

■ *Restart without extensions.* As your iMac starts up, hold down the SHIFT key until you see the message Extensions Off in the Welcome to Mac OS window in Mac OS 9. This starts your iMac without extensions. Now, run the application and see if the error recurs. If it doesn't, there might be an extension conflict. See "Troubleshoot Extensions and Drivers," later in this chapter.

NOTE
You can also restart with extensions off in Mac OS X by holding down the SHIFT key, but this only disables third-party kernel extensions, not Apple's own extensions. Still, it can be useful if you believe a third-party driver is crashing your iMac.

Fix Internet Crashing

Did the crash happen while you were browsing the Web? There may be a corrupt preferences file or a file in your browser's cache. You can delete the cache in Internet Explorer by choosing Edit | Preference, then choosing Advanced. Click the Empty Cache Now button to empty the cache.

There is a special Internet Preferences file that's created by the Internet control panel in Mac OS 9. That Internet Preferences file gets changed and saved often by different applications, which can lead to corruption after a while. If you are crashing in many different Internet applications, try opening the Preferences folder in Mac OS 9's System Folder and dragging the Internet Preferences file onto the desktop. Restart your iMac, reset your Internet Preferences in the Internet control panel, and try out your applications. If the crashing has gotten better, toss the old Internet Preferences file in the Trash.

In both Mac OS 9 and Mac OS X, the preferences, cache, and other files for individual Internet applications can also cause problems if they become corrupt. Open the Preferences folder inside the Mac OS 9 System Folder, or the Preferences folder inside the Library folder inside your personal home folder in Mac OS X. In those folders, you'll find the Explorer folder for Internet Explorer's files and the Netscape Users folder for Netscape files. Generally, you can delete "cache" and "history" files without causing too much trouble; but think twice before trashing bookmarks or Favorites.

Fix Freezes and Hangs

A freeze will bring the mouse cursor to a halt and nothing else will happen on the screen. A hang is a little different—the mouse pointer moves, even though things otherwise seem frozen. Why the difference? A hang results when an application has gone into an endless loop of some sort and can't break out to give control back to the Mac OS. A freeze occurs when an application goes bad and causes the Mac OS itself to seize up.

Freezes are odd problems, because they can be attributed to all the types of problems we've discussed: bugs, conflicts, or corruption. Freezes can also be caused by other applications that are running in the background, or even by trouble with printing or networking.

If it's really a freeze, you probably can't recover from it—the best you can do is restart. But that doesn't mean you shouldn't try some stuff. After all, it's important to know if your iMac has actually frozen, or if it's just a hang. In Mac OS X, this is particularly true, as it's much less likely to freeze than Mac OS 9, but it's susceptible to hangs, although you can almost always switch to another application in Mac OS X (try clicking another item on the Dock or pressing ⌘-TAB to switch to another application.) Here's what to do:

1. Make sure the mouse and keyboard haven't been unplugged accidentally. Try unplugging and replugging them to see if there is a USB problem.

2. Check the screen carefully for any activity.

3. Wait. Get up and grab a cup of coffee or check to see if the mail has come. Five minutes or more might be a good idea.

4. Press ⌘-. (period) to see if you can interrupt the program. Press ESC. If that doesn't work, try ⌘-Q to quit. If none of those keyboard combinations are working, you can try a force quit—press ⌘-OPTION-ESC. In Mac OS 9, if the Force Quit dialog box appears, click the Force Quit button. The application may quit forcefully and return to the Finder without saving data.

In Mac OS X, the Force Quit Applications window appears when you press ⌘-OPTION-ESC. If you see this window, select the application that appears to be frozen and click Force Quit. If you're having trouble with the Finder, you can even select it and click Relaunch.

29

> NOTE   *As a last resort in Mac OS 9, press ⌘-POWER (the POWER key on the keyboard or, if you don't have such a key, the Power button on the front of the iMac). If a dialog box appears, type **G F** (include the space) and press RETURN. You'll either quit the program, you'll really completely freeze up, or you'll get a crash requiring an immediate restart.*

If none of these works, the iMac has frozen. Try to restart using CONTROL-⌘-POWER to force the iMac to restart, or hold down the Power button on the front of the iMac for about ten seconds. If that doesn't work, you'll need to use a paperclip or the Reset button to restart the iMac (see the "How to...Restart Your iMac" sidebar).

If the force quit does work, save work in other applications and restart immediately. After a force quit, your iMac is likely to crash or freeze again pretty soon in Mac OS 9. (In Mac OS X, you can generally continue computing, unless you've been forced to quit more than one application.)

If the freeze recurs after you've restarted and launched the application again, check the application's Read Me file for known conflicts with other applications or Mac OS extensions. Start with extensions off (hold down the SHIFT key through the startup process) and see if the freeze recurs. Check with the software publisher's Web site to see if there are any bug fixes or other suggestions. Contact the publisher's technical support folks to see if they have any suggestions.

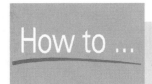

How to ... **Restart Your iMac**

Restarting via the iMac's front POWER key only works on Revision B and newer iMacs (those built in late 1998 and on, including the "flavored" iMacs and the slot-loading iMacs). If you have an original Revision A iMac, you'll need to straighten a paperclip and insert it in the Reset button hole (labeled with a triangle) to restart your iMac.

You may need to press the Reset button to restart a slot-loading iMac that doesn't respond when you press the Power button on the front. If you have a slot-loading iMac, the Reset button is a raised button on the right side of the iMac near the ports. The button has a small triangle on it. (It's shown in Chapter 1)

Troubleshoot Extensions and Drivers

Occasionally, in Mac OS 9 or the Classic environment, your problems will arise from within the System Folder, usually in the shape of an extension conflict. The extensions, stored in the Extensions folder, are small bits of computer code designed to patch or add themselves to the Mac OS as it starts up. For instance, Apple ships extensions that add QuickTime capability—the ability, at the Mac OS level, to work with QuickTime movies. If you started up Mac OS 9 with extensions off, you'd find that it's unable to play QuickTime movies because the proper extensions haven't been loaded.

NOTE *In Mac OS X, extension conflicts with native applications are more rare, but can also be more problematic when they do occur. See the section "Mac OS X Extensions and Drivers," later in this chapter.*

In most cases, an application that's designed to work with Mac OS 9 and/or the Classic environment has been tested fairly thoroughly and shouldn't experience a conflict. (This isn't always the case, and many applications have to be updated slightly when a new Mac OS update is created by Apple since small inconsistencies can affect programs.) But application authors, no matter how diligent, can't test their application with every conceivable extension available for the Mac OS—there are thousands of them. So, you'll sometimes experience a conflict or similar problem, thanks to an extension.

One of the solutions that some folks follow is to simply try not to install too many extensions. If you are the type who wants zero trouble from your iMac, I'd recommend that you avoid most utilities and shareware and some applications that install their own extensions. You should certainly only buy software that specifically mentions the iMac or that has clearly been tested to work well with your version of Mac OS 9. This is particularly true if you work with the Classic environment in Mac OS X often or exclusively; the fewer extensions loaded, the better.

The best way to troubleshoot an extension problem is to hope someone has already figured it out and all you have to do is read about the conflict. If that doesn't work, though, then it's up to you to root out the conflict using the Extensions Manager. Let's take a look.

> TIP
>
> *Want to know if something has been added to your Extensions folder in Mac OS 9? Go open it right now. Select every file in the folder—just click somewhere in the folder and press ⌘-A. Now, choose File | Label and give the files a label. Now, when a new extension is added, it won't have a label and the original extensions will. You can check every time you install a new application.*

Is the Conflict a "Known Issue"?

The Read Me file for the application that seems to be suffering a conflict, as well as any other Read Me files you can come across (especially those for applications or utilities you've recently installed) is the first place you should look when you suspect a conflict. If you've recently installed extensions or control panels, you should look into them, as well. It's possible that the conflict is actually a known issue, and that the software publisher recommends you not use the program in combination with certain extensions or particular applications.

You should also check the technical support Web site for the troubled application and call the application publisher's customer support number. If there really is a conflict, you're probably not the first person to ever encounter it and tech support might be able to point you in the right direction.

> NOTE
>
> *You're definitely going to encounter some situations where an application will work in Mac OS 9, but won't work in the Classic environment. This may be a conflict, but it may also simply be a limitation in the Classic environment. Check the manufacturer's Web site for hints, but realize that in some circumstances, you'll simply need to boot into Mac OS 9 to use the offending application.*

Extensions Manager: Test for Conflicts in Mac OS 9 and Classic

When a conflict occurs between an extension and an application—or an extension and another extension—it's tough to diagnose on your own. But if you can't find information from any of the software publishers that seem to be involved, then testing yourself becomes necessary.

You won't enjoy, this, though. Set aside a few hours one afternoon and grab a book or magazine, because this can take a while. You'll want to use the Extensions Manager—it's a control panel that allows you to selectively activate and deactivate extensions and other control panels that are installed on your iMac.

> TIP
>
> *Conflict Catcher from Casady and Greene (**http://www.casadyg.com/**) does a nice job of automating this process, making it a bit more bearable. Casady and Greene also has a time-limited demo that you can download to test for trouble.*

Here's how conflict troubleshooting in Mac OS 9 and the Classic works:

1. In Mac OS 9, or with a Classic application frontmost in Mac OS X, select Control Panels | Extensions Manager from the Apple menu to open the Extensions Manager.

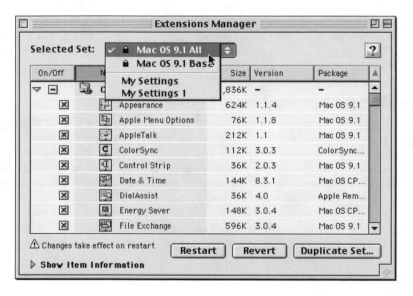

You can open the Extensions Manager from within the Classic environment, or you can open it when starting up Classic by opening the Classic pane in System Preferences, clicking the Advanced tab, then choosing Open Extensions Manager from the Startup Options menu and clicking the Start Classic button.

2. In the Extensions Manager, pull down the Selected Set menu and choose Mac OS 9 All (the name may vary slightly depending on your Mac OS version). This selects only the extensions that Apple originally designed to work with the iMac.

3. Click the Restart button. (If you started up directly into Extensions Manager, select the Continue button.) After your iMac restarts and the desktop appears (or the Classic environment has otherwise fully started up), launch the application that was giving you trouble and see if the same error persists. If it does, then your application may have a conflict with the Mac OS itself. Contact the application publisher.

4. If you get a different error after restarting, it's possible that you disabled an extension required by the application—if the application gives you some indication of which extension it is, go into the Extensions Manager and re-enable that extension. (Click to place a check mark next to any extension that you want to have installed.) Now restart and test again.

5. If you're not having trouble anymore, that's a sign that you're having a bona fide extension conflict. Open the Extensions Manager again and choose View | As Folders. This allows you to see everything that's in the Extensions folder at one time.

6. Make sure you're viewing extensions—the Extensions folder is revealed and a list of extensions appears below it. Now, place a check mark next to three to five extensions at the top of the list. (The first time you do this, you'll be asked to create a new extensions set. Click Duplicate Set, then enter a name like "Test Set" and click Duplicate.) Once you've added three to five extensions in alphabetical order, click the Restart button.

7. Test again for the conflict. If things seem to be working OK, go back to step 6 and keep adding extensions.

8. If the conflict does recur, stop what you're doing, go back and re-disable the last batch of extensions you enabled. (It's not a bad idea to write down the extensions you're enabling each time.) Now, enable the *first* of those extensions and restart.

9. After the restart, open your application and test for the conflict. If the conflict doesn't occur, go back, enable the next extension, and restart again. Repeat until the conflict does occur. When it does, you've figured out which extension is causing the conflict! Actually, you only know one of the extensions causing a conflict. You still need to do a little more testing.

10. In the Extensions Manager again, pull down the Selected Set menu and choose the Mac OS 9 All (or similar) entry again. Now, find the extension you've identified as a problem and place a check mark next to it. (When you do, you'll be asked to create another extension set. Call this one Test 2 Set or something similar and save it.) Click the Restart button.

11. Test to see if the conflict problem recurs. If it does, then you can pop down to the next section, "Resolve the Conflict." If the conflict *doesn't* recur, then you'll need to start the conflict test again—it looks like your conflict may involve two extensions.

12. Add three or more extensions to the Test 2 Set and restart. Test for the problem. Add more extensions if it doesn't recur. If you do encounter the problem, then disable the last set of added extensions and add them back in one at a time, restarting and testing each time. Finally, when you identify the second extension that's causing trouble, you're getting very close.

13. From the Selected Sets menu, choose Mac OS All once more. Place a check mark next to the two extensions you've identified as the problem. (You'll be asked to create a third set—call it "Test 3 Set.") Now, with just the Mac OS extensions and the two potential problem extensions enabled, restart.

14. Test again. If you get the conflict, you've found your problem. If you don't get the conflict, you may be in the absolutely rare situation of a three-way conflict. Pop some popcorn and keep testing.

Resolve the Conflict

Now that you know what's causing the problem, the best way to resolve the conflict is to visit the makers of the conflicting software and see if any of them have a work-around, an admission

29

of guilt, or an upgrade posted that deals with this problem. You might also want to call their customer support line and see if you can get any help that way.

If those things don't work out, you might want to select one of the extensions and leave it disabled if it's not absolutely vital to your daily iMac experience. At least then you won't have to deal with the conflict.

You can try one other thing, too. Sometimes extensions conflict because of the *order* in which they're being loaded. Extensions load alphabetically, so you can change the order by opening the Extension folder in the System Folder and editing the name. Put a space in front of the name to move it to the top of the alphabetical list. If you want the extension to load at the bottom of the extensions list, place a bullet point (OPTION-8) in front of the name. Now, restart with your edited extension names and see if the conflict recurs.

Mac OS X Extensions and Drivers

For the most part, Mac OS X does away with the entire *extensions* concept, and it doesn't allow third parties to "patch" the operating system. This is probably a good thing, as Mac OS extensions, while historically useful, can also be exceptionally problematic.

That said, there are extensions to Mac OS X—called *kernel extensions*—that can be installed by third parties. Instead of adding capabilities to the system, however, these extensions are generally just low-level device drivers for working with third-party peripherals.

If you're having trouble with such an extension, the first solution is to boot with extensions off. Hold down the SHIFT key as Mac OS X starts and only Apple's kernel extensions will load. (You can press SHIFT-⌘-V for the "verbose" version of this startup process.) If you notice that the trouble has ended, then you'll need to get in touch with the company that wrote the extension and let your displeasure be known (or simply see if they have a newer version of the driver).

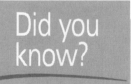

Kernel Panic

Mac OS X is built on top of a tiny, low-level operating system called a *kernel,* and it's this OS that's used to talk directly to hardware devices—that's why many device drivers are kernel extensions. This also opens up a vulnerability—when there's a problem with the kernel, it's one of the few problems that can truly crash the entire Mac OS X system, meaning a freeze or full-blown crash. That's called a *kernel panic.*

In most cases, there isn't much you can do to resolve a kernel panic other than following the instructions for restarting, if you see any onscreen. Otherwise, restart the iMac using the instructions discussed earlier in this chapter in the section "How to...Restart Your iMac." Now, you should carefully watch your iMac to see if it shows signs of trouble, and try to either locate a solution (a new device driver, for instance) or to avoid reproducing the error in the future.

Reinstall, Restore, and Update

Eventually, you may get to the point that you need to reinstall your applications, reinstall the Mac OS, or even update the iMac or Mac OS. As far as reinstalling and restoring go, you can do those things easily using the software CDs that came with your iMac. You can also update your iMac using the updates posted by Apple on the iMac Support Web site.

Uninstall and Reinstall Applications

If you want to get rid of an application, the best way to do it is usually to launch the application's installer program and choose Uninstall or Remove from the Custom Install menu. That's the best way because it removes any special extensions or control panels the application added to your iMac.

If you need to manually uninstall an application, that shouldn't be too much harder. Just drag the application's folder to the Trash. Now, open the System Folder in Mac OS 9, or the Library folder in your home folder in Mac OS X, then open the Preferences folder and drag the application's Preferences file to the Trash, too.

Before doing this, it's a good idea to check the application folder (in Mac OS 9) and make sure you didn't store any important documents in that folder—you can reinstall the application, if necessary, but you can't recover the documents you delete accidentally. You should also stop to consider whether or not you have another application that can read documents created in the uninstalled application. If you don't have one and you think you may need to read those documents at some point, then you might want to translate them to another document format before tossing the application for good.

If you've uninstalled an application in this way, then it's usually pretty simple to reinstall the application—just run the installation program. Before reinstalling, you should probably make sure that the old Preferences file has been deleted, and that there isn't another version of the application already on your hard disk. (Two versions of the same application could cause trouble, and will definitely cause confusion.) Other than that, reinstalling is pretty easy to do.

29

TIP   *You can also get utility programs that help you uninstall applications, such as the popular Spring Cleaning (**http://www.aladdinsys.com**).*

Perform a Software Restore

If you ever get in real trouble with your iMac, you have an out that can save you, get things up and running again, and hopefully go a long way to solving your problems. It's called the Software Restore, and it allows you to reinstall the Mac OS and your applications to the state they were when you first pulled your iMac out of the box and set it up.

Even if that sounds enticing, realize that this is a recourse of last resort. Doing this can wipe out any changes you've made to the Mac OS, settings you made in various control panels, updates you've made to your applications, and so on. It's important that you not perform a Software Restore lightly, since you're in for some extra work—reconfiguring and reinstalling extras— once you've performed the Restore. Still, it's there if you need it.

To perform the Software Restore, you'll be restarting your iMac and booting off the Software Restore CD. Here's how the Software Restore works:

1. If your iMac is on, insert the Software Restore CD in your iMac's CD/DVD drive and restart the iMac. If your iMac is off, start it up, then quickly insert the CD. Place the Software Restore CD in the drive and close it back up.

2. If your iMac doesn't automatically start up from the CD, restart the iMac and hold down the C key after you hear the startup tone.

3. Once the iMac has started up from the CD, double-click the Apple Software Restore icon on the CD.

4. Now choose between the two basic ways to perform a Software Restore. Click the Restore In Place check box if you'd like the iMac to restore the Mac OS and applications to their original state. Choose Erase Mac HD Before Restoring if you'd like the hard disk to be erased before the restoration takes place. (With later versions of the Software Restore application, it will always erase the hard disk. If you don't want to do this, you should use the Software Install CD to re-install the Mac OS and/or your applications.)

NOTE *Choosing Restore In Place won't erase your Documents folder or most of the other folders on your hard disk. It will, however, change settings in the Mac OS and erase anything other than the original iMac bundle. Choosing Erase Mac HD Before Restoring will wipe out everything on the disk, including documents, games, and so on. If you've installed a newer version of the Mac OS or any of its components, you'll need to reinstall those updates and any backed-up documents after the Software Restore.*

5. If you've chosen Erase Mac HD Before Restoring, you can also choose how you want your hard disk formatted—with Standard or Extended Mac OS format. The Extended Mac OS format gives you more efficient use of the hard disk so that you can pack more files onto the drive. (Extended is the best choice, but you might have some reason to choose Standard that you're not willing to share with the rest of the class.) Make your choice from the menu.

6. Once you've made all your decisions, click Restore to begin the process.

Your iMac starts the process of formatting your hard disk (if you chose that option) and restoring the original Mac OS and applications to your hard disk. After this process is over, your iMac is restarted and, hopefully, starts up from its internal hard disk again in all its splendid, restored, glory.

Now it's up to you to go through the process of restoring everything, setting up the iMac again, and copying over documents from your backups. You may also need to reinstall applications, reapply updates, and basically spend an afternoon getting everything back into shape.

Reinstall Mac OS X

In its current iteration, Software Restore doesn't re-install Mac OS X, so you'll need to do that from the Mac OS X CD-ROM. Note that you may have other reasons to do this as well—unlike previous versions of the Mac OS, the Mac OS X installer is good at fixing problems and replacing corrupt files when it's run. If you're noticing trouble with Mac OS X that seems to be at the system level, you might try re-installing from the CD-ROM.

Of course, you should use the most recent CD-ROM version that you have and, if you've downloaded updates to the Mac OS using Software Update (discussed later in this section), then you may need to perform those updates again. Also, the re-installation can actually take quite a bit longer than the initial installation, because it requires the installer to check each system file on your hard disk for changes.

Update Your iMac

Early in this chapter we discussed the fact that you can update the firmware in your iMac. You can also update applications and, occasionally, the Mac OS. In most cases, those software updates use an interface that's exactly like the typical software installer—you choose the installation and tell the installer which drive you want to install on. They aren't tough to use. Check Apple's iMac Support Web site for details on the various updates available for iMac software and the Mac OS.

A firmware update is a slightly different story. You'll also find these on the Apple Support site, but they're installed slightly differently. First, you'll want to download the update from the Web. Then, once the update has been processed by StuffIt Expander, it appears as a disk image. Double-click it to mount the disk. Once the disk appears on the desktop, double-click the Firmware Updater icon.

Here's how the process goes:

1. If your firmware is up to date already, you'll immediately see a dialog box letting you know that. If it's not, all applications are quit in the background and the updater continues.

2. You'll see a dialog box explaining the process. When you click Update, your iMac restarts.

3. Now, after the iMac has restarted, you'll see a small indicator bar that tells you that the update is progressing.

4. When the update is finished, PRAM is automatically zapped (you'll hear a series of startup tones), then the iMac starts up.

5. When you get to the desktop, the iMac should tell you that the firmware was updated successfully.

If all doesn't go well, you may need to go through the process again. There are also some situations where you may be asked by the updater to shut down your iMac and press the Programmer's button. (The Programmer's button is the one under the Reset button. It's shown in Chapter 1.) To do this, click Shut Down in the dialog box.

29

Once the iMac is shut down, press the Programmer's button and hold it down, while pressing the Power button on the front of the iMac. Now the iMac will start up and the updater will be able to update the firmware. (You'll see the progress bar.)

> **NOTE** *Apple maintains a technical document that should help you determine whether or not your iMac requires a firmware update. Visit the Knowledge Base (**http://kbase.info.apple.com/**) and search for article 58174. The article is called "iMac: When to Install Available Updaters." Also, see article number 60385 for more information on firmware updates and possible error messages.*

Update with Software Update

Both Mac OS 9 and Mac OS X include a system software component that enables you to update your iMac over the Internet. Called Software Update in both OS versions, it comes in the form of a control panel in Mac OS 9 and a System Preferences pane in Mac OS X.

> **TIP** *If you use the Classic environment within Mac OS X, you should check the Software Update control panel separately whenever you're booted into Mac OS 9. The Mac OS X Software Update pane doesn't automatically update Classic or Mac OS 9.*

If your Internet connection is active, then launch Software Update and click the Update Now button. Software Update will check with special Internet servers at Apple to see if there are updates available that you don't yet have installed on your iMac. If there are items, you'll see an Install Software window appear (shown is the Mac OS 9 version).

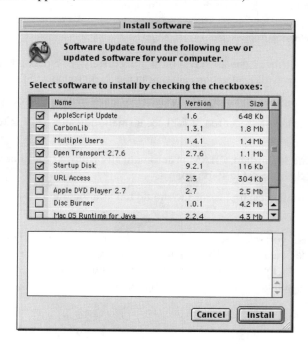

Place a check mark next to the items you'd like to download and install, then click the Install button. Those items will be downloaded (which can take a while over a modem connection) and installed. (You should stick around your iMac, just in case you need to read and agree to licensing agreements and do some other clicking.)

> **NOTE** *You may see some items that are unchecked by default—those are items that Software Update believes aren't necessary for your iMac. If you think it may be incorrect in that assumption, you can download and attempt to install those updates.*

You can also automate Software Update, so that system updates are checked for regularly. In Mac OS 9, turn on the Update Software Automatically check box, then click the Schedule button to choose a time and date(s). In Mac OS X, turn on the Automatically radio button and choose a frequency (Daily, Weekly, or Monthly) from the Check for Updates menu.

Maintain Your iMac

One of the best ways I know to help you get the most out of your iMac is a maintenance schedule. It's important to any iMac that some basic steps take place every week, every few weeks, or once every couple of months.

Here, then, are some of the things you do in the course of iMac maintenance. Let's begin with a schedule for the maintenance, then we'll take a close look at what each schedule item entails.

Schedule iMac Maintenance

A lot of the problems that occur with your iMac's hard disk, Mac OS system files, and other arcana occur slowly—a little file corruption starts to sneak in, causing more problems. Pretty soon things cascade.

What are the things you should do? There are two lists: the daily stuff and the time-based issues. Daily, you should do the following when you're working with your iMac:

- *Turn your iMac on and off no more than once a day.* If you want to shut down your iMac every evening and turn it on in the morning, that's fine. Otherwise, the settings in the Energy Saver control panel (Mac OS 9) or Energy pane of System Preferences (Mac OS X) will conserve energy. After all, it's the iMac's monitor that consumes most of the power. You can also choose Special | Sleep in Mac OS 9 or Apple menu | Sleep in Mac OS X when you walk away from your iMac.

> **NOTE** *Ideally, Mac OS X should be left on all the time, including overnight, because it occasionally runs maintenance tasks at night. The Sleep mode is a good, low-power mode that should save enough power while letting the iMac remain functional. Also, for security reasons, if you do leave your iMac on all night, it's a good idea to disable your DSL or cable modem connection by disconnecting from Internet Connect or pushing the Standby button on your Internet modem, if it has one.*

■ *When shutting down or restarting the iMac, use the commands in the Special menu (Mac OS 9) or the Apple menu (Mac OS X).* You shouldn't just turn off your surge protector or throw a light switch to turn off your iMac. Instead, use the Shut Down and/or Restart commands in the Finder. If your iMac doesn't shut down in an orderly way, then system files and configuration files can be left open, data can be discarded, and problems can ensue.

■ *Restart Mac OS 9 occasionally.* After starting and quitting many programs, your iMac's memory can become fragmented, which leads to errors. If you restart (using the Special menu) after lunch or before a major Internet surfing session, you'll get better performance with fewer errors. (Note that Mac OS X doesn't need to be restarted regularly as a maintenance task.)

■ *Check your hard disk space frequently.* If your hard disk ever fills up or comes close to it, you'll start to see errors in your applications. Make a point of throwing away documents that you're done with. That way you won't fill up your drive, plus you won't have to commit to major purging sessions every few months to regain disk space. Check disk space by selecting your hard disk icon in the Finder and choosing File | Get Info in Mac OS 9. Check the Available entry.

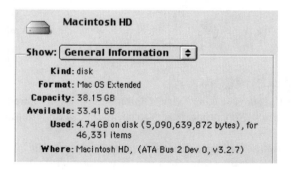

In Mac OS X, you can look at the Finder window's information area, just under the toolbar, to see how much space is available on the disk.

In the rest of this chapter, I'll discuss tasks you should perform weekly and monthly.

Check for Viruses

Since your iMac is designed to live on the Internet, chances are that you're downloading and working with many different files from different sources. This is a great way to catch a computer virus. So, you should buy a virus-checking application and set it to automatically scan your disk and files on a regular basis.

A computer *virus* is a program that attaches itself to other programs and attempts to replicate itself as much as it can, preferably by being transferred via disks, network connections, and the Internet. Not all viruses are designed to cause harm, although they can anyway, by accident. Others really are designed to infect your files, rendering them useless or sometimes deleting or destroying them.

In one sense, viruses on computers work the same way that physical viruses work. The more you're exposed to high-risk situations—the Internet, swapping Zip disks, and using a large computer network—the more likely you are to be infected. And with your iMac, you're probably spending enough time online to be high-risk.

NOTE   *In case you're curious, viruses are computer programs written by people. Virus authors are usually interested in causing consternation and fear around the world. Sometimes that's enough—other times, it's important to the virus author that they also cause trouble and loss.*

If you're online a lot with your iMac, consider getting yourself a virus-protection program. These programs generally run in the background, checking files as they appear on your hard disk or from a removable disk. You can also schedule them to check while you're not using your iMac—late at night or on the weekends, for instance.

There are two major virus packages for the Mac OS—Norton AntiVirus (**http://www.norton .com/**) and Dr. Solomon's Virex (**http://www.mcafee-at-home.com/products/virex/**). Both of these are available from online Mac stores as well as in computer stores and superstores that carry Mac OS products. Currently, only Norton AntiVirus supports Mac OS X.

Most of the time the scans take place in the background. When the virus program detects a file that it thinks may be infected, it'll let you know. Sometimes the detector will automatically move infected files to a particular folder. Other times, it may be able to clean the virus from the file after it's been isolated.

I wouldn't even try to clean a file unless you absolutely need access to its data and you don't have a good backup. (Remember, the backup might be corrupted as well—you should check). If the infected file is a document that you need, you can try to clean the virus from it.

Both of the major virus protection utilities give you the choice of scheduling scans, scanning files as they're added to your iMac (from the Internet or from removable media), or only scanning when you actively ask the program to scan. For maximum protection you should leave the scanner on all the time to check programs as they're downloaded. If you find this is annoying, then I'd recommend scheduling regular scans for when you're away from the computer.

One thing you should definitely do is update your virus definitions. The virus-protection publishers come out with updates, usually every month, that allow the software to detect more viruses, fight them better, and protect against new types of infections. In both programs, you can have the anti-virus software check automatically for updates.

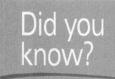

Virus Hoaxes

Viruses are a popular topic for e-mail hoaxes—e-mail messages distributed in chain-letter form, telling you to "pass it on" and "spread the word." These messages offer spurious information about some dire problem. The e-mail warnings generally show up in the form of a virus alert that's been released by "the U.S. government," "Microsoft," "a university lab," or some other organization that seems credible. A dead giveaway is misspellings or grammatical errors in the message.

Most of them also claim that reading a particular e-mail message or loading a particular Web page causes a virus to spread to your iMac. This really isn't the case—a virus can't be spread through the text of a message, so simply reading an e-mail message will not give your iMac a virus. If you *execute an attached document or program,* then it's possible to get a virus, so don't use attachments from people you don't know.

The "open an e-mail" virus alerts are hoaxes, though. Read carefully and you'll see that they probably even have misspellings or bizarre grammatical constructs, considering their supposed source. For the official word on viruses (and many virus hoaxes) the best place to turn is the Symantec Anti-Virus Research center at **http://www.symantec.com/avcenter/index.html** on the Web.

Fix Your Disks

Part of your maintenance routine will require the use of special utility programs designed to help you find corruption, fix disks, and so on. A few of those utilities are free, but others will cost some money. Let's take a look at both.

> **NOTE** *Other tools not mentioned here include Alsoft DiskWarrior (**www.alsoft.com**), which can sometimes magically recover disks (Mac OS 9 and Mac OS X) that suddenly can't be booted, as in those showing a blinking question mark. (The trick is to run DiskWarrior first, before running other applications.) Rewind (**www.poweronsoftware.com**) is a fascinating tool for Mac OS 9 that enables you to actually recover all sorts of deleted files, changed files, and other mistakes you make on your Mac.*

Rebuild the Desktop

Every month you should rebuild the desktop database in Mac OS 9. Do this by restarting your iMac and then holding down the ⌘ and OPTION keys. Hold down the keys all the way through the startup sequence until you see the Rebuilding the Desktop dialog box.

 *You can rebuild the desktop in the Classic environment from the Classic pane in System Preferences—simply open the pane and click the Rebuild Desktop button. You should do this regularly, as well, particularly if you work frequently with Classic applications.*

Disk First Aid

At least once a month you should run Disk First Aid (see Figure 29-1), which is included with your iMac and designed to find problems with the directory structure of your iMac. Run it every month or so since it'll allow you to find directory problems before they crop up. To run Disk First Aid, find it in the Utilities folder and double-click its icon.

 *In Mac OS X, Disk First Aid is part of the Disk Utility application in the Utilities folder inside the Applications folder on your hard disk. Launch Disk Utility, then click the First Aid button to view the First Aid tools. In Mac OS X version 10.1, select disk first and then click the First Aid tab.*

In the top window, select the disk you want to verify—most likely it's the Macintosh HD volume. You can now click Verify to simply have Disk First Aid take a look at the drive and see how everything is doing. If you want to repair the disk while it's being verified, click Repair. This accomplishes two steps in one click.

Now Disk First Aid runs through the disk looking for corruption in the directory structure. If it finds a problem, it'll alert you, asking if you want to fix the problem. (This is true in some cases; in others, it just goes ahead and fixes things.) Otherwise, you'll get through your session and, hopefully, receive a clean bill of health.

 *Disk First Aid can't always fix your startup disk if it's launched from that disk. The solution is to start up from your Mac OS CD-ROM (insert the CD, restart your iMac, and hold down the C key), then launch Disk First Aid from there. If you start up from the Mac OS X CD-ROM, choose Open Disk Utility from the Installer menu.*

MicroMat TechTool and Drive 10

MicroMat makes two versions of TechTool for Mac OS 9. The first is a freeware version you can download from their Web site at **http://www.micromat.com/**. TechTool Freeware is a program that makes it easy to do two things—rebuild your desktop and zap PRAM. Zapping PRAM is a technique used when you're troubleshooting a Mac. Rebuilding your desktop is something you should do regularly and TechTool Freeware makes it easier and does it more thoroughly than the OPTION-⌘ method discussed earlier in the chapter.

Along with TechTool Freeware, MicroMat also makes a version called TechTool Pro, which is commercial software. It adds the ability to analyze your iMac in depth and fix disk problems and file issues, including accidentally deleted files. It's also capable of fixing files on your disk and optimizing them, so it should be run on a regular basis.

29

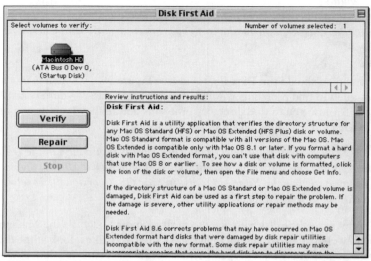

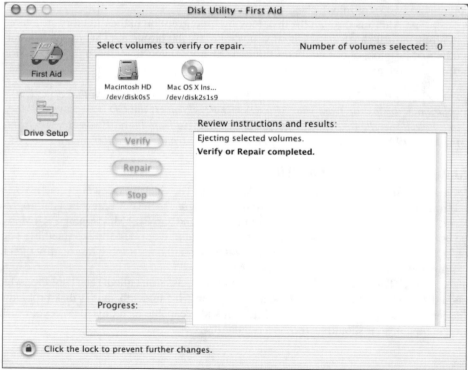

FIGURE 29-1   On the top, disk First Aid in Mac OS 9; on the bottom, the First Aid tools in Disk Utility in Mac Os X

MicroMat's third tool, Drive 10, is designed for Mac OS X. It's also a drive diagnostic tool and, although it doesn't offer defragmentation and optimization features, it will fix damage to the volume structure, which might otherwise require a reformatting.

Norton Utilities

MicroMat's major competitor is Symantec Corporation, maker of Norton Utilities (**http://www.symantec.com/product/home-mac.html**). Norton Utilities offers a number of different programs that help you keep your iMac running smoothly, including:

- **Norton Disk Doctor**   Analyzes and fixes all sorts of trouble with your hard disk.
- **Volume Recover and FileSaver**   Allows you to track and save data from files or entire disks, including removable disks.
- **Speed Disk**   Defragments and optimizes your hard disk for better performance.
- **CrashGuard**   Recovers from some errors in your applications before they freeze or crash your iMac.
- **UnErase**   Tracks and retrieves files you've deleted accidentally.

Norton is a great way to keep your iMac in good shape, guard against trouble, and if you make an occasional mistake, it'll try to bail you out.

29

Appendix A

Upgrade to Mac OS X

How to...

■ Determine if your iMac is compatible with Mac OS X

■ Prepare for Mac OS X

■ Install Mac OS X

If your iMac didn't come with Mac OS X pre-installed, you can probably upgrade to it. Mac OS X was designed to support every iMac that has shipped, from the first 233 MHz model up through the Spring 2001 season of fashionable 600 MHz iMacs in floral and polka-dotted patterns. (Subsequent models have Mac OS X pre-installed.) So, if you'd like to upgrade to Mac OS X, you've got a good chance.

There is one problem—Mac OS X has some fairly stiff system requirements, and it requires a little forethought and prep work before you can move forward with the upgrade. But, if you can get past those hurdles, you can install Mac OS X and get to work with Apple's impressive new operating system.

Determine Your Mac OS X Compatibility

As mentioned, any iMac is technically compatible with Mac OS X—that is, Mac OS X *can* run on any iMac. There are some other statistics you'll need to pay careful attention to, however, before you're actually ready to make the leap. Most pressing are the requirements that Mac OS X has above and beyond the processor that's in your iMac:

■ **128MB of RAM**   Apple recommends that you have a *minimum* of 128MB of RAM installed in any Mac before installing Mac OS X. That may seem like a lot, but I'll reiterate that it's a minimum. I'd recommend having at least 192MB of RAM installed if you plan to use your iMac with a combination of native and Classic Mac OS X applications. For best performance, double the recommendation to 256MB of RAM installed. (See Chapter 26 for more on adding RAM.)

■ **1.5GB of Hard Disk Space**   Mac OS X installs a lot of files—in the basic configuration, it installs over one gigabyte of files simply to get started. In addition, you'll want at least 500MB of storage for new applications, data, documents, temporary files, and so on. That's in addition to a full installation of Mac OS 9.1 (if you intend to use Classic applications and/or boot between the two operating systems). In other words, you probably shouldn't consider installing Mac OS X on a hard disk with less than 5GB of free space. If you use iMovie, iTunes, or other video and audio applications that tend to create large files, remember that installing Mac OS X will take away from your total storage space. Mac OS X can't be installed on external USB and FireWire disks, so you'll need that free space on your iMac's main hard disk.

Beyond those two requirements, there are some other caveats you should consider. Mac OS X is a very graphic-intensive application, and it fares better with Macs that have accelerated graphics chips inside them. The older your iMac, the worse its apparent performance will be when things like windows and icons are drawn and re-drawn on your iMac's screen. In fact, I wouldn't recommend Mac OS X for the original "Bondi" blue iMacs at all, and would hesitate to install it on any iMac that doesn't have a slot-loading CD or DVD drive, as a minimum.

Mac OS X is also a very new operating system and, at the time of writing, it has some compatibility issues. If you've invested in a number of external devices—particularly USB hubs, floppy drives, CD-RW drives, scanners, USB printers, or other interesting video and audio gadgets—you should call or visit the Web site of the manufacturers of those devices to see if they've deemed them Mac OS X-compatible. If they haven't, and those devices are important to you, it might not be the right time, yet, to upgrade to Mac OS X. As time wears on, more and more devices will be compatible and this will become less of a problem. (If you're reading this book in 2002 or 2003, for instance, hopefully all of these compatibility issues are a distant memory, but there may still be some stragglers.)

Upgrade Your Firmware

iMacs have a special bit of internal memory, called *firmware,* that holds very basic instructions for the Mac. This firmware can be updated with utility programs that Apple releases every now and then. The firmware updates can fix problems, change internal settings and, in some cases, make it possible for your iMac to do something it couldn't do before. For instance, in some cases, your iMac may need a firmware update before it can run Mac OS X.

To check, you should do two things:

1. At the very least, you should open the CD Extras folder on your Mac OS 9 CD and look for an iMac Firmware Updater folder. Open that folder and double-click the iMac Firmware icon to launch the updater utility. If your firmware is up to date, you'll see an alert box telling you that. If not, you'll see onscreen instructions that walk you through the firmware updating process.

2. If you're willing to be diligent about your firmware, you should sign onto the Internet (if necessary), launch your Web browser, and visit Apple's Software Update site (**asu.info.apple.com**). Type **iMac Firmware** into the Search entry box and press RETURN, or look for a link to iMac Updates. In the resulting list, check to see if a firmware update more recent than the update on your Mac OS 9 CD has been posted. If so, download that update and run the updater utility to see if your Mac requires this firmware update.

TIP   *The Software Update feature in Mac OS 9 will automatically alert you to new firmware updates. Select Control Panels | Software Update in the Apple menu and click Update Now. (You may need to have signed onto the Internet first if you have a dial-up connection.)*

The next step is to run the update and follow the onscreen instructions—if you want more information, see the section "Update Your iMac" in Chapter 29, which covers firmware updates.

Update Mac OS 9

If your iMac didn't come with Mac OS X pre-installed, then you probably need to update your version of Mac OS 9 before you can install Mac OS X. Mac OS 9 and Mac OS X have to be synchronized by version number in order to work correctly. Mac OS 9.1 works with Mac OS X 10.0 through 10.0.4, while Mac OS 9.2 is required for Mac OS X 10.1. This update-parity issue will probably continue into the future, as Mac OS 9 literally runs as the Classic environment in Mac OS X.

> NOTE *In this appendix, I'll sometimes refer to all versions as "Mac OS 9" and "Mac OS X" for simplicity, but be aware that you should have the latest versions available from Apple.*

Fortunately, a compatible Mac OS 9 CD-ROM is included with your Mac OS X CD-ROM, so installing it won't cost you anything extra. Installing the Mac OS is fairly simple—run the installation program and read the instructions on screen. To begin, insert the Mac OS 9 CD-ROM in your CD-ROM or DVD-ROM drive. Here's how it goes:

1. Double-click the Mac OS Install icon. This launches the installer.

2. After you've read the introductory screen, click the Continue button.

3. You'll see another screen in the Installer that tells you whether or not you have enough disk space for the installation. (If you have more than one disk connected to your iMac, you can select the disk where you'll install the Mac OS from the Destination Disk pop-up menu.) If you don't have enough disk space, you should switch back to the Finder and delete files you don't need. (And you should seriously reconsider whether you can install Mac OS X—it will require another 1GB of available hard disk space at a minimum!) If you have enough disk space, you can consider performing a Clean Install by selecting the Options button and selecting Perform Clean Installation. Then, click the Select button.

4. Now you'll see the Before You Install document, which is simply a Read Me file that tells you last-minute information about Mac OS 9 and its known issues and conflicts. Click Continue when you're done reading.

5. Next, you'll read the Software License Agreement. After dissecting it and running it by your attorney for approval, click Continue. In the box that pops up, click Agree if you agree with the license. If you click Disagree, the Installer reverts to the Welcome screen.

6. Otherwise, you're at the Installation screen. To begin a standard upgrade of the Mac OS, click the Start button.

The installer checks your hard disk for errors, installs a new hard disk driver if one is needed, then begins installing the parts of the Mac OS that have changed compared to your older version. (Or, if your disk had no Mac OS on it, the installer will install a full version.) When it's done, you'll see a dialog box that asks you to restart your iMac. Click the Restart button. When your iMac starts back up, it should be running the latest version of Mac OS 9.

Did you know?

A Clean Install

A Clean Install creates a new System Folder on your iMac's hard disk and installs Mac OS 9 into that System Folder. It then makes it the active System Folder, turning your current System Folder into a folder called "Previous System Folder." This has the advantage of starting you off with a clean, perfect new installation of Mac OS 9. It has the disadvantage of not including your preferences files, any new extensions you've installed, or anything else that's changed in the System Folder. If you have a good backup of your current System Folder and you're not having any trouble with it, you can perform a regular installation that installs over the existing System Folder. It should work fine and it's a lot easier than a Clean Install.

Install Mac OS X

Once you've updated your firmware and updated to Mac OS 9, installing Mac OS X will seem both familiar and anti-climactic by comparison. Here's how it goes:

1. With Mac OS 9 started up, insert the Mac OS X CD. When the Mac OS X CD window appears, double-click the Mac OS X Installer icon.

2. In the dialog box that appears, click the Restart button.

3. Your iMac will restart into a slimmed down version of Mac OS X and the Mac OS X Installer application will appear. Read the welcome message and click Continue.

4. On the Important Information screen, read the document. You may see important updates regarding Mac OS X compatibility with your iMac and/or peripherals. When you're done reading, click the Continue button.

5. On the Software License Agreement screen, read the license agreement, then click Continue. In the dialog box that appears, click Agree if you agree with the license agreement and want to continue the installation process.

6. On the Select a Destination screen, select the hard disk where you'd like to install Mac OS X. Click the Continue button.

CAUTION   *This screen gives you the option to "Erase Destination and Format As:", allowing you to choose Mac OS X Extended or Unix File System. Only enable this option if you know what you're doing—it will erase all files currently installed on the selected hard disk, making them very difficult, if not impossible, to recover.*

A

7. Now you'll see the Easy Install screen. If you'd like to customize the installation, click Customize, then click the check boxes to turn off any items that you don't want to install. Otherwise, click the Install button to begin the installation process.

Now, the installer will check your hard disk and then proceed to install Mac OS X. When it's finished, your iMac will be automatically restarted and Mac OS X will boot. The first thing you'll see is the Setup Assistant, discussed in Chapter 1.

Index

Q

INTERNATIONAL CONTACT INFORMATION

AUSTRALIA
McGraw-Hill Book Company Australia Pty. Ltd.
TEL +61-2-9415-9899
FAX +61-2-9415-5687
http://www.mcgraw-hill.com.au
books-it_sydney@mcgraw-hill.com

CANADA
McGraw-Hill Ryerson Ltd.
TEL +905-430-5000
FAX +905-430-5020
http://www.mcgrawhill.ca

GREECE, MIDDLE EAST,
NORTHERN AFRICA
McGraw-Hill Hellas
TEL +30-1-656-0990-3-4
FAX +30-1-654-5525

MEXICO (Also serving Latin America)
McGraw-Hill Interamericana Editores S.A. de C.V.
TEL +525-117-1583
FAX +525-117-1589
http://www.mcgraw-hill.com.mx
fernando_castellanos@mcgraw-hill.com

SINGAPORE (Serving Asia)
McGraw-Hill Book Company
TEL +65-863-1580
FAX +65-862-3354
http://www.mcgraw-hill.com.sg
mghasia@mcgraw-hill.com

SOUTH AFRICA
McGraw-Hill South Africa
TEL +27-11-622-7512
FAX +27-11-622-9045
robyn_swanepoel@mcgraw-hill.com

UNITED KINGDOM & EUROPE
(Excluding Southern Europe)
McGraw-Hill Education Europe
TEL +44-1-628-502500
FAX +44-1-628-770224
http://www.mcgraw-hill.co.uk
computing_neurope@mcgraw-hill.com

ALL OTHER INQUIRIES Contact:
Osborne/McGraw-Hill
TEL +1-510-549-6600
FAX +1-510-883-7600
http://www.osborne.com
omg_international@mcgraw-hill.com

New Offerings from Osborne's
How to Do Everything Series

**How to Do Everything
with Your Digital Camera**
ISBN: 0-07-212772-4

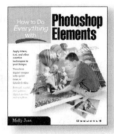

**How to Do Everything
with Photoshop Elements**
ISBN: 0-07-219184-8

**How to Do Everything
with Photoshop 7**
ISBN: 0-07-219554-1

**How to Do Everything
with Digital Video**
ISBN: 0-07-219463-4

**How to Do Everything
with Your Scanner**
ISBN: 0-07-219106-6

**How to Do Everything
with Your Palm™ Handheld,
2nd Edition**
ISBN: 0-07-219100-7

**HTDE with Your Pocket PC
2nd Edition**
ISBN: 07-219414-6

**How to Do Everything
with iMovie**
ISBN: 0-07-22226-7

**How to Do Everything
with Your iMac,
3rd Edition**
ISBN: 0-07-213172-1

**How to Do Everything
with Your iPAQ**
ISBN: 0-07-222333-2